D1602902

Exploring

PEOPLE of the
NEW TESTAMENT

Exploring
PEOPLE *of the*
NEW TESTAMENT

JOHN PHILLIPS

Kregel
Academic & Professional

Exploring People of the New Testament

© 2007 by John Phillips

Published in 2007 by Kregel Publications, a division of Kregel, Inc., P.O. Box 2607, Grand Rapids, MI 49501.

Unless otherwise indicated, all Scripture quotations are from the King James Version of the Holy Bible.

Scripture quotations marked ASV are taken from the American Standard Version.

ISBN 978-0-8254-3387-0

Printed in the United States of America

07 08 09 10 11 / 5 4 3 2 1

Contents

ONE

Mary

The Virgin Mother of Christ

Matthew 12–13; Mark 3:31–35; Luke 1:26–56; John 2; 19; Acts 1

A. MARY AND THE CHILD
   1. The stranger
   2. The danger
   3. The manger
B. MARY AND THE CHRIST
   1. Cana and the commencement of His work
   2. Capernaum and the crisis of His work
   3. Calvary and the climax of His work
C. MARY AND THE CHURCH

Some years ago I was in Vichy, France. I visited a Roman Catholic Church there known as The Church of Our Lady of Healing. It is a church dedicated to Mary. Its dominant feature is a black statue of the Virgin, which is paraded through Vichy with due pomp and ceremony at certain times of the year. The most unforgettable sight in that church, however, is the painting high up in the dome. In that painting, Christ is in the shadows. In the foreground of the picture, dominating everything, is Mary. The picture is so painted that when the sunbeams strike it through the stained glass windows, her whole robe lights up. She stands triumphant, trampling on the Serpent. Christ Himself occupies a lesser and a minor position. Underneath the Virgin, at the base of the dome, is the text, "For God so loved the world that He gave His only begotten Son." But then, in letters that dwarf the Bible text, is the true message of Rome, a quotation from St. Bernard: "It is God's will that we receive all things through Mary."

Let it be said, right from the start, that the Bible knows no such dogma. That is Romish dogma, purely and simply. The worship of Mary first began to develop in the Church of Rome about A.D. 432. Feasts in her honor began about A.D. 650, and the Ave Maria was introduced in the year A.D. 1316. The dogma of the immaculate conception of the blessed Virgin Mary (the dogma that she was born free from original sin) was introduced in A.D. 1854. The dogma of the corporeal presence of the Virgin Mary in heaven was proclaimed by Pope Pius XII in the year A.D. 1950. Thus, down through the ages, Rome has continued to add to its errors.

Every devout Catholic is taught to pray to the Virgin Mary and to say their Ave Marias. Some years ago I was in Rome and went to see the Pontifical Shrine of the Scala Sancta—The Shrine of the Holy Stairs—"Pilate's Staircase" as it is called. According to medieval tradition the Empress St. Helena brought the staircase of Pontius Pilate from Jerusalem to Rome—these were the stairs Christ ascended and descended on the day Pilate condemned Him to death. His back, bleeding from the scourging, and His blood dripping down, the stairs were stained with His precious blood. According to Roman dogma, those who crawl up those Holy Stairs on their knees, meditating on the sufferings of Christ, and praying to the Virgin Mary, can receive from the church a plenary (full) indulgence on certain holy days and a partial indulgence on other days. Thousands upon thousands of Roman Catholics, rich and poor, great and small, noble and peasant alike, have succumbed to this particular Romish superstition.

Nor can any Protestant view those stairs and remain unmoved. In the year 1510, Martin Luther came to Rome as a monk seeking peace for his soul. He had struggled unceasingly against the sinfulness of his heart. He had exceeded all his brethren in watchings, fastings, and mortifications. He had carried his asceticisms to such extremes that he had more than once brought himself down to the very doors of death.

Now he was coming to Rome. Penniless and barefoot, he crossed the Alps, begging for his bread, and heading toward the city of his dreams. "I must see Rome!" cried Paul. "I must see Rome," echoed Martin Luther.

He arrived in Rome at last, only to be shocked and shaken to the core of his being. He found monasteries of marble, and monks, like the rich man in the Lord's parable, faring sumptuously every day. Nevertheless, he hastened to all the holy places. He listened to the legends that surrounded them. And all that he was told, no matter how wild and crude, he implicitly believed. Not even the open profanity of the priests of Rome disturbed his faith at first. But the more he saw, the more disturbed he became. He saw the triumphal pomp of the Pope. He saw cardinals carried in litters, or on horseback, or in carriages ablaze with gems. He grew sick at heart.

He visited all the proper places, seeking to drown his doubts and dismays. He performed all the prescribed rituals. At last he decided to try the Scala Sancta and to climb the steps on his knees, praying to the Virgin Mary as he went. He began the ascent of the cold, hard marble stairs.

On step number one, he prayed, "My Jesus, through the sorrow you suffered in being separated from your dear Mother and your beloved disciples, have mercy on me.

> Holy Mother, pierce me through
> In my heart each wound renew
> Of my Savior crucified."

He felt no better. He painfully jerked his knees up to the second step. He prayed, "My Jesus, through the distress of mind you suffered when betrayed by Judas, have mercy on me.

> Holy Mother, pierce me through
> In my heart each wound renew
> Of my Savior crucified."

And so it went on, praying first to Jesus, then to His mother. Until at last, halfway up, the voice of God rang through his soul: "The just shall live by faith." He rose to his feet. He dusted off his robe. He marched back down those stairs and out of that shrine and right on out of the Roman Catholic Church altogether.

Yet still the deluded climb those steps. You can see them, young and old, rich and poor, great and small—little girls with holes in their stockings and grown men in expensive suits with the pant legs rolled up. And all of them are praying to Mary. Praying to Mary, as though Mary were truly God with the attributes of the Deity—omnipotence, omnipresence, and omniscience.

What is the rationale behind it all? Hear the Catholic theologians: "We are too great sinners to come to Christ Himself, so we need a mediator in the person of His Mother. . . . Is it not natural that if we want something done by the Son, His Mother would influence Him on our behalf when we ask her?" Such is the Mary of *human religion;* the Mary of *divine revelation* is quite different.

The Mary of Rome is not the Mary of the Bible. Catholics, however, are devoted to their Mary. They believe she is "the mother of God." The Jesuit, Theophilus Reynaud, declares that "by reason of her maternity, the Virgin Mary might be worshiped with the worship with which God is worshiped." "One of the Roman Catholic saints canonized by Pope Nicholas V in the year 1450 actually declared, "No creature could obtain any grace or virtue from God except according to the dispensation of His Virgin Mother." He added, "You will see that *Mary has done more for God than God has done for man*" (italics added). Worse still, he declared, "The blessed Virgin Mary is herself *superior to God, and God himself is her subject* by reason of the humanity derived from her" (italics added).

These are statements against which every Protestant must protest, but such is the Mary of Rome. Now let us look at the Mary of Scripture.

A. MARY AND THE CHILD

Mary is, indeed, a woman to be highly honored by believers, in all places, and at all times. She has been pronounced "blessed" by the Holy Spirit. Giving her that which is due is one thing; giving her worship is something else.

1. The Stranger

Mary was a young peasant woman who lived in the despised provincial town of Nazareth. She was a godly and a virtuous woman. Despite her evident poverty she was actually of the Hebrew royal family and could trace her lineage back to great king David through the line of Nathan, one of David's younger sons.

We can picture her going about her ordinary, everyday business when she was accosted by the angel. Doubtless he looked just like a man, for that was the form in which angels frequently revealed themselves to men.

This same angel had been down here on our planet on a similar errand, some six months before. On that occasion he had visited an old priest by the name of Zacharias and had announced to him the coming birth of John the Baptist. To the angel's astonishment, Zacharias had doubted his word!

Imagine what Gabriel must have thought, and what he must have said when he arrived back in Glory! Michael says to him, "Where have you been, Gabriel?"

"Down to planet earth to visit an old priest named Zacharias to tell him that, at long last, his prayers would be answered and his wife would have a son."

"And what did he say?"

"He doubted my word. I smote him dumb for a period of nine months for his unbelief. No one has ever doubted me before!"

Now Gabriel was back on earth again, this time visiting not an old man, but a young woman. His word was not doubted this time, but implicitly believed. Thus, Mary met this visitor from another world, and her life would never be the same.

2. The Danger

She was with child, and she was a single woman. The child stirring in her womb had no human father—but who in all this wide world was going to believe that? At the time the announcement was made to her by the angel, Mary was engaged to be married to Joseph, the village carpenter, so the Jewish law of betrothal would apply to her case. That law was very strict.

When a Hebrew couple wanted to get married, the parents of the man made the necessary arrangements with the parents of the girl. A contract was signed. It constituted an official declaration of intent. The couple were then betrothed. The contract was stringent and could be broken only for the cause of adultery. The engaged couple were already virtually man and wife. A year must elapse, however, between the signing of the contract and the actual marriage. During that year the couple lived with their own parents and were only allowed to meet under the strict eye of an accredited chaperone. To be guilty of a sexual sin was a very serious thing.

A virgin, betrothed to a man, discovered with child, was in peril of her life. The betrothed man himself must denounce her to the authorities. The officiating priest conducted an investigation. If proof were to be found that the woman, indeed, was with child, then he must pronounce sentence of death upon her. She was condemned to be stoned until she was dead. Moreover, the offended fiancé was required to cast the first stone in the execution, and all the community was to join in.

This, then, was the danger which faced the virgin Mary. She was with child. What did Mary do? She went away. That was natural enough. But where did she go? She went to Judea to visit her cousin Elizabeth. Moreover, she did not go to hide her condition but to publicize it! This was very strange behavior for someone who might well have been considered guilty of adultery. Very strange indeed! For Elizabeth's husband was an officiating priest, Zacharias by name. It was his business to denounce the young woman to the council and pronounce sentence of death upon her. He did nothing of the kind. He believed her implicitly when she told the truth about her condition. Her experience had coincided so exactly with his. He had seen an angel; she had seen an angel. The child soon to be born to him was to be the forerunner of the Messiah; the child soon to be born to her was to be the Messiah Himself. He had no doubt about it at all. Thus the danger was past. She had been examined and found innocent of any sexual sin.

Evidence of the stainless character of this noble young Hebrew woman can be gathered from the song she sang. It is called *The Magnificat.* "My soul doth magnify the Lord!" she cried (Luke 1:46). From the depths of her heart the words welled up and spilled over in a torrent of praise. Her hymn consists of ten verses in the New Testament. In those verses, however, Mary cites from memory no less than twenty-three separate Old Testament Scripture passages drawn from twenty-six verses of the Old Testament.

Mary stayed with her cousin Elizabeth for three months. By that time her condition had begun to show, so it was no small act of courage—and one that advertised her clear conscience—for her to return to Nazareth.

Imagine the hurt and bewilderment of Joseph in all this! He was in a real dilemma. In the first place, he simply could not believe that Mary had been unfaithful to him. Everything he knew about her proclaimed her as a modest, moral, and marvelously godly and spiritual young woman.

On the other hand, her story was simply incredible. How could anyone believe that she was still a virgin? How could anyone believe that she had actually been chosen to be the mother of God's own Son? On the horns of his dilemma, he decided to compromise. He would not go through with the betrothal but, on the other hand, he would not denounce her either. He would simply put her away without explanation. True, that would throw suspicion on him, but there it was. He knew he had not touched her. Circumstances would have to take their course.

Then the angel visited *him,* and the cloud lifted from his brow. Suspicion melted like snow before the summer sun. He would marry her! They would both doubtless be the subject of many a gossiping tongue—but let the scandalmongers talk. What cared he or she for that? Now he knew. All was well.

3. The Manger

The time came for the Son of God to be born into this world as the Son of Man. One prominent and popular modern author says in his commentary on

Hebrews that Jesus became the Son of God when he was born at Bethlehem. That is a gross misrepresentation of the truth. Jesus was *always* the Son of God—God the Son, the Second Person of the Godhead, coeternal, coequal, coexistent with God the Father and God the Holy Spirit. Jesus did not become the Son of God when He was born in Bethlehem; He became the Son of Man.

And what a place to be born! Of all places, in a cattle shed with manure for wall-to-wall carpeting, cobwebs for curtains, and bats to fly His honor guard.

Was there ever such a tragic yet typical statement in all the history of this sin-cursed world as this—"There was no room for Him in the inn" (Luke 2:7)? The world gave Him a cattle shed in which to be born and a cross on which to die. The world still has no room for Him. As the little chorus puts it,

> No room in this world for the dear Son of God,
> Only a cattle shed.
> No room in this world for the dear Son of God,
> Nowhere to lay His head.
> Only a cross did they give to our Lord,
> Only a borrowed tomb.
> Today He is seeking a place in your heart,
> Will you say to Him, "No room!"
>
> (Anonymous)

B. MARY AND THE CHRIST

That extraordinary Person, who was born in that Bethlehem barn, was the long-promised, long-prophesied Son of the living God. He was the long-awaited "Seed of the woman," whose coming was first foretold in the garden of Eden when Adam and Eve stood naked and ashamed before God who graciously gave them hope.

What a host of memories Mary must have treasured in her heart! Thirty silent years came and went, broken only once when Jesus was a Boy of twelve. How we would love to know what happened during those years! Where did He go? What did He do? We should like to know all about the Babe. We should like to know all about the Boy. We should like to know all about the Teen. We should like to know all about the young Man. We should like to peer into the cradle, or follow Him to school, or sit behind Him in the synagogue. We should like to see Him at work in the shop. We should like to see Him at play. We should like to observe Him as a Brother and as a Son and as a Neighbor and as a Friend.

Mary could have told us enough to fill a dozen libraries. We'll have to ask her all about it in heaven.

For now, though, we must be content with the three occasions when the Holy Spirit allows us to see Mary and the Christ. The first was at *Cana,* the second was at *Capernaum,* and the third was at *Calvary.* Each time, Mary tried to interfere in His ministry. Each time He gently but firmly put her in her place and refused to allow her to have any part whatsoever in the great work He had come into the world to do.

1. Cana and the Commencement of His Work

The family, including the Lord's disciples, had been invited to a wedding at nearby Cana. Halfway through the celebration, the newlyweds ran out of wine. Mary appealed to Jesus. He abruptly said, "Woman, what have I to do with thee? Mine hour is not yet come" (John 2:4). In our more colloquial English of today we would translate that word "Woman" as "Madam!" He did not acknowledge her as "Mother," and He refused to allow her to influence His decisions. Thoroughly put in her place, Mary turned to the Master of Ceremonies and said, "Whatsoever He saith unto thee, do it." In other words, she recognized that she was no proper mediator between Him and them. She referred them directly to Jesus.

2. Capernaum and the Crisis of His Work

Once His public ministry began, the Lord Jesus left home. He went down to Capernaum on the Lake of Galilee and took lodgings in Simon Peter's house. There was to be no link between Him and His mother in the ministry.

A crisis came. His enemies were gathering their strength. They accused Him of violating the Sabbath. They declared that His many, mighty miracles were performed in the power of Beelzebub, the prince of demons. Jesus told them they were blaspheming the Holy Spirit.

Then His mother and His brothers came. Their intention was to "lay hold on Him." They said, "He is beside Himself." He refused to see them one and all. Then He launched into "the mystery" parables of Matthew 13.

3. Calvary and the Climax of His Work

Three of the Marys of the New Testament came to Calvary. There was Mary,

His mother; Mary, wife of Cleophas, His aunt; and Mary Magdalene. Jesus saw no problem in two of the Marys being at Calvary, but He clearly foresaw the problem of His mother being there. No room must be made to accommodate the extravagant claims the Roman Catholic Church of the future would make in reference to His mother. They would claim she was *co-redemptrix,* a sharer in His redemptive sufferings. So He deliberately sent her away. He referred her to John. He said, "Madam, Behold your son . . ." He said to John, "Behold your mother." Thus, He dismissed her from the scene. There was to be not the slightest ground for any future dogma regarding Mary's being a partner in the great work of the cross.

C. MARY AND THE CHURCH

The crucifixion was over. The burial and the three days and nights of darkness and despair were over. The Lord was alive from the dead! He appeared first to a woman, to one of the Marys who had tarried at Calvary—not to Mary His mother, but Mary Magdalene. Then came the appearances in the upper room and elsewhere and the subsequent ascension into Glory. As the appointed hour for the coming of the Holy Spirit approached, all those who had believed on Him gathered in the upper room to await the birthday of the church. And *that* is where we find Mary. It is the last time we see or hear of her on earth.

We read of the disciples that they "continued in prayer and supplication, *with* the women, and Mary the mother of Jesus . . ." They were not praying *to* her but *with* her. She was just another, like them. Like all the others she was baptized by the Holy Spirit into the mystical body of Christ, the church, when the day of Pentecost was fully come. It is the Lord Jesus, the Word of God, and the Holy Spirit that rule our hearts and lives. Mary is to be honored but not adored.

TWO

Herod

"The Great," So Called

Matthew 2:1–20

A. His DESCENT
B. His DOMINION
C. His DILEMMA
D. His DEMAND
E. His DECISION
F. His DEATH

H e was a monster in human form, a rapacious wild beast wearing the rich robes of a king. A typical afternoon's entertainment for this well-dressed savage was to get drunk with his concubines and invited guests and crucify seven or eight hundred of his subjects on a public platform in the middle of town. Another favorite trick was to trap his unarmed enemies in a narrow place and then send his legionnaires roaring through the doors in full battle dress, armed with shields and short swords, to slaughter the defenseless captives one and all.

One wonders why the soldiers obeyed. Why, indeed, did Himmler's executioners sit on the lips of death pits and mow down boys and girls, women and old men—naked and starved wretches—by the countless thousands, just because they were Jews?

While this vile man's legionnaires hacked away at their butchery and became soaked with blood, the monster himself would stand and watch, licking his lips, and clasping his fat hands together. He would cry, "Death to them! Death to them all! They have opposed me."

His name was Herod. History, with its frequent myopia, has called him Herod

16

the Great. Great in wickedness, indeed. It was during his wretched reign that Jesus of Nazareth—the Son of God, the Savior of the world—was born.

We could subtitle this study "What happens when a thoroughly evil and unrepentant man meets Christ."

A. HIS DESCENT

Herod was an Idumean. He came from Edom and was a remote descendant of Esau, the twin brother of Jacob. There had been little love lost between the two brothers way back in the beginning, and no love at all had existed between the two nations that descended from them. Almost from the first, the nation of Israel and the nation of Edom were at war. Just as Esau and Jacob fought in the womb before they ever saw the light of day, so the two nations have fought ever since.

It is one of the great ironies of history that when God's Son stepped off His blazing throne of light to enter into human life by way of the virgin's womb, He was greeted by a king of the Jews sprung from the Jewish people's most bitter foe. The great red dragon was waiting with open maw to devour the man-child as soon as He was born.

Between the last book of the Old Testament and the first book of the New Testament lie four hundred silent years, during which God had nothing to say to His ancient people of Israel. He was preparing to speak once and for all through His Son.

During these long centuries, Palestine was a constant pawn in the struggles between Egypt to the south and Syria to the north. Not only was Palestine constantly ravaged by war, but the overlords, particularly the Syrians, sought to impose by brute force raw paganism on the people. As a result, a family of guerrilla fighters arose who not only trounced their mighty neighbor but won a measure of independence for their tortured land. These fighters were known as the Hasmoneans. For a while they governed brilliantly, but their family squabbles and power struggles eventually attracted the attention of Rome. Pompey made short work of the whole family, imposed a high priest of his choosing on Jerusalem, and hauled the rival priest off to Rome to grace a triumphal parade through the forum.

But Jerusalem and Judea were not as easy to control. Their constant uprisings were a headache to Rome. Consequently, Rome decided the man to handle the Jews was Herod, the young Idumean. Herod had been born to command.

At age fifteen he had fought Jewish rebels in Galilee. He was glamorous, daring, ruthless, and without conscience. His path to the Jewish throne became strewn with thousands upon thousands of Jewish dead. But Herod cared little for Jewish dead. He was an Idumean, and Edomites had always killed Jews. It was a national sport.

So it was that after various intrigues—after changing sides repeatedly to lick the boots of Pompey, Caesar, Mark Anthony, and Augustus—Herod, still in his twenties, was confirmed in his office as "king of the Jews." A proclamation by the senate, a sacrifice on the Capitol, a royal banquet—and Herod was "king of the Jews."

So much then for his rise to power. The Jews, who were about to crown all their other apostasies and iniquities by murdering their Messiah, who would at home and abroad ratify their decision by persistently and pugnaciously persecuting the infant church, had now been saddled with an Idumean for a king. It nearly drove them mad. It certainly did not lead them to repentance.

B. His Dominion

Herod's dominion turned out to be terrible. He filled Jerusalem and his other domains with foreign troops and councilors, and his cities with spies. No man or woman was safe during his reign. One by one he murdered every rival claimant to the throne. He stamped out the Hasmoneans. He murdered his wife's brother, a lad of seventeen and the darling of the Jews. He murdered his favorite wife and both her sons. Only five days before his own death, he murdered his son and heir. No wonder Caesar Augustus declared, "I'd sooner be Herod's swine than Herod's son." Herod hacked and hewed his way through life, murdering and slaughtering six to eight thousand of the best people in his realm.

"The army hates your cruelty," a tough old veteran of many of Herod's wars once dared to tell him. "Have a care, my lord. There isn't a private who doesn't side with your sons. And many of the officers openly curse you."

Herod threw the old soldier on the rack and tortured him beyond all power to endure. He screamed out worthless confessions and accused officers of treason to the crown. Still Herod did not spare him. The soldier's body was twisted and turned on the rack, jerked and pulled until his joints came apart and his bones cracked. The accused officers were then haled before Herod. He harangued the mob and turned it loose; they tore the men Herod suspected into pieces while the king danced up and down, screaming for their death.

Herod's fiendish cruelties affected his brain. After the murder of his favorite wife, he ran raving around his palace and pleaded for mercy from the ghosts that haunted him. "I killed the fairest Jewish princess the world has ever known," he would scream. "I am condemned!"

Herod would storm among his female slaves, point to this girl and that girl, and shout, "You are not Mariamne." Then one day, walking along the quays at Caesarea, he saw a girl who reminded him of his murdered love. Obsessed with her regal beauty, he seized her, ignoring that she was a woman of the streets. Later, when struck with a filthy disease, he screamed, "I knew it was Mariamne. She has come back to curse me!" Thereafter, a new fire ran through his veins, a fire of madness begotten of the foul infection he had contracted in his besotted state.

The Romans stood back and laughed. Judea was a long, long way from Rome, but the tyrant Herod knew how to butter up Rome. So long as he kept discipline among the Jews, Caesar cared little if a few thousand, more or less, of the hated Hebrews were slain. Besides, any charges brought against Herod were made against a king of the scarlet before an emperor of the purple. So Augustus always sided with Herod. What did it really matter if the most brilliant Jews were killed? That only made it easier for Rome to rule the world.

Herod rebuilt the temple for the Jews to conciliate his hated subjects and to indulge his passion for building. He spared neither men nor money to make the temple the wonder of the world. A thousand vehicles carried up the stone; ten thousand men slaved night and day; a thousand priests were drafted to oversee the work and to assuage the religious suspicions of the Jews. The work went on almost until the time the Romans burned it to the ground. Building Caesarea in honor of Caesar absorbed the revenues of Herod's kingdom for ten whole years, and to rebuild the temple cost him as much again. But Herod cared little about cost. The Jews could simply pay more taxes. Whole armies of virtual slaves spent their lives cutting away the edges of rocks so that the diamond-hard stones could be fitted into perfect walls—each stone uneven and projecting in the center but perfectly aligned along the beveled edge. How many such stones? A million? Twenty million? What cared Herod so long as his visions of grandeur were realized? It took two hundred men to move each stone from the quarries, great distances away, but each one fit like a glove into its appointed place. Yet all would be destroyed soon after the final overlay of gold was poured.

So the royal maniac drove his people to do his iron will. They detested him because he was an Edomite. They loved their temple, but they loathed and hated him.

Everywhere Herod left his mark. He built temples to the gods and to the Caesar. He built and rebuilt towns. In Jerusalem, newly built theaters and amphitheaters proclaimed his Hellenistic tastes, the mighty fortress of Antonia proclaimed his debt to Rome, and the temple served as a means to pacify the Jews and come to terms with their faith. At the northwest angle of the upper city, he built the noblest of palaces in which to live.

Herod's marked contempt for the Jews was always present. He was fully aware that the Jewish law declared, "Thou shalt not make unto thee any graven image, or any likeness of any thing that is in the heaven above, or that is in the earth beneath, or that is in the waters under the earth" (Exod. 20:4). Yet he placed a wooden image of a Roman eagle over the main gate of the temple. Herod knew, too, that no such image had affronted Jewish sensibilities since the dreadful days of Antiochus Epiphanes. When the Jews tore the eagle down, as Herod knew they would, he had them chopped into pieces. In its place he put a larger eagle, and then, in a letter to Augustus, Herod said that he would kill a million Jews to keep the imperial image there.

So the hated Herod reigned over his domain. He was uneducated. He ruled by sheer force of will. And the longer he ruled, the worse he became. He filled the country with fortresses directed not against a foreign foe but against the people he ruled. He constructed huge buildings in foreign cities. He paved the streets of Antioch with marble blocks—two and a half miles of them, adorned along their length with colonnades—and paid for them with taxes wrung from the detested Jews.

Into this man's kingdom came the Son of God—born of the virgin Mary, born in a cattle shed, cradled in a manger, and bedded down in hay and straw. What an unlikely place for God's Son to be born—a foul-smelling stable attached to a wayside inn. What an unlikely time for Him to be born—when a detested Edomite sat on the throne of David and rampaged like a wild beast over the lost sheep of the house of Israel. But born Jesus was, during such a period and in such a place.

C. His Dilemma

What a day it was when wise men came from the East saying, "Where is he that is born King of the Jews?" The question must have thrown the palace into pandemonium. If ever a suspicious, bloodthirsty, ruthless tyrant sat on a throne, it was Herod. If ever a man stained the pages of history with innocent blood at the merest hint or vaguest whisper of a rival claimant to his throne reaching his ears, that man was Herod the "Great."

These imposing foreign nobles from the East arrived in Jerusalem in pomp and power, bearing regal gifts, and telling a strange story about a sovereign and a star. The news took Herod by storm. Herod's servants trod softly about the mad king's palace that day, we can be sure, trembling in every limb at each successive screech of rage that issued from the tyrant's lips.

We can hear him in his rage: "Where are they? Fetch them to me. A king of the Jews! I'll teach them who's king of the Jews. Wise men? Fools to come here publishing such tidings. Where are the guards? Ho, guards. Arrest those men. Where's the inquisitor? Roast them alive until they speak." It does not take much to see it all.

Herod was facing the greatest dilemma of his guilt-ridden life. He was confronted with the birth of a Babe, with the coming of a greater King than Caesar. This newborn King, as Herod well knew, was the rightful claimant to his throne. This child was the long awaited Son of David, Son of the living God, the long-expected Messiah of Israel. This challenge to Herod's sovereignty came from the highest court of all. God, in Christ, had arrived on earth, in Herod's domain. It was a dilemma, indeed. Should he crown this One, or curse Him? It was as simple as that.

Jesus' coming into this world has altered everything. He now challenges every man's throne, hammers at the door of every man's castle, and demands everyone's submission. He comes in seeming weakness—but woe to the man or woman who despises His claims. He comes to us. He demands that we instantly submit to His claims. He is our Maker, God's Son, and the Savior of the world. He knocks at our hearts, putting us into the place of decision. Neutral we cannot be. Will we crown Him or crucify Him? That is the question.

Most people want nothing to do with Jesus. They wish that He had never come into the world, wish He would go away, wish to have no part in such a choice. But the issues are inescapable. Christ has come. We *have* heard about Him. We must decide whether to crown or crucify the Son of God. There is no middle ground.

Herod's wicked life could have been changed in a moment by his simply accepting Christ and submitting to His claims. Herod, however, like so many others, did not want his life changed. He wanted to hang onto life as it was. He wanted to get rid of this choice—and to treat Christ the same way he treated everyone else who crossed his will.

So his great dilemma had come. Would Herod accept the claim of Christ? That would mean abdicating his throne, surrendering his sovereignty, and yielding his will. It would mean a new way of life and a new Lord in his life. From now on Herod could promote the interests of God's Son and become great indeed.

Herod certainly did not want that. Not yielding to Christ's claims, however, was to become even more the enemy of God. Then Herod would court the vengeance of eternal fire. He would go on living in wickedness and sin until God, Himself, finally settled all Herod's accounts.

D. His Demand

"When he had gathered all the chief priests and scribes of the people together, he demanded of them where Christ should be born" (Matt. 2:4). Herod did not know the Bible. He detested it. During this crisis, however, he tacitly confessed that the Bible was the Word of God and that it contained prophecies of great personal relevance.

After World War II, when for a brief time Sir Winston Churchill was back in office as prime minister of England, he became troubled by events on the international scene. He remembered Yalta, that fateful conference in February 1945 when he, Stalin, and Roosevelt had met to decide the wartime fate of Europe. Churchill remembered how Stalin had insisted on a second front and had urged Roosevelt to open it soon to take the pressure off Russia. Churchill remembered Roosevelt's plans for opening a second front across the English channel on the shores of France, remembered the gleam in Stalin's eye as he heartily endorsed the plan, and remembered the flattery of that wicked old fox.

Churchill remembered, too, how he had promoted a different plan. The Allies were already in Europe, fighting their way up the long boot of Italy. He urged that the western powers beat the Russians into the Balkans and into Germany, so that these countries might be truly set free. He pointed out the folly of allowing Russia to get there first.

Churchill remembered Roosevelt's barely concealed jealousy and how the American president fell for Stalin's flattery. Churchill remembered how he had been given the cold shoulder and how his superior statecraft had been ignored. He remembered Yalta.

Churchill remembered how events had happened the way he feared. Half of Europe was enslaved again, only this time to a far more terrible foe than Germany had ever been. He saw that the West had won the war and lost the peace. He saw

Russia astride the world and gaining new strength every day. And that farsighted old warrior-statesman was troubled.

Where could he find light on the things now happening in the world? Ah, there was the Bible. Didn't it say something about these things? Perhaps it could help him now by casting light into the shadows that lay across the world. Perhaps it could speak with authority to the fears that troubled his heart. Like Herod of old, Churchill looked for someone who could chart a course for him through the unfamiliar seas of Holy Writ. An appointment was made for him with a well-taught English Christian, Harold St. John, a former missionary and a careful Bible scholar.

After greeting his guest, Churchill said, "Mr. St. John, I am a very busy man. You have half an hour; make the most of it. Tell me what the Bible has to say about Russia, about the problems confronting us in this dangerous postwar world." So Mr. St. John opened to him the Scriptures. At the end of the half hour Churchill called his secretary. "What other engagements do I have today?" he demanded.

"Sir," she answered, "at ten o'clock you have an appointment with the ambassador from India. At ten-thirty the foreign secretary wants to see you concerning affairs in South Africa. At eleven o'clock the chancellor of the exchequer is to see you about the budget. At twelve you are to have lunch with the chief lord of the admiralty. At one o'clock—"

Churchill cut in, "Cancel them all. Make any excuse you like. Set up new appointments. Anything! I'm spending the rest of the day with Mr. St. John and on no account do I wish to be disturbed."

At the end of that day, the great statesman looked at the humble Christian who had given him a view of the Bible such as he had never seen before. Churchill saw before him a poor man who had spent much of his life in Argentina. He saw a white-haired man with a merry twinkle in his eye. "Mr. St. John," he said, and there was a surprising note of humility in his voice, "I would give half the world for your knowledge of the Bible."

"Sir," replied the courtly old missionary, "I gave all the world for it."

The story does not record how Churchill used the biblical information he received from God's servant, but history does record what Herod did with the knowledge he gained from the priests and scribes of Jerusalem. They told him that Christ would be born in Bethlehem. Thus Herod was confronted for the last time with factual knowledge of Christ, with the fact that God's Son had come into the world and that his own life would never be the same again.

E. His Decision

Herod's decision was automatic and instinctive. It seems that he never gave the alternative so much as a passing thought. He categorically, totally, and unequivocally rejected the claims of Christ. Then he gave full reign to his bitter hatred of God's Son, who had dared to challenge his life. He ordered the cold-blooded massacre of the babes of Bethlehem. It says a lot about Herod's wickedness that Josephus and other historians do not even record the deed. Herod had already massacred so many people. What difference did a few hundred more make? But God recorded it; God records everything.

Herod failed to kill Christ, but he would have done so if he could. People who reject Christ today may not be able physically to assault God's Son, but if they continue to reject Him as Savior, they record their hearts' intentions just the same. God writes down their decisions in His book against the coming day when He will settle accounts at the great white throne. In His tender love and mercy, God sent His Son into this world. To reject Him is an unpardonable sin. That was Herod's decision.

F. His Death

The Bible scarcely gives Herod's death a footnote, but he died horribly. Gone were his sleek good looks. Once lean, he had become obese. He had lost nearly all his hair. Three of his front teeth had broken off. His legs had become great stumps, nine inches thick at the ankles. He could not eat without great pain. A dreadful sickness had spread throughout his body, attacking parts of his flesh and producing ugly, mortifying wounds. He had sores everywhere. His stomach had become so rotten that the guards had to be changed frequently lest they faint from the stench. He was a man of seventy on whose body had been visited all the crimes of his former years. He was foul beyond imagination. His breath was an abomination.

Even as he groveled on his deathbed in mortal agony, his mind ran to murder. He ordered the death of his fifth son. He also remained obsessed with the hatred of Jews. "When I die, I will see to it that they mourn me," he shouted.

He called for his mercenaries—Africans, Cilicians, Egyptians, Persians—the men who had through the years coldly killed off the leaders of Judaism at his command. He raved at them in jumbled sentences: "Go to every city in Judea, arrest the leading citizens, put them in jail, and guard them well. Feed them luxuriously and let them have all comforts. But on the day I die, kill them—kill them all! Go to every city and village; none is too small." He strode about, hacking and thrusting with his right arm, and then fell back exhausted on his bed. Then he gathered himself together again and screamed, "When I die, the Jews may not mourn me, but by the gods they will mourn!"

Herod died as he had lived, a wicked, ungodly man. Laden down with his sins, he died and went to meet his Maker.

Death marks the end of human sovereignty. Napoleon once said of the hated English, "Britain loses every battle except the last." It sometimes seems, in His dealings with men, that God loses every battle. But He does not lose the last one. In the end He sends the angel of death to put an end to an individual's puny sovereignty. From then on God's will is enforced in judgment forever. Thus, we need to ask not only, "What will we do with Jesus?" but also, "What will He do with us?"

At the time of Christ's birth, Herod chose to reject Him; at the same time, wise men from the East came and worshiped Him. The great question is, "Do we take our stand with Herod or with the wise men?"

THREE

Joseph
Husband of Mary

Matthew 1:18–2:23

A. HIS EMPLOYMENT
B. HIS ENGAGEMENT
C. HIS EMBARRASSMENT
D. HIS ENCOURAGEMENT
E. HIS ENLIGHTENMENT
F. HIS ENJOYMENT
G. HIS ENNOBLEMENT

Joseph was not rich. By all accounts, however, he must have been a remarkable man. God would not have chosen a mean man, a miserly man, a moody man, a mediocre man, or a merciless man to be the foster father of His Son. Although we only catch a brief glance of Joseph in the Bible, we see enough to know he was careful, conscientious, concerned, and compassionate—a fitting foster father for Jesus.

A. HIS EMPLOYMENT

Joseph was a village carpenter. He knew what it was like to toil at a workbench. It was hard work. We can be sure he was honest in his business dealings, and we can be sure he worked hard. However, he does not seem to have made much money. We assume he was poor because when the time came for the presentation of the infant Christ in the temple in Jerusalem, the best offering he and Mary could afford was the smallest and least expensive sacrifice the Mosaic Law allowed.

Yet this poor, humble, laboring man was a prince in his own right. We cannot imagine him boasting about his ancestry, but he could have. He could have said to his friends, "I'm a direct descendant of good King Josiah. I am related to King Hezekiah. My family tree goes back to Solomon. I am of the lineage of David. I am a member of the Hebrew royal family. The blood of princes flows in my veins. If I had my rights, I would be sitting on the throne of David in Jerusalem right now in place of that scoundrel Edomite, Herod." (If Joseph had made such boasts, Herod would have had his head.)

Joseph was a direct descendant of David. The fortunes of the imperial house of David had sunk so low, however, that instead of sitting on a throne in Jerusalem, the rightful heir to that throne lived in a despised Galilean village and labored at a carpenter's bench for his daily bread. The tools of his trade were a hammer, an adze, and a saw. As did like tradesmen of the day, he made yokes for oxen, doors for houses, handles for plows, tables and chairs, and other such things.

Joseph, following common practice at that time, brought up his adopted Son to this trade. It is significant that the One who had created a hundred million galaxies labored from His youth at creating things. Being thus employed, Jesus forever ennobled manual labor and the crafting of useful and beautiful objects for the benefit of one's fellow men.

B. His Engagement

A girl in Nazareth caught young Joseph's eye. She was not immaculately conceived, as some say. The Bible does not support any such idea. But she was surely as perfect as any daughter of Adam's fallen race could be. She was surely humble and holy, loving and lowly, patient and pure, thoughtful and kind. God had waited for some four thousand years for this particular woman to be born, so we can be sure that she was as near perfection in character, personality, and disposition as one could be.

Young Joseph knew one thing: he wanted Mary to be his wife. He no doubt felt as any young man feels about a special young woman. His sun rose and set on her. She was all anyone could ever want in a wife. He was thrilled when his proposal was accepted and the betrothal arrangements were made.

There were two forms of betrothal among the Jews. We do not know which form was used in the case of Mary and Joseph. In one form, the agreement was spoken in the presence of witnesses. The vows were confirmed by the pledging of a piece of money. (We can be sure any dowry was small in Mary and Joseph's agreement.) In the other form, the transaction was confirmed in writing.

Either form of betrothal was probably followed by a supper, a benediction, and a statutory cup of wine for the engaged couple. From that moment on, the prospective bride and groom were pledged to be married. Their relationship was as solemn and sacred as the marriage relationship, and any breach of it would be regarded as adultery. The engagement could not be dissolved except by a formal divorce. Yet months—sometimes even a year—elapsed between the engagement and the marriage.

Imagine Joseph's joy! He is the happiest man in Nazareth. Mary fills his whole horizon. He was engaged to be married to a princess of the house of David. She was also related to the priesthood—her mother seems to have been a blood relative of Elizabeth, the wife of Zacharias the priest. This engagement was a remarkable event—not that Joseph would care that much about the lineage of Mary. She was going to marry *him!* That was all that mattered. That good, pure-minded, Bible-believing, spiritual, and capable girl was going to marry him!

For Joseph, heaven above would have appeared a deeper blue, the earth around a deeper green. We can imagine how he would have thought and acted. He whistles while he works. He sings as he delivers his wares to his customers. Each week he looks forward to seeing her in the synagogue on Saturday, and he counts the days and hours to the wedding. He gazes in rapture at the moon. He is going to wed Mary, and all is well with the world. He sleeps with a lock of her hair under his pillow. He dreams of the day when the two will at last become one.

C. His Embarrassment

Then one day Mary approached him. It doesn't take much imagination to picture the scene. "I need to see you, Joseph," she says. "Something has happened. I have something to tell you." His shock is natural as she breaks the news: "I'm going to have a baby."

Joseph is devastated and absolutely stunned. He knows he has never touched her in a dishonorable way. If she is going to have a baby, he is not the father. Joseph cannot believe what he is hearing. He cannot imagine his pure and spiritually minded fiancée doing anything wrong. She is not that kind of girl. She says she has not been raped. She has not committed adultery. She has not betrayed him. She is not interested in anyone else; she never has been and never will be. But she *is* going to have a baby. Joseph cannot believe that Mary is lying to him. He has always believed her honesty and integrity to be above suspicion.

"Well," he says at last, "what *is* your explanation?"

"About six months ago," she answers, "my cousin Elizabeth's husband, Zacharias, was visited by the angel Gabriel. He told Zacharias that Elizabeth was going to give birth to a son. Well, since Elizabeth was too old to have a baby, Zacharias did not believe what Gabriel said. So Gabriel smote Zacharias with dumbness. Then, sure enough, Elizabeth became pregnant. That was six months ago, and Zacharias is still dumb. The whole incident caused quite a stir in the priestly confraternity."

"What does that have to do with you?"

"I'm coming to that, Joseph. The angel told Zacharias that his son would be a special child, the forerunner of the Messiah."

"I still don't see what that has to do with you."

"It has everything to do with me. A little while ago that same angel visited me."

"Come on, Mary! You never told me that."

"I'm telling you now. The angel Gabriel visited me. He told me I was to become the mother of the Son of God—that God was going to send His Son into the world as a baby and that I was the chosen vehicle for that birth. Gabriel told me that I would be overshadowed by the Holy Spirit, that I would miraculously conceive, and that the Son of God would be born of me. Now, just as the angel said, I'm going to have a baby. I waited until I knew for sure before I told you. What do you think of that?"

It is not difficult to understand if Joseph simply could not believe the story, could not believe that Mary was with child. Nor could he believe that she had been unfaithful to her betrothal vows, but he could not believe her explanation. And who else would have believed such a story? Was he dealing with a moral issue or a miraculous issue? Since Mary's explanation was incredible, the issue had to be a moral one.

"You do believe me, don't you, Joseph?" we can hear Mary say.

"I don't know what to believe. I'm going to have to think it over."

"Well, while you think it over, I'm going to visit my cousin Elizabeth. At least she'll believe me."

And so Mary left, and Joseph began to think it over. As far as he was concerned, it was going to take a great deal of thinking over. His mind must have churned: *Pregnant by divine conception indeed!. Who in his right mind would ever believe a story like that?*

D. His Encouragement

Anyone who has suffered a broken engagement will be able to enter into the mind and heart of Joseph. For him there is deep, deep sorrow and a gnawing anguish of soul. There is a sense of shock and disbelief. Perhaps there are sudden surges of outright anger and resentment. But most of all, there is the nagging ache of a broken heart.

The more Joseph thinks over Mary's story, the more it becomes evident to him that, for his own protection under the stern Mosaic Law, he will have to break the engagement. The provisions of that law adds a new dimension of horror to his agony. For a single girl to become pregnant, especially when betrothed, is a capital offense. The law demands the death penalty for the guilty parties. Joseph will have to accuse Mary publicly and go on the witness stand to denounce her. Worst of all, when the death sentence is passed, he will have to cast the first stone.

Can a man like Joseph do that? But can he now marry her? That would be tantamount to admitting his own guilt. Besides, Mary had betrayed him. How else can her condition be explained? How can he believe her story about angelic visitations and a virgin birth? Joseph sadly shakes his head: *She must be living in a dream world, a world of fantasy and wishful thinking and make-believe.*

On the other hand, Mary has kept nothing hidden, and she has always exhibited a stainless character. Moreover, she had rushed right off to Elizabeth of all people. Elizabeth's husband is a priest and would be the first to sit in judgment of an adulteress. Surely Mary's visit to Elizabeth is profoundly significant. If Mary were guilty of immoral conduct, the last place she would go would be Judea, where the laws were more rigidly enforced. The last place she would go would be the house of a priest, who would be duty-bound to report her.

So Joseph, no doubt disconsolate, would have been deeply pondering the situation as he walked the streets of Nazareth. Every corner, every tree, every hill, and every dale would remind him of her. The place would seem haunted now by a ghost. Mary was gone, and Nazareth would seem a place without a soul; his hometown a city of sepulchers, the grave of all his hopes.

Follow along in Joseph's footsteps. The wind in the trees reminds him of the sound of Mary's voice blithely singing the Psalms of their great ancestor David. The village fountain where the girls gather and chat brings back memories. The synagogue is a place of torture. On the Sabbath, Mary's place is empty now. He can only sit and stare at it sadly, choking back his tears. Joseph feels like abandoning the synagogue and its services altogether.

We picture the mental torture that goes on and on until one day, he flings down his hammer and strides out of the carpenter's shop. He goes out of the town and up the hill to the place, perchance, where years later the villagers would seek to throw Jesus to His death. There, perhaps, Joseph halts and, frightened, draws back from the drop. He sinks down to the ground and weeps bitter tears. He has to come to a decision one way or another. In his agony he decides to break the engagement privately and let matters take their course. Exhausted, no doubt, but glad that some decision, however wretched, has been made, he falls asleep.

Suddenly his sleep is ablaze with light. Scripture tells us the angel of the Lord appeared—not Gabriel, but the Jehovah angel. The words of the angel rang in his soul: "Joseph, thou son of David, fear not to take unto thee Mary thy wife: for that which is conceived in her is of the Holy Ghost. And she shall bring forth a son, and thou shalt call his name JESUS: for he shall save his people from their sins" (Matt. 1:20-21).

We can imagine the scene. The storm clouds roll away, and the sun breaks through again. The words of the prophet Isaiah come to Joseph's mind: "Behold, a virgin shall be with child, and shall bring forth a son, and they shall call his name Emmanuel, which being interpreted is, God with us" (Matt. 1:23). Within an hour, Joseph is running as fast as his legs can carry him to Judea. From then on his steps would be ordered of the Lord.

E. His Enlightenment

After Mary and Joseph were married, a decree came from Caesar Augustus. They were to go back to the city of their birth to be enrolled for taxation purposes. Mary was approaching the time of her confinement, but the word of the Caesar had to be obeyed. In the providence of God, the decree meant that, in keeping with an ancient prophecy, the holy Child would be born in Bethlehem. Perhaps the couple was glad to leave Nazareth. Indeed it took a special divine revelation to later bring them back to Nazareth.

The journey from Nazareth to Bethlehem must have taken at least three days. Probably Mary and Joseph followed the route along the eastern bank of the Jordan to avoid going through hostile Samaria. As they approached the heights of Bethlehem, they could see one of Herod's frowning castles perched on the highest hill southeast of Bethlehem. On they went until the mountain ridges of Tekoa came into view. East of the travelers lay the sullen waters of the Dead Sea. To the west, the road wound away to Hebron. To the north rolled the undulating countryside, behind which Jerusalem was hidden. And in front of them at last lay Bethlehem.

Mary must have been exhausted and Joseph not a little anxious to get her settled for the night, for her time had come. But, alas, there was no room in the inn. Thus, the Son of God came from the mansions of glory, from the ivory palaces of heaven, to a wayside cattle shed. We can be sure, however, that Joseph did what he could to clean up the worst of the filth. He found a manger and filled it with straw and hay so that the newborn babe might have a clean and comfortable bed.

The shepherds came and the angels sang. Joseph moved his family into a more convenient place, and the wise men came with their timely gifts. Then the angel of the Lord appeared again and said to Joseph, "Arise, and take the young child and his mother, and flee into Egypt, and be thou there until I bring thee word: for Herod will seek the young child to destroy him" (Matt. 2:13). That child was Lord and Creator of the universe. He could have called ten thousand angels to stop Herod and his men of war dead in their tracks. Instead He fled to Egypt! God had His own timetable for bringing judgment on Herod.

Joseph and his family stayed in Egypt until the death of Herod. And a terrible death it was. The cup of Herod's crimes was full, and his torments and terrors came. He was haunted by visions of a rival to the throne, and he sacrificed thousands of innocent people to that fear, including his favorite wife and various sons. He died, demented by a dreadful disease that devoured his body. According to Edersheim, the visit of the Magi took place in February. In March Herod rounded up all the rabbis he could lay his hands on, locked them up, and left orders for them to be executed on the day of his death. At the end of March or the beginning of April, he murdered his son Antipater, and Herod himself was dead five days later.

He was succeeded by his son Archelaus, who spent the night of his father's death carousing and rioting with his friends. One of his first acts as king was to massacre three thousand Jews within the sacred precincts of the temple. Vile as his father had been, Archelaus was worse. He surpassed him in cruelty, oppression, opulence, pride, and sensuality.

Soon after the death of Herod, Joseph returned to Palestine. It seems he wanted to settle in Bethlehem, a proper setting for great David's greater Son, but Joseph was directed to go back to Galilee and thus Jesus grew up in Nazareth.

F. His Enjoyment

What greater joy could any man on earth have had than the joy of being foster father to Jesus, the Son of the living God? Christ's presence in Joseph's humble home was a benediction.

Jesus grew up giving Joseph the courtesy title of "father." When Mary reprimanded Him for tarrying in the temple on the occasion of His first Jerusalem Passover, she said, *"Thy father* and I have sought thee sorrowing" (Luke 2:48, italics added). So Joseph parented Jesus. Joseph surely surrounded Him with love and kindness and counsel and all the necessities of life. And Jesus responded by being the only absolutely perfect Child and Teenager who ever blessed a human home.

We can imagine how Joseph delighted in the willing, cheerful obedience of Jesus to every command; in His loving, joyful, peaceable disposition; in His uniformly excellent grades at school; in His enjoyment of the Word of God; in His wisdom and universal popularity. There never was such a Boy in all this world, and it was Joseph's privilege to provide the setting for that jewel to be displayed. A humble setting it was: a small, primitive, but comfortable house and a nearby carpenter's shop.

Joseph must have felt an inner glow when the neighbors were impressed. One of them would ask, "How's that boy Jesus doing at school?" And Joseph could reply, "Jesus? He's a straight-A student. He has already memorized the Pentateuch and mops up languages like a sponge." Another neighbor would add to the pleasure: "I say, Joseph, your son Jesus was at our place the other day. He brought my wife some flowers from the field to cheer her sickroom. She says it was a tonic just to have Him visit."

So Joseph played the part of protector, provider, and parent to the Son of the living God; and he no doubt enjoyed every minute of it.

G. His Ennoblement

We will not find this Joseph in *Who's Who in the World,* but we can be quite sure that his name is written down in the book of God's kingdom. When the roll of that kingdom's great ones is called, we will hear the name of Joseph. Yes, indeed, and we will also hear the part of the story that is not recorded in the Bible.

FOUR

The Leper and His Cry

Mark 1:40–45

A. This man's miserable condition
B. This man's marvelous conversion
C. This man's mistaken confession

L eper!" The very word sent cold shudders down the spine. It summed up everything disgusting and horrible and tragic that could happen to a person in this life. Leprosy was a living death. The Jews were terrified of it. They called it "the stroke of God." They thought that a person inflicted with leprosy must be under some special curse of God Himself. The law of Moses legislated stringently against all who had the disease. They were to be immediately isolated from the rest of the population, excommunicated, and banished to some lone place outside the camp of Israel. They were obliged under law to cover their mouth should anyone approach them and give the warning cry, "Unclean! Unclean!" Leprosy was regarded as different in degree and kind from other ailments of mankind. That is evident from the way the Holy Spirit records the Lord's dealings with sick people in general and lepers in particular. He *healed* the sick. He *cleansed* the leper. For leprosy was foul and contaminating and vile.

A. This Man's Miserable Condition

He was a leper. That's all we know about him. We have no idea what his name was or how old he was. We do not know if he was married with a wife and children, or if he was single. We know nothing of his station in life. We do not know whether he came from a rich family or a poor family, whether he was an intellectual or an artisan. We do not know if he was tall or short, good looking or plain, robust or weakly. We do not know from what part of the country he came—if he came from a big city or a little village. We know nothing about his gifts and abilities. We do not know if he had been a carpenter or a fisherman or a farmhand or a scholar or a scribe. All we know is that he was a leper. That is all we need to know. That fact obliterated every other fact. He was a leper.

Nowadays leprosy is known as Hansen's Disease. We know that it comes in two varieties and that it is caused by a bacillus. Now it can be treated, but in Bible times, a person who had leprosy knew that the best he could look forward to was death. Leprosy attacks the nerves near the surface of the face, the arms, and the legs of the victim. It is disfiguring. It renders the victim insensitive to pain—a person with leprosy can cut or burn an infected limb and do terrible damage to himself because he feels no pain. It is contagious and can be spread from discharges from a leper's nose or sores. It can enter a healthy person's body through breaks or cuts in the skin. In severe cases, leprosy can cause blindness. It changes a person's appearance. In Bible times there was no cure. Leprosy was a death sentence, and a terrible one at that.

The leper who approached Christ had the disease in all its horror. "Unclean!" he cried. "Unclean!" The words conjured up the most frightful pictures of decomposition and decay. His disease distorted his countenance and attacked his limbs, spread throughout his body, and rendered his touch a contamination.

Leprosy often began as a small spot that could easily by covered. Perhaps, one day, the victim spilled some hot water on his foot or hand and felt no sensation. His insensitivity was a warning. He had leprosy. The disease would spread. It would reach the point where it could no longer be hidden. All that remained for him was excommunication and isolation from other people. His only companions would be others who, like himself, were lepers.

People were terrified of such people. Travelers in some foreign lands tell how lepers would board trains and accost passengers, exposing their sores and demanding money—or else. They used their condition to terrorize others.

It is not at all surprising that, throughout the Bible, leprosy is a type, a picture, of sin. What leprosy does to the body, sin does to the soul. So the outstanding fact about this man was that he was a leper—that obliterated every other fact. It became the dominant factor in the equation of his life. Nothing else mattered. He was a leper.

Just so, the outstanding fact about every man, woman, boy, and girl in this world is that we are all sinners. That fact obliterates all other facts. Many people deny the fact. They try to hide the fact. But the fact remains. It matters not whether we are rich or poor, black or white, young or old, clever or ignorant, religious or reprobate. The deadly virus of sin courses through our beings. We are sinners.

In the case of the leper, the disease began in a very small way, and it could easily be hidden from the gaze of other people. Just so with sin. People don't usually start off murdering somebody or running off with somebody else's wife. They start off with little lies, with occasional bouts of bad temper, with small hypocrisies. They can put on a good front, go to church, tithe, and give to the poor. They are decent and moral and kind. But they are still sinners for all that; and that obliterates all the rest of it.

In the case of the leper, his disease rendered him insensitive to pain. That insensitivity increased as time went by. It is the same with sin. The more times we perform a wrong act, the easier it becomes to continue that act. We find it increasingly easy to rationalize what we do and say. We become increasingly insensitive to the convicting work of the Holy Spirit. Our consciences eventually are completely cauterized.

The leper's disease is contagious. It can be spread to other people. Worse still, it is more easily caught by children than by adults. So, too, other people are affected by our sin. Some people spread their evil influence without conscious thought. Others—like those lepers who used to board trains in India—deliberately spread their disease, and make no bones about it. They want to spread their wretched lifestyle. It gives them a perverse pleasure to know that other people are following in their ways. And, sadly enough, it is children who are the most vulnerable.

Our society is very tolerant of sin. Pimps and prostitutes, perverts and pornographers have their champions in our society. There is always some newspaper willing to give gambling, drugs, abortion, sodomy, and the like, favorable press. There are always networks that will take up their cause and, during prime time, air programs designed to erode the conscience of the nation and applaud those who deal in wickedness. There are always college professors who delight in tearing down the Christian faith of those they are supposed to educate. And the young are particularly vulnerable to all this.

In the case of the leper, sooner or later, the fact of his leprosy was evident to all. It showed on the victim's face. He had "leper" written all over him.

Our faces are the mirrors of our souls. Someone once asked Abraham Lincoln to appoint a certain man to his cabinet. Lincoln replied, "I don't like his face."

Said the man's advocate, "But surely, the man isn't responsible for his face."

Replied Lincoln, "Oh, yes, he is. Every man over forty IS responsible for his face." For better or for worse, the way we live leaves its marks upon us.

During a recent election campaign, one of the networks aired a program on a well-known senator. It showed him as a freshman senator, handsome, confident, attractive, personable, and popular, lionized as an American aristocrat. Most of the time the camera avoided showing a close-up of this man who was running for reelection. The cameras were kept far enough back so that only a general impression could be seen. Whatever impeccable grooming and styled hair and vigorous speech could do to create a favorable impression was done. But occasionally a camera got too close, and the man's face was all too visible. Years of hard drinking, loose living, and indulged passion could then be seen. The senator, with a sin-ravaged face, was and *is* responsible for his face. And it tells a lot about him. As does every person's face.

Sin leaves its indelible marks upon a person's countenance. It has nothing to do with whether or not a man or woman has natural good looks. Sin etches its lines upon the face. The mouth becomes hard or bitter or slack and weak. The eyes show anger or hate or lust or cynicism. The brow becomes deeply etched with lines of its own. Sin leaves its mark. We can pretend all we like, but we cannot erase the evidence that God Himself stamps on our countenance. When Saddam Hussein was finally caught, hiding in a hole in the ground, we were astonished. He had been a handsome man. No more! Deep furrows crisscrossed his brow. His cheeks were channels etched deep. His face, stripped of cosmetics, was ugly, ravaged, plowed deep by sin. Those who saw it will never forget it.

Sin ends in death. "For the wages of sin is death" (Rom. 6:23). "It is appointed unto men once to die, but after this the judgment" (Heb. 9:27). That was all a leper had to look forward to. Sooner or later he would die. That, too, is all the sinner has to look forward to. Sooner or later death will claim him. No wonder this leper came to Christ. That is what any awakened sinner must do.

B. This Man's Marvelous Conversion

He heard about Jesus. Jesus had left Nazareth, come to Capernaum, and taken up residence in the house of Simon Peter. He was the talk and wonder of the whole fishing village and all the surrounding countryside. People flocked from all over to hear His astonishing teaching and to see His even more astounding miracles. There seemed to be nobody this young Prophet from Nazareth could not heal.

First, it was ones and twos. Then people came in crowds, bringing uncounted numbers of sick people with them. He never lost a case. He never charged a fee. The young Miracle Worker was the talk of the town. There wasn't an inn or shop where somebody did not have some story to tell about some relative or some friend or some acquaintance who had been healed.

Somehow the news filtered into the leper colony, or wherever it was that this leper lived. Evidently this man had some serious debates with himself. His thinking finally reduced itself into two great questions: *Can He?* And *will He?* Can He make me clean? Will He make me clean?

He tackled the first question. *Can He?* It did not take him long to decide that He could. He did not know anybody who had been cleansed of leprosy. Nobody knew anybody who had been cleansed of that remorseless disease. In all the Old Testament only three people had been cleansed of leprosy—Moses, his sister Miriam, and a Syrian general by the name of Naaman. Beyond that, for two thousand years of Hebrew history, going right back to Abraham, the leper could not think of a man, woman, boy, or girl who had ever been cleansed from this foul and fatal curse. But He, this Teacher from Nazareth, had healed some pretty hopeless cases. He *could!* In his heart of hearts the leper knew He *could.* There was not the slightest doubt in his mind. He could!

He was sure that He *could.* He was not quite sure that He *would.*

That is why, when the leper came to Christ, he said, "Lord, if Thou wilt, Thou canst make me clean." It was not a question of *"He would if He could."* That would have been the expression of unbelief. It was a question of *"He could if He would."*

Perhaps the leper could think of reasons why the Lord, with *omnipotence* and *omniscience* at His command, should *not* cleanse the leper. If, indeed, leprosy was the stroke of God, maybe there were reasons why he should go on suffering.

The important thing about this leper is that *he came.* That is the important thing with us, too. We must put away our doubts. We must come.

It must have taken a great deal of courage for this man to come to Christ. Usually Christ was surrounded by a great crowd of people. For that leper to come meant he must defy all custom. He must come in defiance of the Mosaic Law, which ostracized him and excommunicated him and isolated him. He must come in the face of an angry, hostile crowd. There wasn't a man, woman, boy, or girl there who would take kindly to the approach of a leper.

At his cry, "Unclean! Unclean!" they would look up and look around. What is this? A *leper!* Daring to defy all the taboos? A leper, coming toward them! A hundred hands would grope for stones to throw at him to warn him away. Yet, still, he came! What a determined, desperate fellow he was!

It often takes a great deal of courage to come to Christ. The crowd is all against it. The crowd, your particular crowd, may well be hostile the moment you start toward Him. But when your need is desperate enough, you'll come.

One suspects that, instead of throwing their stones, the people dropped them and backed away. One suspects, too, that this man had a path as wide as a well-traveled highway along which to come. If he was coming, they were going.

Presently the leper found himself at the feet of Jesus. He spoke what was in his heart. Like the prodigal, he put his heart and soul into it. "Lord," he said, "if thou wilt, thou canst make me clean" (Matt. 8:2).

Then Jesus did something very wonderful indeed. Before He said a word He revealed His heart. "Jesus," we read, "moved with compassion, put forth his hand, and touched him" (Mark 1:41). That was the kindest thing He could have done. He *touched* him! He touched that loathsome leper! He touched him! It was no doubt the first kind touch the leper had received since the terrible disease had fastened itself upon him. Nobody had touched him like that since he had been thrust out of the camp of Israel as a pariah, an outcast, an untouchable. But Jesus did.

Jesus had no fear of contamination. All He felt was a great, overwhelming compassion for this lost and unhappy and desperate man. A great surge of love must have welled up in this man's soul, too, the moment he realized what Jesus had done. He had touched him! Peter would not have touched him for a king's ransom. But Jesus did. For that's the way He is.

Then He spoke. "I will!" He said, "be thou clean!" That was all. "And as soon as he had spoken, immediately the leprosy departed from him, and he was cleansed" (Mark 1:42). Such was his marvelous conversion.

That's the way Jesus cleanses us from all sin, too. Our cleansing is instantaneous, unmistakable, and comprehensive. No masses. No penance. No pilgrimages. No fasts. No long prayers. No rehabilitation. Instant cleansing. "I will! Be clean!" Just like that.

We see the leper look at where the stumps of his hands had been. He looks at his feet, once so mangled. All traces of his dreadful condition are gone.

C. This Man's Mistaken Confession

Jesus sent him away. That's not what we would do with a notable convert. We would urge him to stay around. We would want him to give his testimony.

We would want to parade him from one meeting to another. We would want to show him off.

Jesus sent him away. Moreover, Mark says, "He straitly charged him" (Mark 1:43). That is to say, "He strictly charged him." He gave him some very specific instructions as to what he should do next with this new life he now had.

"See thou say nothing to any man: but go thy way, shew thyself to the priest, and offer for thy cleansing those things which Moses commanded, for a testimony unto them" (Mark 1:44). He was to show himself to *the priest.*

The Jewish priestly class were, as a group, united in their opposition to Christ. They needed the testimony of this leper. The cleansed leper himself needed the lesson of *Calvary* to be set before him in the rituals prescribed in the Mosaic Law for the cleansing of the leper. They were long, complex, and rich in the typology of the cross. The man needed that. The priests needed that.

In fifteen hundred years of human history, the ritual for the cleansing of a leper had only been performed once. It was performed in connection with the leprosy inflicted on Miriam for her presumption in criticizing that Moses had married someone of whom she did not approve. It must have been a startled priest, indeed, to whom a cleansed leper presented himself with the demand that the ancient ritual be performed.

Moreover, the actual carrying out of the ritual would have confronted the priest with a dramatic picture of Calvary, of the death and resurrection of Christ, and with the amazing authority of the Word of God. The Lord Jesus had as much love for the soul of that priest as He did for the heart of that leper.

But notice what the man did. Jesus sent him to the *priest.* The man went and told the *people.* "But he went out," we read, "and began to publish it much, and to blaze abroad the matter, insomuch that Jesus could no more openly enter into the city" (Mark 1:45).

It was all very well meant, we can be sure. The man, after all, was so excited, so full of the wonder of it all, so deliriously happy, so full of what Christ had done for him that he couldn't wait to tell someone.

Soon he had a crowd. He told them about Jesus. We would applaud the man. We would say, "That's what a new convert should do. He should tell everybody." We would have backed it up with a text: "That if thou shalt confess with thy mouth the Lord Jesus, and shalt believe in thine heart that God hath raised him from the dead, thou shalt be saved" (Rom. 10:9).

So testifying to one and all, the cleansed leper sent crowds of people to Christ.

And he hindered the work as a consequence. Jesus had no need of crowds of sensation-seekers. All they did was get in the way.

What the new convert needs is not the limelight but seclusion. He needs to sit down and think through, in the light of Scripture, exactly what has happened to him and how much light Calvary sheds on it all. That is what the cleansed leper should have done. Then, as the priest and penitent together worked their way through the ritual of Leviticus 14, the experience would have been enlightening for both of them. A week or so later the cleansed leper would have come back not only *cleansed* but *informed*—and he would have been far better off indeed.

FIVE

Simeon

A Godly Watcher

Luke 2:25–35

A. HE WAS RELIGIOUSLY ALERT
　1.　He had in his history a very great background
　2.　He had in his hand a very great Book
　3.　He had in his heart a very great burden
　　　a.　Confronted by unattainable precepts
　　　b.　Confronted by unfulfilled prophecies
　　　c.　Confronted by unexplained procedures
　　　d.　Confronted by unsatisfying provisions
B. HE WAS REMARKABLY ALONE
C. HE WAS REDEMPTIVELY ALIVE

We hardly know this man. He appears for a moment onto the sacred page then shuffles back off it again. Tradition has it that this old man, Simeon by name, may have been the son of the great Hebrew rabbi, Hillel, and the father of Gamaliel, the teacher of the apostle Paul. Edersheim picks up the idea and toys with it in a footnote and puts it back down again. We do know for sure that Simeon was very old. We know also that he haunted the temple precincts, ever on the lookout for something. Never a father and mother brought their newborn babe into the temple to be dedicated but that old Simeon would hover in sight, peering expectantly and then turning away disappointed yet again.

His name means *hearing,* and that tells us all we need to know. For the Holy Spirit declares, "Faith cometh by hearing, and hearing by the word of God" (Rom. 10:17). Simeon, in other words, was a man who listened to that same "still small voice" of God, which whispered into the ears of the great Elijah so many years before. He listened earnestly and expectantly, until at last, the words came, like the chiming of Christmas bells in his soul. He was promised he would not die until he had *seen* God's salvation.

He knew all about that salvation. He knew it from the earliest chapters of the book of Genesis. He knew it from what Moses had said, and from what David had said, and from what Isaiah, and a galaxy of Old Testament prophets had said. He knew it from *hearing* the Word of God. Likely enough there wasn't a messianic passage in all the Old Testament that old Simeon hadn't learned by heart. But he had not *seen* God's salvation.

He was different from all the rabbis, different from the whole college of Pharisees and Sadducees of his day. They read the Bible. They added endlessly to the Bible. They divided it, and dissected it, and discussed it, and distorted it. Simeon read it to *hear*.

He was a latter-day Samuel. He had learned to say, "Speak, Lord, for thy servant heareth" (1 Sam. 3:9) when he pondered the sacred page. So by *hearing,* he knew that he was living in the days of the coming of the Son of man. He knew that Jesus would come in his lifetime. He knew that he would actually *see* God's salvation. And he knew because God had told him so. God told other people, too, but they were too busy to listen.

A. He Was Religiously Alert

There are three things that indicate that Simeon was religiously alert.

1. He Had in His History a Very Great Background

For Simeon was a Jew. In that ancient world, it was a very great thing to have been *born a Greek*. The Greeks had an illustrious history. They were the great thinkers of the ancient world. In matters of the intellect, Athens stood supreme. There were Homer and Hesiod, there were Archimedes and Aristotle. There were Plato and Pythagoras, Socrates, Euripides, and Euclid. There were Zeno and Aesop and Herodotus. But for all their brilliance in art, science, and statecraft, when it came to religion, their pantheon of gods was about as childish as a fairy tale.

In that ancient world it was a very great thing to have been *born a Roman*. The Romans had conquered the world. At the Forum in Rome there stood a golden milestone. From that famous hub, great arterial highways reached out across thousands of miles in all directions. Along those magnificent highways, Rome's invincible legions marched. But when it came to religion, the Romans were no better than the Greeks. Indeed, dissatisfied with their own gods, the Romans borrowed gods from everybody. From Greece, from Syria, from Egypt. In the end it all boiled down to Caesar worship; the worship of the State.

Simeon was not born a Greek or a Roman. He was *born a Jew*. And that gave him an enormous advantage over every other nation in the world of his day. For Simeon grew up with a knowledge of Moses and Melchizedek, of Jonah and Jeremiah, of David and Daniel. Far better to be acquainted with the great names of Hebrew history and God-breathed poetry and prophesy than to know all the names of the petty, peurile philosophers of Mars Hill. Boys growing up in Babylon or Britain, in Greece or in Galatia, in Sparta or in Spain, in Pamphylia or in Partha, grew up surrounded by the customs and the culture of their various lands. Doubtless they were taught the appropriate creeds. But only a *Jew* grew up with a knowledge of God.

Moreover, Simeon was *not just a Jew by birth*. He was *a Jew by belief.* He was "waiting for the consolation of Israel." That is to say, he was anticipating the coming of Christ, and for a very good reason.

2. He Had in His Hand a Very Great Book

The world knows no Book like it. It is unique. It is the only Book, not only written, but *God-breathed*. For "holy men of God spake as they were moved by the Holy Ghost" (2 Peter 1:21). What was revealed to them by divine inspiration was written down by them for all the ages of time. Such is the Bible.

This Book is not a collection of folk lore and "old wives" fables. It is not a record (of varying degrees of accuracy) of the history, hopes, and heritage of the Jewish people. Here we have that same awesome mingling of the human and divine that we have in the Person of Christ. The Lord Jesus combined in His Person both the nature of God and the nature of man. It is impossible to say where the one ended and the other began. It was not that now He acted as God, now He acted as Man. He *always* acted as God and He *always* acted as Man. It is impossible to say where the humanity ended and the Deity began, or where the Deity ended and where the humanity began. In Him the two natures were perfectly blended and could not be separated.

What was true of the historical Jesus is equally true of the written Scriptures.

The *incarnate Word* and the *inspired Word* are *identical* in this—they *both* display that same mysterious mixing and merging of the human and the divine.

So far as the Bible is concerned we can detect the thought patterns and the style and the experiences and the backgrounds of its various human authors. Peter doesn't write like Paul. James does not copy Jeremiah. Job and Jonah, Joel and John lived in different times and wrote under different circumstances. Yet all display the same proofs of divine authority, accuracy, and inspiration. For all were overshadowed by the same guiding, inspiring, controlling Spirit of God. They wrote what *He* wanted written and used the very words He wanted used. Yet, at the same time, they wrote truths that were conceived and nourished and brought to birth in their own souls. Nor was the absolute, plenary, verbal inspiration of their writings a mechanical thing. The Holy Spirit did not simply dictate truth to them. He used them, limited, erring, stumbling human beings that they were, and sovereignly preserved them from making any mistakes.

So it was that Simeon had at hand a very great Book comprised of some thirty-nine books in his day. They were divided into three major segments—the Law, the Prophets, and the Writings. The history of Genesis, the hymns of David, the heroes of the book of Judges, the hopes of the prophets, the heights of Ezekiel, and the hosannas of Isaiah were without doubt all as familiar to Simeon as the gossip of his day. He would have known the books of his Bible and loved them all. The older he grew, the more he would know of the length and breadth and height and depth of God's blessed Book. He likely knew it nearly all by heart, believing every chapter, every verse, and every line.

3. He Had in His Heart a Very Great Burden

He read his Bible, he believed his Bible, he memorized his Bible, he obeyed his Bible. But there was something missing. When he read his Bible, as an honest and believing man, he was confronted by four things that must have burdened him.

He was *confronted by unattainable precepts.* He could count up no less than 613 commandments of the Law. He knew them by heart. He knew they were summed up in the Decalogue. He could check off all Ten Commandments in his soul and could say of the first nine, "All these have I kept from my youth up." He honestly believed that. He could say, "I have never had any God but God, the living Jehovah-Elohim-Adonai revealed in the Book. I have never made a graven image, never bowed down to an idol, never served a false god. I have always revered the infallible Name. I have never profaned the Sabbath. I have even sought to abide by the ever-multiplying rules and regulations of the rabbis. I have always honored my father and my mother. I have never killed. I have never committed adultery. I have never stolen anything. I have never borne false witness against a living soul."

The tenth commandment, however, bothered him the most—just as it did the apostle Paul—"Thou shalt have no evil desire." "The commandment came," Paul could say. "Sin revived. I died." For Paul could not say, Simeon could not say, nobody can say, "I have never had an evil desire" (Rom. 7).

More. Simeon had never loved the Lord his God with *all* his heart and with *all* his soul and with *all* his might. He had broken the first and the greatest commandment just like everyone else. Nor had he ever loved his neighbor the way he loved himself. He had broken the second commandment. All his righteousness were therefore as filthy rags, the same as ours. He had broken one law and was guilty of all. His goodness was only *relative* goodness. But God demands *absolute* goodness.

He was *confronted by unfulfilled prophecies.* God had promised Abraham and his seed a land that would stretch from the Nile, the great river of Egypt, to the Euphrates, the great river of Babylon. When had Israel ever possessed a tithe of that territory? All Israel had ever owned was a strip of land up and down the Jordan.

God had promised David a throne upon which the Messiah Himself would sit. Where was that throne? It was gone. The Babylonians had effectively put an end to Hebrew hopes of an Empire. There was a throne but Herod sat on it, and he was a monster of a man, a tyrant, a pagan, an *Edomite.*

The prophets spoke in glowing terms of a *golden age* when men would beat swords into plowshares and spears into pruning hooks, when the desert would blossom as the rose, and the lion would lie down with the lamb. Was that all mere rhetoric and hyperbole after all?

Then, too, he was *confronted by unexplained procedures.* There were the feast days, for example. The most elaborate rituals surrounded them. Passover. Pentecost. Atonement. Tabernacles. And the rest. To what purpose was all this regulation and ritual imposed on people?

There were the endless rituals connected with the consecration of a priest and the deconsecration of a Nazarite. Even the cleansing of a leper was attended by a multitude of religious rules and rituals. What was the sense of it all? Did God take such great delight in the minutia of ritual? It likely made little sense to him or to anyone else that he knew of.

Worse still he was *confronted by unsatisfying provisions*. What was he going to do about his *sin?* True, there was an elaborate ritual of offerings and sacrifices. There was the *burnt* offering, and the *meal* offering, and the *peace* offering, and the *sin* offering, and the *trespass* offering. There was also the great annual sacrifice on the Day of Atonement.

What was the sense of it all? He had offered sacrifices and, as so many of his contemporaries, had likely grown tired of it. He could have testified with the hymn writer:

> Not all the blood of beasts
> On Jewish altars slain,
> Could give the guilty conscience peace,
> Nor wash away one stain.[1]

So then, he was religiously alert. He had in his history a very great background, at hand a very great book, and in his heart a very great burden. But he never gave up. He kept on listening. "One of these days," he would say to himself, "the living God who spoke to Abraham and to Isaac and to Jacob, who spoke to Moses and Elijah, who spoke in times past unto the fathers by the prophets, will speak again. And when He does, I'll be there listening for my name."

B. He Was Remarkably Alone

Except for one very old woman who haunted the temple area, nobody else seemed to care.

There were thousands of priests—far too many of them, indeed. There were so many of them that a priest waited a whole lifetime for just one opportunity to minister in the Holy Place of the temple. They were experts at carving up the sacrifices, just as the rabbis were experts at carving up the Scriptures. But it was just a job with them. They were ordained at the age of thirty and retired at the age of fifty. They lived off the system and seemed content to let it go at that.

There were even more Levites, experts in the Law of Moses. They could tell you what the law said about this and what the rule was about that. They could rattle off precepts and punishments with practiced ease. But that was the extent of their concern.

---

1. Isaac Watts, "Not All the Blood of Beasts," 1709.

There were plenty of rabbis. The synagogue system, in vogue since the Babylonian captivity, seemed to multiply them. True, they numbered some remarkable scholars in their ranks, but they seemed more interested in what they called the *oral* law than in the *written* Law. Their mastery of this mythical oral law gave them enormous power and influence. They multiplied traditions. They added to the Law. They took the Law, intended by God to be a blessing to His people, and made it a burden. People couldn't do this and they couldn't do that. They mustn't go here and they mustn't go there. They must observe this rabbinical rule and that required regulation. Moreover, the rabbis loved to haggle over details. They would argue for months and months, for instance, over such a statement in the Law as "Thou shalt not seethe a kid in his mother's milk" (Exod. 34:26). They would come up with so many ifs, ands, and buts as to make everyday life in the kitchen a nightmare.

Then there were the Pharisees. There were plenty of them too. They were sticklers for procedure. They were concerned with such things as tithing, and fasting, and ritual prayer.

There were also the Sadducees. And in numbers more than sufficient. They were rationalists, modernists, liberal theologians. For the most part they were rich. They controlled the temple and its precincts. They fattened their purses off the concessions that cluttered up the Court of the Gentiles in the temple.

Worst of all there were the Zealots, red-hot patriots, eager for war with Rome. They were fanatics and radicals whose headstrong ways would surely lead to the dismemberment of Israel and the deportation of the Jews, unless they were curbed.

And so it went on. Old Simeon had nothing in common with any of them. They all seemed to have missed the mark. Each day the old man would visit the temple. He would see all the color and pageantry of his people as the representatives of the various Jewish religious bodies surged and swayed about him. He would peer into their faces. He would scan the faces of visitors from Galilee. He was looking for a special face. All he saw, however, in each face he scanned, were the marks of fallen human nature: ambition, hope, fear, lust, greed, sorrow, anxiety, unrest.

For it had been revealed to *him* by the Holy Spirit that he should not see death until he had seen the Lord's Christ. It had not been revealed to the High Priest. It had not been revealed to the elect priests and elders and rulers of the people who made up the Sanhedrin. It had not been revealed to anyone else. He was remarkably alone. It had been revealed to him.

This old man believed his Bible and was familiar with the remarkable prophecies of Daniel. He would know by heart the prophecy of the seventy weeks of years (490 years). He would know the exact date when *that* particular prophecy was to begin to run its course. It was to start with the decree of Artaxerxes, given in 445 B.C., in the twentieth year of his reign. This was the decree that authorized Nehemiah to go to Jerusalem and build the walls. After sixty-nine of the seventy weeks of years (483 years) something was to happen. Messiah was to be *"cut off."* Simeon would figure it out (483 years from 445 B.C.) and arrived at a date. He would think some more. The Messiah, when unveiled, could hardly be less than thirty years of age—priests, for instance, were not ordained until they were thirty. That would make the Messiah about thirty-three when the mysterious "cutting off" was to take place. He would subtract the thirty-three years and arrive at another date. *That* date fell within the date of Simeon's old age. The Messiah would have to be born about now he concluded. That was as far as human reasoning could go. Then divine revelation broke in, for God spoke to him and told him that the Messiah was about to be born. He would stop looking into the faces of sin-ravaged men, and start watching out for a babe in arms. Especially for a Babe from Bethlehem being brought to the temple for dedication.

C. He Was Redemptively Alive

Then we can imagine one special morning. Simeon gets up and has his breakfast. He spends some time meditating upon the Word of God. He wends his way, as at other times before, toward the temple. It dominates the horizon, all gleaming marble and gold. Herod had lavished a king's ransom on it. He had torn down the temple of Zerubbabel and had conscripted eighteen thousand workmen to build his temple. It was still not finished. But it would be one of the wonders of the world.

Although the old man can walk the temple courts blindfolded, he keeps eyes and ears very much open, indeed. What is this! Yonder, talking to the officiating priest, a couple, obviously peasants, evidently poor, seemingly from Galilee. The man is saying something like this: "This Child is named *Jesus.* We called him 'Jesus' because we were told to by the angel Gabriel. This Child is my wife's, not mine. He is virgin born."

The priest cuts in, rudely enough: "Never mind all that nonsense—and you'd better guard your Galilean tongue, you peasant. What you are saying comes close to blasphemy. What kind of an offering are you bringing for this dedication—a couple of *birds,* well that figures from the look of you. Here, let me have that boy so we can get this thing over and done with . . ."

In a flash it is all revealed to Simeon. *That's Him!* He hurries over. He takes the little Bundle of Humanity into his hands. He gazes down upon the face of Deity in humanity, wrapped in swaddling clothes, the eternal, self-existent second Person of the Godhead. Wonder of wonders! O joy, O delight! "Now lettest thou thy servant depart in peace . . . for mine eyes have seen thy salvation."

Old Simeon speaks a word or two to Mary. Then off home he goes—*saved!* Saved and sure of it! Off home to go to bed, perhaps to wake in the bosom of Abraham and within sight of the gleaming gates of Glory. To depart to tell all those in paradise that the magic moment had come! Christ has come at last! Hallelujah! What a Savior!

SIX

Anna

A Bold Herald of Christ's Coming

Luke 2:36–38

A. HER VICTORY
   1. She could have been bitter at the funeral
   2. She could have been bitter over her family
   3. She could have been bitter over her frailty
   4. She could have been bitter over her finances
B. HER VOCATION
C. HER VISION

Anna was a very old woman. She had been a widow for eighty-four years and had been married for seven years before that. That accounts for ninety-one years. Even if she had married when she was a young teenager, she would still be over a hundred years old. Anna was a woman who had grown old, loving God with all her heart and all her mind and all her soul and all her strength.

Anna was from the tribe of Asher. Asher was the least important of all the tribes. It sprang from Asher, the son of Jacob and Leah's maid Zilpah. Leah was the unwanted wife, and Zilpah was the unwanted slave of the unwanted wife. Asher was the last and least of the four slave-born sons of Jacob.

Yet Asher never allowed that status to bother him. His name means "happy." He made up for the deficiency of his birth by the joy and gladness of his disposition. Just because a person comes from humble circumstances doesn't mean he cannot be happy. Anna was born into the "happy tribe," and she seems to have imbibed the two characteristics of that tribe: she was humble and she was happy.

Anna added another godlike grace—she was holy. She had grown old in godliness.

Her name is so recorded in the sacred text as to be forever associated with the birth of the Lord Jesus Christ. God allowed her to see His Son when He was a tiny infant, a baby six or seven weeks old. She saw a little One who was dependent for every human need upon the ministry of a mother. Yet Anna realized He was the One who hung the stars in space, the Creator and Sustainer of the universe—the One who, even as He was cradled in this mother's arms, upheld all things by the word of His power (Heb. 1:1–3).

The Lord Jesus had been circumcised when He was eight days old, probably on the last and greatest day of the Feast of Tabernacles. After the appropriate lapse of time, Mary now comes to the temple with her Holy Child to offer the sacrifice demanded by the law to cover her ceremonial uncleanness. A mother had to bring such a sacrifice forty days after the birth of a son, or eighty days after the birth of a daughter (Lev. 12:2–5).

On this particular occasion God allowed two people to hold His Son in their arms. One was a woman; one was a man. Both were old. The two who were given a special glimpse of Him at this time were Anna and Simeon.

A. Her Victory

When studying people in the Bible of whom very little is told, we may carefully read between the lines. We may flesh out the stories, put ourselves in their shoes. When we read between the lines of Luke 2:36–38, we can at once see that Anna is a woman who had achieved victory over bitterness.

1. She Could Have Been Bitter at the Funeral

She once was young, she was married, and she was probably happy. She was in her late teens or early twenties when the tragedy happened: her husband died and she was left a widow.

Anna could have been very bitter at her husband's funeral. We all know people who have turned bitter after a tragic bereavement. They blame God for their sorrow; they speak rashly and accuse Him of cruelty—and Satan wins a victory. He traps people into projecting a distorted picture of God. But death is not God's fault; death is our fault. The wages of *sin* is death. We have no one but ourselves to thank that death stalks the earth, invading every home, breaking up every marriage, and turning this world into one vast graveyard. The blame for this blight can all be laid at the door of sin.

Anna might easily have accused God of robbing her of her husband. She could have decided to turn against Him. Millions do. Had she allowed herself to become bitter, in time she would have turned into a sour old woman nobody liked.

With her husband dead, Anna probably had to work to make ends meet. At harvest time, of course, she could glean in the fields. It was hard work and earned the equivalent of a minimal wage. But it would enable her to survive the winter. We can imagine her coming home at night. She sees her husband's work shoes in the corner of the room and his old robe hanging in the closet. The house is empty and silent but full of haunting memories.

Her life would be so dark, so very dark.

But then, perhaps, Anna would take down the old family Bible, find a well-worn passage in the prophecy of Isaiah, and read there of "the *treasures* of darkness" (Isa. 45:3, italics added). Anna learned to trust God in the dark. We can hear her say, "Dear Lord, I don't know why You took my beloved from me, but I trust You anyway. You have promised to be the friend of the widow. Dear Lord, I need You to be my friend."

So Anna entered into victory. She could have been bitter at the funeral. Instead she entered into the treasures of darkness. She decided she would make God's house her home.

The temple courts in Anna's day were both commodious and elaborate. The outer court, as rebuilt and extended by Herod, did not form a part of the sacred area. Gentiles were allowed to walk there, so it was called the court of the Gentiles. The ruling religious authorities had concessions set up in this court. Their agents were always busy there, changing money for buying and selling animals for sacrifices. Anna would make her way across this court until she came to some steps that led to a barrier.

This barrier was known as the middle wall of partition. On the wall, notices in Greek and Latin were posted to warn Gentiles not to penetrate beyond that point. The penalty for not heeding this warning was death. Ritually unclean Jews were also forbidden to go beyond the wall. Nine massive gates led through this barrier. One of the gates was known as the beautiful gate. It was sometimes called the Corinthian gate because it was overlaid with costly Corinthian bronze.

Anna would make her way through one of the gates and enter the court of the women. In this court the temple treasury was located. Jewish men could go farther—into the court of Israel. Descendants of Aaron could go farther still—into the court of the priests. Anna could go only as far as the court of the women.

In this court Anna would find a quiet corner that became her real home. She "departed not from the temple" (Luke 2:37), says the Holy Spirit. It appears she made God her husband, made His house her home, and entered into the treasures of darkness. She said with Job, "Though he slay me, yet will I trust in him" (Job 13:15).

So instead of becoming bitter at the funeral, Anna dedicated her widowhood to God. She determined to be the happiest, holiest widow in Jerusalem.

2. She Could Have Been Bitter over Her Family

Anna could have reacted against God even before she became a widow. She could have nursed resentment at her parents for making her go to the temple so often. Then, when tragedy struck, she might have said, "If that's all the thanks I get for going to the temple so often, that's it. I'll never darken the doors of the temple again." Many people offer excuses like that. They resent the most precious privilege ever granted to a human being—the privilege of being born into a Christian home—a home where parents love the Lord, keep fellowship with God's people, require their children to go to Sunday school and church, and protect their children as far as possible from the wickedness of the world.

Think of it—to have been born into a Hindu home. Until recently little Hindu girls could be subjected to the horrors of child marriage.[1] Others could find themselves destined to serve as temple prostitutes. Hindus have some 300 million gods, they worship idols, and they venerate animals, even rats and vermin. Some time ago *National Geographic* carried an illustrated article showing food actually being set out for the benefit of rats that are regarded as sacred—in a land that traditionally has had trouble feeding its millions of people.[2]

Or one could have been born into a Muslim home. Muslims are taught to worship Allah and to revere the teachings of a fierce and lustful prophet. Their creed revolves around the formula, "There is no god but Allah and Muhammad is his prophet."

---

1. What those horrors were has been amply documented in a harrowing book by Katherine Mayo, *Mother India* (New York: Harcourt and Brace, 1927).
2. *National Geographic,* July 1977, 71.

Or one might have been born into a Communist home and have been indoctrinated with the lie that there is no God. Millions of such practicing atheists die in their sins without God, without Christ, without hope.

Those who are born into Christian homes are greatly privileged. Yet some resent their Christian upbringing and cannot wait to get away from it all. Like the prodigal son, they throw off the restraints and requirements of a godly home. They have been brought up surrounded by sublime truth. They have been taught that Jesus is the eternal, uncreated Son of the living God, that He deliberately incarnated Himself in human form at Bethlehem, that He "went about doing good" (Acts 10:38), that He lives in the power of an endless life, and that He is mighty to save. Atheists prefer to throw such a priceless heritage away.

When a person decides to turn his back on all that is Christian, God sometimes lets him have it his own way. It will be more tolerable for some shrinking cannibal standing at the great white throne on the day of judgment than for such a rebel.

Anna's father must have been a godly man. His name was Phanuel, which means "the face of God." Thus, Anna grew up in a home where her father projected a living image of God to her childish soul. She must have seen the face of God in the face of her father. She knew what God was like, then, because she knew what her father was like.

My own father had his faults and failings like anyone else, but he showed me the face of God. I have never known a man who could pray like my father prayed. When my father stood up to lead God's people in prayer, he lifted them into the very throne room of the universe.

Why do so many Christian parents see their children go astray? Sometimes it is because the children look at their parents and do not see the face of God. Christian parents must do more than talk about what is right. Their supreme responsibility is to live Christ so that their children will think of the face of God whenever they think of their parents.

3. She Could Have Been Bitter over Her Frailty

Even though Anna was not bitter over her family, she could have been bitter over her declining health. A person does not arrive at over one hundred years of age without accumulating at least some of the inevitable physical consequences of advanced years. Perhaps she had arthritis or rheumatism. She might have had a weak heart or bad circulation. She could easily have pleaded her old age as an excuse for no longer going to the temple. But Anna's chief delight seemed to lie where God's people came together.

Her friends might have said, "Granny, you'd better give it up. You could fall down and break your hip on those stairs." "Granny, you can't go to the house of God today. It's raining." "Granny, now that you're so old, why not ease up a little? Why not settle for the Sabbath? Just go to the temple on the Sabbath."

But Anna would have said, "I'm looking for the coming of the Lord, and when He comes I know where I want Him to find me. I can think of a thousand places where I don't want Him to find me. I know where I would like Him to find me; and I know where I'm most likely to find Him—in the temple. You'll never keep me away from God's house."

When Jesus was twelve years old and Mary and Joseph lost track of Him, they went back to Jerusalem and spent three days searching Jerusalem to find Him. Astonishingly, they never thought of looking in the temple. Yet Jesus had haunted that temple. Anna was like Jesus: she loved the place where God's people met. So did Peter and John. Acts 4:23 says that after they were threatened by the Sanhedrin, "being let go, [Peter and John] went to their own company." There is more truth than poetry in the old saying that birds of a feather flock together.

4. She Could Have Been Bitter over Her Finances

Anna could have used her financial status as well as her frailty as an excuse for not going to the temple. There were vested interests in that temple, those who, under the guise of religion, fleeced the widows and the helpless. Jesus spoke of those charlatans who "devour widows' houses, and for a pretence make long prayers" (Mark 12:40).

Under Jewish law a widow could not dispose of her property except through the rabbis, some of whom were cheats. Quite possibly Anna herself had been cheated. But that some people use religion as a cloak to cover up their wickedness would have made no difference to Anna. She would not let their hypocrisy rob her of her own joy in the Lord.

The Holy Spirit says of Anna that she "departed not from the temple" (Luke 2:37). The word *not* is a strong one, expressing full and direct negation; absolutely not. There were no ifs, ands, or buts: Anna lived solely for the place where God had put His name. Her whole life revolved around the temple.

A verse in Anna's Bible told her that the Lord would come suddenly into His temple (Mal. 3:1). She did not know where else He would come, but she knew He would come there. So the temple was where Anna wanted to be.

Anna, it seems, triumphed over all the big and little excuses people make for staying away from the gathering place of the people of God. She was not, we can be sure, infatuated by the temple itself but wanted to be where God Himself had promised to be. Her presence in the temple is strong evidence of her victory over bitterness.

B. Her Vocation

Luke 2:37 tells us that this remarkable woman "served God with fastings and prayers night and day." The word translated "served" signifies "worshiped." Anna devoted her whole life to praying for the Lord's coming. She could see wrongs all about her, even in the temple, and she no doubt longed for the Lord to come and put them right.

When we read of Anna's vocation we can picture an old woman, bent and feeble, *doing what the high priest should have been doing.* (The high priest was Caiaphas, and everyone knew he was more interested in the politics of his office than anything else.) We can also picture an old woman *doing what the shining seraphim and cherubim are doing.* We see Anna, as the hymn says, "gazing on the Lord in glory." We see her, day and night, ceasing not to cry, "Holy, holy, holy, is the LORD (Isa. 6:3). "Thou art worthy, O Lord, to receive glory and honour and power: for thou hast created all things, and for thy pleasure they are and were created" (Rev. 4:11).

Anna brought her body under control and set her spirit free. Her life's work was to praise the Lord and to pray—she would have prayed for her family and friends, for the religious leaders of her nation, for the spiritual life of her people, for those who ruled the land, for God's kingdom to come, and for His will to be done on earth as it is in heaven.

The name *Anna* (Hannah) means "God is gracious." People might have said to her, "God is gracious? He took away your husband in your youth when you had been married barely seven years. God is gracious?" Anna would have replied, "Oh yes! That was His gracious way of wedding me to Himself. Do you think I have been a widow these past eighty-four years? Oh no! I have been married to Another, even to Him who is to be raised from the dead."

Anna's vocation, then, was to pray. God has few saints like her on earth. He has plenty of people who are willing to preach. He has only a few who are willing to pray, and even fewer who feel called to make prayer and fasting the great and controlling ministry of their lives.

C. HER VISION

One day Anna's prayers were answered!

We can imagine that day. It begins like any other day. Anna wakes up that morning at the usual time. With her poor old bones and joints all stiff, she takes a little while to get going. She dresses, goes outside, picks up her pitcher, and hobbles down to the well. There she exchanges a few pleasantries with other women from the neighborhood. Then she goes back home to make herself a little porridge for breakfast.

She takes her well-worn staff, and off she goes to the temple. She knows her way blindfolded, she knows every house and shop, every man and woman, every stick and stone.

She puffs and pants a little as she comes to the temple mount. Rising from the deep valleys, the mount is like an island surrounded by a sea of walls, palaces, streets, and houses. Rising terrace after terrace, the mount is crowned by a mass of snowy marble and glittering gold. Anna pauses to admire the splendor of the view. She has seen it thousands of times, but it never fails to take her breath away. She has seen that gigantic sacred enclosure thronged with as many as two hundred thousand people on high days and holy days.

Once within the temple gates, Anna sees colonnades and porches every-where—the most famous is the ancient eastern colonnade known as Solomon's porch. She sees, too, the pinnacle of the temple, towering 450 feet above the Kidron valley.

Once past the colonnades she enters the court of the Gentiles. As she walks through she looks with disapproval at the way it has been turned into a market. Coming to the middle wall of partition, she labors up the fourteen steps to enter, through one of the splendid gates, into the court of the women. There Anna finds her usual corner and begins her daily round of prayer.

But this day is to be different from any other day, for on this day Jesus comes!

Anna notices a man and a woman entering the court. They are obviously poor and have with them a babe wrapped in a blanket. Anna sees an old man approach the couple. She knows that old man. He is Simeon. She can't help overhearing what Simeon says as he intercepts the couple and takes the baby in his arms:

"Lord, now lettest thou thy servant depart in peace, according to thy word: for mine eyes have seen thy salvation" (Luke 2:29–30).

Anna's heart leaps. *It is the Lord! Hallelujah! He is come! Of course! Of course! He is come as a baby. A virgin was to conceive and bear a Son.* And Anna bursts into thanksgiving and praise.

She now has a new vocation. She speaks of Him to all who "looked for redemption in Jerusalem." She knows every believer in town. "He's here!" she says to each and every one of them. "I've seen Him. His name is *Jesus.* Keep your eyes open. He'll be back in your lifetime. Be sure you are ready."

So instead of becoming bitter, Anna became a blessing. Anna's joy over the coming of Jesus is ample testimony to God's faithfulness in rewarding a life like hers.

SEVEN

John the Baptist

Matthew 3:1–17

A. THE MAN
1. John's sphere of labor
2. John's sense of leading
3. John's style of life
B. THE MULTITUDE
1. John's converts
2. John's critics
C. THE MASTER
1. John's practical word to the leaders
   a. Their faulty character
   b. Their false conduct
   c. Their foolish conceit
2. John's prophetic word to the laity
   a. The barren nation
   b. The believing nucleus

John was born to be a priest, for both his father, Zacharias, and his mother, Elisabeth, came from an ancient priestly family. In Israel, the priesthood was not an open profession. It was the exclusive preserve of members of a single clan and of a single family within that clan. A man had to be of the family of Aaron of the tribe of Levi in order to be a priest. John met the criterion.

John, however, made a decision. Long before he expected to embark on his career as a Hebrew priest, long before he would have performed the ceremonial functions that comprised much of the ministry, John arrived at a decision. John decided that what Israel needed was not another priest after the order of Aaron; what Israel needed was another prophet after the order of Elijah. So John turned his back on an honored, comfortable, and secure profession and headed for the wilderness.

We do not know how old he was when he made this decision, and we do not know how long he stayed in the wilderness. We do know that from birth, he had been set apart to be a Nazarite—one of three lifelong Nazarites in Scripture. That is, John was set apart to live solely for God. And from the time of his birth, he was filled with the Spirit—something very rare indeed.

John grew up in a Hebrew home. He was blessed with godly parents who would have instructed him in the Word of God. They must have often told him the story of the coming of the angel to foretell his birth, and of his father's disbelief, consequent muteness, and eventual deliverance. It is not surprising, then, that he cut himself off from the professionalism of the priesthood and sought the solitude of the vast wilderness in order to listen for the clear call of God. And finally it came. He was to announce to the Hebrew people the imminent coming of Christ.

What a man John was! He was willing to beard the unscrupulous and powerful Herod in his den, denounce him publicly for his immorality, endure the rage of Herodias, and face the headsman's ax. Above all, John was willing to fade into the background when the Christ appeared, as the moon fades before the rising sun.

A. THE MAN

John shook his nation to its foundations. He was, Jesus said, the greatest man born of a woman.

1. John's Sphere of Labor

Matthew simply wrote, "In those days came John the Baptist, preaching in the wilderness of Judaea" (3:1). Luke filled in the details about "those days." John began preaching "in the fifteenth year of the reign of Tiberius Caesar" (Luke 3:1).

Tiberius was born in 42 B.C. In "those days" he was an old man. As a citizen he had distinguished himself as an orator, soldier, and civil servant. As a Caesar he had distinguished himself for tyranny, sloth, self-indulgence, deceitfulness, cruelty, and licentiousness.

Pontius Pilate was governor of Judea. Herod Antipas, another cruel, crafty, carnal man, was a petty princeling in Galilee. Herod's half brother Philip ruled another part of Palestine. Philip the tetrarch was the only "decent" member of the Herodian family, but he really wasn't much better than his brothers.

Annas and Caiaphas were Israel's high priests. Jewish law allowed only one high priest, but that law was modified by the Romans who chopped and changed the office to suit themselves. In the previous 107 years there had been twenty-eight high priests. Annas had been high priest from A.D. 7–14, then the Roman governor had deposed him and in A.D. 18 installed Caiaphas in his place. That change didn't make much difference, however, for Caiaphas was Annas's son-in-law. Luke, in fact, lumped them together (3:2). Caiaphas wore the robes; Annas told him what to do.

So the preaching of John the Baptist is well dated. His advent marked the coming of Christ and the beginning of a new era. John tolled the bell over a decadent age and pealed out tidings of a new beginning for mankind.

In "those days" John came preaching in "the wilderness of Judea." Such was his sphere of labor. That wilderness was desolate and dreary, utterly hostile to life—a tumble of barren ridges running the whole length of the Dead Sea. What a place to begin preaching! We would have suggested that he rent the Royal Albert Hall or Yankee Stadium. We would have told him to train a team, send advance men into town to seek the support of religious leaders, get businessmen behind the venture, send in organizers to recruit counselors, place advertisements in newspapers, buy TV time, announce his meetings on the radio. In other words, we would have told him to mount an intensive campaign to prepare people for his crusade. But John would have ignored our suggestions.

John's pulpit was more likely a rocky ledge frowning down on a vast, unpeopled waste. There he would fast, pray, watch, and wait for God to make His move. John had no crusades, no committees, no choirs, no collections. He was just a man alone with God in the wilds. John did not go to the crowds; the crowds came to him. It has been estimated that, from start to finish, about a million people found their way to the wilderness to hear this desert preacher.

2. John's Sense of Leading

John did not beat around the bush when the people started coming. He thrashed them thoroughly for their sins. He went, as we would say today, straight for the jugular. His one main word was "Repent!" It rang out like a peal of thunder across the wilderness.

The Holy Spirit's great appeal, after all, is not to the intellect or the emotions, but to the conscience and the will. His first word to the sinner is "Repent!" The Spirit of God cannot be fooled, for He knows us. He knows what we have done, where we have been, what we have said, and with whom we have been involved. He knows the time, place, circumstance, and consequence of every act. Uninterested in our excuses and explanations, He pounds away at a single word: "Repent!"

3. John's Style of Life

John's lifestyle, wedded to his compelling personality and natural ability, gave his preaching devastating authority. Everyone knew he was a holy man of God. John prayed passionately. He lived like a Spartan, wore rough clothing, ate coarse food, and underwent endless fastings. He had power with God and with men. John could have been high priest; he could have made it to the top in any profession. And he did make it to the top as a preacher who knew how to make people weep over their sins.

John's baptism was a baptism of repentance. His "altar calls" brought people straight to the water. Their tears helped swell the waters of Jordan. Down into the water they went—publicly, before family, friends, and foes. Up they came, and then away they went with a few practical words from John concerning their conduct in the future.

The crowds would melt away with the gathering shadows. As they hurried home, some would weep over their past; some would worry over their stubbornness and unwillingness to repent; some would shout for joy because their sins were forgiven and they had peace with God. All would be aware that the Christ was coming soon.

John, we can easily imagine, would return to his dwelling, perhaps a lonely cave. After eating a few locusts and a spoonful of wild honey, he wraps a rag around his shoulders to ward off the chill of the night, and he goes back into the presence of God. He weeps and prays for a deeper, more lasting work to be done in the life and soul of the nation he loves.

Such was the man.

B. THE MULTITUDE

1. John's Converts

People flocked to John from Judea and the regions around Jerusalem and

Jericho. They came from Bethlehem and Bethany, Cana and Capernaum, Nazareth and Nain. The old, the young, the rich, the poor, the priest, the peasant, the aristocrat, the artisan, the butcher, the baker, the candlestick maker—one and all, they came to hear a man preach with passion and power. They came to hear a man filled with the Spirit of God.

Some came because they were burdened with their sin, others because they were curious. Some came because others who had come received new life. When they came, they heard John's message. His message was not clever, but clear; not wordy, but weighty; not scholarly, but scorching. Those who came did not hear a learned rabbinical discourse on the law of Corban, or the law concerning the seething of a young goat in its mother's milk. When they came they were stabbed by the Holy Spirit with a sense of their personal sin and guilt.

When they came, the message they heard was simple. Christ is coming! He is already on the way! He had left His Father's home on high and was about to burst upon the nation. Prophecy was about to be fulfilled with a vengeance. John motivated the people to ask, "What shall we do to prepare for His coming?" He told them that they must take a stand for God against their sins—and enormous crowds repented then and there.

Matthew said, "Then went out to him Jerusalem, and all Judaea, and all the region round about Jordan, and were baptized of him in Jordan, confessing their sins" (3:5–6). In the Bible the Jordan River is always a symbol of death. It flows down a tortuous bed and buries itself at last in the bitter waters of the Dead Sea. By being baptized in the Jordan, John's converts owned themselves dead in trespasses and sins and in need of cleansing within.

John did not make repentance easy for them. He did not say, "Every head bowed. Every eye closed. Now who will slip up his hand and say, 'Preacher, pray for me.'" Oh no! He said in effect, "Get up from where you are. Come up front, in front of this crowd of people. Come right into the water, just as you are, clothes and all. I will publicly baptize you if you confess your sin and confess your faith in the soon-coming Christ of God." It was an altar call calculated to strike at the very roots of pride.

2. John's Critics

No matter how popular a preacher is, if he is faithful to the Word of God, he will make enemies. John was no exception. We can be sure that some people found reasons to dismiss both him and his message. Some disliked the way he dressed and did his hair. Some objected to his ragged beard. Others scoffed at his style of preaching. Some sneered at his seeming lack of education. Some people thought him wrong to make religion so personal, so public, and so practical. Religion, they said, should be kept within cloistered walls and surrounded with proper rituals; a religious gathering should be a stately occasion, not a circus parade.

John's critics came, though, from the religious crowd. The harlots, publicans, sinners, and outcasts did not come to criticize; they came to be converted. The response to John's preaching illustrates that while there is no one too bad to be saved, there are many who think they are too good. The religious leaders of Israel—the Pharisees and Sadducees—certainly did not think they had any need to repent.

The Pharisees and the Sadducees came from opposite sides of the religious spectrum. Not much love was lost between them, but they no doubt agreed that John was a religious exhibitionist whose preaching was radical and ridiculous. We can see them come, their robes wrapped around them, looking disdainfully at what was going on.

The Pharisees, who specialized in *ritualism,* attended the synagogue, fasted three times a week, and were scrupulous about the outward aspects of the law. They kept the Sabbath, said long prayers, and paid their tithes. But these paragons of moral rectitude had hearts as cold as clay. In the end they demanded Christ's death. Yet the Pharisees did not consider themselves sinners and certainly did not think that they needed to repent. Above all, they had no intention of making public spectacles of themselves by being baptized in the muddy waters of the Jordan in front of John's rag and bone collection of the lower classes.

The Sadducees, who specialized in *rationalism,* denied the miraculous and watered down the Scriptures. These keepers of the temple were the aristocracy of the nation. They certainly were not going to listen to a fellow like John—a dropout from the priesthood who dressed like a beggar and ranted and raved at publicans, harlots, and other sinners. Yes, indeed, John had critics as well as converts.

C. The Master

To understand John, we must study his relation to Christ. John was a God-sent forerunner or herald. He was commissioned from on high to preach the soon coming of Christ and to awaken the nation to a sense of sin and need. That is why he spoke so scathingly to those he knew would reject Christ. John knew that those who rejected the forerunner would also reject the Christ. The New Testament principle is clear: No John, no Jesus. If there is no repentance (John's message), there is no rebirth (Jesus' message).

In the light of the imminent coming of Christ, John had two things to say. One was practical and the other was prophetic. He had a whip for his nation's leaders and a warning for its people.

1. John's Practical Word to the Leaders

The fact that the religious establishment had rejected him did not deter John. His critics had money and influence at court, but he did not yield to their pressure. They regarded him as a bigot and a radical, but that did not stop John for a moment. He just brought up his heavy artillery and concentrated his fire on his foes. John exposed their character, their conduct, and their conceit.

a. Their Faulty Character

"O generation of vipers, who hath warned you to flee from the wrath to come?" he said (Matt. 3:7). Imagine that! John denounced both the pope and the college of cardinals of his day. He saw right through the religious leaders and called them a nest of snakes, sons of the serpent. And their serpent character would soon be exposed, for within a few years they would succeed in having Christ crucified on Calvary's hill. Religious error always ends up rejecting Christ.

Picture a modern preacher calling respected religious leaders poisonous snakes? That would be quite different from much of today's sermonizing. Many preachers today are more concerned with making friends and influencing people than with telling them that unless they repent, they are going to hell. Many ministers are content with a diluted ecumenicalism and a compromising fellowship with false teachers. No wonder preachers cannot expose the wickedness of those who lead people astray. The Bible reserves its most scathing denunciations for those who teach error in the name of Christ.

b. Their False Conduct

John continued, "O generation of vipers . . . bring forth therefore fruits meet for repentance" (Matt. 3:7–8). The Pharisees and Sadducees were hypocrites. They did not think they needed to repent, yet their lives were a shallow, empty sham. They did not commit the gross sins of the publicans and harlots, but the religious leaders were just as much in need of repentance as the worst people in the land. Their sins were not sins of the flesh. They were sins of the spirit: pride, resentment, jealousy, anger, smugness, and hypocrisy. In God's sight such sins are just as bad as drunkenness, murder, and immorality.

c. Their Foolish Conceit

Exposing the leaders' conceit, John added, "Think not to say within yourselves, We have Abraham to our father: for I say unto you, that God is able of these stones to raise up children unto Abraham" (Matt. 3:9). Being born into an exclusive family did not make the Pharisees and Sadducees acceptable to God; they needed to be born again.

Years ago I took a man to hear an outstanding preacher. The preacher took as his text the Lord's warning to Nicodemus: "Ye must be born again" (John 3:7). After the sermon I asked my guest if he had been born again. He replied that his wife was a descendant of John Wesley. His hope of heaven was based on the fact that he had married into a religious family!

He might just as well have said, "I am a descendant of Noah," but even that pedigree would not make him a candidate for heaven. Eligibility depends on being born again. Being born into a believer's home does not make a person a Christian any more than being born in a stable makes one a horse.

The people to whom John preached prided themselves on their religious ancestry. God was not impressed. So John's practical word was for the religious people who scorned him as well as his message concerning the coming Christ.

2. John's Prophetic Word to the Laity

a. The Barren Nation

The nation of Israel had a rich spiritual heritage and enjoyed many religious privileges. Within a few years, however, it would reject not only John, but also the Christ he preached. John prophetically declared, "And now also the axe is laid unto the root of the trees: therefore every tree which bringeth not forth good fruit is hewn down, and cast into the fire" (Matt. 3:10).

John was not speaking of pruning. That had been done twice: once when the Assyrians had cut off ten of the twelve tribes, and again when the Babylonians had cut off the remaining two. By God's grace, the nation had been replanted in the Promised Land, but now the final test was approaching: What would they do with Jesus?

If the nation rejected Him, the judgment would fall not only on the nation as a nation. The ax would be put not just to the tribal branches this time, but to the *root* of the tree; that is, the individuals who made up the nation, the individuals who rejected Christ, would feel the weight of coming wrath.

b. The Believing Nucleus

John said in Matthew 3:11–12,

> I indeed baptize you with water unto repentance: but he that cometh after me is mightier than I, whose shoes I am not worthy to bear: he shall baptize you with the Holy Ghost, and with fire: whose fan is in his hand, and he will thoroughly purge his floor, and gather his wheat into the garner; but he will burn up the chaff with unquenchable fire.

That prophetic statement embraced both comings of Christ: His coming in grace to baptize believers into the mystical body of the church, and His coming in government to baptize all Christ-rejecters with fire.

John realized that there would be a lasting division among mankind. Some would believe on Christ and be saved. Others would reject Christ and be lost. John's great burden was to awaken the conscience of the people so that when Christ came knocking at the doors of their hearts, they would be open to Him and let Him in.

Our age is the age of grace. Christ has come, and the great division of the human race into those who have accepted Him and those who are rejecting Him is under way. There is still time and opportunity to accept Christ and thus escape God's wrath. The old hymn asks,

> What will you do with Jesus?
> Neutral you cannot be;
> Some day your heart will be asking,
> What will He do with me?[1]

---

1. Albert B. Simpson, "What Will You Do with Jesus?" 1891.

EIGHT

Herod Agrippa I
A Murderous Hand

Acts 12:1–25

A. THE HOLLOW CROWN
B. THE HIDEOUS CRIME
   1. The death of James
   2. The detention of Peter
C. THE HAUGHTY CLAIM

Herod Agrippa I grasped the helm of the Jewish state with a murderous hand. He was a scheming, grasping, treacherous individual. The Herods were a bad lot, true children of Esau; Edomites with hands dyed red with the blood of innocent men, women, boys, and girls. Disregarding the laws of God and of man, the Herods were a law unto themselves. A man would be safer trusting a rattlesnake than trusting a Herod. The family, though, was not without wit, charm, and genius. Herod the Great, so-called, was a magnificent builder, bold ruler, and crafty negotiator. But woe would betide the man who crossed a Herod, or who had something a Herod wanted, or who stood in a Herod's way.

Herod Agrippa I, whom we meet in the early chapters of Acts, is not the Herod we meet in the Gospels. The man who murdered John and mocked at Jesus was Herod Antipas, an uncle of Herod Agrippa I.

A. THE HOLLOW CROWN

The Herods thought they were big men, but they were only as big as God in heaven and Caesar on earth allowed them to be. Nevertheless, they made plenty

69

of noise, splashing their weight around in their own small puddles. If you'd heard them talk and seen them strut, you'd have thought they ruled the world, not just bits and pieces of a little land held in Rome's iron grip. A Herod's crown was usually a hollow crown.

The grandfather of Herod Agrippa I was Herod the Great, the big-time builder. One of his projects was the temple in Jerusalem. It took about eighty-four years to build the temple, and about six years after it was completed it was destroyed by the Romans in accordance with the prophecy of Christ. The Roman general Titus ordered it to be preserved. Jesus said it would be razed. Jesus was right.

Another landmark of Herod the Great's building genius was the Roman city of Caesarea on the coastline of his realm. Caesarea was an architectural marvel because its builders had to overcome enormous obstacles when constructing the harbor.

Herod the Great, however, is best known to us as the one who murdered the babes of Bethlehem in an effort to destroy the newborn Christ of God.

The grandmother of Herod Agrippa I was the beautiful Mariamne. Herod the Great was madly in love with this princess, yet that did not stop him from murdering her and her two brothers. After that he became insane. His nights were haunted by the beautiful woman he had married and murdered, and his days were spent trying to find another woman like her. On one occasion he saw a woman of the streets who reminded him of his dead princess. Despite all warnings he wanted her. He got what he wanted—and more. He contracted a foul disease that rotted his body through and through.

The father of Herod Agrippa I was Aristobulus, who was also murdered by his father Herod the Great. Agrippa's parents were first cousins. Agrippa himself was married to his first cousin, the daughter of an aunt who was married to an uncle. No wonder there was a trace of madness in the Herods.

When Herod the Great murdered Aristobulus in a fit of jealous rage, Agrippa was sent off to Rome by his mother so that he would be out of the reach of his evil grandfather.

Agrippa's uncle Philip married the bloodthirsty Herodias. Then Agrippa's uncle Antipas ran away with Herodias. Agrippa's cousin Salome (daughter of Herodias) performed a provocative dance before her stepfather Antipas. It so inflamed the king that he promised to reward her with half his kingdom or whatever else she desired. Her she-wolf mother urged her to demand the head of John the Baptist on a platter, which she did.

Agrippa's brother, Herod of Chalcis, married his niece Bernice. Later on

Bernice showed up as the consort of her brother Agrippa II under circumstances that caused the tongues of the scandalmongers to wag.

Such was the Herod family. They had no moral scruples. The only law they consulted was the law of their own lustful desires.

While the young Herod Agrippa I was in Rome, he made an important friend indeed—that friend was Gaius, the grandnephew of Tiberius Caesar. Gaius is better known today as Caligula. When Tiberius died, Caligula became the emperor. Caligula remembered his friend Agrippa and sent him back to Palestine as a king. Later on, the emperor Claudius enlarged the domains of Herod Agrippa I so that he actually ruled a kingdom almost as large as that of his grandfather Herod the Great.

The crown, however, was hollow. The king who wore it could never forget that he was, after all, a puppet of the Caesar. When Agrippa was on his way back to Palestine, he spent some time in Alexandria, Egypt. The Greeks openly mocked and derided him. Nor was he liked by his subjects. He was too much the child of Roman vice, too much given to Greek frivolity, too glib with his lip service to Judaism, too much a savage Herod, and too much an Idumean to have been anything but a monster.

So Herod Agrippa I wore a crown, a hollow crown, one that commanded no respect at all from the Jews. True, he could claim descent from Mariamne, daughter of an ancient line of Jewish priest-kings. But the wild blood of Esau ran too strongly in the veins of the Herods for any of them to be able to command much respect in the Jewish promised land. Agrippa, however, tried to make friends among the Jews when he could. He was an old hand at buttering the toast of those who wielded real power. He played up to Caiaphas, Annas, and the college of Jewish cardinals who sat in the Sanhedrin and pulled all the important strings.

B. The Hideous Crime

Agrippa was politician enough to know that if he wanted to gain favor with Caiaphas he must side with the Sanhedrin against the church. Most members of the Sanhedrin viewed the church with hatred. They hated Christ. They hated the "ignorant and unlearned men" who were so successfully preaching Christ and who were fast rendering Judaism obsolete. Caiaphas and his friends were infuriated by the success of the handful of Galilean fishermen who snapped their fingers at the Sanhedrin. How bold they were, these Christians! How complete was their indifference to the commands and threats issued by the Jewish authorities.

It did not take Agrippa long to put two and two together. A good way to ingratiate himself with the Jewish authorities would be to do their dirty work for them. He had no scruples. He would please the Sanhedrin. Such would be the governing principle of his regime—kill off the leaders of the church.

1. The Death of James

"Now about that time [about the time that Paul and Barnabas showed up with a substantial cash donation from the dynamic Gentile church in Antioch for the support of poor Christians in Jerusalem] Herod the king stretched forth his hands to vex certain of the church. And he killed James the brother of John with the sword" (Acts 12:1–2). The Greek word translated "vex," *kakoō,* means "to do evil to someone, especially to harm physically or maltreat someone." In the case of James, the maltreatment took the form of cold-blooded murder—premeditated and malicious. Herod acted without any cause or provocation, and he thought he could get away with it because he sat in a seat of dictatorial power.

James had been a Galilean fisherman. He and his brother John were first cousins of Jesus. James's mother was one of the Lord's most devoted followers and accompanied Him even to the cross. At the call of Jesus, James and John left their fishing business and became the Lord's most intimate disciples. James was one of the three disciples chosen by Jesus to witness the raising of Jairus's daughter, to be present on the mount of transfiguration, and to watch and pray with Him in the garden of Gethsemane.

We can well imagine that in the infant church James was much in demand as a speaker. New converts would be eager to hear him tell over and over again of the many marvelous and mighty works of Jesus. He would recount for them firsthand the Sermon on the Mount, the Olivet discourse, and the Lord's many parables. He would tell how Jesus cleansed lepers, gave sight to the blind, fed hungry multitudes, and raised the dead.

James would tell them with an embarrassed laugh how he and John had persuaded their mother to ask Jesus to give them high posts of honor in His kingdom (Matt. 20:20–28). "How little we understood about the kingdom in those days," he would say. He would look around the group and add, "Jesus said to us, 'Ye know not what ye ask. Are ye able to drink of the cup that I shall drink of, and to be baptized with the baptism that I am baptized with?' [v. 22]. We boasted that we could. Well, He gave us a chance to taste of that cup. He took us to Gethsemane and told us to pray. We fell asleep. We had the chance to follow Him to Golgotha. We ran away."

So James went quietly about his business, telling the story of Jesus to this person and that group until he filled Jerusalem with the knowledge of Christ. James's testimony was so effective that, when Herod decided to vex the church, he thought it would be a good idea first to get rid of James. Thus, James became the first martyr among the apostles. Herod simply ordered his henchmen to execute James, and then the king sat back to reap the approval and applause of the Jewish religious elite.

2. The Detention of Peter

"Because he saw it [James's death] pleased the Jews, he proceeded further to take Peter also" (Acts 12:3). Peter was taken on the anniversary of Christ's murder. It was the feast of unleavened bread, which is closely associated with Passover. Herod was delighted with the new friendliness of the Jewish high priest and his toadies. Arrest Peter! What a cheap and easy way to keep the troublesome Sanhedrin happy and content.

Probably Herod imprisoned Peter in the strongly garrisoned fortress of Antonia, which frowned down on the temple court. Peter was locked up as tightly as any prisoner on death row today. Between him and freedom stood two iron chains, sixteen soldiers, various keepers, and an iron gate. Four relays of soldiers—four guards in each relay—would have guarded him around the clock. Two of the guards would stand at the door; the other two guards would stand one on either side of him. In keeping with Roman custom, Peter would be actually chained to these two. Moreover, the death sentence had been signed and would be carried out the next day.

So what did Peter do? Did he pray, pleading with God to set him free? (God had given him the keys of the kingdom, but a lot of good they were doing him now.) Did he pace the floor of his cell, grit his teeth, and bravely resolve to die like a man? Did he ask God to give him dying grace? No. He simply committed his soul to God, said good night to his jailers, and went to sleep! He was not just a conqueror; he was more than conqueror.

Peter had already learned how to be crucified with Christ. The life that he now lived, he lived "by the faith of the Son of God" (Gal. 2:20). To Peter, death was simply a matter of being "absent from the body, and . . . present with the Lord" (2 Cor. 5:8).

When the angel who visited Peter in his cell reported back to the courts of bliss, we can imagine what he said. "What was Peter doing when I arrived? Bless you, he was sound asleep! I had to give him quite a blow to wake him up. You'd have thought he was safe and sound in his own bed."

Meanwhile the church was praying. The church knew how to pray in those days. Luke wrote, "But prayer was made without ceasing of the church unto God for him" (Acts 12:5). Peter was asleep but his brothers in Christ were wide awake. Across Jerusalem and up and down Judea all-night prayer meetings were in progress. The court of heaven was being bombarded and blitzed by an enormous barrage of intercessory prayer.

The church in those times likely could not imagine itself without big, blustering, bossy, beloved Peter. He had such a happy knack of putting his foot in his mouth and making people love him for it. God had used Peter to perform miracles. Peter was the one who preached on the day of Pentecost, the birthday of the church. Peter was the one who was speaking when the Holy Spirit was given to the Samaritans. Peter had flung wide the door of the church to the Gentiles. Peter was always way out in front of everyone else or else lagging far behind. Peter could tell inimitable stories about Jesus. Peter was famous for his bluff honesty; he would shout a person down one moment and weep with sorrow and regret the next. Peter had bravely faced the Sanhedrin. Peter was one of the chosen three, along with James and John, who knew Jesus best. The church could not imagine itself without Peter, so the church prayed.

On the surface it seemed as if all the odds were with Herod Agrippa I. He had the fortress and the soldiers, the power and the authority. He had the confidence of the Caesar and the great seal to legitimize his actions. Behind Herod stood imperial Rome and its armies of iron. Alongside Herod stood the powerful Sanhedrin, which spoke for hundreds of thousands of Jews at home and abroad.

On the other hand there was a praying church—ordinary men, women, boys, and girls who loved Jesus. An unsaved betting man would have put his money on Herod, especially after the martyrdom of James. The God of the Christians had not lifted a finger to help him.

Then the miracle happened. Down from the heights of heaven came Peter's angel. How we would like to know more about these angels! We each have one. Peter and Paul saw theirs. Little children have angels. Individual churches have angels.

Jacob's ladder swarms with angels. In Genesis 28 we see them ascending and descending that shining stairway. They trudge upwards, weighed down with the sad stories of man's injustices, atrocities, and downright wickedness. They come back down refreshed and revived, their eyes alight with new resolve, returning to earth with new orders from the throne of God.

Peter's angel came right into the jail. What cared the angel for iron gates and iron men? A snap of his fingers, and all the guards would be sound asleep. An imperious beckoning of his hand and Peter followed. (Peter, dazed and still half asleep, thought he was having a particularly interesting and vivid dream.) The door swung open of its own accord. The iron gate felt a sudden miraculous impulse to fling itself open. The gate let the great apostle of the Lamb pass and then shut itself again with a triumphant clang.

How sweet and fresh the night air must have smelled after the fetid atmosphere of the prison. Peter turned around to thank his benefactor, but he was gone! Peter was free—but by no means safe. God never does for us what we can do for ourselves, so Peter set off for the house of Mary, the mother of John Mark. Mary's house was one of the primary meeting places of the Jerusalem church.

We have all chuckled over what happened next. Rhoda, who couldn't believe that Peter was really at the door, left him standing there while she ran in to tell the news to the people who had gathered to pray. It was incredible. God had answered prayer! "It is his angel!" said the people. But Peter's persistent banging on the door at last produced the desired result. We can imagine the hubbub in that house.

Peter prudently decided to go into hiding before the morning came, and off he went into the night. As for Herod, he simply added to his other crimes the execution of Peter's unoffending guards.

C. The Haughty Claim

Herod went back to Caesarea after all this "and there abode," the Holy Spirit says. The Greek word translated "abode," *diatribō,* literally means "to rub away, to spend time." Herod went on rubbing away the little bit of time he had left.

Then a crisis arose in the coastal cities of Tyre and Sidon, old Phoenician trading centers. Herod exerted pressure, things came to a head, and the cities gave in. When the cities sent a delegation to Caesarea to make their peace with the royal tyrant, Herod decided to make an occasion out of it. He would accept the surrender with suitable festivities and all due pomp and circumstance.

On the second day of the festivities, Herod decided to make an especially grand entrance. He put on a gorgeous robe woven throughout with strands of silver. He entered the theater where everyone was assembled at the break of day so that the first rays of the rising sun would shine on him. His robe blazed and flashed as though with fire and the people cried out, "This is a god!"

Then the watching angel smote him. As Herod drank in the adulation of his subjects, God summoned worms to gnaw at his intestines. Five days later he died in agony. The invisible watcher made his report; the invisible worm did his work. Herod was only fifty-four. He had been king for less than seven years.

The judgment of God is not always that obvious, but it is always certain. We may not immediately see the sequence of cause and effect, but we can be sure that it is there.

Herod Agrippa I was dead and damned, "but the word of God grew and multiplied" (Acts 12:24). The Word of God lived on. It lives on still, and will live on and on even when time will be no more. God buries the opposition, and His work and His Word go on.

NINE

Peter in the Spotlight

Matthew 14:27–31; 16:13–28; John 1:40–42; 6:16–21; 18:15–27; 21:1–22;
Acts 2:14–42; 3:1–26; 4:12, 19–20; 8:5–25; 9:32–11:18; Galatians 2:11–16;
1 Peter 1–5; 2 Peter 1–3

A. PETER WITH HIS EYE ON THE LORD
B. PETER WITH HIS MIND ON THE STORM
C. PETER WITH HIS FOOT IN HIS MOUTH
D. PETER WITH HIS TEARS IN HIS EYES
E. PETER WITH HIS BOAT ON THE LAKE
F. PETER WITH HIS LORD ON THE THRONE
G. PETER WITH HIS PEN IN HIS HAND
H. PETER WITH HIS HAND IN HIS POCKET
I. PETER WITH HIS LIFE ON THE LINE
J. PETER WITH HIS FINGER IN THE PIE
K. PETER WITH HIS NOSE IN THE AIR
L. PETER WITH HIS BACK TO THE WALL
M. PETER WITH HIS SHOULDER TO THE WHEEL
N. PETER WITH HIS FACE IN THE MUD
O. PETER WITH HIS NAME ON THE LIST

There used to be a popular program on television called *Candid Camera*. The producers of the show hid cameras in all sorts of unexpected places, set up all kinds of unusual situations, and then caught people during their unguarded moments.

One of my favorite episodes involved a stevedore union in New York. The muscle-bound, hard-bitten stevedores were called into an office one by one and were told that they had to go to a bird sanctuary and spend their vacation time watching birds. I can still see the incredulous look on one tough stevedore's face as he pointed a gnarled finger at his hairy chest and growled, "Me? Watch Boids? Not me!"

Some of the best photographs we take of children (or adults) are snapshots taken during unguarded moments. Such photographs are not posed; they are real-life pictures.

The Bible gives us a number of candid pictures of Simon Peter—impulsive, impolitic, impressionable Peter.

A. PETER WITH HIS EYE ON THE LORD

Peter had a brother, just about the best kind of brother a man like Peter could have had. He had none of Peter's fervor and fire. He was not nearly as flamboyant, impetuous, or outgoing as Peter. Just the same, he led his big, boisterous brother to Christ.

Peter's brother Andrew had become a disciple of John the Baptist. Andrew would spend as much time as he could spare from the family business listening to John and learning how to prepare people for the coming of Christ. Doubtless there were many lively discussions at home about John and his prophecies. Peter perhaps was inclined to be skeptical, while Andrew defended his hero. "He knows what he's talking about, Simon, believe me," we hear Andrew say. In the end, even bluff and businesslike Peter is impressed. Andrew describes the crowds and converts of John the Baptist. He recounts John's confrontation with the authorities and talks about John's character. "He was raised a priest, Simon, but he is far more than a priest. I'll tell you who I think he is. I think he's Elijah, who has come back to prepare the way for the Messiah."

Then one day, Andrew would have burst into that Galilean home. "Simon, where are you? I say, Simon, we've found *Him*. We've found the Messiah; we've found the Christ. I've just met Him—Jesus, the Son of God, the Savior of the world, the promised Messiah!" Andrew insisted that Peter come and meet Jesus too. At last Peter went, finally persuaded by his quietly persistent brother. That day Peter put his eye on Jesus, and he rarely took it off Him again. That day Peter changed. Jesus said to him, "Hello there, Simon. I'm going to call you *Peter*. I'm going to call you *a stone*. There is a rocklike quality about you that I can use." That's our first snapshot—Peter with his eye on the Lord.

B. Peter with His Mind on the Storm

It had been an exciting day. Jesus had preached to an enormous crowd. It had seemed to the disciples as though the prayer Jesus had taught them, "Thy kingdom come," was about to be answered. Jesus had crowned the day by feeding five thousand men, plus women and children, with a little lad's lunch. Peter, who would have seen the boy give his five barley loaves and two small fishes to Jesus, had himself been given bread and fish in abundance to distribute to the crowds. He would have come back again and again for more. The boy's lunch had turned into a banquet with twelve baskets of food left over. Peter had thought it amazing, and the crowd had thought so, too. The people were ready, then and there, to crown Jesus king. Far from accepting the proffered crown, however, Jesus had sent his disciples away, and then the multitude.

Oh well, Peter might have thought, *I expect He wants to be acclaimed king in Jerusalem, not here in Galilee. Probably that would be better.*

Jesus told the disciples to get into a boat and row across the lake where He would meet them later. He would stay behind for a while to pray. We can hear Peter, halfway across the lake, turning to the others and saying, "I say, you fellows, I don't like the look of those clouds. I think we're in for a storm." They all knew how dangerous a storm could be on that lake.

Sure enough, the winds howled, the waves heaved, and the disciples struggled against what now had become a terrible tempest, bringing with it what seemed to be certain death. Then one of the disciples saw it—a shape walking on the water toward them. They were terrified! It must be a ghost, some uncanny specter from the deep. Peter was petrified.

A loved voice called out above the shriek of the gale: "It is I; be not afraid."

Impulsively Peter called back, "If it be thou, bid me come unto thee on the water."

"Come," Jesus challenged (Matt. 14:27–29).

And Peter did. We can see him put one leg over the side, then the other, holding on perhaps to James and John. Feeling the waves unexpectedly solid beneath his feet, Peter takes a step, and another, and another, keeping his eye on Jesus.

Then the noise of the wind dinned in his ears, and the fearful sight of the waves caught hold of his eye. With his eye now on the storm, Peter began to sink. "Lord, save me," he called.

What a picture! What a lesson! We all know what Peter learned that day. He learned that he must never focus his eye on the storm; he must keep his eye on the Lord. All too often we look at the waves and listen to the wind and focus on our adverse circumstances when we should be looking to the Lord. When we look to Him, all will be well.

C. PETER WITH HIS FOOT IN HIS MOUTH

Peter always seemed to put his foot into his mouth, just like most of us do. That is, of course, what is so downright lovable about him.

In this particular snapshot, we catch Peter in one of his more spectacular mistakes. The Lord asked the disciples, "Whom do men say that I the Son of man am?" (Matt. 16:13). They replied that some people said that He was Jeremiah, some said that He was Elijah, and some thought that He was John the Baptist raised from the dead. One and all, people were likening Jesus to the greatest men in their nation's history. But that would never do. He was not to be compared to them.

So Jesus asked the disciples, "But whom say ye that I am?"

Peter quickly replied, "Thou art the Christ, the Son of the living God."

"Blessed art thou, Simon Barjona," the Lord responded to Peter's confession of faith, "for flesh and blood hath not revealed it unto thee, but my Father which is in heaven" (Matt. 16:15–17).

Peter's heart swelled with pride, and Satan got hold of him in an instant. Very few people can absorb large doses of praise.

Jesus began to talk to the disciples about His impending betrayal, His coming crucifixion, about His death, His burial, and His resurrection. But all Peter heard was that one ominous word *crucified*. He blurted out, "Be it far from Thee, Lord" (Matt. 16:22).

Instantly Jesus replied, "Get thee behind me, Satan: thou art an offence unto me: for thou savourest not the things that be of God, but those that be of men" (Matt. 16:23). Peter had put his foot into his mouth.

We have another snapshot of Peter doing the same thing on the Mount of Transfiguration. Peter had been taking a little nap. It is warm, strenuous work scaling the rugged slopes of Hermon, and we can see Peter throwing himself down with a sigh and, before he knows it, falls sound asleep. He awakes, rubbing his eyes with astonishment. Visitors have arrived, men from the past, talking with Jesus on the mountaintop. They are Moses and Elijah, no less, representatives of the law and the prophets, in earnest conversation with Jesus. Peter overhears them talking with the Lord about His "decease which he should accomplish at Jerusalem" (Luke 9:31).

Peter "rose" to the occasion. With magnificent disregard of the proprieties of the situation, ignoring the fact that nobody was talking to him and that the conversation did not concern him at all, he put his foot into his mouth. "Lord," he blurted out, "it is good for us to be here. Let us set up three tents—one for You, one for Moses, and one for Elijah." What folly! Peter wanted to put Jesus on a level with mere men. God broke up the meeting at once. He told Peter to be quiet. "This is my beloved Son," He said, "hear ye him" (Matt. 17:5).

D. Peter with His Tears in His Eyes

The shadow of the cross was now dark and closely impending, and the Lord must have looked sadly at His somber disciples. A prophecy likely came to His mind, a prophecy of Zechariah that had long been slumbering in the womb of time but was now stirring to life and fulfillment: "Smite the shepherd, and the sheep shall be scattered" (Zech. 13:7). Already Gethsemane was looming up against the night shadows. Jesus said, "All ye shall be offended because of me this night: for it is written, I will smite the shepherd, and the sheep of the flock shall be scattered abroad" (Matt. 26:31).

Peter bristled. "Not me, Lord," he states in so many words. "Others might be offended, but not me."

"You think so, Peter?" Jesus replies. "Well, listen for the crowing of the cock. Before the cock crows, you will deny me thrice."

And that is what happened. Shortly afterward, as the Jews bullied and beat Jesus, Peter warmed his hands at the fire. Three times he denied the Lord, the last time with oaths and curses. Then the cock crowed, and at that very moment Peter intercepted Jesus' look (Luke 22:61). It was not an "I told you so" look, but a look of such love and forgiveness that it broke Peter's heart. For immediately he went outside and wept bitterly. Scripture does not tell us where Peter went, but we might not be far wrong in suspecting that he went back to Gethsemane.

Never had Peter experienced a darker night. He was so ashamed, so sorry, so full of repentance and remorse. Had it not been for the Lord's kind and understanding look, Peter might have taken the terrible road that Judas was now pursuing and gone out and hanged himself.

What was it Jesus had said? "Satan hath desired to have you, that he may sift you as wheat: but I have prayed for thee" (Luke 22:31–32). That prayer of Jesus held Peter on the path of sanity and kept him from suicide during that terrible night, and during the days and endless nights that followed, until he met the risen Christ and received full absolution at Jesus' pierced hands.

E. Peter with His Boat on the Lake

After the events at Gethsemane and Gabbatha (John 19:13) and Golgotha, Peter must have thought that he would never lift up his head again. For some time he seemed to be subdued. Perhaps it appeared to him that, although Jesus had forgiven him, the other disciples had not. Likewise, we, ourselves, are not nearly so willing to forgive a brother's fall as Jesus is. We hold it against him, color every subsequent action with suspicion, and act as though we have never sinned ourselves.

Gradually, however, Peter's confidence in the Lord came back and along with it his self-reliance. Jesus had said that after His resurrection He would meet Peter and the other disciples in Galilee. So off to Galilee they went. Back at home in the familiar surroundings of his boyhood and business days, Peter no doubt begin to feel like himself again. After an interval, and still Jesus did not come, we can see Peter wandering around, hating the inactivity. He was essentially a doer, not a dreamer like John. Suddenly Peter comes to a decision: he would go back into business. Living by faith was all right, so far as it went, but now he is fed up with it. He determines to fix up his nets, clean out his boat, see to his lines, and go back to fishing.

We can picture Peter resolutely setting out from his house for the beach. The other disciples see what he is doing and follow him down to his boat. "Figuring on doing some fishing, Peter?"

"Yep, I've had enough," Peter says. "I'm going back into business, starting tonight. You coming?" There is some heated discussion. Finally, some of them make up their minds.

Doubting Thomas says, "I'm with you, Peter."

Nathanael, a man singularly free from guile, says, "I'm coming too."

James and John, Peter's fishing partners during the old business days, find the temptation too strong as well. "Count us in, Peter." Two others, for some reason not named, also side with Peter.

So seven out of the remaining eleven disciples went on a fishing expedition that night. They caught nothing. Perhaps going back into business was not such a good idea after all. They were tired and frustrated, when, as the morning broke, they saw a stranger on the shore. "Cast the net on the right side of the ship," the visitor called out. They did so, and with astonishing results. Immediately John recognized Jesus. "It is the Lord," he said.

In a moment the headstrong, impulsive Peter jumped over the side of the boat and waded with giant strides toward the shore. Breakfast was ready! It was Jesus sure enough, and He had fish sizzling on the fire and bread ready as well. Without a word the disciples sat down and ate the welcome meal. It would not be surprising if they glanced sideways at each other and at Peter, waiting for what might come next. Then it came. The Lord picked out Peter, the born leader of men.

"All right, Peter," Jesus says as we eavesdrop on the scene. "Tell Me, do you love Me more than these? More than these disciples? More than these fish? Do you love Me, Peter?"

Peter cautiously makes reply. He does not dare use the Master's word for love—the all-embracing, all-compelling, all-conquering love that many waters cannot quench, and which suffers long and is kind. "Lord! You know I am fond of You," is the best Peter can trust himself to say.

"Then feed My sheep, Peter. I called you out of the fishing business years ago. You are to be a shepherd, Peter—a great shepherd, a good shepherd—not a small-time businessman on this little landlocked lake. You are to be a shepherd-pastor of My flock."

F. Peter with His Lord on the Throne

At last the day of Pentecost had come. For ten long days the disciples had waited in the upper room, not daring to leave lest they miss the promised coming of the Spirit of God. They had spent the time in preparation and in prayer. Then had come the cloven tongues of fire; the mighty, rushing wind; the promised baptism of the Spirit.

Down the stairs and into the streets the disciples rushed, their voices raised on high. Crowds came running. Now Peter was preaching—preaching as never in all his days he had thought it possible to preach—with passion, with persuasion, and with mighty power. The Bible leaped to life. It seemed to burn in his soul. The crowd was hushed. Boldly, without fear or favor, Peter charged home to the Jews their guilt. They had crucified the Lord of glory. They had murdered the Messiah. A terrible conviction of sin settled down upon multiplied hundreds of hearts. Three thousand people were saved in a moment, in the twinkling of an eye. Up there in the upper room above, the mystical, universal church was born.

Down there, on the city streets, the local church was born. The church that had been born in the upper room expanded into a vast congregation of men and women and boys and girls—a people ransomed, healed, restored, forgiven.

What a snapshot. If only we could take similar snapshots of the church today!

G. PETER WITH HIS PEN IN HIS HAND

It is likely that Peter came to regret his slow start in the great world-missions enterprise of the church. Others had taken the early initiatives. Stephen, one of the church's first deacons, was the first to see that the days of Jerusalem, Judaism, and Judea were over. The Spirit had moved on. Israel's persistent rebellion and unbelief made judgment inevitable. Besides, the tearing of the veil had rendered the whole temple religious-system obsolete. Most Jewish Christians, including Peter, were unable to see that truth. But Stephen did. It cost him his life.

Then Philip—Philip the deacon—was the first to take seriously the Lord's commission to evangelize Samaria. Peter only went there after the work was done.

It was Paul, not Peter, who blazed the trail to the regions beyond, who evangelized Galatia, Macedonia, Achaia, Cappadocia, and Bithynia. It was Paul who left a trail of churches in Pisidian Antioch, Iconium, Lystra, Derbe, Philippi, Corinth, and Ephesus. It was Paul who blazed the trail across Roman Asia and on into Europe.

Peter was a latecomer to the work of Gentile evangelism. Eventually he turned eastward, as Paul had turned westward. He seems to have settled in Babylon. There we see Peter, pen in hand, watching the storm clouds gather. The climate has changed. Roman imperial power has finally stirred itself in anger and rage against the church. Peter thinks particularly of the Christians in Europe, already bearing the brunt of the persecution. He thinks of the many people Paul has led to Christ. He thinks of Gentile churches spaced out far and wide, and now dear to his heart. He thinks, too, of Jewish Christians in so many of those churches. He takes up his pen.

Peter wrote two letters. The first one dealt with troubles from *without*. The other, with the shadow of Peter's death becoming more and more defined, dealt with troubles from *within*. The first letter had to do with a *suffering church*. The second letter had to do with a *seduced church*—persecution from without, and apostasy from within. The church was under attack.

Peter's letters were received with joy. Peter had an enormous fund of goodwill in the Gentile and in the Jewish world. He was respected and revered as a disciple who had been with Jesus from the very first. Peter had walked with Him and talked with Him. Peter had heard all His parables and seen all His miracles. Peter had observed Jesus' flawless life and His fearless death. Peter had been present in the upper room and had attended the last Passover and first communion feast. He had been in Gethsemane and at Gabbatha. He knew all about Golgotha. He had been at the grave on the resurrection morning and on the Mount of Olives when Jesus had ascended into heaven. Peter had been in the upper room on the day of Pentecost when the Holy Spirit came and the church was born. Peter had led three thousand people to Christ with a single sermon. Peter had opened the door of the church to the Gentiles.

So he had enjoyed great goodwill from Christians everywhere. His very faults and failings were endearing to people. Peter was "the big fisherman," the bluff, hearty, warm, and impulsive companion of Christ.

Peter's letters reveal his intimacy with Jesus. Peter used the same illustrative style—telling stories, painting word pictures—and made scores of allusions to his many months with the Master. People read and remembered Peter's words of encouragement and hope, his challenge to remain firm in the face of the foe, and his urgent pleas against the invasion of heresy and the vileness of apostasy. People cherished and preserved his letters. Finally they found their way into the sacred canon of Holy Writ. Little did Peter think—as a boy in Galilee reading Job, Jeremiah, Moses, and Malachi—that one day his writings would appear as a divinely inspired addition to the Word of God.

Dear old Peter! We cannot help but love him! Heaven's photograph album is still open before us, crammed with snapshots as well as formal portraits of all kinds of interesting people. Let us look, though, at some other pictures of Peter.

H. Peter with His Hand in His Pocket

It was three o'clock in the afternoon. Peter and John were on their way to the temple to pray. They had been good friends for many years. In the old days they had been business partners. Now they were partners in the gospel. Far from their beloved lakeshore home in the north, they were living now in the great, busy, impersonal city of Jerusalem. It was the city of many boyhood dreams and many grown men's disillusions. Just the same, the temple never ceased to fascinate the two friends. Peter could not as yet realize that the temple was obsolete and that it no longer served any useful function. Habit drew him back to the temple every time the call to prayer resounded through the city. Perhaps that was not such a bad habit after all.

There were various courts in the temple. Herod the Great had embellished the temple, and enlarged the outer court. The Jews did not regard this enlarged court as part of the temple's sacred area. So the Gentiles were allowed to walk around it, and it was known as "the court of the Gentiles." Steps led up, out of that public court into the sacred temple area. After ascending these steps, the Jews (only they were allowed to go beyond the court of the Gentiles) came to a barrier known as "the middle wall of partition." On this barrier was a notice warning Gentiles to go no farther.

Nine gates led through this barrier. The gate Beautiful appears to have been one of them. Once past the barrier, a Jew entered the court of the women where the treasury was located. Women could penetrate this far into the temple. Jewish laymen might go farther into the court of Israel, and there they had to stop as well, for beyond this court was the enclave of the priests. Within this final court stood the temple itself with the holy place and the holy of holies.

Josephus says that public sacrifices were offered twice a day in the temple—in the early morning and "about the ninth hour" (three o'clock in the afternoon). A service of public prayer accompanied each sacrifice. A final service was conducted in the temple at sunset.

On this day Peter entered the court of the Gentiles, passed the barrier by way of the gate Beautiful on his way into the court of Israel, and suddenly something he saw pulled him up short. At the gate Beautiful lay someone who was anything but beautiful—a lame man, a man who was a beggar. He had been there most of his life. He had been born lame, and now he was more than forty years old. He had become somewhat of a fixture there. Everyone knew him. Day after day his friends laid him at the gates of a powerless religion. The decades had come and gone. His religion did nothing for him. Indeed, it could do nothing for him but let him beg.

With a keen eye for a prospective donor, the beggar sized up Peter and John. He could hope much from them. They were evidently Galileans. Perhaps they would be more ready with a coin or two than were the Jews of Jerusalem. He appealed to them.

Peter put his hand in his pocket. The beggar's eyes gleamed with expectation, but the hand came out empty. Then Peter spoke, and his first words dashed all the beggar's hopes. "Silver and gold have I none; but such as I have give I thee."

Peter's second statement raised the beggar's hopes as high as heaven: "In the name of Jesus Christ of Nazareth rise up and walk" (Acts 3:6). What a snapshot. Peter's pocket was empty, but he was willing to give what he had, and he had something worth far more than a pocketful of gold. He came with power to heal the lame, and to transform the poor, the destitute, and the lost.

I. PETER WITH HIS LIFE ON THE LINE

The lame man's healing and conversion caused a considerable stir. People came running to see what had happened. No wonder! The fellow was leaping and jumping and shouting for joy, hanging on to Peter and John, proclaiming them as his benefactors. A crowd gathered. Peter saw an opportunity to preach. And preach he did! Soon word reached the temple authorities that these Galilean peasants were preaching—without a license. How dare they preach—especially in the name of Jesus, so detested by Jewish authorities.

Peter and John were arrested. They were hauled before the Sanhedrin and told to give an account of themselves. Gone were the cowardly Galilean fishermen, gone was the man who had once been so ready to deny his Lord, all because of the casual comments of a serving girl. In his place stood an apostle as brave as a lion and as terrible as an army with banners. He bluntly told the rulers of his people that they were guilty of the murder of their Messiah. When asked by what authority or in what name he had healed the lame man, Peter boldly told them. It was the name of Jesus. Peter then added without hesitation, "Neither is there salvation in any other: for there is none other name under heaven given among men, whereby we must be saved" (Acts 4:12).

The Sanhedrin ordered Peter and his fellows not to speak any more in the name of Jesus. Fearlessly, Peter replied, "Whether it be right in the sight of God to hearken unto you more than unto God, judge ye. For we cannot but speak the things which we have seen and heard" (Acts 4:19–20).

Peter put his life on the line. The reality of Christ's redemption, resurrection, rapture, and promised return had taken hold of Peter's heart. No man or group of men, however powerful, could intimidate him any more.

J. PETER WITH HIS FINGER IN THE PIE

Since the ascension, the Twelve had largely ignored the Lord's great commission—"Ye shall be witnesses unto me both in Jerusalem, and in all Judaea, and in

Samaria, and unto the uttermost part of the earth" (Acts 1:8). That was all very
well, but who would want to go to Samaria? Jews had no dealings with Samaritans.
A deep-seated hatred of Samaria was born and bred in the breast of every Jew. No
self-respecting Jew would go to Samaria. On a journey he would take the bypass
road and go miles out of his way, rather than go through Samaria.

We can well imagine some of the heated discussions that took place in the
upper room when the question of evangelizing Samaria came up.

"John, you go," says Peter. "You are the youngest. The Samaritans might take
more kindly to a young man."

John answers, "Not me."

Matthew chimes in, "You ought to go, Peter. You're the leader, after all. You
should set the example. You took the limelight on the day of Pentecost. Take it
now, too."

Peter says, "Not me."

Then Thomas would have a word, and with a rare touch of sardonic humor
he says, "I think Simon Zelotes ought to go—Simon the Zealot, Simon the
Jewish patriot."

Simon Zelotes says, "Not me."

Peter speaks up, "Andrew, you should go. You're good at bringing people to
Christ. You and Philip brought those Greeks that time."

Andrew says, "Not me. Not Samaria. I have no leading at all along those
lines."

In the end nobody went. So, because none of the Twelve would go, the Lord
sent somebody else—Philip the evangelist. Then revival soon broke out in
Samaria, and at once Peter wanted a finger in the pie. He headed a two-man
delegation to go down to Samaria to see what was going on, and perhaps add his
apostolic blessing. He found that a very good pie indeed was being baked down
there in Samaria. Sadly it contained one rotten apple. Peter soon detected that
and removed it. His trip to Samaria turned out to be good for Peter. It helped rid
him of his insular prejudice against the Samaritans. Moreover, Peter's endorsement of Philip's mission made the Samaritans full members, without barrier or
bias, in the Christian community.

K. Peter with His Nose in the Air

The Samaritan mission was surely distasteful to Peter, but visiting the Gentiles
was worse. It is certain that he had no intention of doing so. We can almost see

him put his nose in the air with a gesture of religious superiority, and positively refuse to have anything to do with such a visit. He would draw the line when it came to evangelizing Gentiles.

Then came the compelling, heavenly vision and Peter's resolute, "Not so, Lord." The Lord instantly overruled Peter's objections, and off Peter went to Caesarea, the detested Roman capital of Palestine, to visit in the home of a Gentile soldier named Cornelius. By now Peter's nose was not as high in the air, although he still did not relish the idea of being hospitable to Gentiles. Enter a Gentile home? Eat at what he had always considered to be an unclean table? *What if they served me pork or ham?* he would think. *What if they give me bacon for breakfast?* Besides, any meal in a Gentile house would include meat that had been offered to idols and cooked with the blood still in it. Everything about this mission ran against Peter's Jewish grain.

Once Peter met Cornelius, however, and heard of God's dealings with him, all Peter's doubts were swept aside. His racial prejudice, as deep as the sea and as wide as the ages, was gone. The door of the church was flung open to the Gentiles. The Holy Spirit came down, and it was Pentecost all over again. Not many of us can overcome our prejudices as quickly as that.

L. Peter with His Back to the Wall

Peter eventually returned to Jerusalem from his mission to Gentile Caesarea. What a reception committee awaited him there. The exclusive brethren, who made up a major part of the Jerusalem church, were waiting for him, ready to read him right out of the fellowship for breaking one of their religious taboos. Peter, they believed, had disgraced them. He had visited a forbidden home and fellowshipped with religiously unclean people. They had their case against him well in hand.

Peter, however, had anticipated their reaction and had taken some Jewish witnesses with him on his mission. Now he called on them to substantiate what had happened. Then, in words brief but pointed, he recounted the whole story and confronted his critics with what God had done. "There you are, brethren," he said in effect. "You take up *that* matter with the Lord."

When we, like Peter, have our backs to the wall, it is good to know that we have God on our side.

M. Peter with His Shoulder to the Wheel

It finally dawned on the apostles in Jerusalem, and on Peter in particular, that the Lord had been serious about evangelizing not only Judea and Samaria but the uttermost parts of the earth. After Philip opened up Samaria, Peter finally put his shoulder to the wheel. He became active in the Lord's work beyond the boundaries of Jerusalem.

His first venture was not very ambitious. He went down to Lydda on the coastal plain of Sharon, about a day's journey from Jerusalem. It was not much of an effort, but it was a start. The Lord blessed him for making the move. In Lydda he healed a man sick of the palsy. Then Peter was summoned to nearby Joppa for the funeral of a gracious, generous lady named Dorcas. He raised her from the dead, a truly spectacular miracle.

These encouraging blessings on his widened ministry greatly stiffened Peter's resolve to keep on reaching out to the great world beyond Jerusalem's confining walls. The legalism and narrowness of the Jerusalem church had constricted him too long. Then the Lord opened the door to the Gentiles, and Peter's horizons were further broadened. As time went on, his travels widened and so did his interest in the mission field. Eventually we find him writing to believers in far-away places, in fields the apostle Paul had pioneered for the gospel: Cappadocia, Pontus, Galatia, Bithynia, and Asia.

It is a great thing when we set our eyes on regions beyond, when we catch the vision of a lost world and of "untold millions still untold." It is a great thing when we put our shoulders to the wheel. Peter never became the flaming evangelist and tireless missionary that Paul became, but at least Peter threw the weight of his influence and personality behind such a man. We can do that too. We cannot all become Hudson Taylors or David Livingstones, but we can all throw our weight behind those people God has called in our generation to make an impact for Him far and wide in this poor, lost world.

N. Peter with His Face in the Mud

News came to the Jerusalem church that revival had broken out among the Gentiles of Antioch, a thriving metropolis in the nearby country of Syria. Barnabas and Saul had labored there and had tremendously expanded the work. The news filtered back to Jerusalem where it was merely a matter of passing interest. In the view of the Jerusalem Christians, no work could be as important as their work, and no church of Gentile believers deserved such high regard in the sight of heaven as a church of Jewish believers in Jerusalem. Antioch! What a place for a revival to break out. Even Peter was not particularly interested at the time.

Then Paul and Barnabas broke all precedent and boldly carried the gospel to "the regions beyond." At last the Holy Spirit made His move toward what Jesus had called "the uttermost part of the earth." He had waited long enough for Peter; from now on the limelight would be on Paul. Peter probably did not care that much; evangelizing Gentiles did not really appeal to him. True, he had opened the door, but he was content to let someone else press through it. Paul was welcome to assume the work of pioneering in Galatia among wild, barbarous tribes and in other outlandish places.

In the meantime, however, Jewish believers had infiltrated the new church at Antioch and had brought with them typically Jewish sectarian views: Gentiles must be circumcised; they must keep the law of Moses; they must be zealous Jewish proselytes as well as Gentile Christians. It was all so much high-sounding nonsense, but it made its impact. The Jewish believers seemed to have plenty of Scripture references to back up their views. Besides, something had to be done to keep the Gentile church from swamping the Jewish church, for ever-increasing numbers of Gentiles were already flooding into the church. Soon Jews would be a permanent minority in the church, and that in their minds would be a disaster.

What better way for us to keep the Gentiles in their place, the Jews thought, *than by putting them under the yoke of the law?* Such was the new Judaizing creed, and Peter did nothing to stop it. Perhaps he did not see anything wrong with it.

But Paul certainly did, and so did Barnabas. It was not long before a delegation came from Antioch to Jerusalem, asking that this effort to Judaize the Gentile church be stopped. Couldn't the Jews understand that there was only one church, and that in that church there was neither Jew nor Gentile? A heated debate followed. To give Peter his due, he stood up for Paul. Then the Jerusalem church wrote a letter in which they admitted that Gentile emancipation from circumcision, from the Sabbath, from the law, and from the traditions of the Jews was of God. Paul no doubt thanked Peter heartily for his share in getting this principle acknowledged in Jerusalem.

James, the Lord's brother, by now had assumed a dominant position in the Jerusalem church. James was a legalist. He had agreed to Gentile emancipation from the law, but had insisted that some stipulations be included in the letter:

Gentiles must abstain from fornication, from eating blood, and from eating animals killed by strangulation. Peter was intimidated by James.

Just the same, Peter wanted to see for himself what was happening at Antioch. So we see him saying goodbye to James and off he goes. When Peter arrives in Antioch, he is thrilled at what he sees, and grows to love the Gentile Christians. They lionize him. This is Peter, who had spent over three years in the company of Jesus. They press him for details. He spends many hours in the homes of the generous and hospitable Gentile believers, eating at their tables, sharing personal experiences of Jesus with them. What happy times these are. What a grand church this is! Peter does not miss for a moment the stuffy regulations of the Jerusalem church. He feels marvelously free.

Then a delegation from Jerusalem arrived in Antioch. They were sent by James to see what was going on. At once Peter caved in. All of a sudden the same old Peter emerged who had once shrunk from confessing his Lord before a serving maid. Under the frowns of James's legalistic colleagues—separatist and exclusive brethren—Peter retreated. He withdrew from fellowship with the Gentiles and refused all further invitations to their homes. He no longer ate meat with them. Throughout the Antioch church confusion reigned. The Gentile believers were dismayed. What had they done? Hadn't this issue been settled? Did they not have in the church archives the letter Peter and James had signed?

Then Paul came, filled with righteous indignation. We can see Paul taking Peter aside and giving him a piece of his mind. Paul's eyes flash and his eloquence ignites his holy anger. Soon Peter becomes more afraid of Paul than he ever has been of James. Besides, Peter knows in his heart that Paul is right and James is wrong.

With that impulsiveness that made him so beloved, Peter apologized, acknowledged that he had been wrong, and did what he could to put things right. To his credit, Peter never held Paul's actions against him. Peter felt that he had deserved Paul's anger. Years later, when writing to churches Paul had founded, Peter could speak of "our beloved brother Paul."

O. Peter with His Name on the List

We do not know where Peter was living when Nero burned Rome and blamed the Christians. Roman tradition says that Peter was in Rome, but that is doubtful. There is no concrete evidence that Peter ever visited Rome. Indeed, biblical evidence militates against the idea. Be that as it may, Peter's name was on the "persecution list." Nero, a dreadful tyrant in Rome, was disgracing the throne of the Caesars as never before. His name, indeed, has gone down in history as the arch-persecutor of the church and as the supreme type of the Antichrist. Nero so terrorized the early church, the idea circulated that he would come back as the Antichrist in the end times.

Nero was out to rid the world of Christians. He had them rounded up and tortured to death. Some were thrown to lions in the arena or wrapped in animal skins and thrown to wild dogs. Some Christians were burned alive. Some were dipped in wax and burned as torches to light the orgies in Nero's palace grounds. Nero issued orders to the effect, "Get Peter! He's the ringleader. I want him dead . . . crucified, do you hear?"

Peter knew that he would be killed. He had escaped from death at the hands of Herod, but he knew that he would not escape from death at the hands of Nero. Jesus had told him years before that he would one day die for Him and hinted strongly that he would die by crucifixion. Tradition has it that Peter's last request was to be crucified upside down, to make amends for the time he had denied his Lord.

Peter died a hero's death. When at last he drew his final, agonizing, painful breath and his great spirit departed for the courts of bliss, his beloved Lord welcomed him home on the other side. "Welcome home, Peter," we can hear Him say. "Come and see the mansion I've prepared for you on Hallelujah Avenue, just across from Victory Square. Well done, Peter! Ah, here's Gabriel. Gabriel, come and meet Peter, My dear friend."

And we can hear Gabriel saying, "Peter. Oh yes, I've met Peter. Do you remember me, Peter? The last time I saw you, you were sound asleep in prison, and I opened the prison's doors for you. Welcome home, Peter."

"And now, Peter," we can hear the Savior say, "come and meet My Father." And so Peter entered into the joy of his Lord.

TEN

John the Beloved

John 1:35–39

A. JOHN AS A PERSON
B. JOHN AS A PUPIL
C. JOHN AS A PASTOR
   1. A word about the fellowship
   2. A word about the faith
   3. A word about the family
D. JOHN AS A PROPHET
E. JOHN AS A PRISONER

By the time John took up his pen to write his gospel, his epistles, and the Apocalypse, the first century of the Christian era was about to close. As an old man he looked out on a world much different from the one he had known as a boy. Jerusalem was no more. The Jewish people had been uprooted and scattered to the ends of the earth. The church was spreading over the entire world, too, and had already endured the terrible persecutions of Nero and Domitian. The roots of apostasy were everywhere. Gnosticism threatened to change Christianity into something unrecognizable. Peter was gone, James was gone, and the apostle Paul was gone.

John wrote for the third generation of Christians. By its third generation, a movement stands in desperate need of revival, or else it will either disappear altogether or linger on as a ghost of its former self. In the first generation, truth is a *conviction*. Those who hold a conviction, hold it dearly. They do not know the meaning of compromise. They are willing to die for what they believe to be true. In the second generation the conviction becomes a *belief.*

94

Sons hold to the truths they have been taught by their fathers and defend their beliefs in discussion and debate. The keen edge of conviction, however, has been blunted, and adherence to a body of beliefs inherited from the fathers is not so much a passion as a persuasion. In the third generation, the belief becomes an *opinion*. By then some members of the movement are willing to trade in their opinions for anything that promises to be a fair exchange. They feel it is time for a change, they start talking about renewal, and they look to the world for ideas.

John wrote for just such a third generation. He wrote with a sense of urgency. He did not write, as did the synoptists, from the viewpoint of an infant church; he wrote from the standpoint of an infirm church, one that was in dire peril from persecution without and subversion within.

A. John as a Person

John's father was Zebedee, a successful fisherman of Bethsaida on the sea of Galilee. John's mother was Salome and had ambitious plans for her son. She was a devoted follower of the Lord Jesus, and she sometimes traveled with the disciples. She was present at the crucifixion and was at the tomb on resurrection morning. From Matthew 27:56; Mark 15:40; and John 19:25, it may be inferred that she was a sister of Mary, the mother of Jesus. John's brother was James, the first of the apostles to pay the price of martyrdom. The two brothers appear to have been cousins of the Lord Jesus, so they doubtless had known Him most of their lives. The Zebedee family seems to have been prosperous. They likely had hired servants, and "ministered unto [the Lord] of their substance" (Luke 8:3). Moreover, they were influential in official circles in Jerusalem.

A follower of John the Baptist before becoming a follower of Jesus, John the Beloved was one of the first two disciples to be called by Christ (Matt. 4:18–22; John 1:35–39). Along with Simon Peter and his brother James, John was one of the inner circle of three in the apostolic fellowship and, as such, was given a special vision of the Lord's *greatness* at the raising of Jairus's daughter, of the Lord's *glory* on the Mount of Transfiguration, and of the Lord's *grief* in the garden of Gethsemane.

John was one of the four who prompted the Olivet discourse by asking the Lord questions about eschatology (Mark 13:34). John was one of the two sent by the Lord to prepare for the Passover (Luke 22:8). John was called "the disciple whom Jesus loved" (John 21:20), and he was the disciple to whom the Lord

Jesus entrusted the care of His mother (John 19:25–27). Although John was of a contemplative disposition, he was capable of being greatly aroused—so much so that Jesus called him "a son of thunder" (see Mark 3:17).

John was with Peter when Peter healed the lame man at the temple gate (Acts 3:1–8). John appeared before the Sanhedrin with Peter (Acts 4), and the two refused to obey the command to cease from speaking in the name of Jesus. John went with Peter to Samaria to give the apostolic blessing to the Samaritan revival spearheaded by Philip the evangelist (Acts 8:14). John was banished to the island of Patmos by the emperor Domitian and probably died a natural death at Ephesus during the reign of the emperor Trajan (A.D. 98–117).

B. John as a Pupil

If we were to ask John what he learned during the three-and-a-half amazing years he spent with Jesus, he would point us to that wonderful book we know as the gospel of John. In that gospel, we have John's memoirs of Jesus. John wrote his gospel when he was an old man, but he had forgotten nothing. Indeed he had ample time to muse over the miracles of Jesus and meditate deeply for many years on His teachings. A remarkable memory, quickened by the Holy Spirit, enabled John to write a gospel that was *contemplative, complementary* to the works of Matthew and Mark and Luke, and *conclusive* regarding the gnostic heresy.

John's gospel is the basis of our chronology of the life of Christ. We gather from this gospel that the Lord ministered for three-and-a-half years. John recorded the Lord's visits to Jerusalem in connection with the national feasts; and from him we learn that Jesus had six periods of ministry in Judea, five in Galilee, one in Samaria, and one in Peraea.

John's favorite words were *know* (used 142 times), *believe* (used 100 times), *Father* (used 118 times), *world* (used 78 times), *see* (used 105 times), *verily* (used 50 times in 25 pairs), and *love* (used 36 times).

John struck the dominant notes in his gospel again and again. Preeminently he wanted to demonstrate that Jesus was indeed whom He claimed to be: the Son of the living God. To this end, the miracles and messages of Jesus in John's gospel were carefully chosen.

The thoughts, imagery, and language in John's gospel were drawn from the Old Testament. Graham Scroggie said that there are probably 124 references rooted in the Old Testament. Seven times John referred to Scripture being fulfilled.

Scroggie also pointed out that John evidently had Luke's gospel in front of him when he wrote his gospel. What Luke put in, John left out; what Luke left out, John put in.[1]

It is from John that we learn how our Lord Jesus made Himself available to the Father, so that God could in turn make Himself available to the Son. We can enjoy the same type of relationship. As men, we can make ourselves available to the Lord Jesus so that He can make Himself available to us.

John taught us nearly all we know about the Father and much of what we know about the Holy Spirit. John was the writer who emphasized the absolute deity of the Lord Jesus.

The gospel of John revolves around three focal points: the signs, the secrets, and the sorrows of the Son of God. John first sets before us various *signs* and proofs that Jesus of Nazareth was the One who was in the beginning with God, who was God, and who became flesh and dwelt among us as God incarnate. Then John reveals the *secrets* of the Lord Jesus, shared in His heart-to-heart upper-room talks with His disciples prior to His crucifixion. Finally John sets before us the *sorrows* of the Son of God. He bypasses Gethsemane and takes us straight to the trials and the tree.

John was a very good pupil. By the time he started to write his gospel, he had been taught not only by the Son of God but also by the Spirit of God. He gives us facts that the synoptic writers omit from their narratives. He shows us the Lord's thought life.

John lingers long at the cross. About one half of his gospel is devoted to just one week in the Lord's life: Passion week. To him the great wonder of the universe was that the Son of God should die for sinful man.

C. JOHN AS A PASTOR

In the New Testament, a pastor is a shepherd, one who has a heart for the flock. The Lord Jesus is the Chief Shepherd, the great Shepherd of the sheep. A pastor is an undershepherd who cares for the people of God as Jesus cares for them.

When the Lord Jesus from the cross committed the care and keeping of His own mother to His dear friend John, John's work of shepherding began. He took Mary home with him and became a son to her. In later years, when John went to Ephesus to help with the pastoral care of the great Pauline church in that city, he

---

1. W. Graham Scroggie, *A Guide to the Gospels* (London: Pickering and Inglis, 1948), 426, 437–44.

probably took Mary with him. What a blessing that godly woman would have been to that particular flock!

We can formulate an idea of what John was like as a pastor by studying his three Epistles, all of which are short, and two of which are little more than memos. His first epistle deals with fellowship, the second with faith, and the third with family.

1. A Word About the Fellowship

In his first epistle, as in his gospel, John took us back to basics. Peter and Paul had both been dead thirty or thirty-five years, and John was all alone, the only surviving apostle. Old men dwell much in the past. John refers to the past about fifty times. He also refers to "the beginning" ten times (nine of the ten times in connection with Christ and His ministry).

In his gospel, John set forth the life of God *in Christ;* in his first epistle he set forth the life of God *in us.* The life of God is inherent in Christ; the life of God is imparted to us.

The first epistle of John gives evidence of its writer's pastoral care. It was written to *banish distance,* for we are called into intimate fellowship with one another and with the Father Himself. It was written to *banish distress* so that the believer's joy might be full. It was written to *banish deception.* One of John's key words is "light" as opposed to darkness. In this epistle there are no shades of gray. All is either black or white, true or false, right or wrong. The first epistle of John was also written to *banish defilement.* John condemned sin in the life of the believer, called for confession, and reminded us that the blood of Jesus Christ cleanses us from all sin. Finally the epistle was written to *banish doubt.* John listed about two dozen things we can know. We can know that we have passed from death unto life, for instance. We can know, too, that we have been born again.

2. A Word About the Faith

The second epistle of John is a brief memo addressed to a lady. Here again we see the pastor at work, for John was concerned about the well being of that lady. She was in *danger* since the faith was under attack. It was very likely that she would receive a visit from the emissaries of a cult. Someone would come offering new lamps for old as in the story about Aladdin, so she must be on her guard.

Should such a person come, she should not let him get his foot in the *door.*

Christian courtesy did not require her to open the door to a cultist or invite him in to spread forth his wares. The door must be firmly closed on him—in his face if necessary.

When sending this person about his business, she must not even wish him Godspeed. She must not shake his hand or bid him good day. The *duty* of the woman of the house was to send the man packing without even the most common courtesies. John knew how persistent cultists can be. They are not to be given the slightest encouragement to come back.

3. A Word About the Family

The third epistle of John is a brief memo addressed to a man. Here again we see in action a great undershepherd of the sheep. We also learn about four men.

The first man is *Gaius the believer.* We are to *recognize* men like him. Gaius was gentle and hospitable, the kind of man whose ministry is a benediction to a local church.

The second man is *Diotrephes the bully.* We are to *resist* men like him. He wanted to be a local pope and made it his business to decide who could or could not be received into the fellowship. Diotrephes even prated against the highly esteemed, benevolent, and patriarchal apostle John.

The third man is *Demetrius the brother.* We are to *receive* men like Demetrius. He seems to have been a traveling preacher whose ministry Diotrephes rejected. John gave Demetrius his own personal word of commendation.

The fourth man is *John the Beloved.* We are to *respect* men like John. If anyone ever had a right to be a pope it was John, but he held an office better than that of a pope. He was an apostle—and he was not too old to wield the power of an apostle if necessary.

John closed this brief memo with a gentle word. "I hope to see you again before too long," he said in effect. "I plan on coming your way." His glove may have been velvet, but there was a resolute hand in that glove. Many years had passed since John and his brother had been called "the sons of thunder," but let Diotrephes and his kind beware. There are times when even the mildest and most patient of pastors has to assert his authority and power.

John must have been a very good pastor. He had the very best of teachers. He could remember how patiently the Lord had shepherded His own little flock in those far-off Palestinian days. Jesus had even laid down His life for His sheep. John was ready to do the same.

D. John as a Prophet

John was given the task of writing the book that completed the sacred canon of Scripture. Appropriately enough, Revelation is a book that looks ahead; it is in many ways the greatest book of prophecy in the Bible.

John, as mentioned before, was one of the disciples who asked the question that prompted the Lord to give them His great Olivet discourse. In that sermon on eschatology, the Lord Jesus drew together all the threads of New Testament prophecy. Although John did not discuss this prophetic discourse in his own gospel, he doubtless remembered it. Doubtless, too, he had copies of Matthew's account, and Mark's and Luke's as well.

John's Apocalypse, "the unveiling," is saturated with Old Testament quotations and allusions. The gospel of Matthew has 92, the epistle to the Hebrews has 102; but the Apocalypse has 285 references to the Old Testament. John knew his Bible and must have spent many years poring over its prophecies.

The Apocalypse is closely related to the book of Genesis. Three chapters from the beginning of Genesis we meet the serpent for the first time. Three chapters from the end of Revelation we meet the serpent for the last time. There are at least two dozen other comparisons and contrasts involving Genesis and Revelation. In Genesis it all begins; in Revelation it all ends.

In the book of Revelation, all the forces of heaven and hell are seen ranged in conflict, and the chief arena of battle is the planet Earth. Arrayed against God's Lamb, we see the scarlet Beast, the scarlet woman, the miracle-working False Prophet (with the appearance of a lamb and the voice of a dragon), and the red Dragon himself with his seven heads and ten horns! But God's Lamb is no ordinary lamb. This Lamb has seven eyes and seven horns—and all the attributes of deity.

Throughout the book of Revelation the scenes alternate between heaven and earth. God's word is decreed and declared in heaven; and then, in spite of all the power of the enemy, His will is done on earth. Revelation unveils the full and final answer to the Lord's prayer: "Thy kingdom come. Thy will be done in earth, as it is in heaven" (Matt. 6:10). But John's prophetic book is, supremely, an *Apocalypse* (a Revelation, an unveiling), of Jesus Christ.

The book proceeds in an orderly fashion. First there is a series of seven *seals*. These seals are broken so that "the beginnings of sorrows" (Mark 13:8) might overtake the earth. This section of the book is all about man. Man reduces the world to a state of utter chaos, and the terrified people left on the planet desperately look for a man who can bring order out of chaos.

Then there is a series of seven *trumpets*. These are blown to herald the coming of Satan's false messiah, the Antichrist. This section of Revelation is all about Satan. He brings his man to global supremacy over the entire world. He then inaugurates the great tribulation, and unleashes untold woes on a Christ-rejecting world.

Finally there is a series of seven *vials*, outpoured to bring events to a climax at the final return of Christ. This section of Revelation is all about God. He steps down at last into the arena of human affairs. He breaks the Antichrist's stranglehold on the planet. He mobilizes the Asiatic hordes against him. He draws the armies of the world to Megiddo. Now God has His foes where He wants them. He suddenly appears and puts an end to man's mismanagement of the planet.

The account of John's soaring visions ends with a description of the eternal state and the celestial city—as seen from heaven. Thanks to the keen vision of John the prophet, the Bible ends on a triumphant note.

E. John as a Prisoner

In the Aegean Sea, between Asia Minor and Greece, lies a small rocky island called Patmos. About ten miles long and six miles wide, Patmos consists of two segments joined by a narrow isthmus. On this island of rugged volcanic hills and valleys, wrapped by blue waters of the sea, the Romans had a penal colony. Criminals banished to Patmos were put to work in its mines and marble quarries. Among the prisoners was the apostle John. He was banished to Patmos by the emperor Domitian in A.D. 95.

We can picture this venerable old man, bowed down beneath his chains, working at hard manual labor all day long. Perhaps out of consideration for his age, he was allowed to toil at some lesser task, but we can still picture him as a lonely exile—cut off from his home in Ephesus, where he had been respected as a beloved apostle and pastor. Yet this old man was by no means defeated. We can picture him out among the angels and the heights of heaven by night.

All the might of Rome could back the emperor's decree banishing the aged apostle to Patmos. But all the power of hell could not keep John from his dreams and visions. Little did that wicked old tyrant Domitian know that he was setting the stage for a prophet. He put John on Patmos. God put John with his feet on Sapphire highways and streets of gold—and gave him visions of splendor in the Glory Land.

Tradition says the Romans tried to boil the apostle in oil. He had come through unscathed. What could the Devil do with a man like John? Turned loose, he would bless the church and win souls to Christ. Martyred, he would be promoted to glory. Locked up in a penal colony, he was "in the isle that is called Patmos" one moment (Rev. 1:9) and "in the Spirit on the Lord's day" the next (1:10). The Devil himself trembles at the thought of such a man. Well done, beloved apostle!

ELEVEN

James
The Son of Zebedee

Matthew 4:21; 17:1; 20:20–28; Mark 1:19–20; 5:37; 13:3; 14:33; Acts 12:2

A. His FAMILY
B. His FAITH
C. His FIDELITY
D. His FAME

I was once at sea on a troopship. Standing on the deck, I saw in the distance the gray horizon, where the tossing waves met the lowering sky. There was another ship out there. From time to time, riding an especially high wave, she would lift her masts above the skyline. Then she would sink back out of sight again. Such a ship, in such a sea, was the apostle James, who was the brother of John and the son of Zebedee and Salome. Once in a while we catch a fleeting glimpse of James in Scripture, but most of the time he is out of sight. We know he is there (usually when John or Peter is there); we catch the occasional glimpse of James, but most often we don't see him at all.

A. HIS FAMILY

James's father was Zebedee. Even more elusive than his son, Zebedee is seen on only one occasion in the Gospels (Matt. 4:21–22; Mark 1:19–20). He lived at or near Bethsaida on the western shore of the sea of Galilee, where Peter and Andrew were raised. The place, often frequented by Jesus, was probably not far from Capernaum, where the Lord eventually had His headquarters during His Galilean ministry. Later on, the Lord denounced Bethsaida for not receiving His teachings.

Zebedee was a successful fisherman who owned his own boats and paid other men to work for him. He was the kind of employer who kept a watchful eye on his business. His two sons were in business with him, and there seems to have been some kind of partnership between them and Simon Peter and Andrew.

Zebedee probably had a house in Jerusalem, too, and was acquainted with the high priest Caiaphas and his household (John 18:15–16). We can gather that Zebedee moved in the upper social circles.

We do not know anything about his personal relationship with the Lord Jesus. Zebedee does not seem to have done anything to hinder his two sons from giving up the fishing business to become disciples of the young prophet from Nazareth. Doubtless he had hoped that his boys would continue in his fishing business and carry it on after he retired. Still, he allowed them to go with Jesus and put no obstacles in their way. Some have criticized him for not going with them, but perhaps he thought it better to stay home and run the business so that he could contribute to their support.

It speaks well of a father when his boys want to follow in his footsteps. It also speaks well of a father when he unselfishly gives his sons to the Lord's work. Zebedee was a fine, hardworking man and a good father.

Salome, the mother of James, seems to have been a somewhat pushy, ambitious woman who wanted the best for her boys. We do not know how she reacted when her boys abandoned their future in the family business to trek up and down the countryside with the preacher from Nazareth. The early popularity of Jesus and His extraordinary miracles probably reconciled her to the decision her sons had made. Then when it dawned on Salome that Jesus was claiming to be Israel's rightful King, she was enthusiastically in favor of their choice.

She attempted, in fact, to push her sons forward in the anticipated kingdom (Matt. 20:20–28). Unknown to her, the Lord was actually on His way to Calvary when she made her move. She asked Him to give them the two highest and most important positions in His realm. We are not told what the two brothers thought of her behavior. Perhaps they were embarrassed. We do know what the other disciples thought. They were angry. In any case, the Lord denied her request.

It is possible that Salome was the sister of Mary, the Lord's mother. So perhaps Salome was trying to take unfair advantage of her family relationship. If on the purely human level Zebedee and Salome were indeed the Lord's uncle and aunt, they would have known Him from His infancy.

The circumstances of His birth were remarkable enough to have occasioned a considerable amount of gossip in the area. The character of the youthful Lord Jesus would also have been the likely subject of many conversations. He was never known to have said an unkind word or done an unkind deed. Luke said that He grew "in favour with God and man" (Luke 2:52).

Jesus was known in the area for His genius. He was a first-class scholar and a devoted student of the Scriptures. He carefully kept the letter and spirit of the Mosaic Law, which He knew by heart. Stories must have been circulated about His encounter with the Jewish rabbis in Jerusalem when He was a lad of twelve.

For years the Lord labored at the carpenter's bench in Nazareth. We can be certain that nobody ever had reason to complain about His workmanship or ever regretted doing business with Him. He was a craftsman whose creations were no doubt faultless. He was good and clever and kind. Nobody had a bad word to say about Him.

Doubtless He was a frequent visitor in Zebedee's home during the thirty silent years of which we know so little and of which we should like to know so much. So perhaps Zebedee and Salome were not at all surprised when Jesus quit the carpenter's shop and announced Himself to be the Messiah. They, of all people, would have known the truth about His birth and lineage.

Salome became an early and enthusiastic supporter of Jesus. She believed in His kingship. She was one of the women who ministered to Him of her own substance (Luke 8:3). She followed Him on His last journey to Jerusalem. She was at the cross and witnessed His final suffering (Mark 15:40–41). She was one of the women who came first to the tomb to complete the embalming of His body (Mark 16:1). Remembering her devotion to Jesus, we can forgive her for being a bit pushy.

Salome and Zebedee's sons, James and John—the Lord's cousins—would have amazing stories and countless unrecorded details to tell on their occasional visits home. It is easy to imagine Zebedee sitting in his easy chair and listening to it all, and Salome bursting out with one exclamation after another.

Of the two brothers, James seems to have been the older. Apparently it never occurred to James to be envious because his younger brother was closer to Jesus than he was. Maybe James recognized the unusual talents of his young brother, who went on to write five books of the New Testament. James and John had something in common: they both loved the Lord Jesus with an ever-growing love that would unite them in everlasting bonds far more enduring than any earthly ties.

B. His Faith

Reference is made to James in connection with the healing of Peter's mother-in-law, for right after that incident he responded to the call of Christ to become one of His personal disciples. In time James, his brother John, and his fishing partner Simon Peter formed a special inner circle among the disciples. As part of that inner circle, James was chosen by Jesus to be present on at least three significant occasions when his faith was greatly strengthened.

James was present, for instance, in the house of Jairus, the ruler of the Capernaum synagogue, when Jesus had His first ministerial face-to-face confrontation with death. That day James saw something no one had seen for hundreds of years. Not since the days of the prophets Elijah and Elisha had anyone seen a person raised from the dead.

The daughter of Jairus had died, and James saw the grief of the heartbroken parents. He witnessed the struggle in the soul of Jairus as he hoped against hope and battled so bravely with his understandable unbelief. Then James watched Jesus put out the professional mourners and turn His back on their mockery. James, John, and Peter, along with the stricken mom and dad, went into the child's bedroom. They looked at the face of the twelve-year-old girl, a face once fresh that was now cold and fixed in death. They saw Jesus take the little girl's dead hand in His and heard Him say, "Damsel, I say unto thee, arise" (Mark 5:41). They watched the blush return to her cheeks as she came back to life. James would never forget what he saw that day. He saw *the Lord's greatness*. It robbed death of all its terrors.

Later on James saw Jesus raise the widow's son and Lazarus, whose body was already rotting in the grave! No wonder James was such martyr material. He knew Jesus had conquered death and all its power.

James was also with Jesus on the Mount of Transfiguration. Once more in the company of Peter and John, he walked with Jesus into the Anti-Lebanon mountains and climbed to the snow line of Mount Hermon. There he saw the Lord's appearance change. James caught a glimpse of man as God intended man to be—inhabited by God and robed in a glory not of this world. Dazzled by the blazing whiteness of the Lord's homespun robe, James saw His face shine like the sun. James saw Moses and Elijah and heard their conversation with Jesus. James heard them talk of the Lord's "decease which he should accomplish at Jerusalem" (Luke 9:31). James heard Peter's blundering words as well as the voice from heaven. The Lord enjoined silence about the transfiguration, but James would never forget what he saw. He saw *the Lord's glory*.

Then James was with the Lord in dark Gethsemane. He heard the Lord say that His soul was "exceeding sorrowful, even unto death" (Matt. 26:38). Doubtless the mind of James was in a whirl. He had just come from the upper room where the Lord had talked more bluntly than ever before about His impending departure. James had partaken of the emblems of a new feast of remembrance, the significance of which was wholly beyond his comprehension at the time. He was bewildered by the talk of the Lord's body being broken and His blood being shed.

In the garden, James promised the Lord that he would stay awake and watch and pray, but he promptly fell asleep. He was ashamed of himself, but he kept on falling asleep just the same. Jesus excused him and John and Peter graciously: "The spirit indeed is willing, but the flesh is weak" (Matt. 26:41). But James saw the Lord's face drawn with anguish and stained with tears. He saw *the Lord's grief*.

James was with Jesus when Judas arrived with the rabble, the rulers, and the Romans. Like the other disciples, James ran away. Salome went to Calvary, but we have no intimation that James was there. John was there; the Lord consigned the future care of His mother to him, but there's no hint that James was there. If fear kept him away, he must have severely reproached himself for his desertion—until Pentecost changed everything forever.

James was in the upper room when the Lord appeared to the disciples after His resurrection. We can be sure he made up his mind then never to play the coward again. It was small comfort that the others had run away, too. It was small comfort that he had not betrayed the Lord as Judas did or denied the Lord with fisherman's oaths as Peter did. It was great comfort that the Lord had forgiven him. James had learned his lesson and learned it well. He was determined that next time he found himself in a place of danger because of his confession of Christ, he would play the man. To that end he schooled his heart and mind and soul and will.

C. His Fidelity

We see the fidelity of James in an incident that took place shortly after the transfiguration. Jesus had deliberately set His face toward Jerusalem, and each step was bringing Him closer to the cross. His way led through Samaria. Hard feelings had existed between the Jews and Samaritans for centuries, and the city of Jerusalem stirred the religious envy of the Samaritans. When the Lord entered the province of Samaria He pointedly bypassed their holy mountain Gerizim, thus making it evident that He was on His way to Jerusalem. So when the Lord and His disciples passed through a small Samaritan village, they encountered a hostile crowd. Perhaps the Samaritans felt that Jesus had snubbed their holy site. Perhaps they resented a band of Jews taking a shortcut through their village. For one reason or another, the Samaritans gave the Lord and His disciples an uncongenial reception.

James and John reacted at once. They had just seen Elijah on the Mount of Transfiguration—if Elijah could call down fire, they could do it too. "Lord," said James and John, "wilt thou that we command fire to come down from heaven, and consume them?" (Luke 9:54).

The call for fire was indeed appropriate: not penal fire, but Pentecostal fire! Not the fire of God's wrath, but the fire of God's grace! James and John did not yet know of what Spirit they were. They would understand better by and by.

In the meantime, the Lord gave them a nickname. He called the pair *Boanerges,* "sons of thunder" (Mark 3:17). Some think that the designation was given to James and John earlier because of their hot tempers; but, in any case, the term comes to mind in connection with this incident.

They *were* hotheads, but they were loyal hotheads. If their zeal was mistaken, they meant well. They could not bear to see their beloved Master slighted—and by Samaritans of all people! However blameworthy James may have been at the time, the incident certainly gives us a glimpse of his fidelity.

We see another glimpse of James shortly before Calvary. The disciples were exclaiming over the wonders of the temple and the great stones in its foundation when Jesus at once foretold the impending destruction of the temple and the city. Mark 13:3–4 tells us that James was one of those who asked the Lord for more details regarding the prediction. James wanted his faith and fidelity to be intelligent and informed. In answer to James's question, the Lord picked up the threads of Old Testament prophecy and the threads of New Testament prophecy and wove them into the wondrous tapestry of His great Olivet discourse. We might say, even at this belated date, "Thank you, James, for being so thoughtful as to ask that question."

Then, in the last chapter of the gospel of John, we see James on the seashore after the Lord's resurrection. The Lord had promised to meet the disciples in Galilee, so off to Galilee they went. Back to the towns and villages and scenes and memories of their earlier years. Before long Peter, it seems, got tired of waiting for Jesus and announced that he was going back to fishing. James was one of the other six disciples who fell in step with Peter. Down to the shore they went, just like old times. It was as though nothing had ever happened and that the three years they had spent with Jesus were all a lovely but impossible dream. The familiar boat, the ropes, the sails, and the nets were still there. The disciples launched out into the water, let down the nets, and toiled all night. The result was—nothing! They had come back to nothing! Then Jesus came and told them what to do and called them afresh to His work.

Like the others, James sat there shamefaced enough and, in uneasy silence, ate the breakfast the Lord provided. He listened as the Lord dealt with Peter. James heard Him silence Peter when he wanted to know what John's future would be. James heard the Lord's veiled but unmistakable prophesy of the terrible death Peter would die. Then and there, James must have made up his mind: he, too, would die, if need be, for the One who had died for him.

D. His Fame

Around A.D. 44 James was murdered by Herod Agrippa I. The church was just ten years old. The Herods were a cruel and dangerous family. Three or four of them come into the gospel story, and a quick glance at them will be useful.

Herod the Great, as the world calls him, was the man who murdered the babes of Bethlehem in an attempt to get rid of the infant Christ. He was an Edomite sitting on the throne of David and lording it over the people of God. He was such a brutal tyrant that even his own family was not safe. He had nine or ten wives and not only murdered his favorite, but also murdered her two brothers and some of his sons as well. Just five days before he himself died, he ordered the death of his son Antipater. No wonder the emperor Augustus said it would be better to be one of Herod's hogs than one of his sons! When Herod knew his life would soon be over, he rounded up all the leading Jews and gave orders for them to be massacred the day he died. "The Jews will not mourn me," he raved, "but they will mourn." Toward the end of his life he suffered terribly. A horribly painful and foul disease seized him, and his agony was indescribable. His sores stank so badly that people dreaded having to be in his presence.

Next came to power Herod Antipas, the son of Herod the Great. Antipas had a reputation for craftiness and cunning, and one historian called him "a wily sneak." He stole his half brother Herod Philip's wife Herodias, and she in turn goaded Antipas on to murder John the Baptist. That crime so haunted his conscience that he grew superstitious about Jesus, especially as the reports of His miracles circulated throughout the country. Herod Antipas secretly hoped someday to witness a miracle. He thought his time had come when Pilate, find-ing that the trial of Jesus was likely to be a very dangerous business indeed, sent Jesus to Herod Antipas for judgment. Antipas was delighted, thinking now he would see a miracle. Jesus, however, simply ignored him until at last Antipas, enraged by the Lord's silence, mocked Him and poured scorn on His claim to be King. So this Herod began by murdering John the Baptist and ended by mocking Jesus, the Son of God.

Herod Antipas was succeeded by Herod Agrippa I, a grandson of Herod the Great. The Herods had the confusing and unhealthy habit of marrying each other. Herod Agrippa I, for instance, was the child of two first cousins. He married another cousin, who was the daughter of his aunt, who was married to an uncle! Agrippa was a close friend of Caligula, one of the maddest of the Caesars. Agrippa was the Herod who murdered James in an attempt to curry favor with the Jews. Later he accepted divine honors for himself and died under the stroke of God.

James was the first of the apostles to suffer martyrdom. One tradition is that, before his martyrdom, James went to Spain to preach to Jewish captives in exile there. Herod Agrippa I had sent the Jews to Spain as slaves, so if James did, in-deed, go there to minister to them, Agrippa would have thought he had sufficient grounds for executing him. The execution of James pleased the Jews so much that Agrippa, wanting to humor his difficult subjects, went on to arrest Peter.

It is one of the mysteries of God's providence that Peter escaped and James was martyred. But it was only a decade or two before Peter was martyred also. Doubtless Peter was welcomed to his new home in heaven by both Jesus and his old fishing partner, James. James, through his mother, had once made a bid for a crown. Now he wears a martyr's crown in a land of fadeless day where he sits enthroned as one of the mighty apostles of the Lamb.

TWELVE

Nathanael the Guileless

John 1:45–51; 21:2

A. WHAT HE CONTENDED
B. WHAT HE CONFRONTED
   1. He was discerned
   2. He was displayed
   3. He was described
C. WHAT HE CONFESSED

John always called him Nathanael. The synoptic writers called him Bartholomew. *Bartholomew* is a patronymic—that is, a surname consisting of one's father's name or an ancestor's name plus a prefix or suffix. The surname *Johnson*, for example, is a patronymic; thus, *William Johnson* means "William, son of John." So *Bartholomew* is a surname meaning "son of Tolmai." The prefixes *Ben* and *Bar* always signal patronymics. Examples from the Bible include Bartimaeus, Barabbas, Ben-hadad, and Benjamin. Peter is called Simon Barjona because his father's name was Jonah. We do not know which ancestor is indicated by the name Bar-tolmai although we know there was a Jewish sect known as the Tholmaens who were dedicated to the study of the Scriptures.

The name Nathanael is more familiar to us since we are acquainted with the Old Testament prophet Nathan. *Nathan* means "gift" and *El* is a name for God, so *Nathanael* means "gift of God." The choice of the name Nathanael revealed the pious hope of the boy's parents that he would indeed be the gift of God. From what we know of Nathanael's character even before he met Christ, we can be sure those hopes were not in vain.

Nathanael was fortunate in his choice of friends. One of his closest friends was Philip. As soon as the Lord Jesus found Philip, he rushed off to find Nathanael.

Philip was brimming over with great news: "We have found him, of whom Moses in the law, and the prophets, did write, Jesus of Nazareth." Probably the two friends had often pored over the Old Testament Scriptures together, searching out the many prophecies concerning the coming of Christ. They had found Moses' prophecy that the Messiah would be a prophet like him. They had read Isaiah 53; 63; Psalms 22; 69; and Daniel 9. The preaching of John the Baptist had doubtless heightened their expectations.

Nathanael, slumbering under a fig tree, received a momentous awakening when Philip came bursting upon him with, "We have found him!" We can imagine that scene: Nathanael pricks up his ears and leaps to his feet. When Philip adds, "Jesus of Nazareth, the son of Joseph," Nathanael sinks back down.

A. What He Contended

"Can there any good thing come out of Nazareth?" Philip exclaimed. Nathanael knew Nazareth. He was a native of Cana, which was only five miles away from Nazareth. The word *Nazareth* gave him pause.

Sophisticated Jews did not think much of this Galilean town. They regarded the whole region of Galilee with more than a touch of contempt; they called the province "Galilee of the Gentiles" (Matt. 4:15). Remote from the theological stronghold of Judea, Galilee stood astride a busy international corridor, crossed by the great military roads from the north and by ancient caravan routes from the east. "Out of Galilee ariseth no prophet," the leaders of the Sanhedrin sneered when Nicodemus ventured to put in a tentative word for Christ (John 7:52).

They were dead wrong, of course. Barak the deliverer, Elon the judge, and Anna the prophetess had come from Galilee. Jonah, the only prophet to whom Jesus directly likened Himself, came from Gath-hepher, only a few miles from Nazareth itself. Elijah, Nahum, and Hosea had either come from Galilee or carried on much of their ministry there.

The Jerusalem and Judean Jews mocked at the grammatical errors and mispronunciations common among Galileans. Galileans were regarded as stupid yokels. The fact that the region had a mixed population of Phoenicians, Arabs, and Greeks, as well as Jews, increased the contempt in which Galilee was held by her neighbors to the south.

But the Galileans themselves were scornful of Nazareth. This provincial village had some kind of unsavory reputation. Just the same, the Lord Jesus spent thirty years of His life there. He lived in careful obscurity in the most despised province of the country, in the most despised valley of that province, and in the most despised village in that valley. For thirty years He was unknown, unrecognized, and unnoticed. So very ordinary did those years seem to His contemporaries in Nazareth that when, at last, in their local synagogue He proclaimed Himself to be the Messiah, they tried to assassinate Him for blasphemy.

Thus it was that when Philip added the words, "Jesus of Nazareth, the son of Joseph," he punctured the balloon of rising hope his first words had begun to inflate in the soul of Nathanael. He might have argued, "Let us concede that a prophet can arise out of Galilee. Jonah came from Gath-hepher, a town of Zebulun. Hosea was of the tribe of Issachar. Nahum came from Elkosh. Elijah was the Tishbite from Tishbeh in the territory of Naphtali. A prophet can arise out of Galilee—but Nazareth? Philip, show me one passage of Scripture that links Nazareth with the Messiah!"

Philip was a wise man. He did not attempt to argue the point with his friend. He did not try to change Nathanael's opinion of Nazareth. He simply said, "Come and see." He would introduce Nathanael to Jesus and let Jesus do the rest. That is the very essence of soul winning.

"Come and see" is what Jesus said to two disciples of John the Baptist. When they heard their master announce that Jesus was the Lamb of God, they left John the Baptist and followed Jesus. The Lord saw them following Him and asked, "What seek ye?" They replied, "Where dwellest thou?" He answered, "Come and see." The Bible says, "They came and saw where he dwelt, and abode with him that day" (John 1:39; see also vv. 35–39). The reference is to John the Beloved and to Andrew. What a time they must have had! What an endless stream of questions they must have asked Him. Perhaps later, as with the travelers on the Emmaus road, He began at Moses and the prophets and "expounded unto them in all the scriptures the things concerning himself" (Luke 24:27). Whatever happened, John and Andrew abode with Him, and thenceforth they were His!

"Come and see," said Philip. It did not take Nathanael long to discover that some good thing could, indeed, come out of Nazareth! Nothing so good had ever come out of any city in all the long ages of time. Goodness is a rare attribute that belongs essentially to God alone. It is one of the choice fruits of the Spirit. It is a pearl of great price, a gem more valuable than rubies. Nathanael found himself up against absolute goodness. He looked into a pair of eyes that saw right through him, and stripped away all of life's comfortable little disguises. He heard a voice that spoke the truth with a gentleness and candor that left him breathless. The words he heard were undiluted and memorable. He was in the presence of One who was wholly unafraid and awesome and unfathomable. He was confronted by a sincerity that hurt because it made all pretense, sham, and hypocrisy wither on contact. Love, unutterable love, shone out of those all-seeing eyes and resounded through that arresting voice. Nathanael came and saw for himself.

B. What He Confronted

1. He Was Discerned

Jesus said to Nathanael, "Before that Philip called thee, when thou wast under the fig tree, I saw thee." Perhaps that fig tree was in Nathanael's back yard. Perhaps that fig tree was in some remote unfrequented spot, a place where Nathanael liked to get away from it all. Perhaps that fig tree shaded Nathanael from the hot Syrian sun in a place where he could be alone and muse over a verse of Scripture that had caught his attention. Wherever that fig tree was, Jesus had seen Nathanael hidden away beneath its shadow.

Jesus' statement must have been somewhat disquieting to Nathanael. It had been disquieting for Adam and Eve when they first discovered that it is impossible to hide from God. As they cowered among the trees of the garden in their wretched aprons of fig leaves, and as they heard God's voice calling to them, "Where art thou?" (Gen. 3:9), they had known at once it was useless to hide. That voice penetrated every nook and cranny of Eden. The eye of God stripped aside all foliage and made every hiding place bare.

It was a terrifying truth to Adam and Eve that there was no hiding place from God. It was a tender and tremendous truth to poor, unhappy, runaway Hagar. Goaded beyond endurance by Sarah's acid tongue, Hagar had fled from Sarah and Abraham. She was heading for Egypt, totally disillusioned by the behavior of these believers. At sunrise she would cross the Egyptian frontier and go back to her own lifestyle and religion. God had other plans. He could not allow her to go back into the world, back into the dark, back to the demon gods of her people, carrying with her a distorted idea of Himself. So the Lord revealed Himself to Hagar, spoke to her, and gave her as fresh and as real and as unique a revelation of Himself as ever He gave to Abraham. God unfolded the prophetic page before her, giving her an exceeding great and precious promise. He then told her to go back to the one place on all this earth where He had put His name. "Thou God seest me," she exclaimed (Gen. 16:13).

The fact that we cannot hide from God is a terrific truth or it is a terrifying truth, depending on our relationship with Him. "I saw you," Jesus said, and Nathanael wondered what He had seen. Nathanael was to see even more clearly that his innermost thoughts were an open book to the One before whom he stood.

2. He Was Displayed

It could be inferred that Nathanael had been reading his Bible when Jesus saw him under the fig tree. The Lord now referred to Genesis 28:12, apparently the chapter and the verse upon which Nathanael had been meditating when His all-seeing eye was cast upon him. "Hereafter," Jesus said, "ye shall see heaven open, and the angels of God ascending and descending upon the Son of man" (John 1:51).

Genesis 28 tells us of a similar day in the life of Jacob. Jacob's wiles had caught up with him. He had double-crossed his twin brother once too often. Now Esau was breathing out threatenings and slaughter, and Jacob was forced to leave home. His first encampment proved to be memorable, for that night he dreamed of a ladder, a shining stairway linking earth to heaven. Moreover he saw the angels of God ascending and descending that ladder.

This activity of the angel hosts in Jacob's vision is significant. The angels were not descending and ascending; they were ascending and descending. They weren't coming down from heaven to earth and going back from earth to heaven. They were ascending to heaven from earth and then returning to earth from heaven. We cannot miss the meaning—they were already here, stationed down here.

This world is a battlefield, a planet that has been invaded by beings of great power, intelligence, and wickedness. The planet has also been invaded by count-less hosts of angelic beings from the high halls of heaven. The ranks of the holy angels include martial angels, ministering angels, and messenger angels. These beings owe their allegiance to God; they battle Satan's principalities and powers, his rulers of this world's darkness, and wicked spirits he has installed in high places.

The angels of God, it seems, have a shining stairway they use, or used to use, in order to communicate with the great white throne of God. Jacob saw them ascending. Up that endless ladder they went, laden down with sad tales of wickedness and woe. What stories of injustice and tyranny and oppression they carried with them, what tales of hate and malice and envy and rage, what stories of war and famine and pestilence and persecution, what disclosures of treachery, murder, and abuse! That ladder must have seemed a veritable Everest of difficulty and pain for the angels who were weighed down with the consequences of Adam's fall.

Jacob also saw the angels descending. They had made their reports and received new instructions. Down they came, having taken fresh courage from the untroubled calm and confidence that radiates from the throne of God. Iniquity was indeed a mystery to the angels of God. Howbeit, the angels sensed from the peace and power emanating from God's throne that all was well. They were reassured that although God's present purposes may be inscrutable, they are perfect and peerless. So descending the stairway with confident steps, the angels came to resume their duties. What a noble and awesome vision for a runaway young man! No wonder it had changed Jacob's life.

"Well, Nathanael," Jesus said in effect, "I am that ladder. I am that living link between earth and heaven. The angels of God ascend and descend upon Me. I am the way, the truth, and the life, and no one comes to the Father but by Me."

3. He Was Described

The moment Jesus set eyes on Nathanael, He said, "Behold an Israelite indeed, in whom is no guile!" The word translated "guile" here is the same word used in the Septuagint version of Genesis 27:35 to convey the idea of guile or subtlety.

Genesis 27 tells us of Jacob's guile. When Jacob stole Esau's blessing and Esau pleaded, "Bless me, even me also, O my father" (Gen. 27:34), "he found no place of repentance, though he sought it carefully with tears" (Heb. 12:17). He had bartered away his birthright years before and had forfeited the blessing along with it—not that either birthright or blessing was ever really his to sell. Nevertheless, overwhelmed suddenly and too late by the immensity of what he had thrown away, Esau burst out in anguish. Isaac, too, now fully aware of what had really happened, put it bluntly enough to Esau: "Thy brother came with subtlety, and hath taken away thy blessing" (Gen. 27:35).

Jesus used the same word Isaac did when He described Nathanael as an Israelite in whom was no subtlety or guile. John 1:47 has frequently been paraphrased, "Behold an Israelite indeed in whom is no Jacob!"

It took God twenty years to get to the root of the Jacob-nature in the pilgrim patriarch and bring him to the place where He could change his name to Israel. Even then the old Jacob-nature often reasserted itself. Indeed it is not until we come to the closing chapters of Jacob's life that we see him living as Israel.

But here in Nathanael, standing before Jesus, was an Israelite singularly free from the guile, crookedness, and subtlety of Jacob. The Lord appreciated the guilelessness of the man. True to his nature, Nathanael did not depreciate the Lord's comment with false humility, but accepted it at face value. "Whence knowest thou me?" he said (John 1:48). In other words, "How do you know so much about me?"

Nathanael was singularly free from the double-dealing so characteristic of some of Jacob's seed. There was something inherently transparent about Nathanael. He harbored no mixed motives in his heart and was a man who could be trusted. He scorned the use of what are commonly called "the tricks of the trade." People always knew where they stood with Nathanael. The Lord Jesus recognized this rare quality at once and spoke words intended to evoke the response that demonstrated Nathanael's guilelessness.

C. What He Confessed

Nathanael was quick to grasp the truth. "Rabbi," he exclaimed, "thou art the Son of God; thou art the King of Israel."

"The Son of God!" That identification put Jesus on the throne of the universe. Nathanael's statement was an amazing confession of faith. Peter took years to come to a like confession. Nathanael was far ahead of the majority of the nation of Israel in his comprehension of Christ. Nicodemus, learned and thoughtful member of the Sanhedrin that he was, did not rise to that realization until after Calvary. When he sought his famous midnight interview with Jesus, he hailed Him simply as "Rabbi . . . a teacher come from God" (John 3:2).

When we stand at the foot of the cross, we hear another man confess Jesus to be the Son of God—a Roman centurion, the man in charge of the Lord's crucifixion. But that confession was wrung out of him by the sheer weight of the evidence—darkening skies, rending rocks, bursting graves, and terrors in the temple. No such physical phenomena gave birth to the confession from Nathanael's soul. It was evidence enough for him that Jesus had demonstrated His deity by reading him like a book.

"The King of Israel!" That identification put Him on the throne of David. For a thousand years the Hebrew people had looked for the coming of the Messiah. The Davidic kingdom had waxed and waned and had finally been swept away by Nebuchadnezzar. The times of the Gentiles had begun. Cyrus the Persian had eventually restored a remnant of the Jews to the Promised Land. Hope for the restoration of their nation had revived, but Ezra, Zerubbabel, and Nehemiah had presided only over a dependency. Their mandate had been to build a temple, not a palace—to raise up an altar, not a throne.

The terrible sufferings of the Hebrew people during the Syro-Egyptian struggles and the coming of the monstrous Antiochus Epiphanes had hardened the clay of persistent Jewish unbelief. The sects of the Pharisees and Sadducees and the institution of both the synagogue and the Sanhedrin had hardened the clay still further. Rabbinical handling of the Scriptures had caused belief in the Bible to degenerate into adherence to the sterile traditions of the elders. Belief in a coming King had eroded and become buried under layers of dogma and scriptural interpretation.

Then had come the voice of John the Baptist. It had kindled new hope. So, when Christ confronted Nathanael, it took him about two minutes to make up his mind; Jesus was the King of Israel. All the messianic promises could now be fulfilled. The King had come and soon the kingdom would come!

"Thou art the Son of God," Nathanael said. Jesus countered, "Ye shall see heaven open, and the angels of God ascending and descending upon the Son of man." Jesus was indeed that ladder of Jacob's dream. As Son of God He placed His hand upon highest heaven. As Son of man He planted His feet firmly on the earth. God manifest in flesh! He was truly God in every sense of the word. He was truly man as well.

Nathanael was quick to recognize the Messiah. That is about all we know of him. That is all we need to know. We can be sure that a man who began with such a head start finished way out ahead. At the judgment seat of Christ it will be particularly interesting to see and hear what proof Nathanael made of his ministry in those years after Calvary.

THIRTEEN

Simon the Zealot

Luke 6:15

   A. THE MAN HE WAS
   B. THE MAN HE MET
   C. THE MAN HE BECAME

Simon is called the Zealot. That's all we know about him beyond the fact that he was a disciple of the Lord Jesus and one of the twelve apostles of the Lamb. The silence about him in Scripture is all the more arresting because the other Simon in the apostolic company is made highly visible. The name *Simon* means "one who hears." His name may be some kind of clue to the mystery of the Zealot, for "faith cometh by hearing, and hearing by the word of God" (Rom. 10:17). Perhaps we can deduce that he was a good listener, but Scripture does not give us any additional insights. In an attempt to synthesize a character sketch of Simon, we will consider the man he was, the man he met, and the man he became.

As we consider the man Simon was, we will study a man's convictions, and we will see how Jesus chooses a man. As we consider the Man Simon met, we will study a man's confrontation, and we will see how Jesus challenges a man. As we consider the man Simon became, we will study a man's conversion, and we will see how Jesus changes a man.

A. THE MAN HE WAS

When Pompey conquered Judea and Jerusalem in 64 B.C., the country became a Roman province, and thereafter its people were subject to Roman taxation. The

Romans heeded not that the Hebrew people were already heavily taxed—they had to pay a double tithe to support the Levites, priests, and temple. Most pious Jews paid these religious taxes willingly enough, but the new tax was harsh and rapacious, and the Romans farmed out the job of collecting it to self-seeking opportunists. One estimate is that the Jews were paying at least 30 to 40 percent of their income in taxes. So heavy was the burden that it threatened to bring the country to the verge of economic collapse. Neither the religious leaders nor the Roman masters would give way. This situation gave rise to the Zealots.

The Roman administrators of Judea were often insensitive and heavy-handed. Most of them were hack appointees—rough-and-ready soldiers who had risen up through the ranks. They had little or no administrative skill and cared nothing about social niceties. They made crude mistakes and backed them up with cruelty. Their idea of statesmanship was simple: when all else fails, use force.

The Roman procurators were often incompetent. The last of them, Florus, turned out to be the worst. He had learned nothing from the history of the previous governors of Judea. During a Passover celebration he seized the high priest's vestments. Then Florus added insult to injury by violating with obscenities the most sacred beliefs of the Jews. He had a consuming passion for wealth, so it is not surprising that he raided the temple treasury. A riotous demonstration ensued, and Florus chose to treat this demonstration as an act of rebellion. He called in the troops, arrested a number of the leading citizens, crucified them, and then handed Jerusalem over to his soldiers to plunder. This was the last straw, and a revolt against Rome broke out.

The Jews stormed the Roman garrison outside Jerusalem and routed the troops stationed there. Rebellion spread like fire throughout the country, and the Zealots saw the magic moment they had been waiting for. They captured the impregnable fortress of Masada. The tiny Jewish nation had thrown down the gauntlet to Rome, the giant oppressor of the world, and the Zealots became national heroes.

This group of rebels was the party Simon had joined. The Zealots were an intolerant crowd. Josephus described them as *sicarii,* a term that refers to people armed with daggers. Until open insurrection against Rome was possible, the more extreme Zealots relied on simple terrorism to achieve their ends. These extremists would conceal daggers in their robes, mingle with the crowds, and stab those they regarded as traitors.

The Zealots were in the thick of the fight against Rome. At the time the Roman army drew its compass around Jerusalem, the city was in the hands of three rival groups: the city itself was in the hands of Simon Bar Giora; the outer temple court was held by John of Gischala; and the inner courts were held by the Zealot leader, Eliezerben Simon. The unfortunate people of Jerusalem suffered as much from the brigandry, oppressions, and squabbles of these bandit leaders as they did from the Roman siege. When the three rival gangs were not fighting Rome, they were fighting each other and pillaging and ravaging the inhabitants of the city. Anyone suspected of wanting to defect to Rome was killed—often simply flung over the wall of the city to be dashed to pieces by the rocks below. The scenes of horror and terror inside the city were almost indescribable. Josephus heaped much of the blame for the suffering on the Zealots.

The last stand of the Zealots was at Masada in A.D. 71. After a long and bitter fight, the Roman general Silva took the fortress. Masada, a remote "fortress in the sky" in one of the most desolate places on earth, frowned down on the Dead Sea. Herod the Great had made the fortress virtually impregnable, and the Romans were compelled at last to build an enormous and expensive ramp up to the walls. When they finally stormed the fortress, they found only a few people still alive. All the rest had committed suicide rather than fall into the hands of the Romans. To this day, the Zealots' defense of Masada is legendary.

Simon was a Zealot, but not all Zealots were nationalist fanatics. Some were pure idealists. All of them, however, longed to see their country forever rid of the Romans.

When Jesus decided to pour Himself into just a dozen men, one of the men He chose was Simon the Zealot; Simon, after all, was a man of conviction. He may have been inclined to carry his convictions to the extreme, but the beliefs he held, he held with passion. Jesus needed a man like him.

On the purely human level, Simon might have been a potential liability to Jesus. We can be sure that the procurator's palace had a list of men to be kept under surveillance, and high on this list were members of the Zealot party. They were known troublemakers, forever fomenting riot and rebellion. To be marked down as a Zealot in those days would be like being marked down as a Jew by the Nazis or as a Communist in the days of the cold war. Jesus took the risk in His stride. He was as willing to associate Himself with a Zealot as with a publican.

There was considerable variety within the ranks of the apostolate. Simon was a Zealot; Matthew was a publican. They stood at opposite ends of the political spectrum. One was an ardent patriot, the other an outcast collaborator. Peter was a doer; John was a dreamer. Nathanael was a thinker; Thomas was a doubter. Philip was a realist, Andrew was an optimist, and Judas Iscariot was an opportunist. They were as diverse a collection of men as you would find today in the average local church.

Yet they all were attracted to Jesus, and Jesus was attracted to them. He chose them after a night of prayer. He knew what He was doing when He called Simon the Zealot. He knew the man's secret heart. He knew that he ached and longed for the messianic kingdom. Jesus knew that the spark and fire that made him a Zealot would also make him a grand apostle—once all his fiery passions had been extinguished and rekindled by Calvary love.

Simon the Zealot was made out of the same stuff as the Old Testament prophet Jonah, a man who was fearless, single-minded, and mightily used of God. Jesus had a future field of service for a man like him.

So we can surmise what kind of man Simon was: a man of conviction. We never read anything about him except that Jesus chose him and called him—and he came. We do not know how long Jesus knew him or when he was called. We do not know what kind of home he came from. We do not know if he moved in the same circles as Barabbas and his band of insurrectionists. We do not know anything except that he was willing to lay all his passionate convictions at Jesus' feet. In the Gospels he never raised his voice in debate. He never pushed himself forward. He asked no questions. Simon ("one who hears") was just there—listening, learning, longing, looking.

B. The Man He Met

Before Jesus began His public ministry, a notable prophet appeared among the Jews. His voice was raised in the wilderness, his message was strangely stirring to the soul, and his appeal was to the widespread masses. "Repent," John the Baptist cried, "for the kingdom of heaven is at hand" (Matt. 3:2). Thousands of people were moved to the depths of their beings. They flocked in droves to the Jordan to hear John preach. Large numbers responded to his call and submitted to baptism as a sign of repentance.

The religious establishment wrote off John as a public nuisance. Probably that only confirmed to Simon the Zealot that John was indeed a true prophet of God, in the Old Testament sense of the word. The Sanhedrin and the synagogue had sunk to a sorry level of compromise, materialism, hypocrisy, formalism, and impotence. That only inclined Simon all the more to listen to John. Perhaps Simon thought that John was the reincarnation of the prophet Elijah, who was to herald the coming Messiah. Simon kept his eyes and ears open.

Then Jesus came. He took up John's cry: "The kingdom of heaven is at hand." John did no miracles, and he kept himself in the backwoods and in the wilderness. But this new teacher, Jesus of Nazareth, took the Jewish world by storm. Stories of miracles came pouring in from all over the country. Not even in the days of Moses and Elijah had such wonders been seen. It seemed that neither demons nor disease nor even death itself could exist in His presence. Moreover, He was preaching about a kingdom now being offered to Israel. The common people heard Him gladly. The establishment suspended judgment, but, as usual, were inclined to be skeptical.

Perhaps it was the action of Jesus in the temple in Jerusalem that finally persuaded Simon the Zealot of His authenticity (John 2:13–17). Jesus looked around the courts with growing wrath. He used a scourge of cords to drive out the money-changers. He overturned their tables, forcibly driving out the merchants who marketed sacrificial animals. "Make not my Father's house an house of merchandise," He said (John 2:16). When Simon the Zealot heard about the cleansing of the temple, he doubtless said to himself, *Good for Him!* Perhaps Simon remembered the Old Testament text about the promised Messiah: "The zeal of thine house hath eaten me up" (Ps. 69:9). Here was a Zealot indeed.

Perhaps at first, it was the Lord's social program that appealed to Simon. Here was a man who was actually doing something about the sick and the hungry. What had the Zealots ever done? True, they were against injustice, tyranny, and the Roman occupation of their native land. The program of the Zealots, however, seemed to begin and end with clandestine meetings. It was a program of deception, violence, guerilla warfare, and for those who were caught, a cross.

One day the confrontation came. Jesus challenged Simon to become one of His disciples. We know nothing whatever about the meeting. We can be quite sure, however, that Jesus made the issues crystal clear. He was the last, the rightful, and the only surviving legitimate claimant to David's throne—a fact that could be checked by consulting the records in the temple—and He was going to establish a kingdom. He was indeed the Messiah, the King of Israel. He was the Son of God.

Simon was invited to become part of a revolution. Unlike any other revolution, however, this was to be a revolution of love. The problem was much more serious than the Roman occupation. The problem was sin. Jesus had come to destroy sin's empire in the human heart.

Doubtless Jesus said much the same to Simon the Zealot as He said to Nicodemus: "Except a man be born again, he cannot see the kingdom of God"

(John 3:3). Jesus, indeed, was going to found an empire—but the ruling principle in that empire was to be love. There would be a revolution, but it would be based on regeneration. Human nature has to be changed before nations can be changed.

Simon certainly had a lot to think about. He also had to consider that indefinable "something" about Jesus. It was not just His clear thinking, His great vision, His captivating personality, and His demonstrated power. It was not just His radiant humanity. There was His evident deity. He was so essentially good. Indeed, *holy* would be a better word to describe Him. His wisdom, love, and power were absolute, beyond any ever displayed by sinners of Adam's ruined race.

So Simon the Zealot made his decision for Christ. We can imagine how Jesus might have introduced him to the others. "This is Simon Peter and his brother Andrew, fishermen from Capernaum. This is James and his brother John. Their mother Salome and My mother are sisters. They, too, used to be fishermen. This is Thomas. These two are Philip and Nathanael. Here's someone you'll be interested to meet: Matthew or Levi, to give him his Hebrew name. He used to be a tax collector, a publican; but now he is My disciple and My friend. Here's Judas. We have two Judases. This one is Judas Iscariot. He's our treasurer . . ."

Under any other circumstances and in any other setting, the Zealot would have had little or nothing in common with most of these men. What made him one of them, and one with them, was their common love for the Lord Jesus. The apostles were like the spokes of a wheel, radiating out from their common center to the circumference of the circle. As those spokes draw closer and closer to the hub, they draw closer and closer to each other. They depict the secret of the apostolic community. Each of the Twelve, except Judas Iscariot, loved the Lord Jesus. He was the hub that held them all together. As they drew nearer to Him, they drew nearer to each other. Apart from Him there would have been no apostolate. Apart from Him there can be no church.

Simon the Zealot accepted Christ's challenge. He exchanged his membership in a band of hotheaded revolutionaries for membership in a fellowship based on love for the Lord Jesus Christ. He would never regret his decision. The Man he met became all-in-all to him. The Man he met eclipsed all others, dominated all horizons, controlled all situations, filled his heart and mind, and thenceforth ruled his life—for the Man he met was Jesus!

C. The Man He Became

Conversion is both a crisis and a process. The crisis comes when Jesus is enthroned in the heart as Savior and Lord. The process goes on for the rest of the believer's life. The crisis is often sudden; the process is usually slow. We grow in grace and increase in the knowledge of God. Both growing and acquiring knowledge are gradual processes.

Surely it did not take Simon long to realize that his zeal would need to be redirected. The Sermon on the Mount must have convinced him of his need. It would take the death, burial, resurrection, and ascension of Christ, followed by the baptism, indwelling, filling, and anointing of the Holy Spirit to bring him and the other apostles into some measure of the fullness of the stature of Christ.

The high concentration of apostles in Jerusalem was finally broken up. The apostles began to take seriously the Lord's call to be His witnesses to—"the uttermost part of the earth" (Acts 1:8); Simon the Zealot, it is said, headed for North Africa. He journeyed westward through what was called Mauritania and probably took the gospel to the great city of Carthage. Then Simon and Joseph of Arimathea, it seems, went to Britain.

Britain had been conquered by Julius Caesar half a century before the birth of Christ. London was founded in A.D. 43 and within a couple of decades became an important city. When Nero became emperor, the British people, led by the indomitable Queen Boadicea, revolted against Roman rule and a savage war broke out. About this time Simon would have arrived in Britain with the gospel.

One tradition is that the Zealot's activities were brought to the attention of Caius Decius, who nursed in his pagan soul a deep hatred of Christianity. Simon was arrested, given a mock trial, and sentenced to death by crucifixion. He is said to have been martyred at Caistor, Lincolnshire, where he was buried on or about May 10, A.D. 61.

A different tradition is that he did preach to the Latin community in Britain, perhaps even in London, but the Boadicea uprising prompted him to leave the country since the climate was no longer favorable to the gospel. Simon is thought to have returned to Palestine and made his way to Persia, where he was martyred by being sawn asunder.

Simon remained zealous to the end. His vision for the liberation of Palestine from the rule of Rome was expanded by Christ to a vision for the salvation of the whole lost Gentile world. Once, Simon advocated the use of the sword, but after his conversion he proclaimed God's offer of peace to all mankind.

The church needs men like Simon the Zealot. So many Christians are lazy, apathetic, half-hearted, and careless; they cannot find it in their hearts to give even minimal support to the evangelistic and Bible-teaching efforts of the church. We need the zeal of a John Knox, who said, "Give me Scotland or give me death!" We need men like D. L. Moody, who heard someone say that the world had yet to see what God could do through a man wholly sold out to Him. Moody declared, "By the grace of God I'll be that man." We need men like David Livingstone, who was willing to go anywhere as long as it was forward. We need men like George Verwer, who have motivated thousands to get up and get going for God; he is a man driven by the life-text, "Nothing shall be impossible unto you" (Matt. 17:20). The church needs men who are willing to be fuel for the flame of God.

FOURTEEN

Matthew

The Tax Collector

Matthew 9:9–13; Mark 2:14–17; Luke 5:27–32

A. HIS MONEY
B. HIS MASTER
C. HIS MANUSCRIPT
   1. The King is revealed
      a. His person
         (1) The Lord's ancestry
         (2) The Lord's advent
         (3) The Lord's ambassador
         (4) The Lord's adversary
      b. His purpose
         (1) The Lord's men
         (2) The Lord's mandate
      c. His power
   2. The King is resisted
   3. The King is rejected
   4. The King is raised

Matthew is called "the son of Alphaeus" (Mark 2:14). So is James the Less, but it is possible that Matthew's father was not the same Alphaeus who was the father of James the Less. Matthew's name is usually linked with that of Thomas, and it is not at all unlikely that they were brothers. Thomas is called *Didymus,* which means "the twin," so perhaps he and Matthew were twin brothers. Some scholars think that Thomas, Matthew, and James the Less were brothers.

There were several sets of brothers in the apostolic fellowship. Andrew and Simon Peter were brothers. James and John were brothers (since their mother Salome is thought to have been the sister of Mary, the Lord's mother, James and John may also have been the Lord's cousins). James the Less and Jude (Judas) may have been brothers. Half the company of the disciples was made up of pairs of brothers.

Matthew always referred to himself as Matthew. Mark and Luke always referred to him as Levi. We usually think of Matthew first as a tax collector.

A. His Money

At one time Matthew had plenty of money. The trouble was that his money had been treasured up at the price of infamy, for he was a publican, a tax collector for the Roman government. Most Jews branded him an outcast, for they considered the publicans to be traitors in the pay of a detested occupying foreign power.

Moreover tax collectors were not at all scrupulous about how they amassed their private fortunes. They used the system to their own advantage. Roman officials farmed out the actual job of collecting taxes and gave each collector a quota. What he collected over and above the quota was his to keep. As a result, extortion was common, and the tax collectors preyed on rich and poor alike.

Matthew had an office in Capernaum, a busy town on the northwest shore of the sea of Galilee. There he collected taxes from the fishermen and from the caravans that came that way. We do not know how he came to be so employed. His choice of a profession must have broken his parents' hearts, for he was born a Levite.

To be born a Levite was considered a privilege, for that Hebrew family had been set apart by God to handle holy things. Children of the Levites were well-grounded in the Scriptures. Matthew's familiarity with the Old Testament is evident throughout his gospel. The Levites were also experts in Mosaic Law and rabbinic traditions.

Their tribal history was unique. Every other tribe was given a province of its own, but the tribe of Levi had no such territorial holding. Instead, it was given a number of cities (including six "cities of refuge") scattered throughout the territories of the other tribes. Thus the Levitical tribe was intended to have a godly, leavening influence on the more secular tribes. The Levites were denied property in this world so that they might lay up treasure in heaven. The Levitical tribe derived its income from the tithes and offerings of the other tribes.

Young Matthew seems to have taken a dim view of this arrangement. When his mother would ask him what he wanted to be when he grew up, he probably did not say he wanted to be a Levite. When she insisted, "What are you going to be?" he likely replied, "Rich!" The Levitical system of living on handouts from other Israelites apparently was not for him. Matthew, it seemed, was sick of that kind of life. His intent, as it turned out, was to get rich as fast as he could. When, in his bed at night or in his wanderings here and there, his thoughts likely turned to how to get rich quick. One sure way became obvious. He would become a tax collector.

Why not? He would reason. *I might as well accept the situation as it is. The country is occupied by Rome, and that's a fact of life not likely to change in my lifetime. So what if tax collectors are despised and classified with harlots and sinners? I don't need to be an extortioner. I'll just make a fair commission. My parents are wedded to the old ways, trying to earn a living by teaching the Mosaic Law. But surely the only law that really matters is Roman law. I can't spend the rest of my life tied to my parents' apron strings. I'm sorry they'll be upset by my decision, but it's my life after all. I'm going to become a tax collector.*

To that end, Matthew would have given attention to his education so that he would be literate and at home in both the Jewish and Roman worlds and able to handle basic arithmetic and bookkeeping. Eventually he became a publican and joined a small, tight-knit community of rich social and spiritual outcasts. Shrugging off any vision of his parents' anguished faces and their shame, he went about the business of making money.

Matthew probably knew Zebedee and his sons quite well. They were prosperous fishermen and doubtless paid their taxes to him. So did Jonas and his boys, Andrew and Peter.

It is probable that Matthew saw Jesus when He visited the area. He would have known of His reputation for integrity, workmanship, generosity, and plain old-fashioned goodness. His reputation would have preceded Him even before He gave up the carpentry business in Nazareth, went down to Jordan to be baptized of John, and then reappeared as a preacher and miracle worker. Jesus showed His scorn of gossip and cutting public opinion merely by stopping to pass the time of day with Matthew.

B. His Master

It is unlikely that Matthew was really happy. He may have laughed and joked when he was with his own company—that tight little circle of tax collectors who shrugged off the scorn of their fellows by throwing lavish parties for each other and hiring entertainers of questionable morals and few scruples. But the snubs and sneers of the Jews, his excommunication from temple and synagogue, and the pained, stricken looks on the faces of his parents must have cut deeply into Matthew's soul. Perhaps he had already discovered that money—lots and lots of money—couldn't make a man happy.

Then one day, like a bolt out of the blue, a voice of authority and command offered the opportunity of a lifetime. There was Jesus of Nazareth hailing him, and there was a handful of His new disciples. The disciples were looking him over with mixed feelings indeed, but the Master was looking into his very soul. The disciples saw the publican; Jesus saw the person. Jesus saw the real man beneath the empty mask of indifference and bravado. "Follow me," He said. That was all. It was enough; Matthew did not hesitate for a moment. We can see the scene as he hands his account book over to his assistant, appoints a successor, and then walks out of the tax-collecting business forever. Matthew is a changed man.

The Master's call came to Matthew as an unexpected challenge. Perhaps he had been thinking about a change for a long time. No doubt he had heard some of Jesus' sermons, seen some of His miracles, and maybe talked to Him privately at night like Nicodemus. Perhaps Matthew had been longing and yearning for just such a call. In any case, it did not take him long to make up his mind. He didn't say, "I'll think it over." He rose up instantly and followed Jesus.

Matthew's decision no doubt caused quite a stir in and around Capernaum. The gossip spread from village to village: "Guess what! Jesus of Nazareth has a new disciple—a publican. He must be hard up for disciples."

But Jesus wanted Matthew. He wanted him for Himself—He saw beneath the surface to the sound quality of the man. But He also wanted the skills that Matthew had. They would be invaluable later on in establishing His kingdom in the hearts and lives of men. He wanted the businessman in Matthew.

Most of the Lord's disciples were only average people. Judas was the only Judean; the rest were Galileans, and the Galileans were despised in Jerusalem as provincial. Most Galileans had a very limited education. But Matthew could read, write, keep records, draw conclusions, weigh the pros and cons of a situation, and make firm decisions. He was used to assessing the value of all the different kinds of merchandise carried by the caravans along the great Damascus-Tyre highway that ran through Capernaum. His work as a tax collector had called for a wide range of knowledge. He would be an invaluable man to have in the apostolic circle.

Like most Jews, the disciples had well-trained and retentive memories and would be able to recall much of what they heard and saw in their three-and-a-half years with Jesus—especially when their capacious memories were quickened by the Holy Spirit. It was in the interest of everyone to have someone along who could write things down. Making notes seems to have been Matthew's particular job, for he never opens his mouth in the Gospels. We see his name in the various lists of the apostles, but we read little else about him.

No sooner had Matthew responded to the "royal invitation" to become a personal follower of the Christ of God than he did a very sensible thing. He threw a party. He invited all his former friends, the whole fellowship of publicans and sinners, to be his guests. He also invited Jesus and all his new friends in Christ. It was Matthew's way of introducing his former associates to Jesus. It was his way of saying to his old crowd, "I'm through with the old way of life. Come and meet the Master. Come and meet the Man who changed my life completely. Perhaps you would like to enthrone Him as Savior and Lord of your lives too."

We have no idea how many responded. Perhaps it was news of Matthew's changed life that touched the heart of Zacchaeus. In any case, Matthew's dinner party marked a complete break with his old way of life. He had a new Master, a new fellowship, and new friends. His old friends could come and join him, but he would not be joining them anymore. What a wonderful way to begin a new life in Christ!

Committed now beyond recall, Matthew spent the next three years of his life in the personal company of Jesus and His disciples. He trudged the length and breadth of the Promised Land with Him. He saw His many miracles (only a scant three dozen of them are recorded in the Gospels). He heard His wonderful sayings. He saw how Jesus handled Himself in various situations. He listened to the Sermon on the Mount and made copious notes—Matthew was the only gospel writer to give us the full text. He listened avidly to the Olivet discourse—and again Matthew gave us the fullest account of that remarkable sermon on things to come. He watched the growing opposition. He was in the upper room for the Lord's farewell messages. He had firsthand knowledge of the trial, the terrible miscarriage of justice, the crucifixion, the burial, and the resurrection. And all this time his pen was busy writing and recording. Of the 1,068 verses that make up Matthew's gospel, 644 contain actual words of Christ; so about three-fifths of his gospel is made up of the recorded words of the Lord Jesus.

C. His Manuscript

If Matthew never did anything else, he performed a service of the highest order for the world and for the church when he wrote the gospel that bears his name. His gospel was initially intended for the Jewish people. He wanted to demonstrate that the man Jesus, whom the Jews had so terribly rejected, was, indeed, their Messiah. Ample evidence of this intent is found in the nature and content of the gospel itself. Consider the following examples:

1. The gospel of Matthew traces the Lord's ancestry back to David, the founder of the Hebrew royal family;
2. This gospel traces that ancestry through Joseph, the lineal descendant of Solomon and the foster father of Jesus;
3. This gospel makes constant reference to "the holy city" and refers also to "the holy place";
4. This gospel in various places calls Jesus the Son of David;
5. This gospel shows the fulfillment of Old Testament prophecy regarding the coming of Christ;
6. This gospel alone makes reference to the kingdom of heaven. This kingdom of heaven is not the same as the kingdom of God. The kingdom of God is eternal, spiritual, and free from sin. It can only be entered by means of the new birth, and its empire is established in the hearts of the regenerate. The phrase "the kingdom of heaven" refers to God's purpose and plan to establish a kingdom on earth. Its fortunes have fluctuated with the course of history, and its establishment is still being postponed until the second coming of Christ. Matthew's understanding of the Jewish role in the kingdom of heaven led him to tell us most of what we know about it;
7. The gospel of Matthew alludes frequently to Jewish customs, the Mosaic law, and the Hebrew prophets. Matthew generally assumed his readers were familiar with such quotations and allusions.

It is thought that Matthew's gospel was written just before the destruction of Jerusalem and the temple by the Romans in A.D. 70. By that time Jewish rejection of the claims of Christ, both in the homeland and among the Diaspora, was deeply entrenched.

Matthew's plan was to group his material, not necessarily in chronological order, but in a logical order to produce a cumulative effect. For instance, Matthew kept the remarkable Sermon on the Mount intact, whereas in Luke the substance of the discourse is found scattered here and there throughout the gospel. Matthew recorded twenty specific miracles of Jesus and, in keeping with his pattern of grouping his material, half of these miracles are recorded in just two chapters (chaps. 8–9).

Matthew recorded about forty of the Lord's parables. He alone tells us about the wheat and the tares, the hidden treasure, the pearl of great price, the fish net, the householder and his treasure, the unmerciful servant, the laborers in the vineyard, the ten virgins, and the talents. Nearly all the parables recorded by Matthew alone are in keeping with his purpose of emphasizing the fact that Jesus was Israel's Messiah.

At least seven of the forty parables recorded by Matthew are parables of judgment. Doubtless the terrors inflicted on his native land as the Romans pursued their relentless war colored Matthew's writing. Jesus had warned that judgment would come to the apostate nation of Israel. But the judgment at the hand of the Romans was only preliminary. Matthew focused on end-time judgments too. In keeping with the judgmental aspect of his gospel, Matthew recorded the Lord's denunciations of the Jewish leaders. In this gospel the Lord's public ministry begins with eight beatitudes (Matt. 5:3–10) and climaxes with eight curses (Matt. 23).

Matthew's gospel can be divided into four parts: (1) in chapters 1–9 the King is *revealed;* (2) in chapters 10–16 the King is *resisted;* (3) in chapters 16–27 the King is *rejected;* (4) in chapter 28 the King is *raised.*

1. The King Is Revealed

a. His Person

First, the gospel of Matthew reveals *the Lord's ancestry.* Jesus was the Son of David and the rightful heir to David's throne. When Matthew wrote, the temple was still standing, and anyone could verify the Lord's genealogy by consulting the registers in the temple.

Next, the gospel reveals *the Lord's advent.* Matthew recorded how it came to pass that Jesus was born, as prophesied, in the town of Bethlehem. Matthew told of the visit of the wise men from the East—the Gentile magi who bore tribute to Jesus as the King of the Jews. Matthew told also of the fulfillment of another prophecy: "Out of Egypt have I called my son" (Matt. 2:15).

The gospel then reveals *the Lord's ambassador*. Matthew told of the coming of John the Baptist, in the spirit and power of Elijah, to herald the imminent unveiling of the King.

Moreover the gospel reveals *the Lord's adversary*. Matthew gave us the fullest account of how the Lord was tempted in the wilderness and how He routed the ancient enemy of mankind.

b. His Purpose

The King's purpose is revealed in the choice of *the Lord's men*. Matthew tells us how the Lord chose His disciples, the men with whom He intended to share the administration of His kingdom. Those who judged only by outward appearance thought the disciples were an undistinguished and insignificant collection of nobodies. It was obvious that here was a King who loved ordinary folk. He bypassed the religious establishment as represented by synagogue and Sanhedrin and went straight to the common people for His followers.

Matthew also revealed *the Lord's mandate*. The gospel records the famous Sermon on the Mount in which the King issued a series of astonishing principles for the government of His kingdom. The Lord took the light of the Mosaic Law (in itself impossible to obey), passed it through the prism of His divine intellect, broke that white light up into its glowing colors, and then lifted it like a rainbow as high as the heavens themselves. Then in answer to those who wrote the word *impossible* over His precepts, He lived by them—moment by moment, day after day, in all the various circumstances of life.

c. His Power

Then, too, Matthew revealed the King's power. The gospel tells how Jesus cleansed the leper, stilled the storm, and raised the dead. He fed the multitudes, healed the sick, and gave sight to the blind. He made the dumb to speak, the deaf to hear, and the lame to walk. Such power had never before been demonstrated on earth.

2. The King Is Resisted

In chapters 10–15 of his gospel, Matthew records mounting resistance to the King. We would have expected His contemporaries to cheer Him all the way to Jerusalem, to Rome, and to the empire of the world. Instead the Jewish religious establishment instigated a rising tide of opposition. That resistance was *foretold* in Matthew 10, *felt* in Matthew 11, and *focused* in Matthew 12–15. When the Jewish leaders finally accused Him of doing His marvelous miracles in the power of Satan, He gave a series of parables ("the mystery parables") in which He officially postponed the establishment of the kingdom of heaven until an unspecified future date. The Christ interposed the age of grace (the church age in which we live), a period of time during which God would work out quite a different purpose of grace—He would build a spiritual *church* rather than establish a material *kingdom*.

3. The King Is Rejected

Matthew 16–27 tells of the King's rejection. After Peter's confession and the subsequent transfiguration, the Lord began to talk increasingly about His forthcoming death on the cross. He pronounced a series of woes upon the leaders of the Jewish religious establishment, and then, in His great Olivet discourse, He foretold the impending destruction of both Jerusalem and the temple and set the stage for end-time events and for His coming again.

Events happened swiftly after these warnings. Judas defected to the Sanhedrin and betrayed the Lord while He was praying in Gethsemane. A series of mock trials followed, and Jesus was handed over by the Romans to the executioners. And so the Jews rejected their Messiah, and the Romans collaborated with them in His murder. An age had come to an end.

4. The King Is Raised

In the final chapter of his gospel, Matthew told us of the King's resurrection. Matthew 28:1 says it was "the end of the sabbath" when Jesus rose from the dead. It was the end of the Sabbath indeed! It was a new dawn, a new day, a new dispensation. Everything now centers not on the dead Jewish Sabbath but on the first day of the week, the resurrection morn, the day the King came back. The Sanhedrin did their best to squelch the tidings, but they might as well have tried to put out the sun. Today the tidings of a risen Christ are heralded around the globe.

Well, Matthew, you took good notes! The Holy Spirit inspired you as to how to use them, and we are grateful to you. Little did you know on that day you walked out of the Capernaum customs office that you would eventually write a bestseller—a book that would become part of the divine library, a book that would be read and studied and loved and taught throughout the whole world, a book that would be translated into hundreds of languages, a book that would make your name famous for the rest of time. That was a good bargain you made when you forsook all to follow the Christ of God.

FIFTEEN

Judas and His Crime

John 13:21–30

A. How he deceived the saints
B. How he despised the Savior
    1. He despised all the Lord's works
    2. He despised all the Lord's words
    3. He despised all the Lord's warnings
C. How he destroyed his soul

The story of Judas Iscariot is like flotsam and jetsam scattered across the entire manuscript of the historical books of the New Testament. Rarely did such a ship set forth in the morning—laden with such a cargo of rich opportunity, guided by such a brilliant Star, with such high hopes of a prosperous voyage—only to make such utter and total shipwreck before nightfall. The wreckage of Judas's life is strewn far and wide. We pick up a piece of the story here, another piece there, still another piece somewhere else. We find a verse or so in Matthew, a couple of comments in Mark, a saying or so in Luke, a splinter or two of information in John, and a final piece in the book of Acts. And that is it.

We sit down and try to patch the pieces together, but we are left with many questions and few answers. When, where, and why did he become a disciple of the Lord Jesus? What was the home like in which he was raised? Did he have any brothers and sisters? What did his father think of it all? At what point did things go sour in the life of Judas? Suppose he had not betrayed the Lord, what then?

We look at the wreckage. Gone now are the brilliant opportunities and the glowing hopes, the bright promise, the great prospects. For the opportunity Judas was given in life was enough to make the angels gasp. He might have had his name engraved in royal gems and embedded forever into the foundation stones of the Celestial City. Throughout all the endless ages of eternity, the redeemed of all ages would have stopped to admire that name, along with all the others, adding its own unique luster to the city of God. In their endless comings and goings, the angels might have pointed out his name to each other as one of the twelve apostles of the Lamb. Instead, his name rings down the centuries as a synonym for treachery and shame.

Possibly Judas might have done the work for which the Holy Spirit later called, saved, anointed, and commissioned the apostle Paul. He might have turned the world upside down for Christ. He might have written a score of epistles. Letter after letter might have begun, "Judas, an apostle of Jesus Christ . . ." He might have become the very chiefest of the apostles. Instead, he did the Devil's work and stands forth as the very chiefest of all apostates from the Lamb. As we grope amidst the wreckage of Judas's life, we notice three outstanding things about the man: he deceived, he despised, and he was destroyed.

A. How He Deceived the Saints

There can be no doubt Judas was a good hand at playacting. He put up a good outward show of pretending to be a sincere and devoted disciple. The other disciples thought the world of him at the time. It was not until afterward that they saw through him. During most of the time he trod with them over the highways and byways of Palestine, they thought that he could do no wrong. Perhaps that was because he was the only Judean in the small Galilean band of the Lord's disciples. That, in and of itself, would give him special status. Indeed, he came from the same royal tribe as the Lord Jesus. We know how the Judeans prided themselves on being pure-blooded Jews and how contemptuously they referred to people from Galilee. "Can there any good thing come out of Nazareth," they sneered when seeking to discredit Jesus Himself. Judas came from Kerioth on the southern border of Judah. The Galileans, in contrast with the Judeans, were often of mixed blood. They spoke their native Aramaic with a thick north-country accent. They tended to be rustics, fisher-folk, provincials. As a Judean, Judas had a head start, at least in the thinking of the other disciples.

The only other disciple who seems to have had any claim to sophistication was Matthew, but then, his claim was tarnished by his having been a tax collector for the occupying Roman power. Judas had no such handicap. He was universally known among the disciples as Judas Iscariot, "inhabitant of Kerioth," a Judean.

The other disciples were quite prepared to give him all the deference that title might command.

Not that it was such a difficult thing to deceive the saints. Many a person has succeeded in doing that. In the first place, the membership of Judas in that small apostolic fellowship was in good order, so far as the others could see. His credentials were never called in question. He was accepted by them as one of them. He was treated by the others as a brother in the Lord. They would greet him with "a holy kiss" as they would each other. Or, as we would say, they shook hands with him heartily and warmly on each occasion they met, giving him what the Bible calls "the right hand of fellowship." So far as all outward appearances went, he was in full and hearty fellowship with those who loved the Lord.

Then, too, he had been a gospel preacher. He had done evangelistic work in a gospel team. On one occasion Jesus sent out his immediate disciples two by two to preach the gospel throughout the land. On another occasion Jesus sent out no less than seventy disciples on a similar mission. Judas was one of those who went. The commission was comprehensive and clear: "Go to the lost sheep of the house of Israel. And as ye go, preach, saying, The kingdom of heaven is at hand. Heal the sick, cleanse the lepers, raise the dead, cast out devils: freely ye have received, freely give. Provide neither gold, nor silver, nor brass in your purses . . ." (Matt. 10:6–9). When the traveling evangelists regathered after their mission, they were overjoyed and overwhelmed. "Even the devils are subject unto us!" they cried (Luke 10:17).

There is not the slightest hint of an exception in the case of Judas. God honored His Word when it was proclaimed by James or by John, and He honored His Word when preached by Judas. So then, Judas had "lived by faith" as we would put it today. He had been a traveling preacher. In the name of Jesus he had called upon men to repent. He had preached the coming of the kingdom. He as well as the others had success stories to share.

There was even more. He was recognized by the others as a kind of "elder," for he was the only one who had an "office," a position. He was the treasurer of the group. When the question arose as to who should take care of the finances, Judas was elected. After all, he was a cut above the rest, at least on the human level. So he was entrusted with the bag. When someone wanted to share financial fellowship with the Lord's work in those days by contributing some money toward the expenses of the Lord's followers, it was Judas who received the money, wrote out the receipt, and sent a "thank you" letter of acknowledgment. When one of the disciples, or the Lord Himself, saw a special case of need and it was decided to extend a helping hand by means of a gift, it was Judas who took care of things. It was Judas who looked up the needy one, who left the parcel of food, or who gave the agreed sum of money. Indeed, in this way, Judas was able to acquire a very cheap and easy reputation for caring for the poor. Many an orphan, many a widow, many a beggar by the wayside blessed Judas for the generosity extended to them.

In keeping with his reputation for watching over the common purse, it was Judas who protested when Mary of Bethany poured out that costly perfume over the feet of Jesus. "Why was not this ointment sold for three hundred pence," Judas demanded indignantly, "and given to the poor?" (John 12:5). It was not until many years later that John exposed the secret sin of Judas. "Not that he cared for the poor," John said, "but because he was a thief, and had the bag" (John 12:6). At the time, however, the disciples thought Judas had spoken out of compassion for the poor and, on similar occasions, they even echoed his sentiments.

Moreover, Judas took his place at the Lord's table. When the disciples sat down to "break bread" together and to "drink the cup," the Lord Jesus being "in the midst," Judas took his place along with the others. Even when he had the blood money jingling in his pocket, Judas still professed himself to be loyal to the Lord and to His cause. Not one of the others suspected him for a moment.

It is all too easy to deceive the saints, to go through all the motions of being a believer. It is particularly easy to playact the part of a believer if one has been raised in a Christian home and taken from earliest days to church and Sunday school. It is easy enough, then, to speak well the language of "Canaan." It is easy to come and go in a local fellowship of believers and be accepted as a believer and all the time have a heart as black as pitch and a conscience seared with a hot iron.

B. How He Despised the Savior

Judas never failed to pay lip service to Jesus. He never, though, knew Him as personal Savior and never once acknowledged Him as Lord. He customarily addressed Jesus as *Rabbi* ("Teacher"), never as *Lord*! His stolid refusal to pay to the Lord Jesus the proper tribute due to both His Name and His character was evidence enough that "the root of the matter was not in him." He was not in love with Jesus, and, in fact, despised Him in his heart of hearts. It was a long time before that carefully concealed wickedness showed, but it was there all along.

1. He Despised All the Lord's Works

Never before or since was there such an extraordinary life lived on this planet than the life of the Lord Jesus. Judas had the rare, first-hand opportunity of observing that life at close quarters. He spent three-and-a-half years in the immediate company of the Lord Jesus. He saw Him perform the most astonishing collection of miracles that could be imagined. The gospel narratives confine themselves to a scant three dozen miracles of Jesus, but John tells us that the world could not contain the books that could have been written about Jesus. Judas saw these mighty miracles. Some of the Lord's miracles were performed in private, but Judas knew about them just the same.

He knew, for instance, that Jesus could turn water into wine. He was there when the hungry multitudes were fed, when Jesus took a little lad's lunch and used it to found a feast. He was one of the Twelve who distributed that miraculous meal to the people. He was one of those who gathered up the twelve baskets full that remained when it was all over. He saw the lepers cleansed. He saw blind men given their sight, crippled men healed, the deaf and dumb made both to hear and speak. He saw the Lord Jesus raise the dead. He saw even the fiercest and foulest demons flee at a word from Christ. He saw crooked men made straight, profligate men made pure, greedy men transformed. It all made no lasting impression on him.

One suspects he became irritated by all these miracles. After all, what was the point and purpose of them? They did not seem to bring Jesus anywhere nearer the throne of David. Indeed, after the feeding of the five thousand, when the enthusiastic crowds wanted to make Jesus King, then and there, Jesus simply sent them away. We can well believe that Judas was astounded. What a golden opportunity lost! Perhaps it was at that point that he began to make his secret plans to salvage what he could for himself before deserting such a lost cause as the one to which he had joined himself. Why didn't Jesus take advantage of His miraculous powers? Anyone who could still the storm and walk upon the waves and multiply loaves and fishes and turn water into wine could step right up to the throne of the world if He went about it with any pragmatism at all. Or so Judas would think.

2. He Despised All the Lord's Words

Even the Lord's enemies exclaimed, "Never a man spake like this man" (John 7:46). It was obvious to any thinking person that Jesus spoke "with authority, and not as the scribes" (see Matt. 7:29). There was a freshness, a fervor, a fragrance, and a force about the words of Jesus that attached to no one else's words then or now. Judas listened to all the Lord's marvelous teaching and tuned Him out.

Judas heard all the Lord's parables, each one a miracle in words. He heard the beatitudes as they fell one by one from the lips of the Lord. He doubtless thought them idealistic and impractical. The entire Sermon on the Mount must have seemed to him as the words of a dreamer. He heard the Lord's great prophetic statement on the Mount of Olives and realized that whatever the Lord had taught about a kingdom, it certainly was not coming in his lifetime. He had heard some of the heart-to-heart talks Jesus had with His disciples in which He told them He was going to die and be buried and rise again. Judas must have been greatly disturbed by the increasing emphasis on a cross. He heard the Lord pronounce His eight curses on the religious leaders of the day. The entire Jewish establishment, so far as Judas could see, was up in arms against Him. What was the sense in deliberately provoking the most powerful men in the land? The more Judas listened to Jesus the more he tuned Him out. At last, surfeited by miracles and parables, he became thoroughly "gospel hardened." He came to the place where he no longer paid the slightest attention to the Lord's words. He was thinking, instead, how he could salvage something for himself from this hopeless cause with which he was identified.

We recognize the same pattern today. It is possible for a person to be familiar with all the wonderful teachings of Jesus, to be able to repeat His priceless parables, to be able to recite the Sermon on the Mount and to expound the Olivet Discourse and be as lost as a pagan. One of the greatest of all perils is to be familiar with divine truth and to refuse to act upon it but, rather, to turn against it and despise it.

3. He Despised All the Lord's Warnings

Over and over again, the Lord Jesus let Judas know that, while he had successfully deceived the saints, not for one moment had he deceived the Savior. The Lord could read his innermost thoughts like an open book. Again and again the Lord let Judas know that He knew. "Have not I chosen you twelve," He said on one occasion, "and one of you is a devil" (John 6:70). What was it that Judas did that caused the Lord to use such strong language? He had not committed murder and insurrection. So far as we know he was not an adulterer, nor a licentious man. Yet he committed the sin of all sins. He betrayed the Lord

Jesus Christ, the Son of the living God, the Creator of the universe, in the days when He trod these scenes in history. Worse still, he betrayed Him with a kiss. He did not spit upon Him as some vulgar men did; he kissed.

C. How He Destroyed His Soul

In the upper room Jesus plainly declared, "One of you shall betray me." Eleven of the twelve men in the room were astounded. Twelve men in that room cried out, "Is it I?" (see Matt. 26:21–22). One of those twelve was Judas. "Is it I?" he said, with thirty pieces of silver burning a hole in his purse. Over and over again the Lord let Judas know that He knew.

Peter could not stand the suspense. He beckoned to John who was closest to the Lord in that upper room. John asked the Lord, "Who is it?" Jesus answered that it was the man to whom He would give the daintiest morsel when He had dipped it in the sauce. Having said that He gave that morsel to Judas. The wonder is that Judas did not choke on it. The warning was about as blunt as a warning could be. Judas despised it, as he had despised all the other warnings.

Then, in Gethsemane, Jesus gave him one last chance. "Friend," He said to him, "why have you come?" (see Matt. 26:50). "Friend!" Jesus would have still saved him. "Friend!" The word can be rendered "Comrade!" It occurs elsewhere in the New Testament. The Lord used the word to describe, for instance, those who had *a contentious spirit*. When He told His story about the children playing at weddings and funerals in the market place, He used the word "comrade" to describe the contentious children at play.

He used the word in the parable of the laborers and the generous employer. When the pay was distributed and the one group complained because the other group received as much as they did for far less work, Jesus again used the word "comrade" to describe those with *a covetous spirit*.

He used the word in His parable of the king who invited all and sundry to the marriage of his son. The state occasion called for formal wear, and the appropriate garments were provided by the king. One fellow came strolling in wearing his own soiled raiment. "Comrade, why did you come without your wedding garment?" The king took this as an act of contempt and sent him to the executioner. He saw right through this *contemptuous spirit*.

Now He used the word to describe Judas, the man with all three spirits held and nurtured in his breast. He had evaluated the Son of God and had sold Him for the price of a female slave. He had a contentious spirit, a covetous spirit, and a contemptuous spirit all in one. *"Comrade!"* said Jesus. Surely He wanted to recall to Judas the other three occasions when He had used the word. Surely He was making one last appeal to the soul of Judas. But Judas despised all the Lord's warnings, right down to this very last warning of all.

The moment Judas had received the tasty morsel from the hand of the Lord of Glory, he pushed back from the table and left the room. The others thought, so great was his ability to deceive, that he had gone to give something to the poor or else to buy some further provisions for the feast. Jesus called after him, "What thou doest, do quickly." He went out "and it was night," the Holy Spirit declares. The darkness of blackest midnight wrapped him around within and without. "Satan entered into him," the Holy Spirit says. He was now sold out to Satan.

Why did Judas do it? Perhaps he thought he could get away with it. He had seen the Lord Jesus in many a tight corner. There was that occasion in Nazareth, for instance, when the infuriated mob tried to push him over a cliff. He had simply walked away. Time and again the Sanhedrin had tried to arrest Him, but always in vain. Judas perhaps thought, *I'll lead the agents of the Sanhedrin to Gethsemane, and they'll try to arrest Him. He will put forth His power and walk away from them as at other times before.*

It did not work out that way. Judas hoped to invest his ill-gotten gains and go on playacting the part of a disciple. Instead, Jesus allowed Himself to be taken, and all the crafty schemes of this wretched man came crashing down around his head. The Lord Jesus allowed Himself to be taken by wicked hands and slain. Judas knew that his little scheme had recoiled upon him. Suddenly those coins began to burn like live coals in his purse.

He was filled with remorse, not repentance. He was sorry for what he had done, but not sorry enough to seek forgiveness of the One he had wronged. He went to the priests. "I have sinned," he said. They scoffed at him. "What is that to us?" they sneered, "see thou to that" (Matt. 27:4). He took those cursed coins, and he flung them on the floor. We can almost hear them roll and rattle across the marble mosaic of the temple court. The priests scramble after them, scrape them up, and use them to buy some property.

Judas went out and hanged himself. About the time they were preparing to nail the Son of the living God to a tree, Judas found a tree for himself and from that tree hurled himself into a lost eternity.

"He went to his own place," the Bible says. He went out into a deeper darkness than that of the darkness into which he had walked from the upper room. He went out into eternal night. If only he had gone to Calvary! If only he had found his way to the cross. If only he had flung himself at the pierced feet of the Son of God and had said to Him, "God be merciful to me a sinner." Doubtless, even then, he could have been saved. But he had crossed a line in Gethsemane from which there was no turning back. He had sold the Son of God for thirty pieces of silver. He never spent a penny of it. Jesus called him "The son of perdition." Literally, He called him "the son of waste." For it was a waste of the precious blood of Christ to have been shed for him. It was a waste of God's creative energy ever to have made him. Judas wasted every opportunity Jesus gave him to be a true apostle of the Lamb.

He has been in "his own place" now for some two thousand years, suffering the pangs of eternal remorse. All he has to look forward to is the Great White Throne when, standing naked and undone, he will see the Lord in all His glory. He will hear Him say, "Depart from me ye cursed. I never knew you."

And all for thirty pieces of silver. The tragedy is that millions sell Jesus for even less. They sell Him for a godless friendship, for some vile habit they hug to their hearts, for a robe and a ribbon, and the applause of godless men. And for them "their own place" awaits, just as it did for Judas.

SIXTEEN

Jude the Obscure

Matthew 10:3; Mark 3:18; Luke 6:16; John 14:22; Acts 1:13

A. His name
B. His fame
   1. A very important test
   2. A very important truth
   3. A very important trio
C. His aim

We can be quite sure that the Lord made no mistakes when He chose the Twelve. Indeed, He waited some time before He selected His disciples out of an ever-growing crowd of followers, and ordained those twelve to be apostles. He made His selections after a night of prayer. Besides, He was incarnate omniscient wisdom. But why did He choose such a pale-faced nonentity as Judas (Jude), the brother (or perhaps son) of James?

Two other men by the name of Judas are prominent in the New Testament: Judas the betrayer, the man who sold the Savior for a handful of coins; Judas the author of the book of Jude, the little memo on apostasy near the end of the New Testament. The latter is commonly thought to be one of the Lord's half brothers.

But who was Judas, the son of James? He is barely mentioned outside the lists of the apostles, and he is often overlooked by the average reader because in some of the lists he is not called Judas.

A. His Name

He bore a name of infamy. After the nefarious and notorious behavior of Judas Iscariot, the name Judas was a heavy enough cross for anyone to carry. "Oh! So you're Judas?" people might say, having only heard of the other Judas and not knowing that he was dead.

"No! No!" Jude the Obscure would say. "I'm not *that* Judas."

"Who are you then?"

"I'm Judas the son of James."

The title "Judas the son [or perhaps brother] of James" opens up a complex field of investigation. Three people by the name of James appear in the New Testament. Two of them were disciples of the Lord, and one was James the brother of Jesus. This third James was an ascetic. He became prominent in the Jerusalem church and wrote the epistle that bears his name. He was not one of the Lord's disciples during the days of His earthly ministry and was an unbeliever until the Lord met him and saved him after the resurrection. This James is not thought to have been the father of Judas.

The disciple James the Less was the son of Alphaeus and is sometimes called James the Younger. We know next to nothing about him. Some scholars think that he and Judas were brothers—these relationships are not always as clear as we could wish.

Other scholars think that the disciple James, who was the brother of John and the son of Zebedee, was the father of Judas. This James, the first martyr among the apostles, was one of the Lord's inner circle along with Peter and John. If Judas was the son of this James, he was the grandson of Zebedee and the nephew of the apostle John.

If he is undistinguished in all else, this son (or brother) of James is outstanding among the apostles in that he has three names. In Matthew 10:3 he is called "Lebbaeus, whose surname was Thaddaeus." In Mark 3:18 he is called Thaddaeus. Luke 6:16 and Acts 1:13 refer to him as "Judas the brother [or son] of James." John 14:22 speaks of "Judas . . . not Iscariot." We gather that Judas (Jude), Lebbaeus, and Thaddaeus are all names for the same individual, for the names always appear in the same position in the various listings of the Twelve.

Perhaps out of kindness and consideration, Matthew and Mark dropped the name Judas. Luke used it to help us identify the man. John wrote at the end of the first century when it no longer mattered that there were two men by the name of Judas, one of whom was infamous and the other more or less anonymous. By that time Jude the Obscure may have been dead. Just the same, out of respect for the memory of the faithful Judas, John distinguished him from the traitor by adding the words "not Iscariot."

Both *Thaddaeus* and *Lebbaeus* suggest the idea of being dear or beloved or close to the heart. Probably these were nicknames given to Judas either when he was young or after he became an apostle. In any case, he apparently was looked upon with affection.

Jesus deliberately chose this Judas. If he was the grandson of Zebedee and Salome, Jesus knew him well. Salome was His mother's sister. So Jude's grandmother was the Lord's aunt, his grandfather was the Lord's uncle, and Jude's father James was the Lord's cousin! During the silent years of Jesus' life, He and His family must have made many trips from Nazareth to the seaside to visit His mother's family. Jesus would often have observed little Judas growing up. Perhaps He saw in him the character traits that earned the nickname Thaddaeus. Judas may well have been a lovable little fellow. Jesus and young Judas were attracted to each other, and by the time Jesus was ready to call James to be a disciple, He had made up His mind to call young Judas as well.

Jesus knew Judas would never be a boisterous leader like Peter. He would never be a great visionary like his Uncle John. He would never stand tall or stand out, but Jesus saw something in him. When we get to the judgment seat of Christ and the books are opened, we will understand why Jesus added this youngster to the apostolic band. Perhaps Jesus valued his youthfulness, which made him quiet and retiring around the older men. Perhaps Jesus desired diversity in age as well as in temperament and background among the Twelve. In any case, Judas found his place among the disciples. He was a follower rather than a leader, a listener rather than a talker. Indeed he only speaks once in Scripture, but what he said is very much to the point.

Judas Iscariot tarnished a great name—that of Judah. Young Jude the Obscure went a long way to redeem it, this name of the royal tribe. Judah is the tribe of which Jesus was born, and the names *Judah*, *Judas,* and *Jude* are synonymous.

B. His Fame

Jude is famous for only one thing: a question. The place was the upper room. The time was the last Passover and the institution of the Lord's supper.

By the following night Jesus would be dead and buried. Within an hour He would be weeping His heart out in Gethsemane. Soon Peter, usually so forward, would have denied the Lord three times, once with oaths and curses. Only Jude's Uncle John would show any semblance of courage, and he would become the tender guardian of Mary, the Lord's mother. Judas Iscariot would be both dead and damned—his name blotted out of God's book and indelibly written into the history of this world as the archetype of all traitors. In time, and one by one, the scattered disciples would find their way back to this upper room. Jude the Obscure and the other disciples—wishing they were as obscure as he was—would huddle there behind barred and bolted doors, dreading to hear the footfall of the temple police or of Pilate's officers.

But let us refocus on Jesus' sharing the last Passover meal with His disciples. Judas Iscariot had left their midst. A sense of foreboding prevailed in the upper room as Jesus addressed a hushed and unhappy group of men. "I'm going away," He said in effect. "I'm going home. But don't let that bother you too much. You know where My Home is and how to get there." He went on to speak of other things. He told them about the Holy Spirit. He told them they could expect the hatred of the world. He talked to them about the true vine. He prayed for them. Jude the Obscure sat there at the table with all the others listening, hardly believing his ears, wondering what kind of world it would be without Jesus.

The Lord was interrupted three times. First Thomas *contradicted* Him. He told the Lord that *he* did not know where He was going, and he certainly didn't know the way. Then Philip *confronted* Him. He said in effect, "You keep on talking about the Father. Who is this Father You talk about? Show Him to us, and we'll be satisfied." Then Jude *consulted* Him. He asked Him a question.

There are various kinds of questions. The *scientist* asks *why*. Why does a magnetized needle point north? Why does light travel at the speed of 186,000 miles per second?

The *pragmatist* asks *how:* "So what if the square of the hypotenuse is equal to the sum of the squares of the two sides containing the right angle! How does that affect practical everyday life?" One answer to his question leads to the three-four-five-triangle, which enables us to lay out perfectly angled ninety-degree buildings.

The scientist asks why mass and energy and the speed of light are interrelated, and he comes up with an equation ($E=MC^2$) that explains the relationships of space, matter, and time. The pragmatist shows us how that equation relates to the real workaday world. He invents the atomic bomb and the nuclear power plant.

Jude the Obscure heard what Jesus was saying. He followed the conversation and the interruptions. He heard Jesus say, "He that hath my commandments, and keepeth them, he it is that loveth me: and he that loveth me shall be loved of my Father, and I will love him, and will manifest myself to him" (John 14:21). The word *manifest* arrested young Judas. The original Greek word *emphanizō* means "to cause to be manifest or shown plainly and clearly; to see something that otherwise would not be recognized by the unaided mind or eye." Jude quickly extrapolated something of profound significance: Those who loved the Lord and were loved by Him would be enabled to see things hidden from the general run of men and women. This revelation of the Lord Jesus, in other words, would be a secret revelation.

At once Judas asked his question: not why, but how. "Lord, how is it that thou wilt manifest thyself unto us, and not unto the world?" (John 14:22) The question was penetrating and went to the heart of the matter.

All the disciples had expected the Lord to manifest Himself to the world. They had anticipated an earthly kingdom. They had looked forward to the day when He would come suddenly into the temple, announce Himself as the promised Messiah, take over the reigns of government from the ruling and unbelieving establishment, mobilize His forces, rid the country of the Romans, sit on the throne of His father David, and extend His empire to the ends of the earth. Jude had probably gulped at the revelation that Jesus intended to do no such thing now. He could take in his youthful stride the total upset of all the conventional ideas about the Messiah. But the practical problem remained: How could Jesus possibly manifest Himself to some people and not to other people? And how could He show Himself if He was going home to heaven?

The Lord did not deal with Jude's question directly. The answer on the pragmatic earthly level would be known soon enough. Within the next few days and weeks, the resurrection, the Ascension, and the coming of the Holy Spirit would answer Jude's question more fully than anything the Lord could say that night. Moreover, Jude and the others would be better equipped to understand the answer later on.

The last time the world saw Christ was when the authorities sealed Him into Joseph's tomb and set a guard to patrol the grounds. Nobody witnessed Christ's resurrection. Early in the morning, just as the dawn was tinting the eastern sky, Jesus rose through the grave clothes and stepped silently through the walls of the tomb. Nobody saw Him rise. For sometime afterward, the sentries continued to patrol up and down before an empty tomb. They did not know it was empty until the angel came and rolled back the stone to show to one and all that the tomb was tenanted no more. We can imagine that one sight of that angel was enough for even those Roman veterans; with a howl of terror, they fled toward the city.

Then Jesus began to manifest Himself to His followers. He manifested Himself in His *resurrection* body. He appeared here and there to this one and to that one. He appeared to Peter and to James. He appeared to the two on the Emmaus road. He appeared in the upper room. He appeared again to convince Thomas. He appeared by the shore of the Sea of Galilee. On one occasion He manifested Himself to about five hundred believers at one time, but never to the world.

He also manifested Himself in His *rapture*. He gathered the entire band of believers together and led them to the Mount of Olives. He talked and answered questions as He went. Then, right before their eyes, He stepped from the earth into the sky and thence back into heaven.

The Lord manifested Himself in *revelation* as well. In the upper room on the day of Pentecost, the Holy Spirit came. The eyes of the disciples' understanding were then fully opened. They understood at last and in the full blaze of that understanding went out to evangelize the world and write the various books of the New Testament.

Jude the Obscure was, of course, to be involved in all these events. The Lord had no need to give an explanation ahead of time. Everything would be made plain in the course of the next six or seven weeks. Instead, the Lord went to the heart of Jude's question and taught him some very important lessons that are recorded in John 14:23.

1. A Very Important Test

"If a man love me," He said, "he will keep my words." This statement presents the ultimate test of genuine love for the Lord: Those who love the Lord do what He says. Those who love the Lord treasure His Word. His slightest wish is their command. Love can never do enough for the Beloved. If we say we love Him, but spend little time reading His Word, and even less time doing what He says, there is something radically wrong with what we call love.

2. A Very Important Truth

"If a man love me, he will keep my words," Jesus said, "and my Father will love him." Imagine being the special object of the love of the Father. The Lord

Jesus was always talking about His Father. God is rarely called Father in the Old Testament—probably fewer than half a dozen times—but the name Father was constantly on the lips of the Lord Jesus. In His first recorded utterance He said to Joseph and Mary, "Wist ye not that I must be about my Father's business?" (Luke 2:49) As a boy of twelve He already knew who His Father was, and He had already made it His goal to "do always those things that please him" (John 8:29).

Speaking His last words on the cross He said, "Father, into thy hands I commend my spirit" (Luke 23:46). Jesus spoke the name again in His first conversation after the resurrection. He said to Mary Magdalene, "I am not yet ascended to my Father" (John 20:17). Almost the last word He uttered on earth was *Father*. On the way to Olivet He told the disciples to go back to Jerusalem and wait for the promise of the Father. Jesus knew that all times and seasons are in the Father's sphere of authority.

The Lord Jesus loved His Father, and His Father loved Him. Now if we love the Lord Jesus with the kind of love that does what He says, and if we treasure His Word, the Father will love us too. He will love us with the *agape* kind of love—the kind of love that is stronger than death, the kind of love that many waters cannot quench, the kind of love that suffers long and is kind. What a truth! Imagine being the object of God's personal affection and tender loving care.

3. A Very Important Trio

"My Father will love him, and we will come unto him, and make our abode with him." What a trio! The Father, the Lord Jesus, and the person who loves the Lord Jesus and does what He says will dwell together. The Father and the Son will come and take up their abode with such a believer.

Think for a moment of what that promise means. God the Father and God the Son will move in with us. They will live in our houses. They will ride in our cars. They will join us where we work. They will be with us when we gather with others of like precious faith. Imagine it! Sometimes we read this awesome statement and hardly let its significance penetrate our minds. The two most wonderful, most powerful, most loving, most infallible persons in the universe will take up Their abode with us.[1] They control all the factors of space, matter,

---

1. The coequal Holy Spirit's ministry is not in view in this passage.

and time. They are the objects of the ceaseless adoration of the angels and the theme of the seraphs' song—and They choose to come and live with us!

The word translated "abode" in John 14:23 is the same word that is translated "mansions" in John 14:2. The Father and the Son will turn even the humblest cottage into a mansion, into a place more important by far than the White House or Buckingham Palace.

Jude the Obscure listened to Jesus' words and took them all in. He said to himself, *I love Him. I intend to do what He says; I love His words. So I'm going to count on having some very exclusive and magnificent company from now on.*

C. His Aim

Aided after Pentecost by the baptizing, indwelling, filling, and anointing of the Holy Spirit, Judas set out to live the life of one who keeps the words of Christ.

For some time he tarried in Jerusalem with the other apostles. He witnessed the great influx of souls after Pentecost and helped organize and supervise the church. He probably came in contact with Paul and heard his impassioned defense of liberty in Christ for an ever-growing Gentile church. Perhaps Judas and Barnabas had some long talks about the work in Syria, especially in Antioch.

Then the time came to move out of Jerusalem. Reasonably reliable Christian tradition leads us to believe that Jude the Obscure headed north to Syria. He is thought to have helped plant the gospel in Armenia and to have gone to Mesopotamia and Persia. So as Paul headed west with the gospel, this little-known foot soldier of the cross went East. In the end, it is believed, Judas suffered martyrdom in Persia. Wherever he went, this unsung saint of God carried another presence with him. God the Father and God the Son accompanied him on his travels and stood by him in his efforts to spread the glad tidings of salvation.

For the most part, Judas remains obscure, but one day the books will be opened. When they are, we will join hands with him around the throne in heaven, and he'll invite us to come along and see his heavenly mansion eternally graced by the abiding presence of the Father and Son.

SEVENTEEN

Andrew

The Soulwinner

Matthew 4:18–20; John 1:40–42

A. ANDREW THE HOME WORKER: ANDREW AND HIS BIG BROTHER
B. ANDREW THE CHILD EVANGELIST: ANDREW AND THE LITTLE LAD
C. ANDREW THE FOREIGN MISSIONARY: ANDREW AND THE FOREIGN FIELD

Charles H. Spurgeon once said, "It takes more grace than I can tell, to play the second fiddle well." Andrew, one of the Lord's very first two disciples, was a second-fiddle man. Like Isaac in the Old Testament, he was overshadowed. Isaac was overshadowed on the one side by his illustrious father, Abraham, and on the other side by his equally illustrious son, Jacob. Andrew was overshadowed by Peter, James, and John, who formed an inner circle in relation to the Lord. Andrew is the New Testament counterpart of old Benaiah, one of David's mighty men, of whom the historian says, "He was more honorable than the thirty, but he attained not to the first three . . ." (2 Sam. 23:23).

Probably Andrew was used to it. He was always, it seems, in Peter's shadow. At the synagogue school, when they were boys, Peter would always be the one who had the answers, even if they were the wrong answers. Peter would be the one who knocked down the school bully, and the one the girls liked. When it came to games, Peter would always captain the team that usually won. It was Peter who would have the most to say about the family business, with everybody doing things Peter's way. Andrew would be used to playing second fiddle to his forceful brother. People would say to Andrew, "Sorry, I've forgotten your name." "Andrew," he would reply. "Oh yes! Andrew—Simon Peter's brother."

Andrew, however, was not jealous of Peter. He was proud of him. He loved him. The Holy Spirit says "love envieth not." Andrew did not know what it was to be jealous of his famous brother. When Jesus took Peter into the house of Jairus to witness His greatness, and on up to the heights of Hermon to witness His glory, and into Gethsemane to witness His grief, Andrew was content. He did not say to himself, "Well, I like that! I was His disciple before Peter was. I was saved the same day John was. Why have I been left out?" Andrew was not like that at all.

Andrew was the son of a woman named Joanna and of a man named Jonah. He was born at Bethsaida, about twenty miles east of Nazareth, on the west bank of the Sea of Galilee—one of the cities the Lord afterward denounced for not receiving His teachings. The village itself appears to have been very close to Capernaum, if not actually a suburb of that city.

Before he ever met Jesus, Andrew felt the call to go to Bethany, beyond Jordan, way down the Jordan Valley, where John the Baptist was preaching. He was soon converted and became one of John's most zealous disciples. He was there the day John the Baptist announced Jesus to be the Messiah. He had often heard John preach about the coming of Christ so he was ready. When John said, "Behold the Lamb of God, which taketh away the sin of the world," Andrew immediately left John to follow Jesus (John 1:29–40).

He was not alone. John, son of Zebedee, Andrew's friend and another disciple of John the Baptist, joined Andrew on this personal quest. Presently Jesus, who knew they were following Him, stopped, turned around, and asked them what they wanted. Then He invited them to come and spend the evening with Him. It must have been a memorable time! When John wrote his gospel, nearly seventy years later, he still remembered the actual time of day. "It was the tenth hour" he said—that is, it was four o'clock in the afternoon (John 1:39).

It was not only a memorable hour both for Andrew and John, it was a golden hour of opportunity. It was when they made their life-transforming decision. They spent the rest of the day and the following night with Jesus. Neither John nor Andrew was ever the same again. Nobody ever is who spends such time with Jesus.

Andrew remained true to Jesus until the day of his death. One tradition is that he went to Scythia. (We locate that in southern Russia in the area around the Black Sea.) One account has it that he was first stoned, then crucified there. Another tradition is that Andrew suffered martyrdom in Greece. Another tradition is that he went to Asia Minor, to Ephesus, indeed, where both Paul and John had labored for the Lord. This particular tradition has it that Andrew suffered martyrdom at Patras.

There could well be truth in all these elements of traditions. Perhaps he went first to Ephesus to be with his old friend John. Then maybe he went on to southern Russia, to Scythia. The great land bridge between Russia and Greece is Asia Minor. So perhaps Andrew returned to Ephesus that way and then went on to Greece in his later years. One tradition is that he earned the wrath of the governor by winning the governor's wife to Christ. Tradition is that he suffered on a cross that was shaped like a letter "X." Certainly that kind of a cross has become known as a St. Andrew's cross.

There are three chief occasions when Andrew is given special mention in the Gospels. Each time he is seen introducing someone to Jesus. The first time it was his big brother, the second time it was a little lad, the last time it was a couple of men from Macedonia. The first time, we see Andrew as a home worker, the second time he is a child evangelist, the third time he is a foreign missionary.

A. ANDREW THE HOME WORKER:
ANDREW AND HIS BIG BROTHER

The history of the church is the history of little men who led big men to Christ and who, ever afterward, reveled in what the big man was doing, and thanked God for the joy of having led that one to the Lord. In the narrow way we write history, we tend to overlook the little man. We forget that he, too, is often a very big man in heaven. Who could name the man who led Dwight L. Moody to Christ? It was a man by the name of Edward Kimball. But where did he live? What was his trade? How old was he? What did he look like? We know all these things about Mr. Moody, but the man who led D. L. Moody to Christ has faded into obscurity.

Who was it who brought John Knox to Christ? It was a Dominican monk, of all people! We do not remember the man's name, however, although the entire Christian church knows of John Knox.

Charles Spurgeon preached the gospel to millions and, through his books, he speaks on to this very day. But who was the nobody who led Spurgeon to Christ? Spurgeon was only a boy, just fifteen years of age at the time. He was looking for a place to worship on that Sunday morning, January 6, 1850. A blinding snow storm decided the matter for him. He turned into a little Primitive Methodist Chapel on Artillery Street, where only a dozen to fifteen people were present. Spurgeon sat under the balcony, way at the back. He watched the whispered consultations as the elders anxiously awaited the overdue minister. Evidently he was snowed in. Presently a poor, thin-looking man, a shoemaker, a tailor, or something of like sort (so Spurgeon later described him) yielded to the murmured pleadings of his peers and climbed the pulpit steps. He looked nervously around at the nearly empty chapel. Almost all the three-hundred seats were vacant—but not quite. He knew the handful of people before him, all except the boy beneath the balcony at the back.

Says Spurgeon, "The man was really stupid, as you would say. He was obliged to stick to his text for the simple reason he had nothing to say. His text was, 'Look unto me and be ye saved, all the ends of the earth.' He did not even pronounce the words correctly . . . He said, 'Young man, you look very miserable.' Well, I did; but I was not accustomed to having remarks made from the pulpit on my personal appearance. However, it was a good blow, and well struck . . ." The preacher continued, and Spurgeon, already under conviction, listened. "Young man," the preacher shouted, as only a Primitive Methodist preacher could shout, "look to Jesus. Look! Look! Look!" Says Spurgeon, "I did, and then and there the cloud was gone, the darkness had rolled away, and that moment I saw the sun." Thus Spurgeon was saved. But who was that unknown preacher? Doubtless Spurgeon has been introducing him to people in heaven ever since he joined him there.

Andrew, too, was a second-fiddle man. After that memorable visit with Jesus, John went on home to find his brother James, and Andrew went home to find his brother Peter. Peter would preach to thousands and perform miracles. Peter would be given the keys of the kingdom of heaven so that he could fling wide the door of the church to Jews and Gentiles alike. Peter would write two important epistles of the New Testament. Andrew would do none of those things, but he knew a man who had all the makings for just such a work for God, so he hurried home and brought that man to Jesus.

That was the very next day. Andrew wasted no time in getting down to work. He became a home missionary. He, indeed, began in his own home. Often the home is the most difficult place of all to witness for Christ. Peter does not seem, however, to have argued with his brother when he told him the good news. There was something good and sincere and convincing about Andrew, a genuineness beyond question.

We can see Andrew, at the back of the crowd, on the morning of Pentecost. Peter is way up front, preaching to thousands. The words pour out of his mouth. And what words! Words supplied by the Holy Spirit Himself. The crowd falls silent and then deep conviction of sin comes down upon one and all. "Men and brethren, what shall we do?"(Acts 2:37) they cry as the enormity of their guilt in rejecting Christ comes home to their hearts.

Then, down to the river for a mass baptism. Three thousand souls were saved that day and added to the church. Andrew was full of "joy unspeakable and full of glory" as he remembered the day he said to his brother, "We have found the Christ." Now three thousand more had found Him too! Andrew must have been so full of joy in his soul that he could hardly speak.

That was the beginning. The next time we see Andrew, he is at it again, bringing someone to Jesus.

B. ANDREW THE CHILD EVANGELIST: ANDREW AND THE LITTLE LAD

"Suffer the little children and forbid them not, to come unto me," Jesus had once said, "for to such belongeth the kingdom of heaven" (Matt. 19:14 ASV). That was all Andrew needed to go and bring this little lad with his loaves to the Lord.

We can picture this little boy setting out that morning from home. The whole countryside is full of stories of Jesus, His understandable teaching, and His miracle-working power. Everyone had been to the synagogues, of course, and had heard the rabbis. Every now and then a special rabbi would come from Jerusalem, but they were all dry-as-dust. They made much ado about nothing. With their religious maxims, they levied heavy burdens, unwieldy, impractical, and burdensome, impossible to be born.

Then Jesus came with His practical wisdom, His encyclopedic knowledge of the Bible, His total indifference to the traditions of the rabbis and their much quoted Midrash and Mishna commentaries. The common people heard Him gladly for "He spoke with authority, and not as the Scribes" (see Mark 1:22). His teaching was down-to-earth, inspiring, full of illustrations from field and farm, from kitchen and workshop, from home and hedgerow.

So the little boy had won permission to go and hear Him. Probably it was not far away, and he was a good and able lad. Doubtless, he was hoping against hope that he would see a miracle. Everybody knew that Jesus healed the sick and gave sight to the blind, made the dumb to speak, the deaf to hear, the lame to walk. He even cleansed lepers and cast out evil spirits.

We can see the little boy now as he hops with excitement while his mother lovingly packs him a lunch—five pieces of barley pocket-bread and two small fishes.

The boy sits spellbound all day. He has clean forgotten about his lunch! Then his appetite awakens and he pulls out his package and gazes hungrily at his loaves and fishes. He has enjoyed the teaching, but oh, how he wishes he could see a miracle. Just as he is about to tuck into his meal he overhears some whispered conversation. The great Teacher is telling His disciples to feed the multitude. The little boy had secured a seat for himself in the front row. No back seat for him! He wants to be where he can hear everything and see everything. He wants to see a miracle.

He hears one of the Master's men say, "We have no bread. How can we feed all this crowd? There must be five thousand men not counting women and children. Two hundred pennyworth of bread would not be enough to give each one so much as a couple of mouthfuls . . ." (see John 6:7).

A thought flashes into the little boy's mind. He is hungry! Everybody is hungry! No doubt Jesus is hungry! An especially lovely thought takes hold of his heart—he will give his little lunch to Jesus. At least Jesus can have something to eat. He deserves it. He has been talking for hours.

We can see him run a speculative eye over each of the disciples. He does not dare approach Jesus Himself, but which apostle might take him to the Master? That one called Peter? No. He is too big, burley, and blustery. The one they call Thomas? No. He wears too heavy a frown upon his brow. The one they call Judas? No! The boy does not like the shifty look in his eye. He would probably eat the lunch himself. The one called Matthew? No. He is too businesslike, busy with paper and pencil, ciphering how much food it would take to feed five thousand men and an equal number of women and children. The one called James? No. He looks too much like a thunderstorm. The one called Philip? He is as bad as the one called Matthew. He has already set a price on even the merest snack.

The little boy's eyes fall on Andrew. Yes, he can approach him. He has a kind face, a twinkle in his eye, and a pleasant smile. And, sure enough, Andrew responds right away. In a moment he has an arm about the little lad's shoulders. He asks his name, guesses his age, and has the little boy chatting to him. "Yes sir, my mother was glad I wanted to come. It's been wonderful. I especially liked the story about the treasure hid in the field. Oh, and by the way, sir, I do have a little lunch here. My mom packed it for me. I haven't touched it. I wondered if Jesus would like it . . ."

"Well sonny, let's go and see. I'll introduce you to Him. Come along. This way . . ." And so Andrew introduces the little lad to the Lord, lunch and all. And the boy sees his miracle! He will never stop talking about it. We can be sure, when he becomes an old man, his grandchildren will climb up on his knee and he will tell them about Jesus. "Let me tell you about the time I met the Master. He did a miracle that day . . ." "You actually saw a miracle, grandpa?" "Oh yes. As a matter of fact, I was part of it . . ."

C. ANDREW THE FOREIGN MISSIONARY: ANDREW AND THE FOREIGN FIELD

The Lord was on His way to Calvary. He had just performed the greatest of all His many miracles—He had raised Lazarus from the dead. The whole countryside was agog with excitement. It was at this very time that certain Greeks come into the gospel story. They had just one request, "Sir, we would see Jesus" they said (John 12:21). They appealed to Philip. But Philip did not know what to do. He had once heard Jesus say, "I am not sent but to the lost sheep of the house of Israel," and these men were Greeks (see Matt. 15:24). They may be lost sheep, but they were not of the house of Israel.

Philip appealed to Andrew. Andrew would know what to do. "I say Andrew, there are some Greeks here. They want to see Jesus. What do you think? Should we send them away? After all, they are Greeks, not Jews." Andrew would have another word of Jesus in mind. A much more recent saying: "Other sheep I have, which are not of this fold: them also I must bring" (John 10:16). Andrew was not to be put off, just because the people wanting to see Jesus were not his kind of people.

It is amazing how we let differences of class, color, country, and creed stand in our way of bringing people to Jesus. We put obstacles where God sees none. Racially the Greeks were Gentiles, and the Jews as a race despised Gentiles. They considered them unclean and called them dogs. Greek cities were notorious dens of vice. Greek culture was sophisticated. Greek philosophy was persuasive and had once posed a terrible threat to Jewish ways of thought. Antiochus Epiphanes, who had terribly persecuted the Jews, a veritable Antichrist before his time, had been a Greek.

Religiously, the Greeks were utter pagans. They peopled Mount Olympus with gods made in the image and likeness of fallen man—gods who lusted and whored and hated and murdered. It was said that it was easier to find a god than a man in Athens, so crowded was their famous city with images.

Andrew swept all prejudices aside. Thus it was that Andrew took the lead in world evangelism. In so doing, he brought a moment of special joy to Jesus.

Jesus exclaimed: "They shall come from the east, and from the west, and from the north, and from the south, and they shall sit down in the kingdom of God" (Luke 13:29). Thus it was that, on that Palm Sunday, when the Jewish authorities were making their plans to get rid of Him, Jesus saw, in the coming of those Greeks, the day when people from all over the world would be drawn to Him. It was sunshine in His soul and music in His heart. It cast a bright gleam of glory across a path that was leading Him step by step to Gethsemane, Gabbatha, Golgotha, and the grave.

There is still joy brought to the heart of Jesus when some quiet, unassuming Andrew brings another soul to Him. There are more Andrews than there are Peters because we need more Andrews. It is the Andrews who undertake the greatest enterprises for Jesus. They are always quietly, unassumingly, bringing people to Jesus.

In 1555, Catholic Mary, Queen of England, had Hugh Latimer burned at the stake in Oxford. He was known as the terror of evildoers, the idol of the common people, and "the most honest man in England." He and Bishop Ridley were in the forefront of the Protestant movement in England. By sheer force of character, Latimer raised himself from a plowman's cottage to a bishop's palace. When "bloody Mary" came to the throne, Latimer refused to change his coat as so many others did. People who heard him preach fell under the spell of his eloquence. For years he had been as stout a champion for Rome as he afterward became for the true cause of Christ. Hugh Latimer was led to the Lord by a nobody, by one of God's magnificent, insignificant Andrews.[1]

There was a man in Cambridge, in the days when Latimer was still Rome's champion, whose name was Thomas Bilney. He was a man of no account. They called him "Little Bilney." He had come to Christ himself by reading the New Testament, and he coveted the soul of Hugh Latimer for Jesus. Nobody paid much attention to Little Bilney—but if he could win Latimer to the Lord, why, there was a man. Latimer could sway the multitudes.

So it was that one day Little Bilney went to the church where Latimer was preaching. He accosted the popular priest on his way down the aisle. "Please, Father Latimer," said Little Bilney, "may I confess my soul to you?" It was a request not to be denied, and they went into the confessional. That day, Hugh Latimer heard a confession the like of which he had never heard before. Little

---

1. As F. W. Boreham tells the tale in his book *A Bunch of Everlasting* (New York: Abingdon Press, 1920).

Bilney told of the coming of Erasmus. He told of the purchase of a book. He told of the hunger of his heart. "Father Latimer," he said, "I went to the priests. They pointed me to broken cisterns. They told me to do penance, to go to mass, to do good works. These things only mocked at my soul's deep need. I bore the load of my sins. I was crushed. Then, the light of Scripture burst into my soul. I read, 'This is a faithful saying . . . Christ Jesus came into the world to save sinners.' And then and there I was saved." Latimer was taken that day by storm, and he gave his heart to Christ. The popular Roman priest had been won by one of God's illustrious nobodies, one of the many Andrews He puts into the harvest field to be unsung home missionaries, cheerful children's workers, and unassuming foreign missionaries. They are the nobodies in this world, but they are the aristocracy of heaven.

EIGHTEEN

Philip the Plodder

John 1:43–45; 6:5–7; 12:20–22; 14:8–9

A. WHAT PHILIP FOUND
B. WHAT PHILIP FIGURED
C. WHERE PHILIP FALTERED
D. WHAT PHILIP FELT

Philip had a Greek name. The most famous Philip in Greek history was Philip of Macedon, the father of Alexander the Great. After Alexander's conquests, Greek culture had a pronounced influence throughout the Middle East. Perhaps that is why Philip, the Lord's disciple, had a Greek name. The fact that Philip had a Greek name may have been one of the reasons Jesus chose him.

This disciple may have been named after another Philip, closer in time and territory: Philip the Tetrarch, one of the sons of Herod the Great. Philip the Tetrarch's brother Herod Philip married their niece Herodias, who afterward eloped with her husband's half brother, Herod Antipas. Herod Philip and Herodias had a daughter, Salome, who was a major player in the drama of John the Baptist's murder. Philip the Tetrarch married Salome. The Herods were a bad lot. Philip the Tetrarch was the best of them. Like his father, Philip the Tetrarch was a builder. One monument he left behind him was Caesarea Philippi at the foot of Mount Hermon. He was well-liked by his subjects. Doubtless it was not at all unusual for people in those days, as in our own day, to name their sons after well-known figures such as the tetrarch.

The fact that Philip, the Lord's disciple, had this Gentile name suggests that his parents were not narrow-minded Hebrews, but more liberal-minded Hellenists. But even Hellenists would have made sure that their son had a thoroughly Jewish education.

163

Philip came from the city of Bethsaida, which is called by the gospel writer "the city of Andrew and Peter." Perhaps John was suggesting that these two leading men in the apostolic company were friends of Philip. (At the time Jesus was choosing His disciples, Andrew and Peter were living in Capernaum [Mark 1:21, 29]; but Bethsaida and Capernaum were quite close, possibly twin cities.) Not long after Andrew and Peter gave themselves to Christ, Philip did the same. Andrew had been a disciple of John the Baptist before he became a disciple of Jesus. We can imagine how Andrew would have talked enthusiastically about the Baptist and the imminent coming of Christ. No doubt Philip had been included in some of those impassioned conversations.

Philip apparently did not make much of an impact on the other disciples. If John had not rescued him from complete anonymity, all we would know about Philip would be his name and the fact that he ranks as number five in the general listing of the Lord's disciples.

A. WHAT PHILIP FOUND

There can be no doubt that Philip was interested in what Moses had to say about the coming of Christ. Philip knew that the Messiah was to be a kinsman-redeemer, just like Moses. "A Prophet . . . like unto me" was Moses' way of describing the Messiah (Deut. 18:15). Christ would come armed with might and miracle, and He would redeem Israel.

Philip, we can be sure, was at home with the glowing prophecies that spoke of the coming Son of David, who would put down all His foes and reign in wisdom, love, and power. One day the desert would blossom as the rose, the lion would lie down with the lamb, a child would be able to play with a scorpion, and a man would be a mere youth at a hundred. Jerusalem would become the capital of a new world empire, and the Gentiles would lay their tribute at this mighty Messiah's feet.

But Philip also knew about strange, somber, and startling prophecies that spoke of a suffering Messiah. Philip would read Isaiah 53, Psalms 22 and 69 again and again and puzzle over seeming contradictions. The Messiah was to be born in Bethlehem, yet He was to be called out of Egypt. He was to be militant, yet He was to be meek. He was to be the happy man of Psalm 1, yet He was to be the man of sorrows of Isaiah 53. Philip likely pondered often over the prophetic Scriptures. He may have been slow on the uptake, but he was a patient plodder. He was not the kind of man to be in a hurry to make up his mind, but he was the kind of man who arrived at a conclusion in the end. No doubt he thought, *When we finally find the Messiah, we'll see that He has fulfilled prophecy just as it is written.*

Actually Philip didn't find the Messiah, for we read that the day after Andrew brought his brother Simon to Jesus, Jesus found Philip. Philip thus became the archetype of all those people who have a personal encounter with Christ without the aid of any intermediary. They find Him by reading the Scriptures. Or they find Him simply by being found by the Lord Himself. The seeking Savior finds the seeking sinner. Jesus found Philip, yet Philip said to Nathanael, *"We have found him,* of whom Moses in the law, and the prophets, did write, Jesus of Nazareth" (John 1:45, italics added). So Jesus found Philip, and he found Jesus! The seeking sinner meets the seeking Savior.

Over and over again in the Bible we see God seeking men and men seeking God. The first question asked in the Old Testament is "Where art thou?" (Gen. 3:9), and the first question asked in the New Testament is "Where is he?" (Matt. 2:2)—a seeking Savior and a seeking sinner. There can be only one outcome: each finds the other.

"We have found him," said Philip to Nathanael. We all like to find things. We are especially pleased if what we find turns out to be valuable. We are even more pleased if we can tell other seekers that we have found what they have been looking for.

The perennial appeal of Robert Louis Stevenson's *Treasure Island* lies in the book's being all about searching for buried treasure. We are intrigued with the story from the day young Jim Hawkins finds the map in the old sea captain's trunk and only narrowly escapes being killed by pirates. We follow with interest the fitting-out of the *Hispaniola* and Squire Trelawney's careless way of engaging a crew. We hold our breath when he recruits Long John Silver, the one-legged cook. We hide with Jim Hawkins in the apple barrel and learn of the plot by the remnant of Flint's old crew—now enlisted seamen aboard the *Hispaniola*—to seize the ship, murder the squire and the captain (and their loyal subordinates), find the treasure, and set sail for the Spanish Main.

Our interest mounts when Jim Hawkins becomes Long John Silver's prisoner and is dragged along on the pirates' final treasure hunt. "Look out for squalls," advises the squire's friend, Dr. Livesey, who had given the map to the rascally cook. Our interest is sustained to the climax: the map leads the pirates to the place where the treasure was buried, but the treasure is gone. All that is left is a big empty hole. The pirates discover that all their crimes have been for nothing.

Poor old Ben Gunn, marooned on the lonely island long ago, had found the treasure and removed it to another hiding place.

The pirates sought treasure and found an empty hole; Philip sought the Messiah and found Him! "We have found him," said Philip, and he invited his friend to come and find Him too. Those who find Him find a treasure beyond the price of buried gold and precious stones.

Philip was still trying to sort out the clues in his treasure hunt when the Lord Jesus turned the tables on him and found him instead. Philip was still poring over the old prophecies in the sacred text. He was still pondering about the new preacher in the wilderness. He was still searching his Bible when he found that he had been found.

B. WHAT PHILIP FIGURED

John next mentions Philip again in connection with an incident that took place near Bethsaida-Julias (not the same Bethsaida where Philip was raised) on the east bank of the Jordan River where it runs into the Sea of Galilee. Jesus and His disciples had retreated to this area, which was a few hours' sail from Capernaum and an even shorter distance by land around the head of the lake.

The Passover feast was approaching, and many caravans were forming as pilgrims prepared to set out on the journey to Jerusalem. Jesus could see the crowds gathering—thousands of men and an uncounted number of women and children—and His heart was moved with compassion. John the Baptist had been recently murdered and buried. And here were all these "sheep" without a shepherd. So Jesus taught them, hour after hour throughout the day. Toward evening the disciples suggested it was time to send the crowds away. Having gathered in a desert place, the people would need to scatter to find food and lodging. "Send the multitude away," the disciples urged (Luke 9:12). "Send them away."

Philip was of the same mind as the other disciples when the Lord challenged him: "Whence shall we buy bread, that these may eat?" (John 6:5). Philip was astounded. He had already been doing his homework and had arrived at an estimate of the size of the crowd—about five thousand men plus the women and the children. He had already figured how many loaves would be needed just to give each person a few mouthfuls. "Two hundred pennyworth of bread is not sufficient," he said (6:7). Perhaps that amount was the sum total of what was in the bag, or perhaps the amount was Philip's estimate of how much money would be needed. In any case, two hundred pennyworth represented a considerable sum since a penny was a working man's daily wage.

The Lord had asked Philip the question only to test him. Philip failed the test. He was too much focused on mathematics and money to be fully occupied with the Master. "Two hundred pennyworth of bread is not sufficient." Those words were Philip's final offering at the altar of truth and trust. "No way!" he was saying. "Not with our resources. We don't have enough money, so there's no way we can feed the people."

It was a pity that Philip had not read his Bible with more attention. Had he done so he would have balked at using the number *two hundred,* for it was a number of ominous significance. The number *two hundred* is used, for instance, in connection with Achan. After the overthrow of Jericho, Achan was tempted. He knew that all the spoil of Jericho was God's first fruit and was not to be touched. Yet he stole some gold and a garment—and *two hundred* shekels of silver (Josh. 7:21). Those two hundred shekels of silver were *insufficient* to redeem his life from destruction when the day of judgment came.

The number is also used in connection with Absalom, the young rebel who sought to overthrow his father, David, and seize the kingdom for himself. Absalom was popular with the people; he had charm, charisma, a persuasive tongue, and he found a ready ally in the golden-tongued Ahithophel, the cleverest man in the kingdom. Moreover Absalom was handsome, and his good looks were framed by a remarkable head of hair, his crown of glory. In counting up his assets, Absalom did not overlook his hair—he weighed it at every year's end. "He weighed the hair of his head at *two hundred* shekels after the king's weight" (2 Sam. 14:26, italics added). Yet that hair caused his death. When, in the battle with David, the tide turned against Absalom and he fled, his hair was caught in the branches of an oak. He hung there until Joab's darts put an end to him.

The number *two hundred* is used in connection with Micah's graven image (Judg. 17). First this unscrupulous man stole eleven hundred shekels of silver from his mother. Then, frightened by her curses, he gave them back to her. Then his mother took *two hundred* of those shekels and had them melted down and made into a couple of images. Next Micah persuaded a landless Levite to be the priest of his idol temple for an annual salary of ten shekels, a suit, and his meals. Later the tribe of Dan persuaded the young Levite to abandon his patron, take Micah's idols, and become priest to the whole tribe. (The young Levite's name was Jonathan. He was the son of Gershom, the son of Moses. So incensed were the later Hebrew scribes with this defection of a grandson of Moses that they changed the name of the grandfather from Moses to Manasseh—to spare Moses' name and memory.) Those two hundred shekels of silver and the silver idols made from them brought disaster on the tribe of Dan. Its name is blotted out from the blessing recorded in Revelation 7.

When Ezra brought his contingent of Jews back to the Promised Land, he had with him *two hundred* singing men and singing women (Ezra 2:65). When they arrived back in the land and inaugurated the true worship of God, Ezra realized that his two-hundred-voice choir was *not sufficient:* the people needed to hear him read the book of the law. He "opened the book" and taught the people out of the Word of God (Neh. 8:1–8).

So Philip ought to have sensed at once that there was something wrong with his thinking when he arrived at the ominous number *two hundred.* He even labeled the number himself as "not sufficient." "Two hundred pennyworth of bread is *not sufficient,*" he figured. His figuring was wrong. He figured without Christ.

C. WHERE PHILIP FALTERED

John 12:20–22 provides another glimpse of Philip. It was three days before the Passover. The Lord had just cursed the fig tree, thus pronouncing doom upon the nation of Israel for its apostasy and unbelief, and we can only imagine how full of sorrow His heart was. With His death just a few days ahead, Jesus was in the temple teaching.

Then it was that certain Greeks approached Philip and asked to be introduced to Jesus. These men were not Hellenists (Greek-speaking Jews). They were Greeks who had come up to Jerusalem for the Passover feast. In other words, they were proselytes of the Jewish religion. These Gentiles had groped their way to the portals of Judaism and, having heard and seen something of Jesus, evidently realized that their adopted Judaism was a poor substitute for Him. Doubtless they were awed by the temple and captivated by the tremendous crowds thronging around Jesus. Then they heard a man, one of the Lord's personal disciples it seems, being addressed by his companions as Philip; they ventured to approach him. Here was a disciple of Jesus who had a Greek name! Maybe he would introduce them to Jesus.

But poor old Philip muffed it again. We can imagine all the doubts and difficulties that came up in his mind: *Proselytes they may be, but they are Gentiles. When Jesus sent the twelve of us on a messianic mission to the tribes, He expressly told us, "Go not into the way of the Gentiles, and into any city of the Samaritans enter ye not: but go rather to the lost sheep of the house of Israel"* (Matt. 10:5–6). *When the Syrophenician woman besought the Lord to heal her child, He said, "It is not meet to take the children's bread, and to cast it unto the dogs"* (Mark 7:27).

Pondering these words of Jesus, Philip was not at all sure the Lord would want to be introduced to any Greeks, however devout they were. Philip had failed to grasp the total change in dispensations that had been ushered in by the Jewish rejection of their Christ and the subsequent cursing of the fig tree. So instead of joyfully bringing a couple of would-be-converts to Christ, it appears that he gave them the cold shoulder and probably told them he would have to make inquiries. Even then he didn't go directly to Jesus with his predicament; he went first to Andrew. It's a wonder the Greeks didn't go away with their feelings hurt.

D. What Philip Felt

Finally John shows us Philip in the upper room. The last few hours had come, and the Lord and His disciples were together. Jesus had washed their feet and declared He was about to be betrayed. He had also told Peter that he was about to deny Him three times.

Then the Lord began His last heart-to-heart talk with His disciples. "I'm going home!" He told them in effect. "Let me tell you about My Father's house. It is a house of many mansions . . ." He saw their sad faces and the dawning of the realization He really was going away. They would be left as orphans in the world. They could not imagine life without Him. The last three-and-a-half years had been absolutely marvelous! They thought of all the miracles they had seen and the tremendous teaching they had heard. They thought of His wisdom, His love, and His power. They thought of His goodness, His greatness, and His grace. What would life be like without their beloved Master?

"Let not your heart be troubled," Jesus said. "I'll be coming back. I'm only going to get things ready for you. I'm going to pave the way for you to the Father." Then it was that Philip blurted out what was in his heart: "You keep on talking about the Father. Show us the Father, and it sufficeth us. That will be sufficient." The same old calculating mind came up short once again. Before he had said, "Not sufficient." This time he said, *"That* will be sufficient"—just show us the Father. It speaks volumes for the patience of our Lord Jesus that He simply took Philip's comment in His stride. The Lord's answer was sublime. John 14:9 gives us His exact words: "Have I been so long time with you, and yet hast thou not known me, Philip? he that hath seen me hath seen the Father; and how sayest thou then, Show us the Father?"

In effect He said, "What you are asking for is redundant. There is not one particle of difference between the Father and Me. What He is, I am; what He says, I say; what He does, I do. If you have seen Me, you have seen Him. If I were to show you Him, I would simply be showing you Myself. Don't you realize that for the past thirty-three years I have been the visible expression of the invisible God? I am God as He is God—except that I am God manifest in flesh. Ever since I was born I have been demonstrating a moment-by-moment, three-dimensional, full-color, audio-visual manifestation of God." At least Philip's blundering statement gave Jesus the opportunity to explain that great truth.

What happened to Philip? He was in the upper room on the day of Pentecost, so he, too, was baptized by the Spirit of God into the body of Christ. He, too, was endued with power from on high, so we can be sure that Philip let his light shine in some small corner of this world.

Tradition tells us he went to Scythia—part of southern Russia—and settled in Hierapolis in Phrygia. Hierapolis was a resort town that attracted people from all over the Roman world. It was near the great medical center at Laodicea. There, Philip would not have been far from his dear friend John, who settled at Ephesus.

Thus if tradition and conjecture are true, careful and methodical Philip helped carry the gospel tidings into Europe. He reminds us that the Lord can use ordinary, prosaic, and dull people just as He can use clever and quick-witted people.

NINETEEN

James the Less

Matthew 10:3

A. His DESIGNATION
B. His DISTINCTION
C. His DESTINATION

He is called James the Less (sometimes James the Younger), and that's about all we know of him—just a name. But that's about all we know of hundreds of people whose names appear here and there in the Bible. At least his name *occurs* in the Bible—and that's more than can be said of the Pharaoh of the oppression in the days of Moses. That's more than can be said for Alexander the Great or for the philosophers and scholars of Athens. That's more than can be said for Julius Caesar. There were millions of people on earth when James responded to the call of Christ, and the vast majority lived and died and were forgotten. Yet James had his name written in the Bible five times. That's better than making *Who's Who.*

A. His Designation

He is called "James the son of Alphaeus" (Mark 3:18). Matthew is also identified as the son of Alphaeus (Mark 2:14). If both references are to the same Alphaeus, Matthew and James were brothers and James was a Levite. Thomas is also thought to have been a brother of this James.[1] The tribe of Levi was the priestly tribe, and the Levites were the legal experts of the day.

---

1. The family ties among the twelve disciples can become very confusing—mostly because opinions of commentators vary. W. Graham Scroggie stated his

One tradition is that before responding to the call of Christ, James the Less was a Zealot. If that tradition is true, Matthew and James could have had little or nothing in common until they both met Christ. Matthew, a Roman tax collector, was a detested publican, a collaborator with Rome, and a traitor to the Jews, while James, a vehement foe of all things Roman, was determined to strike the blow that would shake off the hated shackles of the occupying power.

The name Alphaeus is the Greek form of the Hebrew name Cleophas. The Cleophas mentioned in the New Testament was the husband of that Mary who went with the mother of Jesus and other women to Calvary on the day of the crucifixion (John 19:25).

The Bible tells us nothing else about James the Less. He asked no questions and did nothing to distinguish himself as an individual. He simply marched in step with the others. He was a listener, not a talker; a follower, not a leader.

But James stands at the head of a long line of men and women who love the Lord and seek to live for Him quietly and inconspicuously in the daily rounds and common tasks of life. We do not know the names of the majority of those who were thrown to the lions in the days of the persecuting Caesars. We do not know the names of those hewers of wood and drawers of water who built St. Paul's Cathedral or Westminster Abbey. We do not know the names of millions who, down through the ages, have made up the rank and file of the faith. James the Less heads the procession of the foot soldiers of the cross.

There are four lists of the twelve apostles in the New Testament. Three are in the Gospels (Matt. 10:2–4; Mark 3:16–19; Luke 6:14–16), and one is in the book of Acts (1:13, 26). In each list the names are divided into three groups of four disciples. The same disciples are always grouped together, and in every case each group is headed by the same apostle. The first group includes the more prominent and conspicuous apostles and is always headed by Peter. The second group includes less well-known disciples and is always headed by Philip. The third group includes the least known disciples; they are obscure except for Judas

interpretation as follows: "Most of (the disciples) were closely related to Jesus or to one another. There were two pairs of brothers, Peter and Andrew, James and John. Tradition says that Thomas, Matthew and James of Alphaeus were brothers. Jude was either brother or son of James of Alphaeus, so that, perhaps, a father and a son were in that chosen circle. And James and John of Zebedee, Thomas, Matthew, and James of Alphaeus were first cousins of our Lord, and Jude was a first cousin once removed; so that the 'Twelve' and their Master were a family group." W. Graham Scroggie, *The Gospel of Mark* (Grand Rapids: Zondervan, 1979), 65.

Iscariot, whose name always appears last, covered with infamy. This third group is always headed by James the Less. His place in the list suggests that he had at least some leadership qualities.

We can also more or less positively infer from Scripture that James came from Capernaum. Jesus made Capernaum His headquarters during the early part of His ministry; Peter and Andrew lived there; Matthew had his customs office there; the Lord performed many of His greatest miracles there.

It is not at all unlikely that the Lord kept an eye on Matthew and James the Less for quite a while. He saw something in this obscure James that rang true, and when the time came for Him to make up the list of His personal disciples, He decided that James would make an excellent apostle.

We would have chosen someone who cut a more dashing figure. We would have wanted a banker or a millionaire. We would have thought that someone like Nicodemus or Joseph of Arimathea was better than the retiring James. But when we stand at the judgment seat of Christ, we will applaud with cheers and hosannas the Lord's choice of this man. The Lord chose him as He chose only eleven other men in all the history of this world. And the Lord made no mistakes—not even when He chose Judas Iscariot and certainly not when He chose James the Less.

B. His Distinction

James's distinction lies in his almost complete anonymity. He is conspicuous because he was inconspicuous. He is outstanding because he is obscure. Some of the greatest forces in the universe work silently, secretly, and unseen. Silently the snowflakes fall, building barricades and stopping the march of armies. Silently the atoms whirl, their electrons rushing around their nuclei billions of times in a millionth of a second. Silently great forests grow.

In the church James the Less is the precursor of all those who have trusted Christ, who have walked humbly with their God, and who have sought to serve Him in some small corner of the harvest field. They are unknown, unsung heroes of the faith. Consider the impact of such inconspicuous men on John Wesley, Alexander Cruden, William Booth, John Knox, and John Bunyan.

Let us begin with John Wesley. The Irish historian William Lecky, who cannot be suspected of any bias toward Christianity, declared that the Wesleyan revival saved England from the blood bath of the French revolution. He went so far as to say that the religious revolution, begun in England by the preaching of the

Wesleys, was more important than all the splendid victories won on land and sea under the British prime minister William Pitt.

Conditions in England at the time of the Wesleys were terrible almost beyond belief. The stage was decadent, the royal court reeked of licentiousness, and the church and religion were openly scorned. Infidelity and drunkenness were epidemic. In London one house in every six was a gin mill. Bands of thugs sallied forth from the taverns to commit mayhem on ordinary citizens. The priests of the Church of England were fox-hunting parsons, and a converted minister was as rare as a comet. Every kind of immorality was championed by the press. It was taken for granted that Christianity was defunct—no longer even a subject for inquiry. Then John and Charles Wesley came on the scene.

But how did John Wesley come to know Christ? He had always been religious. He admitted that as a young lad he stole from his mother's purse—but he always tithed what he stole and gave some of it to the poor! He had crossed the Atlantic to be a missionary only to discover that he himself was not right with God. Returning to England, he groped in a kind of twilight zone for some time. "What have I learned?" he asked himself. "I have learned that I, who went to America to convert the Indians, was never myself converted."

His journal tells us that he came to Christ in the middle of a persistent and passionate quest for the truth of God. One evening he went reluctantly to a meeting of a Christian society in London where someone was reading Luther's preface to the epistle to the Romans. About a quarter of the way through the reading, the light suddenly dawned in John Wesley's soul. The man who was destined to bring revival to England passed from death unto life. But who invited John Wesley to the meeting? And who was reading Luther's commentary? One of the church's nobodies.

John Wesley went on to write 118 books and articles. He and his brother Charles published 49 books of hymns and poetry. John traveled some 250,000 miles, mostly on horseback; preached 40,000 sermons; and led countless thousands to Christ. But who led *him* to Christ? It was one of the fellowship of James the Less.

Think also of Alexander Cruden, born in Aberdeen on May 31, 1701. He was known as Crazy Cruden, since on several occasions, he displayed evidence of mental instability. He became first secretary to the Earl of Derby, and later he worked as a tutor. Cruden saved his money, and in 1732 he rented a shop in London just a stone's throw from the royal exchange and went into the bookselling business. Shortly after he moved into the shop, he began work on the project that made him famous: the compilation of a concordance of the Bible. There is no way we can estimate how helpful that concordance has been to the cause of Christ. Anyone knowing just one word in any Bible verse can find that verse with a *Cruden's Concordance,* a work still being published more than two hundred years after its completion.

Today there are other more sophisticated resources available to us—concordances, lexicons, word studies, and computer programs undreamed of in Cruden's day. Yet in his day and for generations afterward, armies of Bible students rose up to call Crazy Cruden blessed. But who led Alexander Cruden to Christ? Nobody knows. It was a member of the fellowship of James the Less.

Another member of that fellowship had an impact on the man who became known as General Booth. Called "the prophet to the poor," William Booth was born among the poor in Nottingham on April 10, 1829. He was born again at the age of fifteen. He launched his new mission in 1865, and in 1878 called it the Salvation Army.

In Booth's day, London's East End was a squalid slum of half a million people. Gin shops beckoned on every corner, and some of the shops even had steps up to the counter so that the smallest child could be served. Booth took the East End by storm. Uniformed Salvationists formed brass bands and marched through the streets, and thousands of people were saved. These militant Christians stirred up fierce opposition throughout Britain. The mayor of one English city advised the people to take the Salvation Army flag, tie it around the necks of the Salvationists, and hang them with it. In the early 1880's, tavern keepers, enraged because so many of their customers were getting saved and giving up drink, urged people to attack Salvation Army soldiers in the streets. When William and Catherine Booth visited Sheffield in 1882, they were attacked by a gang of toughs. General Booth, surveying his troops covered with mud and blood and egg yolks, said, "Now is the time to have your photograph taken." In one year nearly seven hundred Salvationists were assaulted on the streets of Britain simply for preaching the gospel. Some were even punched and kicked to death.

Booth's army went after the poor and the wretched. It was designed, the founder said, for "wife-beaters, cheats and bullies, prostitutes and thieves." C. H. Spurgeon said, "If the Salvation Army were wiped out of London, five thousand extra policemen could not fill its place in the repression of crime and disorder."

General Booth died—or as his fellow soldiers would say, "He was promoted to Glory"—on August 12, 1912. During his lying-in-state 150,000 people filed past his coffin and 40,000 people, including Queen Mary, wife of King George V, attended his funeral. In Booth's lifetime the Salvation Army had grown to include 15,945 officers serving in 58 countries.

But who led William Booth to Christ? Some biographers say that his conversion took place in Nottingham when the revivalist Isaac Marsden was conducting a campaign. Others say Booth was converted in a small prayer meeting. Nobody knows for sure. The person who led William Booth to Christ is another member of the fellowship of James the Less.

Consider next the case of John Knox. When George Wishart was burned at the stake as a heretic, his colleague John Knox escaped arrest, but he watched his mentor die. Knox saw him being led to the stake by the executioner, and Knox heard about the words of forgiveness that Wishart spoke to that man. Knox watched the flames leap up around Wishart as he ascended the ladder of martyrdom to his heavenly home. That martyr made a deep and a lasting impression on Knox.

In 1547 John Knox himself was arrested and sent to France where he was condemned to be a galley slave for nineteen months. While toiling at the oars of a French galley, he showed the stuff of which he was made by boldly defying the ship's Roman Catholic chaplain who tried to intimidate him.

When John Knox returned to Scotland from his enforced exile, he began to preach. He bluntly declared the Mass to be idolatry and boldly stated that Catholic churches and monasteries should be closed. He lived to see Protestantism established as the national religion of Scotland. When Mary Stuart came to the throne in 1560, she promptly had John Knox arrested and tried for treason, but the court acquitted him. The triumph of the Scottish Reformation was complete. Thomas Carlyle, the famous Scottish essayist and historian, said that in the history of Scotland he could only find one epoch: the Reformation wrought by John Knox. Carlyle described it as "a resurrection from the dead" for Scotland.

John Knox went to his rest in 1572, but his soul goes marching on. And who led him to Christ? We know that he was profoundly moved by Wishart, but who took the Bible and pointed John Knox to Calvary? It was another member of the fellowship of James the Less.

We might also ask about the conversion of John Bunyan. He's not so well-known today; but for three hundred years he was the best-known, best-loved, most-read author in the Christian world. His *Pilgrim's Progress* stood side by side with the Bible in almost every Christian home. He was born in Bedford, England, in 1628. Just a humble tinker by trade, he was arrested in 1660 for preaching without the permission of the established church. He remained in the Bedford jail for nearly thirteen years during which his wife, his little blind daughter, and his other children suffered much. He was in jail when the terrible bubonic plague ravaged England, and he was there when the great fire of London reduced much of the city to smoking ashes and rubble.

The Devil could lock Bunyan up, but he couldn't shut him up. During his incarceration he wrote his famous allegory of the Christian life. "As I walked through the wilderness of this world," he began, "I lighted on a certain place where was a Den, and I laid me down in that place to sleep; and, as I slept, I dreamed a dream . . ." The den was Bedford jail. The dream became *Pilgrim's Progress* with its host of colorful characters who have delighted Christians from that day to this. How can we ever forget Mr. Obstinate and Mr. Pliable, or Christian in the Slough of Despond, or Mr. Worldly Wiseman and Madam Bubble, or the man with the muck rake in his hand, or Mr. Hypocrisy, or Mr. Formalist, or Mr. Mistrust, or Giant Despair? And who can forget the Delectable Mountains, the Interpreter's house, Doubting Castle, By-Path Meadow, and Vanity Fair? To spend an hour or two with John Bunyan is to be thoroughly entertained and greatly helped on the straight and narrow way that leads to life. Who can measure the power, influence, and impact of a book?

For a long time before his conversion, though, John Bunyan was tormented by his sin. He felt as though the sun in the sky begrudged the light it gave him. He felt as though the cobblestones of the street and the tiles on the houses banded together against him. Who led him out of this darkness into light? Bunyan mentioned being associated with a Master Gifford. He also mentioned overhearing a cluster of poor women discussing the kingdom of God as they sat in the sun outside their doors, and he mentioned being influenced by the members of the little church at Bedford. But who led him to Christ and thus gave the world *Pilgrim's Progress, The Holy War,* and *Grace Abounding to the Chief of Sinners?* We'll have to wait for the answer, for it was a member of the fellowship of James the Less.

James the Less stands in the forefront of a multitude that no man can number—anonymous men and women and boys and girls who are washed in the blood of the Lamb and whose names are written down in glory. They may stand as silent sentinels on earth, but they will be numbered among the aristocracy of heaven. No bright lights shine on their names down here, but they will shine as the stars in the firmament forever over there.

C. His Destination

One of these days the trumpet will sound. "The dead in Christ shall rise first: Then we which are alive and remain shall be caught up together with them in the clouds, to meet the Lord in the air" (1 Thess. 4:16–17). We will all be there, small and great—those who made a mighty mark for God and are mentioned in church history books, and little old ladies and shy retiring men who loved the Lord and, like Mary of Bethany, did what they could. Those who had the gifts of apostle and prophet; evangelists and pastors and teachers who filled great pulpits; those who blazed gospel trails into dark continents; those who founded missions and movements—all will rise together, with countless ordinary folk, toward the sky.

We will all arrive at the celestial city. Before us will be the vast bulk of that city foursquare. We will see its jasper walls stretching far away on either side and soaring upward mile after mile until they are lost in the sky above. Our eyes will be drawn to the great foundations of that wondrous city, the city that haunted Abraham's dreams. He looked for "a city which hath foundations" (Heb. 11:10), and here he will find a city with twelve foundations ablaze with precious stones. Twelve names are engraved on those foundations for all the universe to see. And just as prominent as the names of Peter, James, and John is the name of James the Less.

We will all go in and stand at the judgment seat of Christ. The books will be opened. The name of James the Less will be called, and we will hear what he did and where he went and what he said and whom he won to Christ. James the Less will be James the Less no more! All those of his unsung fellowship will stand with him, honored and applauded "in the crowning day that's coming by and by."[2]

---

2. D. W. Whittle, "The Crowning Day," 1881.

TWENTY

Thomas the Twin

John 11:16; 14:1–6; 20:24–29

A. HIS CAUTION
B. HIS COMMITMENT
C. HIS CONCERN
D. HIS COLLAPSE
E. HIS CONFESSION

He is usually called Thomas, but sometimes Didymus. Both names mean "the twin." Because he is usually paired with Matthew in the various listings of the twelve apostles in the New Testament, it has been surmised that he was the twin brother of Matthew.

One commentator, Matthew Poole, speculated that Matthew was the original prodigal son, for before his conversion he was a renegade Jew who sunk so low as to sell his soul to Rome. The far country is not always defined in terms of miles; it can often be defined in terms of morals. If Matthew was indeed the prototype for the prodigal in the Lord's parable, Thomas (if he was Matthew's twin) must have been the original elder brother. In the case of twins, being the elder brother can hinge on a matter of minutes. Esau and Jacob were twins, but Esau was always considered the elder and Jacob the younger even though their births were only minutes apart. These are interesting speculations, but probably nothing more.

Archbishop Trench saw a connection in Thomas between being a twin and being twin-minded. The twins of belief and unbelief battled each other in Thomas's heart just as Esau and Jacob struggled in Rebekah's womb. Regardless of whether there is any truth in these suggestions, the fact remains that Thomas was a twin and that somewhere he had a twin brother or twin sister. It would be interesting to know whether he or she also became a follower of the Lord Jesus.

We are indebted to the apostle John for all we know about Thomas as a person. The synoptic writers only mentioned him in their various listings of the twelve apostles. John, writing toward the end of the first century and looking back to those wonderful years of his youth, evidently thought of Thomas as one who was a personality in his own right. Perhaps they had been boyhood friends, since both were Galileans.

A. His Caution

We call him Doubting Thomas, but it might be fairer to say he was cautious. He always wanted to be sure of his ground. He was not the kind of man to sign a document without first reading it all the way through. In a debate, his favorite defense would be "Prove it!" He was the kind of man who had to see things for himself. Once he was convinced, he would hold tenaciously to what he believed.

It is not a bad idea to be cautious, especially about what we accept as the articles of our faith. The Bible, in fact, urges us to be cautious. In his first epistle, John warned against deceiving spirits that lurk in the unseen world. He warned us not to accept ideas just because they were imparted by ecstatic utterance or by a so-called prophet. The Holy Spirit commended the people of Berea because they put even the preaching of an apostle to the test. They searched the Scriptures daily to see if the teachings of Paul were true.

At the high school I attended in Britain, a high brick wall enclosed the playground. The wall was topped with a thick layer of cement in which was embedded pieces of jagged broken glass. The idea, of course, was to discourage boys from scaling the wall. I once saw a cat walking along the top. He took each step with great caution. He would put out a paw, gingerly feel the surface, and when he was quite sure that cement and not glass was beneath his foot, he would take the next step. That cat's name might well have been Thomas! Thomas wanted to be sure of his ground before he made a move. There's not much fault to find in that philosophy of life.

But sometimes even the most careful of men will throw all caution to the winds. Thomas did so and thus earned honorable, although, gloomy commendation in John's memoirs of Jesus.

B. His Commitment

It will be helpful to review the circumstances surrounding the time when Thomas made his daring commitment. The Lord Jesus was in Peraea, a rural area beyond the Jordan River. Originally Peraea was the tribal territory of Gad and Reuben. The northern section was densely wooded; the southern section was rich pastureland fading off to widening tracts of desert as the area reached toward the Dead Sea.

Jesus had been up to Jerusalem to keep the Feast of Tabernacles, a joyful occasion. Jews from the far-flung lands of the Diaspora made their pilgrimage to the holy city to pay their tithes and taxes. The Lord had been watched with great suspicion by the Sanhedrin as He taught in the temple. Their spies were everywhere.

Between the Feast of Tabernacles and the last Passover feast was a period of about six months, which the Lord spent in Peraea. There His ministry was mostly a teaching ministry devoted to parables and discourses. The time in Peraea was interrupted by a brief visit to Jerusalem in December for the Feast of Dedication. This feast was personally significant to the Lord Jesus, for it was at the time of His birthday.

There was speculation among the Jews as to whether or not He would come to Jerusalem at all, since official opposition to Him was mounting in the capital. But come He did. He appeared suddenly in the temple and taught the people. He claimed that He was the true Shepherd, and they were not His sheep. When He said that He was coequal with the Father, "the Jews took up stones again to stone him" (John 10:31).

He escaped and went back across the Jordan to Peraea. Except for a brief interlude when He went to Bethany to raise Lazarus from the dead, He stayed in Peraea. With the river rolling between Him and His enemies, He gathered the people around Him. There, near the scene of the early labors of John the Baptist and not far from the place where He had been baptized, He taught the people.

What wonderful stories He told on those Peraean hills! We are indebted to Luke for the preservation of most of them. They poured out of Him: stories of the good Samaritan; the importunate neighbor; the rich fool and his barns; the barren fig tree; the great supper and the silly excuses made for not coming; the lost sheep; the lost silver; the lost son; the unjust steward; the rich man and Lazarus; the unjust judge; the self-righteous Pharisee; the unmerciful servant. Meanwhile, the shadows of His rejection were gathering deeper and darker in Jerusalem. The Lord prepared Himself, the people, and His disciples for what lay ahead.

Then came the urgent message: "Lazarus is sick. He's going to die. Please come! Come quickly" (see John 11:3). But Lazarus was already dead and Jesus knew it. However, He sent the messenger back with a word of hope and cheer, and He stayed where He was. The disciples must have breathed a sigh of relief. The last place they wanted to go was the vicinity of Jerusalem. Two days later Jesus suddenly announced that He intended to go to Bethany to deal with the unfinished business of His friend Lazarus. Immediately a storm of protest arose from the ranks of the disciples. They remembered the angry mob. They could still picture the stones in the hands of the crowd. They could have been stoned with Him.

To his lasting honor, Thomas spoke up. "Let us also go, that we may die with him," he boldly said. Thomas had no doubt whatsoever that if they once ventured back into the vicinity of the capital, the Sanhedrin would orchestrate their deaths. But if Jesus was determined to go to His death, Thomas was determined to go to his, too. Thomas's commitment made him willing to die for Christ if the call of duty demanded such a sacrifice.

So the disciples rallied around this unexpected leader and trooped back toward Jerusalem. Instead of facing the anticipated stoning, they witnessed the greatest of all the Lord's miracles: the resurrection of a man already dead, buried, and decomposing.

C. HIS CONCERN

When Thomas spoke up in Peraea, he spoke with the voice of his heart. When he expressed himself in the upper room, he spoke with the voice of his mind.

So much happened between the two occasions. Jesus had entered Jerusalem triumphantly, and the disciples, their hearts no doubt pounding with excitement, thought that at last He was going to seize the reins of power and reestablish the throne of David on earth. But the excitement passed, and even the densest of them could see that the storm clouds were gathering thick and heavy across their sky. The Sanhedrin was openly plotting to get rid of this unwanted Messiah.

In the upper room Jesus and the disciples observed the Passover, and the Lord instituted a new feast of remembrance. The Lord, performing a servant's task to teach a lesson in humility, washed the disciples' feet. Judas departed on his unexplained mission.

Then Jesus began to talk again about the subject they dreaded. Over the past few months He had kept coming back to it. He was going to die, by crucifixion of all things. He was going to be buried, but they were not to worry. He would be back three days later. Then He would go home to His Father. "In my Father's house are many mansions," He told them. Although heaven is infinitely better than earth, in some ways that other world is very much like this one, He assured them.

Adding to the consternation and confusion of the disciples, Jesus said, "Whither I go ye know, and the way ye know." That was too much for Thomas. He blurted out what was probably on all their minds. They did not have the faintest idea where He was going or how to get there. "We know not whither thou goest," Thomas said. "How can we know the way?" (John 14:5). In all this incomprehensible talk, one ominous and terrifying fact was clear: He was going away. Thomas spoke up for them all. They did not want Him to go away.

Thomas's outburst gave the Lord Jesus an opportunity to make one of His greatest statements: "I am the way, the truth, and the life: no man cometh unto the Father, but by me." In His reply to Thomas, He answered the three most important questions of the human heart. Man asks, "How can I be saved?" He replies, "I am the way." Man asks, "How can I be sure?" He replies, "I am the truth." Man asks, "How can I be satisfied?" He replies, "I am the life." So long as the disciples knew Him, they knew the way because He was the way.

How comforting to know the way. To find out what it is like in a more mundane sense to be lost, for a nominal fee one can go into the Hampton Court maze. Hampton Court is the famous palace built by Cardinal Wolsey in the days of England's notorious Henry VIII. Having seen the covetous gleam in the king's eye when that imperious monarch saw the palace, Wolsey deeded it over to the king. The maze on the grounds of the palace consists of narrow lanes bordered by high and impenetrable hedges. All paths seem somehow to lead to the middle. When I was quite young, an uncle of mine took me into the maze; and, sure enough, we ended up in the center where the authorities had thoughtfully provided a seat where one could sit down and think things over. We wandered in the maze for a considerable time; and just when I was getting weary, an attendant came along and offered to show us how to get out. Very soon we were on the outside. The secret to all those perplexing pathways was a man—a man who knew the way.

Likewise Jesus knew the way—the way home. In essence Jesus was saying to Thomas and the others, "Don't worry about the way. I am the way. Just follow Me. If you know Me, you know the way because I am the way!"

D. His Collapse

Thomas was almost as overwhelmed by the arrest, betrayal, trial, crucifixion, and burial of Jesus as Peter was. Thomas played the coward and sought to save his own skin, as all the disciples did. Some of them recovered sooner than others, and slowly the sad little group began to reassemble in the upper room. They would at least stay around Jerusalem for a few more days to see what might happen. If they kept a low profile, doubtless the authorities would leave them alone.

The Lord's tomb was sealed and guarded. There was no point in going anywhere near it. A couple of days passed. Then early Sunday morning some of the women decided to take the risk. Perhaps they could find someone to open the tomb for them so they could finish embalming the body. Soon they returned with news: The tomb was empty! The guards were gone. The women had seen some angels who told them that Jesus was alive. Peter and John went to see for themselves, but they saw only an empty tomb and some discarded wrappings.

By evening all the disciples were back in the upper room—all except Thomas. The Lord appeared to them all—all except Thomas. Around the absence of Thomas, scores of suggestions have been gathered and countless sermons have been preached.

Why did Thomas stay away? Why did he make himself the patron saint of believers who stay away from the meetings of the Lord's people? We can suppose that he made the usual excuses people make today.

Thomas might have said, "I'm too tired, too overwrought. This has been a terrible few weeks. I need a rest." Or "I'm too busy. I have to get my life reorganized and pick up the threads of my old fishing business." Or, "It's too dangerous to go out right now. The political and religious climate in Jerusalem is particularly unhealthy for believers in Jesus of Nazareth. The city is swarming with Sanhedrin spies. Why, the moment I step outside this house I'm likely to be arrested. I didn't mind dying for Christ when there was still time for another miracle to happen. But all hope for a miracle is gone." Or, "I'll stay home and read my Bible. I can get just as much out of Moses and the Psalms as I would get out of a meeting with the others. All they'll do is pool their ignorance anyway. Besides, Peter will probably be there, and he'll do all the talking. The last thing I need is to hear that man talk after the way he cursed and swore the other day. But he'll be up at the front, as bold as brass, telling everybody what to do." Or "It's going to rain." Or "I can't imagine a meeting without Jesus in the midst. Any meeting without Him will be dead and dull and meaningless."

So Thomas stayed home and missed Jesus. That evening He came in—through the walls! He talked to those who were there, let them handle Him, ate a meal with them, and then vanished. And Thomas missed everything.

We can be sure that when he did bump into one of the other disciples and heard the astounding news, he was quite taken aback. Then his native caution would have come to his aid. He would have said, "I don't believe it. You're all mistaken. You've been seeing things." The united testimony of the other ten made no impression on him at all. "Except I shall see in his hands the print of the nails, and put my finger into the print of the nails, and thrust my hand into his side," he said, "I will not believe" (John 20:25).

The first time Thomas spoke, he spoke with the voice of his heart. The second time he spoke with the voice of his mind. Now we hear the voice of his will. In the last analysis, the outcome of the battle between doubt and faith always hinges on the will. We doubt, not because we *cannot* believe, but because we *will not* believe.

E. HIS CONFESSION

Thomas did not miss the next meeting. The following Sunday he was in his place in the upper room, as skeptical as ever, but there just the same. He was still muttering to himself, "I won't believe. I have to see. I have to feel . . ."

Then, all of a sudden, Jesus was there in the midst of the disciples! The doors were barred and bolted. There was no knock at the door, no hailing voice asking to be let in. He was just there! Having proved His omnipotence by coming through a barred and bolted door, He proved His omniscience by singling Thomas out and responding to his skeptical words. "Reach hither thy finger, and behold my hands; and reach hither thy hand, and thrust it into my side: and be not faithless, but believing" (John 20:27). Sad to say, the Lord used the same word (translated "faithless") He had used to describe the chronic unbelief of the world in Matthew 17:17. Those were the words of Thomas.

Thomas was won over. "My Lord and my God," he exclaimed, placing Jesus on the throne of his heart ("my Lord") and on the throne of the universe ("my God"). "Thomas," the Lord rejoined, "because thou hast seen me, thou hast believed: blessed are they that have not seen, and yet have believed" (John 20:29).

We, of course, are among the blessed. We are in that succession of multitudes of men, women, boys, and girls who have believed without seeing—who have simply taken God's word that the gospel is true. With all such believers, the Lord is well-pleased.

After John 20:28 the Bible records no more words spoken by Thomas. It does, however, include his name in John 21:2, and in the roll call of the apostles present in the upper room on the day of Pentecost (Acts 1:13). He was, therefore, one of those upon whom the Holy Spirit came with mighty power.

Eventually, tradition says, Thomas went eastward with the gospel—first to Babylon, then across the Euphrates to Parthia, and then on to India. Everywhere he went he told about the One who was risen from the dead, who could walk through walls, who still wears the nail scars in His hands, and who is now in heaven preparing a place of many mansions. All Thomas's doubts were replaced by certainties once Jesus became not only his Lord, but also his God.

TWENTY-ONE

Philip
The Dynamic Deacon

Acts 6:2–5; 8:5–40

A. THE CLAN
B. THE MAN
C. THE PLAN

There was a problem in the Jerusalem church—too many apostles in too small a space. They were all there. Their horizons began and ended in Jerusalem, their native Galilee, and surrounding Judea. The Lord's last words had been plain enough: "Ye shall be witnesses unto me both in Jerusalem, and in all Judaea, and in Samaria, and unto the uttermost part of the earth" (Acts 1:8). But no one took these words seriously, except Philip—and he wasn't even an apostle.

A. THE CLAN

In those days Christianity was clannish. One had to be a Jew to get into the church. One had to subscribe to a temple-oriented, ritual-related, legalistically leavened form of Christianity. Peter endorsed that idea, as did James. Even though James was a latecomer, the fact that he had been the Lord's brother gave him special leverage within the Jerusalem church. James was a born legalist, a dedicated ascetic, and a convinced *Jewish* Christian. The other Christians were all intimidated by James.

The church was a Jewish church. The central and pivotal point of gathering was the temple. Christians tried to keep the peace with the Sanhedrin, the synagogue, and the sanctuary. The martyrdom of Stephen had rocked the boat; Christians had to be careful. They tried not to do anything that would cause offense.

The church, let it be said, was a big clan because a great many Jews had become Christians. That is, they had become Jewish Christians—law-keeping, circumcision-advocating, Sabbath-observing Christians. In their minds Christianity was just another form of Judaism, albeit an elevated and enlightened form. A great many priests had become Christians, and the Pharisees were inclined to lean toward a Christianity that upheld the Mosaic Law.

Peter, James, John, Thomas, Matthew, Philip, Nathanael, and the rest of the apostles were at the heart of the clan. We can be sure they were all very busy because there were thousands of people in the Jerusalem church alone.

Doubtless the apostles were popular speakers. They would be in demand for all kinds of meetings: gatherings in the temple courts, meetings for teaching doctrine, meetings for fellowship, meetings for breaking of bread, prayer meetings, home meetings, and baptisms. Many people would want to hear the authentic story of Jesus firsthand from those who had spent three-and-one-half years in His company.

The apostles were the proper custodians of the gospel. They could describe the Lord's many miracles and recount His wonderful teachings word for word. They knew by heart His parables, His famous Sermon on the Mount, His Olivet discourse, and His teaching in the upper room. None of Christ's words had as yet been written down, so the memories of the apostles were vital.

So the apostles were kept busy enough speaking. And it was still the age of miracles. Was anyone sick? Let him call for an apostle. Gifts of healing were still part of the accrediting phenomena of an apostle. Peter had even raised the dead.

The apostles would receive messages from all over the country. "Can Peter come to Capernaum and preach in the synagogue for the next three Sabbaths?" "Can John come to Joppa? A brother here is desperately ill." "Can Thomas come to Tiberius and tell how the Lord convinced him that the resurrection was real?" Invitations kept pouring in. How could the apostles respond to these calls when they could hardly keep up with the work in Jerusalem?

The social side of the gospel continued to be somewhat of a headache also. The poor seemed to be getting poorer. There was no longer any question of unfairness in the distribution of funds, but there never seemed to be enough money to go around.

The church was all very correct, very conservative, very clannish, very careful, and reasonably comfortable. But God never intended for the apostles to be comfortable. He intended for them to get going to the ends of the earth. A ship tied up in harbor is usually very safe. But ships are built for the high seas—for breasting angry waves and defying storms.

The clan had comfortably forgotten the words of the Master (Acts 1:8). The apostles had evangelized Jerusalem and Judea and were content. Actually, Jerusalem and Judea had more or less evangelized themselves. With the tremendous impetus of Pentecost, the gospel had quickly spread over the homeland. But what about Samaria?

We can imagine the apostles themselves discussing that question. Jude the Obscure says, "What about Samaria? Aren't we supposed to evangelize Samaria? That would be a good job for you, Peter. You always seem to like the lead and the limelight. Why don't you take the lead and go to Samaria?"

Peter responds, "Well, I like that! Don't you people forget that I'm the apostle to the circumcision. John, you wanted to call down fire on Samaria some years ago. Now's your chance. Go and call down some Pentecostal fire on Samaria. You're just the man for the job."

John replies, "I don't feel any leading in that direction at all. Thomas, you're a converted skeptic. That would be a good place for you to go. We all know how skeptical the Samaritans would be if one of us Jews showed up and offered to be friendly. As a cured skeptic, you'd be just the man to break down their barriers."

Thomas says, "Thanks for nothing. Matthew's the man for that job, it seems to me. After all, he was a tax collector at one time. He had no scruples in those days, so scruples shouldn't bother him now. We Jews have scruples about the Samaritans. Evangelizing *them* would be a good job for Matthew."

Matthew replies, "Let's put our hands on Simon the Zealot. What a marvelous job for him!"

Finally the Holy Spirit left them to their complacent inaction and turned to one of the new deacons instead. He said in effect, "Come on, Philip. You come with me. You and I will go on down to Samaria. We'll show them how it's done."

So Philip went to Samaria and revival broke out. Lives were transformed. Miracles happened. People were saved. The whole place turned upside down. "And the people *with one accord,*" Luke said, "gave heed" (Acts 8:6, italics added). Luke said the same thing of the disciples when, just before Pentecost, they were in the upper room eagerly awaiting the coming of the Holy Spirit: "They were all with one accord" (Acts 2:1).

There was great joy in Samaria, just as there was great joy in Wales when the revival broke out there. G. Campbell Morgan recorded his impression of the

Welsh revival: "No song books, but ah, me! I nearly wept tonight over the singing of our last hymn. No choir did I say? It was all choir. And hymns! I stood
and listened with wonder and amazement as the congregation sang hymn after
hymn without hymn books. No advertising. The thing advertises itself. All over
the country people were converted just by reading the newspaper accounts."

Revival came to Samaria and sure enough the Devil had his counterfeit all
ready and waiting, a scoundrel by the name of Simon Magus. All sorts of extraordinary and extrabiblical stories are told about Simon Magus.[1] It was said that he
could make statues walk. He could roll himself in fire without being burned. He
could turn stones into loaves, open bolted doors, melt iron, and produce phantoms at banquets. He could cause vessels in his house to move about and wait
on him at the dinner table. Probably mesmerism was involved. Still, the stories
circulated and continued to be circulated after his apostasy.

Simon Magus was fascinated by the power of the Holy Spirit displayed by
Philip. In fact, Simon made a profession of faith in Christ and was baptized.
It must have been the talk of the town. "Have you heard about Simon the
sorcerer?"

"No, what has he done now?"

"He has become a Christian. He has been baptized. Can you believe it? They
say he sits right up front at all the preacher's meetings."

Meanwhile, the news of the revival in Samaria filtered back to Jerusalem and
made its belated impact on the clan. The apostles decided they must get involved
and sent both Peter and John.

Inevitably, Simon met Simon. Simon Magus watched with astonishment as
the Samaritan believers received the Holy Spirit when Simon Peter laid his hands
on them. The laying on of hands was a method that was essential in the case of
the Samaritans. The centuries-long animosity between the Jews and Samaritans
made it absolutely necessary that the leaders of the Jerusalem church extend
some special gesture of goodwill to the Samaritans so that they would not feel
themselves to be second-class citizens in the kingdom of God.

Simon Magus was fascinated by the signs that accompanied the giving of the
Holy Spirit. It was not long before he betrayed himself. "Sell me the secret," he said
in effect. "I'd like to be able to give the Holy Spirit by the laying on of hands."

Peter turned on him in a flash. "Thy money perish with thee. . . . Thou hast
neither part nor lot in this matter: for thy heart is not right in the sight of God. . . .

1. G. H. Pember, *Earth's Earliest Ages* (Glasgow: Pickering and Inglis, n.d.), 295–99.

Thou art in the gall of bitterness, and in the bond of iniquity" (Acts 8:20–23). But Peter did not act beyond reading the innermost secrets of this unregenerate soul. Death had followed the sin of Ananias and Sapphira because they were truly saved and came under apostolic jurisdiction. But Simon Magus was not genuinely saved, and Peter left his punishment to God.

Simon Peter exposed the man as an impostor and turned away and left him. Frightened, Simon Magus asked Peter to pray for him. But that was not what the wretched man needed; he needed to pray for himself. If tradition is to be believed, he went back to his sorcery and founded one of the Gnostic cults. He is said to have turned up in Rome, where he performed his magic tricks even in the court of the Caesar.

The events in Samaria made a deep impression on the clan; Peter and John "preached the gospel in many villages of the Samaritans" (Acts 8:25).

As for Philip, God called him away to another task.

B. THE MAN

God is just as interested in individuals as He is in nations. He cared about an Ethiopian eunuch as much as He cared about Samaria.

Any one of the apostles might have had the opportunity of meeting the man from Ethiopia, leading him to Christ, and being instrumental in planting the church in the heart of Africa. But no! The Holy Spirit knew that Peter's and John's hearts were in Jerusalem even while they were touring Samaria. So the Holy Spirit whispered again to Philip the deacon, saying something like, "Come on, Philip, You and I have an appointment with the secretary of the treasury of the kingdom of Ethiopia."

Responsive as always to the Holy Spirit (one of the qualifications required of a deacon in the Jerusalem church) Philip went off to the desert. He left behind him a flourishing revival. Philip had no question, no quarrel, and no quibble about leaving the limelight to Peter. Philip responded quickly and quietly to the Spirit of God.

So Philip went toward Gaza and to the high road to Egypt. There he waited, until on the distant horizon, he saw a cloud of dust that soon resolved itself into a group of chariots. They carried the chancellor of the Ethiopian exchequer and his escort.

Like the Samaritans, this man stood in a kind of "half relationship" to the nation of Israel. The Samaritans were pagan cousins; the Ethiopian seems to have been a proselyte cousin. He had gone to Jerusalem to worship, but apparently, he was bitterly disappointed. Possibly he was as disappointed as Martin Luther when he arrived at Rome, the city of his dreams, and found it full of religious arrogance, pomp, power, and pride. He turned from it with disgust and dismay.

We can picture this Ethiopian as he wandered around the city about which he had read and heard so much. Jerusalem was associated with Melchizedek, David, Solomon, and the Queen of Sheba! Jerusalem was the city of poets and prophets, the home of the temple, and the heart of a spiritual empire.

No doubt the Ethiopian attended the Jerusalem synagogues and listened to the rules, regulations, and accumulated religious rubbish that the rabbis propounded in the name of God. He probably went to the temple, only to find himself shut out of most of it. The court of the Gentiles would be about as far as he could go, and that was more like a mercantile exchange than a sanctuary. He probably wondered, *Why don't the temple authorities make a clean sweep of all this temple traffic?* We can imagine his shock when he discovered that the authorities owned the concessions.

Wandering around the markets of Jerusalem, perhaps he found a shop where portions of the Scriptures were for sale—hand-copied, authorized, and very expensive. While browsing through a beautiful copy of the prophecy of Isaiah the word *Ethiopia* would have caught his eye, and he would decide to buy it. He could not have made a better choice if he'd asked the chief rabbi himself for advice.

Maybe the Ethiopian heard rumors about the church and went to Annas or Caiaphas with his inquiries. (A man in high social and political position would go to the top.) We can well imagine what kind of answers the high priest and his crowd would have given. And we can wonder why Andrew or Thomas did not lead the Ethiopian to Christ. Perhaps the church avoided him because he was black and a Gentile.

We can speculate that he was sad at heart, empty of soul, and disillusioned as he wandered about the holy city. We know for certain that he had gone to Jerusalem to worship and that he had come away as hungry of heart as when he arrived.

Still seeking, still longing, the Ethiopian headed for home. His entourage arrived first at Gaza and then headed on toward Egypt. Ahead of him lay a journey of hundreds of miles back to his native land.

When Philip caught up to him, the Ethiopian was reading the prophecy of Isaiah. He could not understand, though, what he was reading. Nevertheless, he had persevered through fifty-two chapters and was in the middle of the fifty-third when suddenly he heard a voice that seemed to come from heaven itself. Philip anticipated his bewilderment: "Excuse me, sir. Do you understand what you are reading?" The Ethiopian looked up and saw the evangelist running alongside his chariot. He was very earthy, very dusty, and quite out of breath.

The Spirit had been waiting until this critical moment. We can hear Him whisper to Philip, "Run, Philip. That's the man, the one in the first chariot, the one reading that book. Run!" Thus the text, the teacher, and the traveler all converged—on Isaiah 53:7. The Ethiopian was reading these inspired words: "He was led as a sheep to the slaughter; and like a lamb dumb before his shearer, so opened he not his mouth. . . . His life is taken from the earth" (as quoted in Acts 8:32–33).

"Of whom speaketh the prophet this?" asked the Ethiopian. "Of himself, or of some other man?" Could anyone have asked a more appropriate question? What an opening for a soul winner. And Philip "began at the same scripture, and preached unto him Jesus" (Acts 8:34–35). Of course he did! Fortunately for the Ethiopian, Philip had not studied at a liberal seminary. If he had he would have begun, "Well you see, sir, I subscribe to the deutero-Isaiah hypothesis. Before I can answer your question, we must first settle which Isaiah we are talking about."

Philip did not expose the inquirer to that kind of high-sounding nonsense. Philip was simply a humble, Bible-believing preacher. From that magnificent text he led the Ethiopian straight into the arms of Jesus. The preaching of Philip is a veritable classic in personal evangelism.

Philip also instructed the new convert in the first steps of the Christian faith. He told the Ethiopian he needed to be baptized now that he had accepted Christ. The Holy Spirit, still in charge, arranged for another of those divine "coincidences" that so often occur in soul winning: an oasis was nearby. The Ethiopian wasted no time. "See, here is water," he said. "What doth hinder me to be baptized?"

In front of his wondering entourage, this high-placed government official stopped his chariot and followed Philip into the water. Having acknowledged the Ethiopian's confession of faith, Philip immersed his illustrious convert.

What happened next is one of those mysteries we will explore with greater understanding when we receive our resurrection bodies and stand with the Ethiopian in heaven. Then we will hear his testimony from his own lips. We can imagine what he will say:

"I came up out of the water, I rubbed the water from my eyes, and I turned to say something to the man who had appeared out of nowhere, but he wasn't there. He had vanished back into nowhere. I asked my servants, 'Where's that Jewish preacher I picked up a little while back south of Gaza?' 'He seems to have vanished, my lord,' one of them replied. 'Well, he can't have gone far,' I said. 'The country is as flat as a pond. Stand on the high point of the chariot and find out if you can see him.'"

But Philip had vanished. The Holy Spirit gives us the only explanation we will have this side of glory: "The Spirit of the Lord caught away Philip, that the eunuch saw him no more." The Ethiopian, however, had no doubt that God had sent him a special messenger. "He went on his way rejoicing" (Acts 8:39).

Meanwhile Philip had been miraculously and instantly transported twenty miles up the coast to the old Philistine city of Ashdod (Azotus).

C. THE PLAN

The divine plan, of course, was to evangelize the whole Gentile world. The Lord's mandate was to "be witnesses unto me . . . unto the uttermost part of the earth" (Acts 1:8). Nothing could be done about the mandate, however, until the apostles took the divine plan seriously.

The Lord was about to jolt Peter out of his complacency and send him, whether he liked it or not, to the home of a Gentile. Even then the Jerusalem apostles would still be content to drag their feet, but once the door was officially open to Gentiles, the Lord would call and anoint a new apostle—Paul.

In the meantime, Philip made tentative attempts at Gentile evangelism himself. He made his way up the old Philistine-Phoenician coastline and visited city after city. Ashdod, Lydda, and Joppa were all on his route. On and on he journeyed northward until, at last, he came to Caesarea.

Caesarea was a bustling modern city with an atmosphere like Rome's. Caesarea was as unlike the sleepy old Palestinian towns as one could imagine. It was the seat of the Roman government in Palestine. An engineering marvel, Caesarea was a bustling seaport. It was the home of the occupying garrison and had such Roman necessities as baths and a stadium. The Jews shunned the place like the plague.

Here, Philip took up his residence. Long after Peter had come to Caesarea to win Cornelius and his family to Christ, Philip settled down in this strategic, outward-looking Roman city. Here he brought up his family for God and sought to be a witness for Christ in a thoroughly Gentile atmosphere. He and his family (including four prophetess daughters) were still in Caesarea twenty years later when the great apostle Paul was imprisoned in this city (Acts 21:8–9). Paul was attended by his Gentile companion Luke who recorded Philip's story in the book of Acts.

Philip was one man who readily entered into the divine plan to evangelize the whole world. The last glimpse the Holy Spirit gives us of Philip is in Caesarea. The next time we see him, we will be in heaven.

TWENTY-TWO

James

The Lord's Brother

Acts 12:17; 1 Corinthians 15:7; Galatians 1:19

A. JAMES AND THE LORD OF GLORY
   1. What confused James
   2. What convinced James
B. JAMES AND THE LAW OF GOD
C. JAMES AND THE LIFE OF GRACE
   1. What we see
   2. Why we sin
   3. Where we slip
   4. Who we snub
   5. What we say
   6. Why we squabble
   7. Who we serve
   8. What we show
   9. When we suffer

Were it not for a passing comment by the apostle Paul, we would never have known. In a letter to the churches of Galatia, Paul mentioned the austere man, the man whose knees, tradition says, were so calloused from continual kneeling in prayer the church called him "camel knees." He was the Lord's *brother* (Gal. 1:19). That piece of information, alone, is invaluable. It tells us that James had grown up in the same home as the Lord Jesus Christ. He could have traded on that. Nowadays he would have been a popular guest of TV talk shows and featured on the front page of periodicals and in lead articles. James, himself, never so much as mentions it. Perhaps it is because for the thirty some years he spent in the same home as the Lord Jesus he was a convinced unbeliever.

The long-established belief is that James died a cruel, martyr's death in Jerusalem. He was caught by the Scribes and Pharisees at the southeast angle of the temple wall where the pinnacle of the temple stood. That was where Satan had once urged the Lord Jesus to cast Himself down. James was cast down from there by his enemies. He fell near the place where the cloth-fullers had their workshop. They, finding him still alive, finished him off with their hammers.

A. James and the Lord of Glory

1. What Confused James

Let us spend some time, in thought, in that Nazareth home. James was a born Pharisee. The tradition is that he was a Nazarite. It is not likely that he was a lifelong Nazarite in the sense that Samson was or Samuel or John the Baptist. But it is quite consistent with what we know of his character that, at a young age, James took a Nazarite vow. If so, he drank no wine, ate nothing that came from the vine, ate no animal food, kept clear of funerals, and allowed his hair to grow long. He was zealous for the Mosaic Law. He fasted often, prayed long prayers, tithed with meticulous care, was attached to rabbinic Judaism, and was scrupulous in the externals of the Jewish religion.

What confused James was that Jesus was not at all like that. Jesus had a disconcerting way of seeing God in things which had nothing to do with religion. Jesus would just as soon go out on the mountains to pray as attend the synagogue, although He was punctilious in keeping all the demands of the Mosaic Law. Jesus had not come to destroy the Law but to fulfill it. Each of the Ten Commandments was kept by the Lord in that Nazareth home as those commandments had never been kept before, and as they have never been kept since. He kept them in the letter and in the spirit. He kept them in the way He later interpreted them in the Sermon on the Mount. By precept and example, He simply took those laws, lifted them far beyond all reach, explained what they were all about, then He kept them. He kept every jot and tittle of the Law and every one of its high and holy intentions.

But James could not see that. James felt that keeping the law meant keeping it the way he was taught by the local rabbi in the nearby synagogue. To keep the Sabbath, for instance, meant keeping all the tiresome, tedious traditions of the elders.

By the time of Jesus, the Mishna was well on its way to replacing the Bible. Instead of the one concise statement of the Mosaic Law, for instance, concerning the keeping of the Sabbath, the Mishna spelled out some forty different kinds of labor that were forbidden. It was forbidden to untie a knot, to sew two stitches, to light a fire, or to carry anything from one place to another. A tailor might not take his needle in his hand before nightfall on Sabbath Eve because he might forget he had it and go out with it, and that would be work. It was forbidden to read by lamplight on the Sabbath because the reader might tilt the lamp, and that would be work. A person could suck a candy on the Sabbath only if he put it in his mouth before the Sabbath began and only if it was done to keep his breath sweet. If it fell out of his mouth and he put it back, he broke the Sabbath, for that would be work.

James thought that kind of thing was necessary. Jesus thought it was nonsense. He was no Nazarite, no Scribe, no Pharisee. That confused James. He would have been far more comfortable with Jesus if He had been an ascetic like John the Baptist, or a radical like Saul of Tarsus. James would have found it far easier to believe in his Brother if Jesus had worn a raiment of camel hair and made His diet of locusts and wild honey, and if He had His dwelling among the rocks and caves of the wilderness. He would, indeed, have been more comfortable with Jesus if, like Bar Cochba, He had led a revolt against Rome.

There is something fascinating about the thought that Jesus and James lived together for so long under the same roof. Imagine, thirty years eating every meal at the same table with Jesus! Thirty years going to bed in the same room with Jesus! Working six days a week in the same workshop with Jesus! Going up on the seventh day to the same synagogue with Jesus! They played together and went to the village school together. Imagine having such an older brother as Jesus! He would keep a watchful eye on James until James was old enough to keep a watchful eye on Joses. He would protect him from school bullies. He would help with his homework. They learned their psalms and sacred history and the commandments of the Law together.

With the other brothers and sisters, He went through the baptism of sorrow when Joseph died, and Mary was left a widow. We can be quite sure that Jesus had some precious, wonderful words to say to the bereaved family that night after the funeral. There would be a word, too, of assurance. Everything would be all right. He would take charge of the family business. James must have often marveled at the craftsmanship of Jesus. No shoddy work would ever come out of that shop and no poor person, we can be sure, was ever pressed to pay his bill.

Then, when Jesus was about thirty years of age, news came to Nazareth. Down there at Bethabara beyond Jordan, a fiery evangelist preached repentance and the imminent coming of the Christ. Weekday and Sabbath day alike, it was the talk of the town, as it was throughout the length and breadth of the land.

At last a band of farmers, fishermen, and tradesmen decided to go off and see for themselves what was going on. Jesus of Nazareth, still known only by that Name, went too. Then it happened! They went to hear John preach. They saw the crowds, saw the hostility of the religious authorities, saw long lines of people coming forward at the invitation to publicly repent and to declare their desire to be ready for the coming of Christ by being baptized in the Jordan. And to their astonishment Jesus went forward to be baptized.

James must have stared. For whatever he may or may not have understood about Jesus, he knew full well that a more godly, gracious, kind, compassionate, or truly holy man than Jesus had never lived. Why would *He* need to submit to a baptism of repentance? Certainly James felt that he himself, wrapped in all his rabbinical and Pharisaical righteousness, had no need for *that*.

But there was more. The preacher saw Him coming. First he remonstrated with Him, then he baptized Him, and then the miracle happened. The heavens opened, the Spirit of God came down like a dove and abode upon Him. John the Baptist, moreover, proclaimed to the people that this Man, Jesus, was "the Lamb of God that taketh away the sin of the world" (see John 1:29).

We can be sure that word of the event must have spread through Nazareth like a forest fire driven by the wind. What did James make of it all? He simply did not believe it. He could not and would not accept the fact that the Boy he had known, that the Teenager he had known, that the Man he had known, was the promised Messiah. The town carpenter? God over all, blessed forevermore? Never! Jesus was a *good* Man—James would be the first to acknowledge that—but the *God*-Man? It was blasphemous. His mother could have told him it was true. Perhaps she did, but James did not believe it.

Then Jesus came back home and on the Sabbath went as usual with the family to the synagogue. Every eye was on Him now, but, as He Himself declared, "A prophet is not without honor except in his own country and among his own people" (see Matt. 13:57). After a while He stood, went forward, took the Isaiah scroll, and read a messianic passage everyone knew by heart. Then He announced that He was the One of whom the prophet wrote.

The synagogue broke into an uproar, and there was a determined and concerted effort to get rid of this blasphemous carpenter. They rushed Him out of town, convinced it would be doing God a service to throw Him headlong over the heights above the city. Nobody could ever explain what happened next. Doubtless, no two stories were alike. The only thing people knew was that Jesus had eluded his captors. James must have been acutely embarrassed by the whole affair.

Then news came that Jesus was preaching far and wide and, by all account, performing the most astonishing miracles that could be imagined. James did not believe. He endorsed the story that Jesus was mad and tried to persuade his Brother to give up His unorthodox proceedings—for the sake of the family if for no other reason. He wrote Him off as a religious fanatic whose strange ideas had somehow turned His head.

So there we have what *confused* him. James was too close. Jesus was too human. The sheer, magnificent *humanity* of Jesus blinded James to His *Deity*. James could not see the forest for the trees.

2. What Convinced James

James must have suffered tortures when Jesus was arrested, arraigned, condemned, and crucified. What an utter disgrace! What shame upon the whole family! To think he, James, a Pharisee of the Pharisees, had a Brother who was crucified like a common criminal alongside other criminals. He was so shamed, and so callous, he could even leave his mother to go to the cross by herself. He, James, was not going to be seen at the public execution of his Brother. Not him! Thus it was that Jesus consigned the care of His mother to His close friend and disciple, John; a charge John carried, likely with great joy.

So then, what did convince James? Jesus did! We have the golden words of Paul, written about Him long afterward. "He was seen of James . . ." he says (1 Cor. 15:7). No details are given of that momentous meeting. We do not know when it was or where it was, but we can picture a likely enough scene.

James has come home and is busy in the carpenter's shop. He hears a noise and looks up, and there, smiling at him, is Jesus. "Shalom James," He says. James is soon convinced. He, like doubting Thomas, is invited to come and inspect the nail prints for himself. From then on he becomes a committed believer in the Lord Jesus.

He won over the family too, it seems. For they were all together, in the upper room in Jerusalem, when the day of Pentecost came and the church was born. James was one of the charter members of the church. He became, indeed, one of its most important figures, a veritable pillar of the great Jewish congregation in Jerusalem.

B. James and the Law of God

James never did, however, shake off his addiction to Judaism. He was the most Jewish of all Jewish Christians. Although he became a believer of believers, he remained to the very end a Hebrew of the Hebrews.

Paul would describe himself thus in later years: "Circumcised the eighth day, of the stock of Israel, of the tribe of Benjamin, an Hebrew of the Hebrews; as touching the law a Pharisee . . . touching the righteousness which is in the law, blameless" (Phil. 3:5–6). Paul learned to write that worthless inventory off, but James never did.

James was half a Pharisee to the very end. He became the presiding elder of the Jerusalem church and did as much as anyone to keep it narrow, exclusive, and legalistic. He was chief elder of a church that remained exclusive and legalistic to the end, a church that soon stagnated in the backwaters of Christianity until, at last, its members were scattered and its center destroyed.

Paul met James in Jerusalem. After his spectacular conversion, Paul had gone off to Arabia to sort things out. He needed to rethink his theology. He had to unlearn all the traditions the rabbis had pounded into his head. He had to rethink his Old Testament in the light of the cross. He had to think much about the person of Christ whose resurrection appearance had convinced him that He was indeed alive from the dead and that He was God's eternal, uncreated, self-existing Son. Paul came back from Arabia with New Testament doctrine well established in his orderly and brilliant mind.

Some time later Paul came to Jerusalem for a two-week period with the special intention of meeting Peter. The two must have spent an unforgettable two weeks together. We can picture the scene: "First, I will take you to the place, Paul, where Jesus wept over the city. Ah! And this is where I was when I denied Him. Here is the Pavement in front of Pilate's Palace. Now we will go to Golgotha. Then I will take you to the garden tomb."

For some reason Paul did not meet any of the other apostles, just Peter and James. We can be sure that James did not quite know what to make of this cultured, educated, Hellenist Jew, once so prominent in the councils of the

Sanhedrin, once so distinguished for his rabbinical training, his elegant Greek, and his Roman citizenship.

Paul came from a different world than James. He was no Galilean peasant like James. He was a clever, capable cosmopolitan with a trained mind, the vision of an Alexander, and a boundless store of energy and enthusiasm. James and Paul came from opposite poles. It was almost inevitable that they would clash.

James, we can be sure, was more than a little suspicious of Paul's theology. As for his claim to be an apostle to the Gentiles no less, well, James would have a great deal of trouble with that. For James was a legalist from first to last. It was doubtless well-known to James that Judaizing legalists dogged Paul's footsteps, that they tried to subvert his Gentile converts with false teaching—if they were to be Christians, they must be circumcised and keep the Law of Moses.

Things came to a head in Antioch. Then one day an indignant Paul, trailing a band of troubled followers, appeared in Jerusalem to insist that a stop be put to this kind of thing once and for all. Moreover, he had brought a Gentile by the name of Titus with him, determined to make him a test case. Would the Jerusalem church accept a saved but uncircumcised Gentile into its fellowship? They could talk as much as they pleased, but *that* would force them to declare themselves once and for all.

There was a conference and a very hot one it was, indeed. James was the presiding elder. He listened respectfully to Barnabas—Barnabas was a sound man. He listened to Paul and heard him tell the long tale of conversions among the Gentiles. Not that he was greatly impressed by that. He was more impressed by the size and importance of the Jerusalem church and by the fact that many Jewish priests had been saved. He listened with growing astonishment as Peter stood up and endorsed the Gentile cause. Then everyone turned to him.

For a moment everything swung in the balance. James was a legalist to the core. He would have dearly loved to have thrown the full weight of his position and prestige on the side of Judaizers, but he did not dare. The Holy Spirit would not let him. Reluctantly, but resolutely, he endorsed the principle of the freedom of Gentile converts from the shackles of the Mosaic Law. It is evident, however, that his heart was not in it. He endorsed the restrictions appended to the letter that ultimately emerged from that conference.

In the intervening years, Paul continued his mission and came back to Jerusalem after his third triumphant missionary journey. This time he brought with him a larger sampling of his Gentile converts. He also brought a large cash donation for the Jerusalem church from Gentile converts in churches far and wide. So far as the record goes, James never so much as said, "Thank you." On the contrary, he tried to shackle Paul with his own legalistic scruples, sent him off into the temple area with some Nazarites who were terminating their vow, and saddled him with the very considerable combined expense that was entailed in that process. Then, there in the temple court, Paul was attacked, arrested, and thereafter in danger of his life. So far as we can see, James and the Jerusalem church did nothing. They washed their hands of him and left him to fend as best he could, a prisoner of Caesar.

C. James and the Life of Grace

We are not yet quite through with James. He wrote a book. In fact, it was probably the very first New Testament book. Typically it was addressed to Jews. In terms of its contents it belongs, in some ways, more with the Old Testament than with the New. It was probably written just before the Jerusalem Conference, the Conference that struck Jewish shackles forever off the wrists of Gentile Christians.

The book is remarkable for its poetic vein. Perhaps James derived his poetic flair from his mother, whose magnificat is a marvel of inspired poetry. James throws everything into picturesque and dramatic form in his book. It abounds in passionate exclamations, rapid questions, and graphic word pictures. Indeed, it reads more like a harangue than a letter. It has all the fiery sternness and vehemence of an Old Testament prophecy. James attacks all kinds of things—pride, greed, strife, wealth, selfishness, and partiality. He deals with temptation, good works, and sins of the tongue.

He parades across his pages diverse Old Testament characters—Abraham, Rahab, Job, and Elijah. He alludes to seventeen Old Testament books, and he makes at least fifteen allusions to the Apocrypha.

More than any other book, it reads like the Sermon on the Mount, even though James was probably not there when it was given. That sermon, however, was already famous and well known to Peter and John, who were friends of James. Better still, James could think back to the astonishing thirty years when the contents of that sermon had been *lived* before him in that Nazareth home.

His book is almost as remarkable for what it leaves out as for what it includes. Christ is named only twice. There is no reference to the incarnation, to the work of redemption, to the resurrection, or to the Ascension. Moreover, the morality upon which James insists is not founded on Christian principles but upon Jewish legal principles. Indeed, James was not trying to write a theological treatise at all. He was making a moral appeal, demanding that Christians have a belief that behaves. Paul's great word is *faith*. Peter's great word is *hope,* John's great word is *love,* and James's great word is *works*.

He writes about *what we see.* "When you read your Bible," he says, "it is like looking in a mirror. Be careful you don't go away and forget what it was you saw" (see James 1:23).

He writes about *why we sin.* We sin because we lust. The father of sin is the Devil, the mother of sin is lust. When lust conceives it brings forth sin. When sin is through it brings forth death.

He writes about *where we slip.* Someone comes along in obvious financial need. We have enough and to spare. If all we do is pass along some pious platitude to the needy one, James says, we are spiritually bankrupt.

He writes about *who we snub.* Two people come into the local gathering of God's people. One is dressed in poor clothes and the other is richly clad. We show preference to the rich man and snub the poor man. James says we are partial and guilty of evil thoughts.

He writes about *what we say.* He likens the tongue to something untamable, to a fire, a world of iniquity. He says that the person who can control his tongue is perfect.

He writes about *why we squabble.* It is because we have a worldly spirit. Don't we know that friendship with the world is enmity with God?

He writes about *who we serve.* We are to submit to God; resist the Devil; draw near to God and He will draw near to us.

He writes about *what we show.* We show men whether or not we are truly saved—by our works. Faith is important, but faith without works is dead.

He writes about *when we suffer.* If we are sick, we should look to the cause. If it is spiritual in nature, then the healing must be spiritual in nature.

There is no doubt that grace transformed James. Although he was a rigid man and narrow in his views, he evidently practiced what he preached. It must have been no small task to shepherd the Jerusalem church. It was very large, and its members came from all walks of life. Many of them came from the cultured elite of Judaism and brought much of their religious baggage with them. The Sanhedrin frowned upon it all. Volatile passions could quickly erupt. The Jerusalem church needed a practical man, one who commanded the respect of the Jews. James was just such a man.

TWENTY-THREE

Nicodemus

A Man Born Twice

John 3:1–15; 7:50–53; 19:39

A. Nicodemus and the Christ
    1. His plan
    2. His plight
    3. His plea
        a. Three sudden stops
        b. Three simple steps
B. Nicodemus and the crowd
C. Nicodemus and the cross

Some scholars think that the Nicodemus who came to Jesus by night was Nicodemus ben Gorion, the brother of Josephus the historian. If so, Nicodemus was one of the three richest men in Jerusalem. If so, he became one of the poorest men, too, for his daughter was later seen gathering barley corns for food from under horses' hooves. If so, doubtlessly his poverty resulted from the persecution he suffered after becoming a Christian. If so, Nicodemus is certainly one of the richest men in heaven today.

We learn three things about him. In the book of John, the only gospel that mentions Nicodemus, we read about Nicodemus and the *Christ,* about Nicodemus and the *crowd,* and about Nicodemus and the *cross.* The first mention sets before us the *conversion* of this man. The second tells us about the *confession* of this man. The third records the *consecration* of this man.

A. NICODEMUS AND THE CHRIST

Nicodemus was "a man of the Pharisees," which tells us something about his *religion;* he was "a ruler of the Jews," which tells us something about his *rank.* He was unquestionably religious.

Normally, we equate the Pharisees with hypocrisy, because most of them were hypocrites. They acted a religious part on the stage of life. Most of the Pharisees, as the Gospels record, were avowed enemies of Jesus. But Nicodemus was not a hypocrite. He was sincerely religious. He fasted twice a week; tithed his income scrupulously, right down to the mint and herbs in his garden; kept holidays as holy days; and knew much of the Bible by heart. He was a religious conservative who espoused traditional teaching of the Scriptures and engaged in private and public prayer.

1. His Plan

Nicodemus had heard about Jesus. Indeed, it would have been difficult in those days for him not to have heard about Jesus. The young Preacher from the north had taken Jerusalem by storm—so much so that the Sanhedrin was considering what action to take against Him. Jesus had dared to call down God's wrath on those in the temple courts who were acting as money-changers and merchandisers, selling animals for sacrifice to visiting Jews. He had done even more. He had actually driven the men of commerce from of the temple and had called it "my Father's house."

The temple was the Sanhedrin's special preserve, and its concessions very profitable to certain high-placed members of that body. But the Sanhedrin was cautious in their response to Jesus because large numbers of people believed that He was a prophet.

Nicodemus came up with a plan. He would meet with Jesus privately. He would talk with Him man to man, perhaps counsel Him to temper zeal with caution, and try to get Him to see that it would do Him no good to infuriate the establishment (of which Nicodemus was a part).

He wasted no time in putting his plan into action. He arranged for a night visit, and he began in a condescending and confident way. "Rabbi," he said, giving Jesus the benefit of the doubt, "we know that thou art a teacher come from God: for no man can do these miracles that thou doest, except God be with him" (John 3:2). The stage was thus set for a revolution to take place in Nicodemus's soul. He was about to learn that Jesus was not just another man God had sent. Jesus was a man inhabited by God, a man who actually was God. And He was not just a rabbi or a teacher. He spoke with authority, not as the scribes spoke. In one sentence, Jesus would sweep away everything on which Nicodemus had been depending for salvation.

2. His Plight

The Lord summarily dismissed the patronage of this influential, well-disposed, and devoutly religious senator. "Verily, verily, I say unto thee," Jesus said, "Except a man be born again, he cannot see the kingdom of God" (John 3:3). Jesus swept away all Nicodemus's scrupulous attention to the ritual requirements of the ceremonial law; all his punctilious observance of religious rules; all his fasting, tithing, and praying; all his almsgiving and good works; all his reliance on circumcision, keeping of the Sabbath, and observance of the feasts; all his sacrifices and offerings; all his trust in racial pedigree, attainments, and status as a member of the Sanhedrin. Jesus said, in effect, "What you need, Nicodemus, is to be born again."

Nicodemus was so utterly dead in sin, not the least of which was religious sin, that there was only one remedy—a new birth!

Strange to say, Jesus' revolutionary, radical statement struck a responsive chord in this old man's soul. He was already acutely aware that all his religious observances, all his moral rectitude, and all his good works and attention to ritual had not stilled the small voice of conscience that told him such practices were not enough. Nicodemus did not question Jesus' startling statement. He did not ask, "Why?" He knew why. If *he* was not satisfied with himself, how could he expect God to be satisfied? If he was aware of unconfessed, uncleansed, and unconscionable sin deep, deep within his soul—how much more was God aware of it?

Yes, that was what he needed. He needed to be born again. The most obvious thing about a newborn baby is that he has no past, only a future. So the Lord not only revealed the plight, He gave a hint as to the remedy. And Nicodemus seized it. Instead of asking, "Why?" he asked, *"How?"* "How can a man be born when he is old?" (John 3:4).

The Lord replied, "Except a man be born of water and of the Spirit, he cannot enter into the kingdom of God" (John 3:5).

Doubtlessly that startled Nicodemus too. The recent preaching of John the

Baptist had shaken the whole land from Dan to Beersheba, including all Jerusalem and Judea. "I indeed baptize you with water unto repentance," John cried, "but he that cometh after me . . . shall baptize you with the Holy Ghost" (Matt. 3:11). Note John's reference to water and the Spirit. John had been baptizing thousands of people in the Jordan river. He had been preaching *repentance;* his baptism was one of repentance. To be "born of water" simply meant repentance. To a man, the Sanhedrin, led by the Pharisees, had rejected John and all that he stood for—especially his baptism of repentance.

Jesus brought Nicodemus back to that teaching. No John, no Jesus. That was the formula. If there were no water baptism there could be no Spirit baptism. Without repentance, there could be no regeneration.

In effect Jesus said, "What you need, Nicodemus, is to go down to John at the Jordan river—religious man that you are, respectable man that you are, rich man that you are, ruler that you are—and repent and be baptized. When you have received John's baptism after confessing your need of repentance, your heart will be ready to receive the next work of God, the baptism of the Holy Spirit—*regeneration*. Then you will be born again."

That was strong medicine for Nicodemus. It is strong medicine for every religious person to face the fact that religion will not save him, that only repentance and regeneration can effect the kind of new birth that puts a child of Adam's ruined race into the family of God.

3. His Plea

"How?" Nicodemus asked again. "How can these things be?" (John 3:9). He had studied the Bible since he was a boy. He had been a diligent pupil of the rabbis. He had absorbed the precepts of the great religious teachers of the age. One of his colleagues was the learned Gamaliel. Yet his studies had all been in vain. His Bible teachers had been blind leaders of the blind. Nicodemus, too, had become a blind leader of the blind. He was a walking Bible encyclopedia, but he had missed the most important lesson of all—he needed to be born again. Learned scholar that he was, biblically literate as he was in the schools and seminaries of men, Nicodemus confessed to Jesus that he did not know how to be born again. Is there a sadder page than this in all of the Bible? Here was a sincere, studious, and scholarly old man who was as lost as any pagan in spite of having spent his life in religious pursuits.

"How can these things be?" Nicodemus asked. We can thank God for this word *how* because most religious people ask *why* and want to challenge the statement that their personal morality, religious observances, and good behavior will not get them into the kingdom of God. Nicodemus's question led to his salvation.

Consider Jesus' reply. (If you want to know "how," it's all there.) Jesus answered the question in two ways. We must look at the *illustration* Jesus gave right here in John 3, and we must look at the *illumination* Jesus gave in John 1.

We begin with what Jesus said in John 1: "He came unto his own, and his own received him not. But as many as received him, to them gave he power to become the sons of God, even to them that believe on his name: which were born, not of blood, nor of the will of the flesh, nor of the will of man, but of God" (vv. 11–13).

These verses contain the nearest thing we have in the New Testament to a formula, the nearest thing to an equation of salvation. Notice the three *sudden stops* in verse thirteen and the three *simple steps* in verse twelve.

a. Three Sudden Stops

The following three negatives strike down all man's natural hopes for salvation: "Which were born, not of blood, nor of the will of the flesh, nor of the will of man."

Man's salvation is "not of blood"; that is, it is *not of human descent*. It has nothing to do with *the purity of one's pedigree*. The Jews, of course, thought that salvation had everything to do with blood. They thought that they had an automatic ticket to heaven just because they were Jews and were "Abraham's seed."

Many people today believe the same thing. They think that they are Christians because they were born into a "Christian" country or because they were born into a Christian home. Years ago our neighbor attended a church service and heard a message on the subject of being born again. Afterward I asked him, "What did you think of the message? Did you feel any need to be born again?"

His answer was ludicrous, especially from an otherwise intelligent man. "My wife," he said, "is a descendant of John Wesley." That would be like asking a man if he were married and hearing him say, "I had an aunt once who went to a wedding."

I replied, "That's interesting. Your wife is a descendant of John Wesley. Well, John Wesley certainly knew what it meant to be born again. He was a preacher for years before experiencing the new birth for himself. But being a descendant of John Wesley is not going to help you very much. I'm a descendant of Noah myself, and that didn't help me."

Being born into a Christian home does not make a person a Christian any more than being born in a stable would make him a horse. Our salvation is "not of blood." It is not of human descent. It has nothing to do with the purity of our religious pedigree. Jesus said so.

Then comes another sudden stop: "Nor of the will of the flesh." Salvation is *not of human desire*. It has nothing to do with *the fervor of one's feelings*. Few things in this world arouse the passions of men more than their religious beliefs. They will die for those beliefs; they will massacre and murder people over their religious beliefs. People feel strongly about their religious beliefs, and most people put a great deal of confidence in their feelings. But no amount of wishful thinking, no amount of religious ecstasy, will put a person into the family of God.

There is one more sudden stop: "Nor of the will of man." Salvation is *not of human design*. It has nothing to do with *the confession of one's creed*. Men have invented all kinds of creeds and a thousand ways to get to heaven. To be saved, people are urged to do this, that, or the other. They must make this pilgrimage or engage in that fast. They must give to this cause or that one. They must subscribe to this or that set of rules. They must undergo this ritual or perform that rite. The Holy Spirit rules out all such effort. Salvation is not of the will of man.

So God says to the religious person, "Stop!" To become a child of God and an heir of heaven is not a matter of birth, breeding, or behavior. It is not a matter of desiring or doing. Salvation operates on an altogether different principle.

Here we should look at the Lord's *illustration* in John 3. He reminded Nicodemus of a historic day in Israel's history. The children of Israel, on their way from Egypt to Canaan, were murmuring, grumbling, criticizing, and complaining almost every step of the way. God sent a plague of fiery serpents among them as punishment. A serpent's bite meant certain death, and there was no human remedy. In His mercy, however, God provided a way of escape, a means of salvation. Nicodemus knew the story well.

Moses made a serpent of brass and hung it on a pole. He told the smitten Israelites simply to look and live. Just look at that brazen serpent—it was a picture of Christ "made . . . sin for us" (2 Cor. 5:21)—hung upon a cross. Look! And live!

This remedy makes no sense at all to human reasoning. The scientist would say, "What nonsense. There is no correlation at all between serpent venom and a brass serpent on a pole. There is simply no way that looking at that thing can save anyone."

The psychologist would say, "We must look for the cause of our problem in some childhood inhibition, some aberration of personality brought about by repressive parents. The thing for us to do is to express ourselves. There is no way that looking at that brass serpent will effect a proper personality adjustment and remove the psychological cause of these painful feelings."

The Christian Scientist would say, "Our problem is simply an error of mortal mind. There is no such thing as pain, and death is not real."

The liberal theologian would say, "There was no such person as Moses, and even if there were, he would not have been able to read and write. So we can discount the whole story as Hebrew mythology. In any case, there could not have been a miraculous cure because all miracles have a rational explanation."

The medical doctor would say, "Serpent venom is a highly complex chemical. We need to develop a serum and immunize the population. It is obvious to medical science that just looking at that serpent on the pole is no antidote to snake venom."

The legalist would say, "We need to get back to the law and do our best to keep it. We can only be saved by our good works."

The religionist would say, "What is needed is for each individual to offer a costly sacrifice."

The optimist would say, "I'm related to Moses. I'm sure that is going to help me."

But the solution to the Israelites' problem was "Look and live." That is still God's answer to the venom of sin that courses through our spiritual veins, bringing death in its wake. That serpent, nailed to that cross, pointed to Calvary and to the time when the Lord Jesus, who knew no sin, was to be made sin for us. All we have to do is look and live.

b. Three Simple Steps

In John 1, not only are there three sudden stops to consider; there are also three steps. "As many as received him, to them gave he power to become the sons of God, even to them that believe on his name" (John 1:12). There is the formula: Believe! Receive! Become! Two of these three action words refer to our part in being born again. The other refers to God's part in the process. Our part is to believe and receive. God says, "Become!"

The first thing we must do is to *believe*—but not just anything. We are to believe on something specific—His name. His name is *Jesus!* When Scripture tells us to "believe on his name," it simply means that we are to believe on that for which His name stands. His name has a special and significant meaning. When the Lord Jesus was born, the angel said to Joseph, "Thou shalt call his name JESUS: for he shall save his people from their sins" (Matt. 1:21). Therefore, to "believe on his name" means that we acknowledge our sins and need for a Savior. It means that we believe that the Lord Jesus Christ can and will save us from our sins. He is the One whom God has provided to save us from sin's penalty, power, and presence. The Lord Jesus can do this because of the cross. He told Nicodemus that He would deal with the universal problem of sin on the cross. He, the Lord Jesus, would bear the world's sins in His own body on the tree.

We must also *receive.* The salvation promise is given to as many as receive Him. We can believe something in our heads without believing it in our hearts. We can give intellectual assent to a truth, yet never allow that truth to change our lives. I can believe that Jesus is *the* Savior yet not be able to say that He is *my* Savior. To make Him ours, we must receive Him.

Suppose someone were to offer you a book. You believe that he is sincere in offering it to you. You believe that the book is valuable, well worth owning, and that it would be a help to you. You really believe that the person intends for you to have it. Does that make the book yours? Of course not. You must receive it. The book is not yours until you do.

Likewise, God offers us Jesus as our only possible Savior from sin. We must receive Him. We must respond, "Lord Jesus, I believe You died on the cross to save me from my sin. I take You as my Savior. Come now and live Your life in me."

That is man's part: believe and receive. When we do our part the miracle happens. God does His part. He says "become," and He gives us instant "power to *become* the sons of God"! Instantly the miracle of new life takes place in our souls. We are regenerated: born again; born from above; born of God. The Holy Spirit of the living God comes, takes up permanent residence in our lives, and imparts to us the very life of God. That is the way we are born again. Nicodemus asked, "How?" That's how.

B. Nicodemus and the Crowd

The second time we read about Nicodemus, he is with his own crowd—the other members of the Sanhedrin. Everyone has his crowd, and any crowd can be intimidating. The Sanhedrin was a Christ-rejecting crowd. It was a jeering, scoffing crowd.

We see Nicodemus standing up for Christ against that crowd. He is not overly brave about it. He does not say much when they sneer at him and suggest that he is ignorant and out of touch. But at least he puts in a favorable word for Jesus. It is always a good sign when a person who has been born again stands up for Christ—even when his old friends become new enemies because of Jesus.

C. Nicodemus and the Cross

Nicodemus did not really begin to live for Jesus until the significance of Calvary dawned on his soul. When he finally saw what the world was like by what it did to Jesus, then he broke with the world once and for all. By means of Christ's crucifixion, Nicodemus was crucified to the world and the world was crucified to him. After Calvary he no longer cared what his crowd thought about his allegiance to Christ. Nicodemus lost all fear of what the world might do. The cross revolutionized his thinking about his evil world—all its values and vanities. He was through with it. He stood up to be counted for Christ, boldly and triumphantly.

Perhaps he said to himself, *I may have been too big a coward to be anything but a secret disciple of the Lord Jesus during His life, but I certainly intend to identify with Him in His death and resurrection. Right now He needs a royal burial. Joseph of Arimathea has a tomb. I have the treasure. I'll invest the price of a king's ransom in spices and see to it that Jesus' body is wrapped in the rarest ointments and the costliest linens. He may not need the tomb for long, but it will be His for as long as He needs it.*

That type of response is always a good sign of a genuine new birth. When a new believer looks at his world in light of the cross, and thereafter dies to that world and lives for Jesus, it is proof enough that he has been born again.

The cross made the difference in Nicodemus's life. We have no evidence that he actually visited the cross, although the likelihood is high that he did. Certainly the implications of the Sanhedrin's dreadful decision must have stabbed his conscience into full wakefulness at last. He knew that he should have taken a bolder stand for Christ years earlier. Now Christ was nailed to a Roman cross, and Nicodemus's cowardice and compromise came home forcefully to his conscience.

Enough was enough. Nicodemus decided not to compromise any longer. He sought out his colleague, Joseph of Arimathea, and bared his soul. The two old men looked at each other, horror-struck at how the fast-paced events of the previous dreadful day had overtaken the nation. Jesus, the Christ, had been crucified! It was too late now for them to undo whatever damage their silence had done. We can picture the scene as it might unfold.

"Well, Joseph," Nicodemus says, "there's still something we can do. We can give His body an honorable burial."

"I've picked up a rumor," Joseph replies, "that our unscrupulous colleagues in the high priest's party are quite prepared to have the body thrown into Gehinnom."

"Never! Not so long as I have a breath in my body!" Nicodemus exclaims. "Aren't you building a tomb here in Jerusalem, off the Damascus road?"

"Indeed I am," Joseph says, "but it's His tomb as of now. Moreover, I'm going to Pilate right now to beg for the body. I have a feeling that he'll give it to me, if only to spite Caiaphas."

"Yes indeed," says Nicodemus, "and what's more, my friend, you and I will be fulfilling an ancient prophecy. Remember the words of Isaiah? 'With the rich in his death' [Isa. 53:9]. You supply the sepulcher, and I'll supply the spices."

And so Nicodemus purchased one hundred pounds of costly aromatic spices with which to embalm Jesus' body, and has been loved for doing so all the ages of the church on earth.

It was the cross that did it. What happened at Calvary opened the eyes of Nicodemus, took away his fear of his fellows, and put the cross between himself and the world. Had he known the deathless words of Isaac Watts in the following hymn, "When I Survey the Wondrous Cross," Nicodemus might well have said,

> When I survey the wondrous cross
> On which the Prince of glory died,
> My richest gain I count but loss,
> And pour contempt on all my pride.
> Were the whole realm of nature mine,
> That were a present far too small:
> Love so amazing, so divine,
> Demands my soul, my life, my all.[1]

---

1. Isaac Watts, "When I Survey the Wondrous Cross," 1707.

TWENTY-FOUR

The Woman at the Well

John 4

A. THE WOMAN AT THE WELL
   1. The harsh realities of life
   2. The hidden realities of life
   3. The hypocritical realities of life
B. THE WOMAN AND HER WITNESS
   1. Her silent witness
   2. Her spoken witness

She was likely the loneliest woman in the world. The trouble was, she was far too good looking and far too popular with the men. One can well imagine the gossip that surrounded her name, for human nature hasn't changed a bit, not even in two thousand years.

We can see two women from the city meeting for a few minutes in the market. Says Mrs. Bigmouth to her friend, "You'll never guess the latest."

Says Fanny Gossip, "Oh yes I can. Mrs. Snoop told me when I called in on her this morning. Liz is back on the market. Husband number five has just tossed her out on the street."

Says Mrs. Bigmouth, "My, you are a one for old history aren't you, Mrs. Gossip. Haven't you heard the very latest? She's just moved in with Sniffles the magistrate."

Says Mrs. Gossip, "Oh yes, I did hear that. Well you mark my words, she will make a muggins out of him before she is much older."

Not that the men are any better. When Liz walks by, their eyes follow her down the village street and their tongues wag as hard as any. Some of the idlers are sitting in the shade outside the Sychar Tavern. There is old Mugwart. Liz passes him on her way to the well. She walks straight and tall, her water pot held high, her eyes straight ahead, her nose tilted in disdain. Says Mugwart, "There goes Liz, fellas."

Says young Gribbles, "Liz who? Liz Boozer, wife of the winemaker? Or Liz Bigfoot, wife of the sexton? Or Liz Mizer, wife of the goldsmith? Or Liz Faceache, wife of the apothecary? Or Liz Jingleslap, wife of the jailer? Never can keep up with which Liz she is."

Says Wiggles, "Haven't you heard boys? She's just shacked up with Sam Sniffles. You mark my words, she will take him for a bundle before long."

And so this woman was the butt of the village gossips. And certainly it seems that, to some extent, she deserved the likely remarks made behind her back and even to her face. We do not know her name. We do not know her age. We do not even know why she was so shopworn and soiled. We simply know her as the woman at the well, for it is as such that we are introduced to her by the aged apostle John.

A. The Woman at the Well

On her way to the well that day, this woman met twelve men, all Jews, all disciples of Jesus. They would have passed her by on the other side. She, we can be sure, gave them her haughtiest look, and they kept the width of the road between her and them. For she was a woman of Samaria, and between Jews and Samaritans little love was lost.

The racial prejudice was very old and its roots ran very deep. When the Assyrians invaded Israel hundreds of years ago, destroyed Samaria, and carried away into captivity ten of the tribes, they left behind them a spoiled and plundered land. Into that land they sent immigrants from other parts of their Empire, foreigners, pagans. Before long these pagans picked up a kind of pseudo-Judaism, a jumble of truth and error, a weird mixture of faith and falsehood. As time went on they considered themselves every bit as good as the Jews still living in Judea to the south. After Nebuchadnezzar carried the Jews themselves into captivity, they considered themselves a good deal better.

When the Jews came back from captivity, the Samaritans were quite prepared to offer them the right hand of fellowship, treat them as equals, as coreligionists, as heirs together of the same vital truths. The indignant Jews would have no part of it. And bitter hostility was born, hostility that lasted for centuries.

So the Lord's disciples certainly had no intention of lowering themselves to talk to a Samaritan woman. And the Samaritan woman had no intention either of passing the time of day with a dozen Jews trespassing in Samaria. So they passed each other by. The Lord's disciples went on their way, wrapped in religious prejudice, congratulating each other that they had not demeaned themselves in talking to a Samaritan woman. They had shown her! Maybe they had. But they had certainly not shown her Christ.

So that lonely woman went on her way to the well. As she drew near she saw something that must have annoyed her immensely. There was someone already there. The sole reason why she went to the well at the hour of high noon—when the sun was at its hottest, when sensible people found a shady spot for their midday meal and siesta—was so she could avoid people. Now there was someone at the well. Worse still, it was a man. And horrors, worst of all, another Jew.

Jesus ignored any contemptuous look she might have darted at Him as she came bustling up to the well, right to where He was sitting. He would have to be sitting on the well, of all places. Why couldn't He sit somewhere else? Not right there. Why? Because He had come that way just to meet her. She did not know it yet, but this was the day she was to meet Jesus. Her whole life was about to be changed.

He asked her for a drink. She must have almost dropped her bucket right down the well. That was how it started. In a simple, sublime, and, to the woman, utterly startling way. He asked her for a drink. He, a Jew, asked her, a woman of Samaria, for a drink. The Lord Jesus deliberately opened Himself to insult, to misunderstanding, to scorn, and to refusal. He did it because He wanted to win this lonely woman to Himself. "Give me to drink," He said.

And she tossed her pretty head and said, "How is it that thou being a Jew askest drink of me which am a woman of Samaria?"

And that is how it all began. With a caustic comment from a woman who considered herself every bit as good as, if not a good deal better than, this Jew. Now follows one of those wonderful conversations that take up such a large part of the gospel of John.

1. The Harsh Realities of Life

Jesus deals with her first along the line of the *physical*. Just for that woman to get sufficient water to drink and for the domestic uses around the house was very hard work. The water was heavy, the way was long, the sun was hot. She had to walk all the way from the village in the oppressive heat, carrying her water pot.

She had to get the water out of the well, which was very deep. She would have to let a bucket down about one hundred feet, draw it up, pour it into her water pot, and do it until her water pot was full. Then she would have to get that water pot on her shoulder or on her head, and she would have to carry it all the way back home. And if she did not use the strictest economy with that water, back she would have to come for more. Life was hard. So the Lord talked to her at the most convenient point of contact—water, thirst, need, desire.

For it was not only water that made her life hard. There were other things. She had other thirsts, other longings, other cravings besides water. Her life was filled, in fact, with unsatisfied longings. As a fresh young girl she had doubtless dreamed romantic dreams. She had always been able to get all the men she wanted. But, somehow, it had not satisfied.

She had thought she would be happy when she got married. That did not last. The honeymoon was soon over. Then she thought she would be happy when she got her divorce from husband number one. But divorce did not make her happy. Then she thought she would find happiness, perhaps, in a single's bar where she could meet another man. Then husband number two came along, and she thought he would make her happy. But that did not work out either. Nothing she had tried had satisfied the deep thirst of her soul.

She tried the broken cisterns of life, but she was still thirsty. Solomon had tried them too, many long centuries ago. He tried wisdom, but that did not make him happy. He tried collecting doctor's degrees, becoming the world's greatest intellectual, having his name and fame carried far and wide, being visited by celebrities. It was all so much emptiness. He soon grew tired of it when the novelty wore off.

He tried women, a thousand of them. Indeed, he must have spent much of his life going to his own weddings. He thought, *Maybe this one will be the one.* Then, *Maybe that one will make me happy.* It took him a thousand tries before he discovered that there was not a woman in the world—no matter how lovely she was, no matter how clever she was, no matter how exotic or different or desirable she might be—who could really meet the deepest hunger of his heart. Except one, perhaps, but she turned him down stone cold.

He tried wealth. He made money, lots of money. He had the Midas touch; everything he touched turned to gold. He was the smartest, the most successful Jewish businessman in all the world. Money flowed in a golden stream into his bank accounts, and he spent it as fast as it came in. He grew tired of it all. He thought he might just as well commit suicide. But, in the end, he wrote the book of Ecclesiastes instead—a sad dirge over the utter inability of anything under the sun to satisfy the deep, spiritual hunger of a human heart.

Like Solomon, this poor woman at the well was still thirsty. We are all born thirsty. The first need a baby has is to satisfy its thirst. The first time a baby cries is because it is thirsty. And as time goes on and we grow older, our thirsts increase. We take on new thirsts. We actually go out of our way to create thirsts that God never intended for us to have. A thirst for drink, a thirst for drugs, a thirst for tobacco, marijuana, angel dust, cocaine, and heroin. Until, at last, life for some becomes one vast craving for something that will satisfy.

Several years ago, at a church service in North Carolina, I met a nurse who shared her story with me. She said, "When I was a teenager, I thought I knew it all and nobody else knew anything. I had all the answers. But then I became a drug addict, and I continued being a drug addict until the Lord saved me after eleven long, miserable years.

"When I first started going with the crowd I thought I was doing something smart, but when I got hooked I found I was not so smart after all." Thousands of thousands of milligrams of tranquilizers, barbiturates, and other pills became her regular diet. She wanted to quit but could not. The habit took all the money she could make. It took food off the table, clothes off her children's back. She wanted to quit.

She tried the usual methods of withdrawal, and a doctor was able to get her off the habit by gradually reducing her dosage in a hospital. She was sent home cured. But twenty-four hours later, she started having withdrawal pains. She said, "I would break out in a cold sweat, I would be sick. My facial muscles would draw, my tongue became thick, when I tried to talk my mouth would distort round to the side of my face, the muscles on my legs and arms would draw, I would have severe stomach and abdominal pains. I would have hallucinations and horrible nightmares. I would have sold my soul for a fix. I lied, I stole, I cheated, I sold drugs to get money to get drugs."

And so it went on and on for eleven years of living hell. Time and time again she tried to quit, but each time, as soon as the withdrawal symptoms started, back she went again. Then she began to lose her eyesight. She lost weight. Her hair began to fall out, her teeth became loose. She became so desperate she took a can opener and slashed her flesh and licked the blood. Then one day she was saved.

She said, "I fell on my face before God. I cried, 'God have mercy on me. I am sorry for my life. I am sick of my life. I cannot go on this way. Please save me.'

And all that heavy burden lifted. I did not know it at that moment, but I had been born again. As the days went by I began to realize I had not the first desire for drugs, and I had not had a single withdrawal symptom."

It was five months before she could go back to work. She felt a sense of mental depression, but after awhile even that cleared up. She says, "For years now I have been on the nursing staff of a hospital. I put my hands all the time on the narcotics and drugs I used to use, drugs I used to steal. It is just as if I never had the habit. I am a new creature in Christ."

What Jesus did for this woman is what He intended to do for the woman at the well. Only her problem was not drugs but men. One would be tempted to think she had been born with that thirst. As she grew older she thought that she could fill the emptiness in her heart with men, when all the time she was really thirsty for God.

So Jesus offered her living water. "If thou knewest the gift of God," He said, the gift of God is eternal life through Jesus Christ our Lord. "If thou knewest the gift of God, and who it is that saith to thee, Give me to drink; thou wouldest have asked of him, and he would have given thee living water" (John 4:10).

After a moment's hesitation she said, "Where is this water coming from?" She still thought He was talking about literal water from Jacob's well.

He said, "Whosoever drinketh of this water shall thirst again: But whosoever drinketh of the water that I shall give him shall never thirst; but the water that I shall give him shall be in him a well of water springing up into everlasting life" (John 4:13–14).

She said, "Sir, give me this water, that I thirst not, neither come hither to draw" (John 4:15). She was tired of her life. She was still unsure what He was offering her, but she wanted it. The Lord Jesus had dealt with the harsh realities of life. He had planted in her heart a desire for a new way of life.

2. The Hidden Realities of Life

He dealt with her now along the line of the *moral*. She said, "Give me this water." He said, "Go, call thy husband, and come hither" (John 4:16). He deliberately touched a raw nerve and He knew it. But she could never have life everlasting until she faced the realities in her life, the deep hidden things, the things she thought He knew nothing about—her sin. He knew all about it. He did not condemn her, but neither did He cover up the festering moral sore in her life.

She brushed off the suggestion immediately with a half truth. "I have no husband," she said (John 4:17). Then Jesus showed her quite plainly that He knew all about the things that, for very shame, she would try to hide. He knew the whole sad story of husband after husband, until finally she decided just to move in with the next man without even bothering about the formality of marriage. The woman at the well embraced the moral climate so characteristic of our own day and age. It says that since marriages do not last anyway, why bother to get married at all—just shack up with whoever suits your fancy.

"Thou hast had five husbands," Jesus said bluntly, "and he whom thou now hast is not thy husband; in that saidst thou truly" (John 4:18). This woman's problem went much deeper than unsatisfied longings. It lay in her disregard of God's moral law. Until squarely, honestly, and uncompromisingly, she faced the sin question in her life, there was no way she could have that everlasting life of which Jesus had spoken to her. Standing there, before the kind but searching eyes of the Son of God, this woman felt suddenly ashamed of her immoralities, of her libertarian views, of her *sin*. Jesus never once mentioned the word. He did not need to. She knew her life was stained with sin no matter how hard she might try to brazen it out.

3. The Hypocritical Realities of Life

He deals with her along the line of the *spiritual*. The woman hastily changed the subject. She raised the question of comparative religion. "Our fathers worshipped in this mountain," she said, "and ye say, that in Jerusalem is the place where men ought to worship" (John 4:20). Jesus had said nothing of the kind. This was just a ploy to get Him off the subject of her sin. She was quite willing to discuss religion with Him. But the religion she professed to espouse had never satisfied her longings, had never dealt with the sin question in her life, and had never brought her anywhere near the everlasting life Jesus offered.

Jesus politely answered her comment. Then He confronted her with the true nature of God. "It is not a question of shrines or sacred places at all," He said (John 4:21, author's translation). "God is a Spirit: and they that worship him must worship him in spirit and in truth" (John 4:24). We must worship Him in spirit because of what He is. We must worship Him in truth because of what we are. Again He confronted her with what she was, a sinner, and now a hypocritical sinner trying to evade the issue by raising an argument about religion.

Then Jesus introduced a startling revelation. "The Father," He said, "seeketh such to worship him" (John 4:23). That was His favorite name for God—Father. His Father could be her Father. Indeed, His Father was actively seeking people willing to be honest, willing to be born again, born of the Spirit, to worship Him. That is exactly why Jesus had come to the well.

The woman again changed the subject. But she is now no longer evasive, just wanting to make sure. "I know that Messias cometh, which is called Christ: when he is come, he will tell us all things," she said (John 4:25). She is ready now for the final revelation of Christ to her soul.

"I that speak unto thee am he," He said (John 4:26). Now she knew it all. Knew her sin, knew her Savior, knew that she had come to the crossroads of life, knew that she was face to face with her decision. Then came one of those interruptions that so often occur at the critical moment when a soul is face to face with Christ. The disciples came back. All twelve of them, blundering in, breaking up this all important meeting at its most crucial moment. The woman quietly left. But she left a changed woman.

B. The Woman and Her Witness

The woman's witness was twofold.

1. Her Silent Witness

We read, "The woman then left her waterpot, and went her way into the city" (John 4:28). There were two reasons why she left that water pot. She left it for Jesus to use. It was her way of saying, "Lord, you have given me the greatest experience of my life. Now let me leave what little I have at Your feet for You to use. You have ministered to me, now let me minister to You. There is not much I can do for You, dear Lord, but I can at least let You have my water pot."

There was another reason why she left that water pot. She now had that wondrous water welling up in her soul. She was satisfied at last! The old physical nature, with its desires and demands, with its cravings and longings, was forgotten in the surging rush of new life that was now hers.

2. Her Spoken Witness

We read, "The woman . . . went her way into the city, and saith to the men . . . ," to the men she had lived with, to her five former husbands, and the man she had just moved in with, she said, "Come, see a man, which told me all things that I ever did: is not this the Christ?" (John 4:28–29). Then she brought the men to Jesus. And they, too, believed on Him. That was her spoken witness. What had happened to her was too good to keep to herself. She simply had to share it with others. Whom better with which to share her new birth than those who had shared her past life.

TWENTY-FIVE

The Prodigal Son

Luke 15:11–24

A. THE FAR HORIZONS
1. What the prodigal figured
2. What the prodigal forgot
3. What the prodigal found
    a. Fair-weather friends
    b. Far-reaching famine
B. THE FATHER'S HOUSE
1. His decision
    a. His situation
    b. His sin
2. His discovery
    a. A gracious father
    b. A glorious feast
    c. A great forgiveness

What is the finest short story ever told? Should we search the works of Rudyard Kipling, Jack London, or Edgar Allan Poe? The finest short story ever told was written nearly two thousand years ago. It is the story of the prodigal son. Not counting the appendix that deals with his older brother, the story of the prodigal is told in fewer than 350 words. Yet this story never grows old, never fails to charm, and never ceases to hammer home the greatness of our God.

This story is one of Jesus' deathless parables. Every one of His parables is a miracle in words. Every parable is an earthly story with a heavenly meaning; each is a matchless, priceless pearl of wisdom. The story of the prodigal son is essentially the story of a father's love.

Jesus came to teach us a new name for God. God had often revealed Himself in the Old Testament by means of His names. He was *Elohim, Jehovah, Adonai, El Elyon,* and *El Shaddai.* He was *Jehovah Jireh, Jehovah Shalom,* and *Jehovah Nissi.* He was the great I AM. He was the Creator, God Almighty, the Lord who provides, the Lord who is our peace, and the Lord who is our banner. The ages rolled by, and God lived up to the names by which He had progressively revealed Himself. Then Jesus came. He taught men a new name for God. He taught them that God is our *Father*—and nowhere more so than in the story of the prodigal son. This story, together with the companion story of the older brother, is simply the story of God as Father. Jesus speaks of God the Father twelve times in twenty-two short verses. If we miss God the Father, we miss the whole point of the parable.

Yet this parable is not without its detractors. Carping critics have found fault with this, the sweetest story ever told. Some say that there is no element of *search* in the parable. The father did not run after his wayward boy. He did not search the brothels, bars, and bawdy houses of the far-off country. He did not search through the dives and dens of sin. He did not haunt the gambling joints, the pleasure palaces, the back alleys, and the slums of the far country. He just let him go.

Others say that the parable has no element of *sacrifice* in it. God does not smile, nod, and lightly forgive. His holiness demands sacrifice. As Hebrews 9:22, says, "Without shedding of blood is no remission."

As usual, the critics are wrong. There *is* an element of search. When the prodigal son was far, far away, not a day passed that the father's heart did not follow the son into the distant country. The father did not run after his son because that never does any good.

Every day, however, the father searched the horizon for the first sign of the prodigal's return. Not a day passed when the father did not take up his watch on some vantage point and stare with tear-filled eyes down the dusty road that led away from home. We know that because when the prodigal decided to come home, "when he was yet a great way off, his father saw him, and had compassion, and ran, and fell on his neck, and kissed him" (Luke 15:20). Oh yes, the element of search is there. It is not overly emphasized in this story because the search has already been fully treated in the sister story of the lost sheep.

The parable of the prodigal also contains an element of sacrifice. It is astonishing how critics could have missed the feast's being founded on sacrifice. The father said, "Bring hither the fatted calf, and kill it; and let us eat, and be merry." Of course, there is an element of sacrifice. Jesus would not overlook that.

The story of the prodigal son revolves around two focal points: *the far horizons* and *the father's house*.

A. THE FAR HORIZONS

How do we measure the distance to the far country? Do we measure it in terms of *miles* or in terms of *morals?* Or do we measure it in terms of both? In the end the prodigal discovers that the far country is very distant indeed from the father's house—both in terms of miles and morals.

We could measure how far the prodigal traveled in terms of miles if we knew his starting point, (such as Jerusalem or Capernaum or Nazareth) and where he ended up (in such places as Antioch or Corinth or Rome). It would be simply a matter of mathematics or geography.

Suppose the prodigal headed north to Caesarea from Jerusalem. That would be about sixty-five miles. If he then sailed to Myra on the seacoast of the Roman province of Lycia, that would be another five hundred miles. Suppose he changed ships there and headed on to Malta, that would be another nine hundred miles. If he went on from there to Rome, landed where Paul had landed at Puteoli, and headed north up the Appian way, that would be another five hundred miles or so. By that time, he would have traveled some two thousand miles from home. In those days, given the road conditions and the even worse sea conditions, that would have been a journey to a far country indeed.

It would be possible, then, to calculate how far the prodigal went if we measure the distance in miles—no matter whether he headed north to Antioch, east to Babylon, west to Rome, or south to Egypt. We have no way, however, to measure how far he went in terms of morals.

When he came back, say, from Corinth or Carthage, from Galatia or Gaul, the road had a beginning point and an ending point. But when the prodigal came back from his immoralities and indecencies, from his debaucheries and drunkenness, there is a sense in which part of him remained in the far country. It is not inconceivable that, there, he left behind unhappy young women whom he had helped to ruin, and addicted young men whom he had helped to destroy with drugs and alcohol. In the far country remained, then, men and women who were much worse now than they had been before the prodigal had come their way.

In that far country, too, would have been mothers who wept because this young man had come their way with his good looks and daredevil ways, with his fine clothes and bulging wallet. These mothers would have cried their hearts out because he had swept their daughters off their feet, seduced them, and then laughingly gone on his way, leaving them forever soiled and shamed. In that far country there would be fathers bowed and bent because this young man had met their sons and taught them how to plunge into "all sin" and how to debauch themselves.

So the prodigal came back. Others continued in the wild ways in which he had encouraged them. How far was the far country in terms of morals? As someone has said, his sin was "a rebellion against the entire universe, an anarchy against society, an outrage on everything, a crime against everybody." His sin had contaminated the planet. Even the far country had become worse as a result of the prodigal's having passed that way in his sin.

How can we measure our waywardness in terms of example, influence, and cause and effect.

1. What the Prodigal Figured

Picture this young man. He grew up in a good home. He becomes increasingly impatient with his father's devotions, his father's duties, and his father's discipline. The father has lofty principles and high moral standards. He is kindly, but he is firm.

The prodigal decides, at last, that he has had enough. He is tired of family devotions, tired of the daily tedium of sitting through the reading of the Scriptures. He is tired of listening to his father's pious prayers. He is tired of hearing his father say "no" whenever he wants to go to this shady place or that questionable house. *If I leave home,* he thinks, *I will be free.*

That is always the Devil's first lie. "Be free," he says. "Please yourself. Get out from under these restrictions and restraints. Do your own thing." It was the very essence of what the serpent said to Eve (Gen. 3). The prodigal follows the Devil's lead when he decides he has had more than enough of the rules that are part of living at home.

2. What the Prodigal Forgot

The path of sin is expensive. Part of "having fun" is spending money—on things he covets but cannot afford. He heartlessly demands his share of the family fortune and then wastes no time in converting it into cash. Then he packs his bags, lines his purse, and goes out—thoughtless young fool that he was—to live on his capital. The money soon, of course, runs out. Easy come, easy go. Money pours through his wastrel hands. Into taverns he goes, the big shot calling for drinks all around. Into gambling joints he goes crying, "Increase the stakes." Into fairgrounds he rushes announcing, "Come on, fellows. Everything's on me." The far country is expensive. It takes everything and gives nothing.

3. What the Prodigal Found

a. Fair-Weather Friends

In the far country the prodigal finds fair-weather friends. Jesus said, "When he had spent all, . . . he began to be in want." His friends soon leave him when the cash flow comes to an end.

Look at the prodigal as he pokes ruefully into his purse and turns his pockets inside out. See him now. He approaches a friend on the street looking for the price of a drink. "Say, Marcus, could you loan me some money?"

"Sorry, old fellow. Wish I could, you know, but I'm short myself. Why don't you get your old man to send you some more? See you around."

b. Far-Reaching Famine

It is the worst possible time to run out of funds because a famine is coming. Hard times for all. Even those who might have been disposed to help him are too occupied with their own needs to care about him. "He began to be in want."

There are thirteen famines in the Bible, all significant. This one is significant both for its timing and its tenacity. It was "a mighty famine," the Lord says, and it comes just when the prodigal is most vulnerable. God sends such circumstances into our lives to drive us to Himself. We forget about Him when things are all going well.

Earth's pleasures soon dry up for the prodigal. His resources disappear. The fun has gone out of life. He has no more food. He has no more future. He comes to the end of the line. He has been having so much fun; but it is no fun to be hungry, homeless, and hopeless far, far from home. He has no resources left and no respect left. He has come to the end—but not quite the end. He has to sink lower still before he gives in.

"He went and joined himself to a citizen of that country; and he sent him into his fields to feed swine," Jesus said. This young man is a Jew. For a Jew to have anything to do with swine is against the Mosaic Law. Hogs are unclean. No Jew would contaminate himself with such creatures. Swine-herding is a dirty business. For this well-bred young Jew to sink so low as to take a job feeding swine is an indication of how low, indeed, he has sunk and how desperate his need has become. For him to take a filthy job like that would be like a man today making a living by peddling pornography.

He "joined himself," Jesus says, to the man who owns this unclean business. The word translated "joined himself" is interesting, for it means "he cleaved to" and comes from a word that means "to glue together." The prodigal finds a man who has a job opening, even though it is a detestable kind of job, and he glues himself to this man. The prodigal sticks to him. Surely he can sink no lower.

But he does. "He would fain have filled his belly with the husks that the swine did eat." He sits there by the pig swill. He watches the animals rooting in the garbage. He is so hungry he begins to devour the slops in the pig pail. There he is, look at him. He has a lean and hungry look. His rags and tatters reek of the swine trough, and his face and hands are grimy with filth. See him now as he scrapes out the bottom of the pig pail and stuffs into his mouth the scraps even the pigs have left behind. He not only engages in a filthy business, he stuffs himself with the garbage he handles. The prodigal truly has hit bottom. He has discovered that the Devil is a cruel master and that the end of the road in this world is a very cold place to be.

B. The Father's House

As long as the prodigal's money, friends, and good times lasted, he did not think at all. He was having too much fun. That is why God allowed him to become friendless and forsaken, homeless and hungry, beggared and abandoned. Now, in extreme need, he begins to think.

1. His Decision

a. His Situation

"How many hired servants of my father's have bread enough and to spare, and I perish with hunger!" It is the first kind thought the prodigal has nurtured concerning his father since the seeds of rebellion took root in his soul. His father is a good man, a generous man, and a gracious man. His father would not allow even a hired hand to starve to death on his doorstep. *Yet here I am,* he thought, *miles from home, grubbing around in the garbage pails of sin, sitting with swine, trying to stave off my hunger pangs with slops from a pig pail.* He begins to feel sorry for himself. *What am I doing here?*

b. His Sin

"I will arise and go to my father, and will say unto him, Father, I have sinned against heaven, and before thee, and am no more worthy to be called thy son: make me as one of thy hired servants." That is a giant step forward. There can be no conversion without conviction. Not until the prodigal comes to himself can he come to his father.

Not until we see our own desperate need of a heavenly Father's love, compassion, and grace can we make the first move toward home. We must first confess that we are poor, lost sinners. It would have done no good for this young man to return home as rebellious and as riotous in soul as when he left.

See the prodigal as he goes to the big house on the hill. The swine are still rooting in the field. The pig trough is almost empty of slops. Holding the pig pail, he bangs on the farmhouse door. "Here, Mister," he calls, "here's your pig pail. I won't be needing it any longer. I'm going home."

Now see the farmer as he eyes the young man up and down. He looks at the prodigal's tattered finery, his emaciated form, his straggly beard, his unkempt hair, his filthy face, his dirty hands, and his bare, mud-covered feet. He holds his nose at the stench of the pigsty that reeked through the ruins of the young man's robes. "You're going home? Looking like that? After what you've done to your father's fine name? If you were my son, I'd turn the dogs on you. That's what I'd do."

Now hear the prodigal: "Mister, I daresay you would. But you don't know my father."

2. His Discovery

The poor young fellow with a new look in his eyes strides out of the gate and heads along the highway for home. He has a long, long way to go. The outward trip had been so easy; it had been all downhill, all fun and frolic. The way back is steep and hard.

His heart fails him at times. What if he is too late? What if he has sinned away the day of grace? What if his father, tired of the long wait, has barred and bolted the door?

On and on he goes, footsore, weary, and hungry. One fixed hope guides him: his father will be gracious and forgiving. At last the prodigal tops the last rise. There it is on yonder distant hill—the family home. At this point his feet falter. He catches the neighbors' scornful looks as he goes past their doors. He hears the crowd's caustic comments. Moreover, he catches a fresh look at himself in the reflecting waters of a pool.

He sits down on a worn stump and puts his head in his hands, groaning in the bitterness of his soul. Coming home had all sounded so easy in the far country, but now . . . he dares not go on.

Then he hears a call; he hears his name. He lifts up his head and sees an old man running toward him at top speed. It is his father! For "when he was yet a great way off, his father saw him, and had compassion, and ran, and fell on his neck, and kissed him." Yes, his father kisses him. He kisses him despite the filth, the stench, the vermin, the disgrace, and the shame. He kisses him.

"Father," the prodigal said, "I have sinned against heaven, and in thy sight, and am no more worthy to be called thy son."

a. A Gracious Father

The father calls for his steward. "The best robe," he cries, "a royal ring!" He will not even hear the part about his son being made a hired servant. Likewise, our heavenly Father forgives us. He does not say, "Well, we'll see. We'll put you to work for a while. We'll need some good works out of you before we can receive you back into the family." Salvation is not of works. We come just as we are, wearing all the rags and tatters of our lost estate, and He receives us just as we are. He clothes us and crowns us, gives us the robe and the ring, arrays us with the righteousness of Christ. He gives us a position in the family—a position of love and trust, and sonship and responsibility. What a gracious Father we have!

b. A Glorious Feast

"My boy is starving," says his dear father. "Where's the fatted calf?" What a feast there is—what music, what dancing! What a gathering there is in that home to welcome back the prodigal son.

That is just like God. First, He saves us, then He satisfies us. The prodigal has not had such a feast since he left home. It is good, wholesome food, too, not the fine, fancy food on which he had squandered his wealth, nor rare, exotic wines of distant lands. It is the good, plain, wholesome food of his father's house. Likewise, God will feed us. He will feed us on His Word and on all the good things that grace can provide.

c. A Great Forgiveness

"*My son,*" says the father. "This my son was dead, and is alive again; he was lost, and is found." The son experiences full and free restoration to the family.

Dead! Alive! Lost! Found! In just four words we have the whole story of redeeming, regenerating grace. God is willing to pick up poor, lost sinners who are dead in trespasses and sins, and breathe into their souls eternal life. God will take rebels and reinstate them into His family. All we have to do is come—just as we are.

TWENTY-SIX

The Elder Brother

Luke 15:25–32

A. HIS SIMPLE DISCOVERY
B. HIS SINFUL DISPLEASURE
C. HIS SURLY DISPOSITION
    1. His self-righteousness
    2. His secret regrets
    3. His sinful resentments
D. HIS SEEMING DECISION
    1. How he was loved
    2. How he was left

When Jesus told the parables found in Luke 15, He had a threefold audience in mind. First there were His disciples. They needed teaching; they needed instruction in the truths of God, in the great facts of the faith. To the disciples, these parables were parables of *faith*. The stories of the lost sheep, the lost silver, and the lost sons were intended to instruct the disciples in the great principles and precepts of the Christian faith.

Jesus also had the publicans and sinners in mind. "All the publicans and sinners" were there, Luke said. The statement is a hyperbole. Luke wanted us to know that there were many of them. They were crowding to Christ. To them, these parables were parables of *hope*. These men and women—the outcasts of society, the dregs of humanity, the wretched flotsam and jetsam of the human tide—heard these parables with dawning hope. Although, for the most part, these people were outside the pale of Judaism, Jesus loved them. Theirs could be the kingdom of heaven.

Finally, but perhaps most of all, Jesus had in mind the scribes and Pharisees.

They were there too. They were Christ's constant, carping critics. "This man receiveth sinners, and eateth with them," they sneered (Luke 15:2). So Jesus focused these parables on lost ones. To the scribes and Pharisees, these stories were intended to be stories of *love*. God loves lost people. The scribes and Pharisees found this truth hard to understand.

Jesus added an appendix to the last parable. Having told of the wayward prodigal, He painted a portrait of a Pharisee, for that is who the elder brother was. In spirit, in soul, in scorn, and in all his acid sourness, the elder brother was a Pharisee. He was a smug Pharisee, keeping to the letter of the law, and never plunging into open, shameful sin. Yet he was lost. Sin is sin. It is repulsive and hateful to God. He loathes and detests sin for what it is in itself and for what it does in us. Somehow, we feel that the flagrant sins of the prodigal were almost attractive compared to the dispositional sins of the elder brother.

The elder brother is a standing biblical portrait of people who, while they never stray into the far country, manage to shed a shadow of gloom over everything and everybody. They never go to excess, they commit no crimes, and they violate none of society's laws. Yet they succeed in depressing everyone and in making everyone feel uncomfortable and unhappy. Their sins are not sins of debauchery; they are sins of the disposition. These people are self-righteous, complacent, moody, touchy, spiteful, niggardly, and bad-tempered.

We can picture the two brothers being sent out to play when they were boys. Mother would say, "Now don't play near that stream. And mind you, don't climb those trees. And stay away from the road." The younger brother would always come home soaking wet, having fallen into the stream. Or, having fallen out of a tree, he would come home with a torn coat. "Well, I was only bird nesting, Mom," we can hear him saying. "I saw a super nest on one of the branches. It had three little birds in it. Any anyway, what about him? He didn't climb the tree, but he threw stones at the birds." The elder brother, on the other hand, never came home with his shoes soaked or with his shirt torn off his back.

Mark Twain captured the spirit of these two boys when he created the characters of Tom Sawyer and Sid. We all like madcap Tom much better than his prim and proper stepbrother Sid. We feel smug when Tom punches the tar out of Sid for some sneaky act of betrayal. But of course the reason is that (as Paul wrote to the Corinthians) we are yet carnal and walk as men.

The parable of this unpleasant elder brother can be broken into three parts.

A. His Simple Discovery

It has been a hard day in the field. The elder brother has been busy—plowing, weeding, gathering in a harvest, herding cattle, making hay, picking fruit, mending fences, tending sheep. Whatever he was doing, we can be sure that he was doing it conscientiously and competently. Now tired, hot, and bad-tempered, he is coming home for his supper and looking forward perhaps to a quiet meal, his easy chair, and an early bedtime.

As he approaches the house, he hears music and dancing. He hails a servant and demands an explanation. "Thy brother is come; and thy father hath killed the fatted calf, because he hath received him safe and sound."

At that moment the elder brother makes a discovery. He discovers how much he hates his young brother. How bitterly he is jealous of him. He hates him for his easy laughter, for his carefree ways, and for leaving him with all the work to do. He hates him for running away from home with half the working capital of the business and for wasting all that hard earned capital with riotous living. He hates him for dragging the good, respected, family name in the muck and mire, and he hates him most of all for coming back home.

More, if the elder brother does not actually hate his father at that moment, he comes very close to it. He hates the thought of his father showing any kind of welcome to the prodigal. *The prodigal,* he thinks, *should be confined to the servants' hall or, better still, be driven from home. He made his bed, so let him lie on it. It is foolish of my father to make this kind of fuss just because the wretched wastrel has come home.*

The younger son might have gone to the Devil, as we would say, in the far country. The elder brother entertains a thousand devils right in his own heart, right there at home. There are devils of injured pride, self-love, self-righteousness, bad temper, malicious spite, and all their kin. The elder brother heartily welcomes each and every one of those demons and gives them the full run of his soul as he stands there, stock-still in the field, glowering at the servant who has brought him the news.

B. His Sinful Displeasure

"And," we read, "he was angry, and would not go in." *What?* He thinks. *Go in there? Go in there and shake that young criminal's hand? Go in there and sit down with him as though nothing has happened? Go in there and sing and dance like an idiot? Not me.*

Harold Begbie spent much of his life investigating some amazing spiritual miracles. Those miracles were wrought by God in the Salvation Army in the early days when its soldiers marched into the slums of London to seek out the lost. In his book, *Twice Born Men,* he told stories of the Puncher, Old Born Drunk, the Plumber, and half a dozen more. Wonderful stories they are of prodigal men and women who were won from the far country and brought back to the Father's house. Begbie wrote about similar miracles wrought through the Salvation Army in India. Few books have ever done more to show the contrast between callous Hinduism and compassionate Christianity.

Having delved deeply into stories taken from real life, Begbie turned his hand to writing a novel called *The Vigil.* It is a story of a young minister's spiritual struggle. The minister is earnest about his parish duties but knows nothing at all about saving grace in his own soul.[1]

The crisis of the story revolves around the death of Dr. Blund, reputed to be the most wicked man in Bartown. That is quite a reputation, for Bartown prides itself on being "the wickedest little hole in England." Dr. Blund spends most of his time drinking gin and playing billiards at the local inn. The only person who believes in him is his broken, bedraggled wife, whose life has been spent in the shadow of his debaucheries. Halfway through the book, the minister receives an urgent call to come to the doctor's bedside. Dr. Blund is dying and needs spiritual help.

The liberal minister has little patience with the case. He goes with utmost reluctance to the doctor's bedside. He cannot see why a man who has lived so hideously should be allowed to avert his just punishment in another world by availing himself, in the eleventh hour, of whatever discharges Christianity might offer. In any case, what can he say? If the truth were to be told, the minister is not saved himself. Religion, to him, is a comfortable profession, the one at which he makes his living, as he would had he become a lawyer or a teacher or an engineer.

He bends over Dr. Blund and speaks to him professionally of repentance and forgiveness, but the words do not come from his heart and do nothing to comfort the dying man. It does not take the doctor long to see through the minister's facade. "Isn't there something in the Bible about being born again?" Blund asks

---

1. Harold Begbie, *The Vigil* (New York: Dodd, Mead, and Company, 1908).

desperately. "What does it mean?" Completely out of his depth, the minister flounders hopelessly. At last the doctor, to whom each moment is precious, fixes his eye on the wretched vicar. "Tell me," Blund says, "have you been born again?" The minister hangs his head in silence. "You don't know," cries the doctor. "You're pretending. You can't help me! You don't know." Covered with confusion and shame, the unconverted minister flees from the room to seek another preacher, one who knows what being born again is all about.

The focus of the story passes from the soul of the doctor to the soul of the minister. The doctor is saved and passes peacefully into eternity, and to the minister this does not seem fair. Why should a man who lived so abominably, he thinks, be absolved of all blame at the last?

The minister is engaged to a young woman who is born again. "Do you think," he asks her, "that a deathbed repentance atones for a whole life of evil?" Her answer is one of the noblest in all literature. "No," she replies, "but Calvary does!"

> It is not thy tears of repentance nor prayers
> But the blood that atones for the soul;
> On Him then, who shed it, thou mayest at once
> Thy weight of iniquity roll.[2]

The minister's problem was exactly the same as the elder brother's problem in the parable. He was angry and would not go into the house because he could not see, for the life of him, why the prodigal should be pardoned and receive forgiveness so full and so free. This was the reason for the elder brother's sinful displeasure. His trouble was that he knew about religion, but he knew nothing about redemption. He had a creed, but he did not have the Christ. He had dead works, but he did not have living faith. He knew nothing of Calvary love.

C. His Surly Disposition

The elder brother's sins were all dispositional sins. The Lord Jesus exposed him. Like a surgeon exposing an inner cancer, the Great Physician opens up to our gaze the meanness and malignancy of this man's soul. The elder brother had not committed a single crime for which society could ever arrest him, but his utter lostness was as real, as terrible, and as Satanic as that of the prodigal in his most abandoned state.

2. A. M. Hull, "There Is Life for a Look at the Crucified One," 1860.

1. His Self-Righteousness

"Lo, these many years do I serve thee, neither transgressed I at any time thy commandment." In effect, he says, "I do this, and I do that, and I do the other." This was his religion. His whole religious outlook was one of self-sufficient, moral rectitude.

That is exactly why God cannot take anyone to heaven on the basis of his imagined good works. In the first place, the elder brother's proud and petulant spirit offset his good works. When God exposes any person's works to the fierce light of His burning holiness, the sins, flaws, and imperfections of those works will show themselves—glaring, ugly, and utterly condemning. God *judges* men on the principle of *work,* He *saves* men on the principle of *faith.*

Suppose God were to take people to heaven on the basis of their good works. They would do just what this elder brother did—begin to boast: "I am here because I did this, because I did that, or because I did the other. I am here because I did not do this, that, or the other. I am thankful that I was not a sinner like other people." Boasting is a manifestation of pride, and pride was the original sin. It was the sin of Lucifer, the morning star, the anointed cherub, the highest archangel of glory. It was pride that inflated him until he was filled with such a sense of his own importance he was changed from angel to devil.

If God were to take people to heaven on the basis of their good works, moral rectitude, or imagined self-righteousness, they would have to be cast out again for the same reason Lucifer was cast out. The elder brother is proof of this. He took pride in his own imagined goodness. He congratulated himself on how much better he had been than his brother. And that attitude kept the elder brother out of the father's house.

2. His Secret Regrets

"Thou never gavest me a kid," he says to his father, "that I might make merry with my friends." The elder brother had the far country in the dark depths of his own unregenerate heart. He was not one bit better than his brother. Both brothers wanted the same thing. The elder brother wanted to take the father's resources and spend them on himself, just as much as the prodigal. The only real difference between the brothers was that the younger brother was more honest. He did not nourish and cherish his lusts secretly in his soul but had the courage to bring them out into the open.

God knows our secrets. He searches our hearts. He knows where our secret fires burn. He knows the motives that control us, knows "those places where polluted things hold empire o'er the soul."

The elder brother's crowd might not have been the same crowd as that of the prodigal. Their idea of "making merry" might not have been the same as his. The elder brother's crowd probably would not have become drunk. They would not have hired women off the streets to share their lusts. They would not have caroused, rioted, taken drugs, and brawled. They would have sat around and gossiped, tearing to shreds the characters and reputations of people they disliked. They would have been spiteful, malicious, hateful, and angry.

3. His Sinful Resentments

"Thou never gavest me a kid," complains the elder son, "that I might make merry with my friends: but as soon as this thy son was come, which hath devoured thy living with harlots, thou hast killed for him the fatted calf" (Luke 15:29–30).

"Thy *brother* is come," says the servant. "This thy *son*," says the elder brother to his father. The brother wants nothing to do with a fellowship that includes such a reprobate as the prodigal. "Thy *brother* was dead, and is alive again," replies the father. The elder brother was totally out of spirit with his father. He was as utterly lost as the prodigal was during his worst and wildest days. The elder brother lived in his father's house and worked within a stone's throw from it, but he was a million miles away from it in spirit.

This elder brother was moral and religious, but he had nothing in common with his father. Nothing. God's people convene various meetings from time to time so that they can commune with their Father in heaven. For all his respectability and religion, this elder brother would have participated in none of them.

We convene the prayer meeting, for instance, so that we can talk to *the Father* about those of our lost loved ones who are far from God. At the prayer meeting, we plead Calvary love for family members who are away from the fold. The elder brother, on the other hand, never once talked to his father about the lost prodigal. The elder brother knew nothing of Calvary love.

Then, too, we convene the evangelistic meeting so that we can tell a lost world the news that "Calvary covers it all," that God is a God of infinite grace. At the evangelistic meeting we tell *others* about Calvary love. The elder brother, however, made no attempt to bring his brother back. He knew nothing of Calvary love.

We also convene the worship meeting so that we can remind *ourselves* of the cost of Calvary love. At this meeting we think through the nature of Christ's great sacrifice for sin. This meeting is a feast of remembrance, a time when the Father spreads the table for us as a tangible token of His grace. We gather to enjoy His love and tell Him how much we appreciate Him. The elder brother, on the other hand, refused to come to just such a feast. He knew nothing of Calvary love. He had no appreciation of his father or his father's love.

We also convene the weekly Bible study so that we can learn more and more about the Father's grace, goodness, government, and glory. There, we are exhorted to become more like Him so that we also might radiate Calvary love. The elder brother knew nothing of that love.

We convene the testimony meeting, also, so that we can tell others how we ourselves came to respond to Calvary love. But the elder brother had never responded to his father's love and, of course, had no testimony.

We convene the missionary meeting to commission others to go to the world's remotest boundaries and seek the lost ones to tell them of Calvary love. At the missionary meeting we pay heed to our Father's heartthrob for a lost and dying world. We each say, "Here am I; send me." The missionary meeting touches our hearts so that those of us who cannot go can be exercised to give and to learn more of the needs of the lost. As far as the elder brother was concerned, however, the prodigal was in the far country and that was that. The elder brother had not the slightest interest in his brother's lost condition. He knew nothing of Calvary love.

Instead of participating in these meetings, or at least in what they represent, the elder brother's soul was full of sinful resentments and self-righteousness. His surly disposition was an ugly reminder that his soul knew nothing of the father's love and grace. His only regret was that he had not had his share of this world's pleasures too.

D. His Seeming Decision

1. How He Was Loved

Now comes the most wonderful part of the parable. The father loved that mean-spirited, self-centered, canting, hypocritical elder brother just as much as he loved the prodigal. "Son," he pleads, "thou art ever with me, and all that I have is thine." What a picture—the father standing out there in the field, pleading with the elder brother, and urging him to respond to his grace.

2. How He Was Left

We do not know how the story ends. All we know is that at last sight, the elder brother remained outside, still making the wretched choice, still showing that he would rather starve than come inside.

There is nobody too bad for Jesus Christ to save, but some people think that they are too good. The elder brother was just such a person. He saw no need in his soul for his father's grace; he had done no wrong. So he stayed outside—unsaved—but the father still pleaded. In time, however, the father's patience doubtless ran out. He would go inside and sadly shut the door, leaving the elder brother to think malicious, evil thoughts. There would be no more point in running after the older rebel than there was in running after the wayward prodigal. But Jesus ended the story before it reached that point. This is still the age of grace.

TWENTY-SEVEN

The Ten Lepers

Luke 17:11–19

A. THE THOUGHTLESS ONES
1. I have my family to think of
2. I have my friends to think of
3. I have my finances to think of
4. I have my frustrations to think of
5. I have my faith to think of
6. I have my followers to think of
7. I have my failures to think of
8. I have my feelings to think of
9. I have my future to think of

B. THE THANKFUL ONE

Of all men these must have been the most miserable. They were lepers, all ten of them. They were ostracized by society and cut off from the benefits and blessings of family and friends, religion, employment, and public recreation. They were "untouchables," outcasts of society, hated, feared, detested, and universally shunned. Their haunt was the distant hills. Their home was the leper colony. The vilest criminal was held in higher esteem than these wretched wraiths.

But beyond all hope they had hope. They had heard that Jesus of Nazareth was in the neighborhood. In a body they came to Him. "Him that cometh to me," He said, "I will in no wise cast out" (John 6:37). People fled before the lepers as they came. Their leper cry: *"Unclean! Unclean!"* made a path for them as wide as they could wish. Some of the bystanders would have stones ready should these pariahs venture their way. Jesus, however, stood willing and ready and eager to receive them.

He looked from one ravaged face and form to another. Then He sent them away. "Go and show yourselves to the priests," He said. It was the duty of the priest to examine a leper who claimed to be cleansed and to pronounce him clean or unclean. If, by some mighty miracle beyond all thought, they should be seen to be clean, then he had to prescribe the appropriate ceremonial of readmittance to the Jewish religious congregation and to the Jewish secular community. The ritual seems to have never once been performed as prescribed. Only three lepers had been cleansed in the Old Testament. Moses was one, his sister another, and the other was a Gentile soldier. The law of the leper had *not yet* been given when Moses became a leper; it does not seem to have been enforced with Miriam; and it had no bearing on Naaman, a Gentile.

So Jesus sent them to the priests. Either it was a cruel hoax—or it was a pledge and promise of cleansing from their dread scourge somewhere between where He was and where the temple stood.

With eager anticipation, with renewed hope and with daring faith, off they went. And on the way they were cleansed, saved by faith in the Lord Jesus Christ.

Consider these ten cleansed lepers. Most of them represent the "Sunday morning only" members with which all churches are familiar.

A. THE THOUGHTLESS ONES

There were nine of these thoughtless ones. We gather that they were all Jews for otherwise the Lord would not have told them to go to the priest and report their cleansing. In their mutual misery, they had tolerated the company of a Samaritan. Now that they were cleansed, they were probably just as glad that he elected to go back to Jesus. They did not relish his company and certainly did not want to go to the priests and the temple in the company of a Samaritan.

One would have thought that, sooner or later, they would all have found their way back to Jesus, but apparently they never did. Jesus said, "Were there not ten cleansed, but where are the nine?" As He watches the people who make professions of faith in Him in our churches today, doubtless He notes how many never come back. Many never find their place at His table, or in the fellowship of the local church, or in the forefront of the battle for truth. "Were there not ten cleansed?" He says, "but where are the nine?"

What was it that kept these thoughtless ones from coming back to the Master? Perhaps we should ask them. Here's one of them. Let's ask him.

1. I Have My Family to Think Of

"Sir, aren't you one of the ten lepers who came to Christ?"

"Oh yes."

"Have you truly been cleansed?"

"Oh yes, indeed."

"You are quite sure."

"There's no doubt about it at all."

"Aren't you grateful to the Lord for what He has done for you?"

"Of course!"

"Are you going back to where He is, back there in the midst of His people, where you found Him?"

"No, I don't plan on doing that."

"May we ask you why?"

"Well you see, ever since I became a leper I have been neglecting my family. I think my wife has first claim on my time. Then, too, my children have seen little enough of their dad. I need to spend time with my boy. My boy is very interested in sports, and I need to get out and play some ball with him.

"Then there's my daughter. She has been busy growing up all the time I have been a leper. She is very nearly of marrying age. I need to be giving thought to her needs.

"So you see, the demands of my family are such right now, I'll not have any time to spare. Christ and His people will simply have to wait until my family no longer makes so many demands upon me. I have my family to think of."

The second man has another excuse.

2. I Have My Friends to Think Of

Like the first man, he is sure he is saved. He has no doubt, either, that he owes his salvation to the Lord Jesus Christ. But before it was discovered that he was a leper, he was a very popular kind of man. He had a great gift for making friends. When we ask him whether or not he's going back to Jesus he replies, "Now just now. You see I have a lot of friends and most of my friends are old friends. They have been friends of mine for a very long time. Many of them stood by my family when I was in the leper colony. I can't just desert my friends. The trouble is, you see, that most of my former friends have no use for Jesus.

"Many of my friends belong to the same club I do. It is a very exclusive club.

We have a strict rule in our club that there are two things about which we do not speak—politics and religion. There are more fights over those two things than anything else, so we have agreed not to talk about them.

"Besides, many of my friends are intellectuals. I was an intellectual myself in the old days. I find these friends of mine stimulating to talk to. They don't have a very high opinion of Jesus. If I mentioned His name they would simply put me in my place. They would remind me of where He came from. He was just a village carpenter, you see. And Nazareth is somewhat of a dump, after all.

"Of course, I'm not ashamed of Jesus—not after what He did for me. But I'll have to go really slowly with these friends of mine. I'm going to let them see the change in my life first. It would only turn them off if I started being too "fanatical" (which is what they would call it) about this salvation of mine. They would think me really a radical if I became an active disciple and follower of Jesus.

"I'm not ready at this stage to give up my old friends. The people Jesus has around Him are anything but intellectuals. I simply can't see rubbing shoulders with a few ignorant fishermen and a tax collector. My friends would laugh at me if I gave them up in order to associate myself with people like that. Eventually, of course, I hope to persuade my friends to think better of Jesus. In the meantime, I'm going back to them."

The third man has yet another excuse.

3. I Have My Finances to Think Of

We ask him if he intends to go back to Jesus, to thank Him, to put the rest of his life at the disposal of the One who provided so great salvation for him.

He says, "Well, you see it's like this with me, I have been sick for a very long time. You should see my medical expenses—not that the doctors ever did me the least bit of good. Indeed, as soon as my condition was diagnosed as leprosy, they refused to see me any more. I was chased out of town. And, what do you know? They keep on dunning my poor wife for their past 'services' to me. She has been driven to distraction.

"Then, you see, there's my farm. It has been terribly neglected all the years I have been a leper. Some of the barns and buildings are about to fall in ruins. The farm house needs fixing up, too. And those scurrilous doctors have put liens on my property.

"So, you see, I shall be terribly busy for the next few years getting my finances back in shape. My wife has a long list of things she needs. My children will soon be going to college. So Jesus and His people will have to get along without me for the next few years."

The fourth man, too, has his excuse.

4. I Have My Frustrations to Think Of

We ask him if he intends to go back and express his gratitude to the Lord Jesus by throwing in his lot with Him and with His people.

"Later," he says. "You see, before I was treated as a leper I was a bit of a play-boy. You can't imagine how frustrated I have been all these years. I've been cut off from every bit of fun. No parties! No dances! No nightclubs! Nothing like that at all. Well, now I simply must have some fun. I don't think that handful of people who rally around Jesus have any fun at all. That fellow Judas, for instance, I think a smile would crack his crafty face. And Simon the Zealot! An absolute fanatic! And that dour-faced Thomas, full of doubts and scruples. And Peter with his foot in his mouth half the time. . . Imagine—all night prayer meetings and all-day Bible classes. Well, that's not for me—not yet anyway. I'm very fond of sports. It's ages since I last went to the arena. I like to have fun. It's years since I had any fun at all. That leper colony was a nightmare.

"Then, too, on cold winter's nights I like to work at my hobby. I made models. I'm going to make a model of the temple. It's something I can do with my wife. She can make the veil and the hangings while I work on the cloisters and courts.

"I simply have to get all my frustrations worked out of my system before I think about going to meetings—even if Jesus of Nazareth is there. I'm going to have some fun out of life for awhile—then I'll find Him and tell Him how grateful I am for the good life He has given me."

The fifth man has another excuse. He's grateful enough for the miracle which has been wrought in his life. It has been quite a charismatic experience for him, he says. But . . .

5. I Have My Faith to Think Of

For, before it was discovered that he was a leper, he was a Scribe. He says, "You see, I already have my religious convictions and I'm not at all sure I go along with all that this rabbi Jesus of Nazareth teaches. Some of His ideas are way out. I was raised in the synagogue. I have taken training under Gamaliel and the other learned Jerusalem rabbis. None of them believe that Jesus is the Messiah. The

High Priest thinks He is an imposter. I understand that Jesus actually claims to be the Son of God. True, He can work marvelous cures. I'm proof of that, but I'm not at all sure that entitles Him to claim to be the Son of God. Some of my friends in the Sanhedrin think Jesus' saying that borders on blasphemy.

"I understand, too, that He simply brushes aside all the time-honored traditions of the elders. I'm not at all sure I can go along with radical ideas like that. So I'm going back to the synagogue. I shall double the attention I pay to the religious aspects of Judaism. I shall be a stronger supporter of the temple and its rituals. I shall pay my tithes. I shall adhere to the old paths.

"Besides, that's a pretty ignorant and unlearned crowd He has around Him. Fishermen! Tax collectors! Zealots! Nobodies! Galileans! Anybody can get a following of people like that. The Jewish intellectuals have looked into His teaching and rejected it. All this talk of a virgin birth and an immaculate life and of being the one and only Way to God . . . well, I think I'll stay with the old religion in which I was raised. The rabbi of my local synagogue is a very good and learned man. He came around and warned me against the teachings of Jesus just last night. I am going to stick with the faith in which I was raised."

But here comes another one. Let's see what he has to say. He seems to be a forceful kind of an individual. We ask him, "Well, sir, now that you're cleansed are you going to make Jesus absolute Lord of your life?"

This man has a different excuse.

6. I Have My Followers to Think Of

"You see," he says, "before I met Jesus of Nazareth, I was a leading advocate of social and political action to improve the well-being and the living conditions of the people. I am a great one for advocating causes. And, although I say it myself, I find it quite easy to recruit followers. Just before I was isolated from society by my leprosy, I was a strong advocate of human rights. My thing was slavery. I think slavery should be abolished throughout the Roman Empire. I think the way to achieve this goal is to organize the masses and sponsor mass demonstrations. I also think the problem should be attacked by means of social, political, and economic pressure. We should educate the masses. There should be marches and civil disobedience and things like that to draw attention to our cause. I have a lot of followers. They will be looking for me to get back into the fight. As for this Jesus of Nazareth, He does seem to have some feeling for the poor and the sick, but His methods are too slow. Why, I even hear He has refused a popular demand that He be made King. That was His big mistake. He should get into the government. He should ally Himself with the Jewish Establishment. He has the charisma to mobilize the entire Jewish Diaspora. I have no patience with His methods.

"Barabbas used to be one of my men. I'm going to look him up and see if we can't join forces in a mass crusade against Rome. I don't think the world is ready yet for the kind of teaching Jesus advocates. Maybe I can help get the world ready for Him. Nobody really understands what He is talking about when He speaks of being born again and dying in order to live. I will lead my followers. We'll get things ready."

Here comes yet another one.

"Sir, are you cleansed?"

"Yes, I think so. It looks like it. But you can never tell. Leprosy is a mysterious malady. Perhaps it will come back."

"Are you going to go to Jesus and thank Him for what He has done for you?"

"Not just yet."

7. I Have My Failures to Think Of

"You see sir, I have always been a very weak sort of person. I have all these bad habits. I have a real weakness for wine. I need to take care of that. I have a foul mouth. I need to take care of that. I can't resist temptation. I always fall. I've tried to reform my life, but it never works. As for Jesus, I can't follow some of His teaching at all. I always thought the standards of the Mosaic Law were high enough. Then I heard Jesus give the Sermon on the Mount. There's no way I can live up to such terms as He expects. They are impossible, at least for me. I think I had better try to overcome some of my failures before I join up with Christ and those who follow Him."

"Well man," we reply, "if Christ has the power to cleanse you, don't you think He has the power to control you? Surely He would enable you to live life on His terms."

"I never thought of that," he says, "but you don't know how weak I am."

Here comes yet another one. Let's ask him if he intends to become an active follower of the Lord Jesus, now that he has been cleansed.

8. I Have My Feelings to Think Of

"Of course I'm grateful to Him for what He has done for me. But I'm not going back just yet. You see, I'm very tired. I have been desperately ill for a very long time. You have no idea how debilitating and depressing it is to be a leper. I'm going to take it easy for awhile. My feelings are still very raw. The last thing I want to do is tramp up and down the country as one of His disciples, always being jostled by crowds, always in the public eye.

"You see how it is," he concludes, "I go by my feelings. Maybe later on I'll feel better about becoming a committed follower of Christ. Right now I don't feel like doing anything."

Which brings us to the last of the thoughtless ones.

9. I Have My Future to Think Of

"You see," he says, "I don't want to get that involved. Jesus demands total commitment. I've heard Him tell people they couldn't be His disciples because they put family first.

"Me? I have a career ahead of me. It's been interrupted once already by my leprosy. I don't intend to have it interrupted again. I'm going into Law. That means I shall have to devote the next half a dozen or so years of my life to a comprehensive study of the Levitical code, of Roman law, and of rabbinical fundamentals. I shall have to work my way through law school. I certainly can't afford to have my career and my future messed up by getting too close to this itinerant teacher from Nazareth. He might want me to give up Law altogether. What if He asked me to be a missionary! What if He wanted me to run a leper colony? What if He wanted me to go to Parthia or to the Tin Islands of Britain as His disciple? I once heard Him say something about a *cross!* The very idea! Oh, no! I have my future to think of."

So we turn in relief to the tenth man.

B. The Thankful One

Of all the ten cleansed lepers, this was the only one prepared to do the good, the right, and the honorable thing and go back to give thanks to the One who had done so much for him. Jesus had saved him through and through. All the decay and death of the past had dropped away. He was a new creature. Old things were passed away, all things had become new. He would go to Jesus and pour out his heart in thanksgiving and praise. The others, Jewish to the core, were just as glad to see the last of this tenth man. After all, he was a despised *Samaritan!*

It is easy to take a great liking to this man. As each one of his former companions would offer his miserly excuse for not going back to Jesus, this man brushed all excuses aside. He was going to enthrone Jesus in his heart as Lord.

So back he came. There he stood before the Master and lifted up his voice in thanksgiving, worship, and praise. He was the only one, and he a Samaritan stranger. Jesus looked at him, and we can be quite sure He warmed toward him. But His thoughts were on the other nine. "Were there not ten cleansed?" He said, "Where are the nine?" There was so much more He wanted to do for them. They had their cleansing; He wanted their consecration. He had removed their leprosy; He longed to revitalize their lives. They were not grateful enough to so much as tender their thanks to Him.

We see it all the time. The gospel is preached. The invitation is given. This one, that one, and the other one come forward. They are counseled. They kneel at the altar. They ask the Lord Jesus to cleanse their hearts from all sin. They are presented to the church. They give a brief word of testimony. They are warmly welcomed and congratulated by the members of the church. And that's the last you see of them. They don't come back Sunday night. The special meetings continue all week. You never see them. They seem to have melted back into the world from which they came. They do not get baptized. They do not join the church. They do not grow in grace and increase in the knowledge of God. They do not support anything, give to anything, help with anything. *"Where are the nine?"* Jesus says it still.

But thank God for that Samaritan! Let us make up our minds to be like him.

TWENTY-EIGHT

The Good Samaritan

Luke 10:25–37

A. RUIN
   1. The human race is on a downward path
   2. The human race is on a dangerous path
B. RELIGION
   1. The priest: The rites of religion
   2. The Levite: The rules of religion
C. REDEMPTION
   1. A person
   2. A process
   3. A promise

The story of the good Samaritan was told by Jesus to a man who was quite confident that he could do something to inherit eternal life. Moreover, he was a man who was quite contemptuous of Christ. That comes out right at the start. He stood up and *tempted* Christ.

The word is a singularly strong one in the Greek, being an intensive form of the usual word. It is used only two other times in the New Testament. When Satan tried to persuade Christ to cast Himself down from the pinnacle of the temple, trusting in angelic arms to hold him up from harm, Jesus turned on him: "Thou shalt not tempt the Lord thy God," He said (Matt. 4:7). That is, you must not put Him to the test. The other place using the intensive form of the word is 1 Corinthians 10:9, where Paul warns men not to tempt Christ by their ungodly behavior.

So then, this man, a lawyer, put Christ to the test. Before the conversation was over Christ put him to the test.

The story of the good Samaritan is really a parable of the human race. It is a story in three parts.

A. Ruin

"A certain man went down from Jerusalem to Jericho and fell among thieves" (Luke 10:30). That is the first thing that we notice.

1. The Human Race Is on a Downward Path

This is quite contrary, of course, to the popular philosophy of the day in which we live. Men today have convinced themselves that man is on an upward path. We are facing today the philosophical fruits of the widespread sowing, for over one hundred years, of the false doctrine of evolution. Man has cast out that grand old creed that has served the human race so well for hundreds upon hundreds of years: "I believe in God the Father, Almighty, Maker of heaven and earth; and in Jesus Christ His only Son our Lord . . ." That creed has been the confession of faith in Christendom almost since apostolic times.

Today's creed is quite different. It goes like this: "I believe in man, maker of himself and inventor of all science. And in myself, captain of my own soul and master of my own destiny. I should not suffer anything painful or unpleasant. I believe that man will one day sit exalted above all worlds. I believe in the spirit of progress, which spake by such men as Darwin, Freud, and George Bernard Shaw. I believe in modern administrative, ethical, and social organization. I believe in the gradual progress of the human race toward unity, peace, and progress through the works and organization and scientific discoveries of man, world without end."

Just one look at the kind of world in which we live—with its concentration camps and mass murders; with its organized violence, terrorism, and atomic bombs; with its publicly paraded pride in being a pervert; with its crime syndicates dedicated to the spread of drug, sex, vice, and pornography—persuades us that the human race is on a downward path, not an upward path. "A certain man went *down* from Jerusalem to Jericho . . ." Man is on the way down. The Bible says that in the end times, "evil men and seducers will wax worse and worse" (2 Tim. 3:13). That sounds like a better evaluation of our times than the bleatings of the humanists and the libertarians.

Two extremities are underlined in the parable. The one is Jerusalem, the other is Jericho. The man is going down from Jerusalem to Jericho. The actual road from Jerusalem to Jericho is about eighteen miles long, and it descends from the Judean hills to Jericho, some three thousand five hundred feet lower, which is eight hundred and twenty-five feet below the level of the Mediterranean Sea.

Jerusalem to Jericho! The phrase measures more than miles. It measures morals. It was only a short way from Jerusalem to Jericho in terms of miles. It was an infinite distance in terms of morals. Jerusalem was the city of peace, the city of Melchizedek and of the Messiah, the city of the great King. It was the center of worship and spiritual life for God's people. It was where God had come down to be enthroned amongst His people. It was the place where God had put His name and where He took up His residence on earth. In spiritual terms, Jerusalem was the place of blessing, the place where God could be known.

But Jericho! Jericho was the city of the curse. When Israel first entered Canaan and conquered the land, the first obstacle they faced was Jericho. And when it finally fell, God put the place under a curse. It was never to be rebuilt. Its location was desirable, it enjoyed a tropical climate, it was an exceedingly fertile place, but it was under the curse.

We do not need a great deal of imagination to get the spiritual message. The man going down from Jerusalem to Jericho represents the whole human race. It did not take Adam long to exchange his place of blessing—Eden, where God came to meet with him, to walk with him, and talk with him—for a world placed under the curse. Down! Down! Down! Even until today, we wonder how much lower the human race can sink.

2. The Human Race Is on a Dangerous Path

"A certain man went down from Jerusalem to Jericho and fell among thieves, which stripped him of his raiment, and wounded him, and departed, leaving him half dead." The human race, at the commencement of its downward course, fell into evil hands. It fell into the hands of Satan, who, with his hosts of demons and evil spirits, did not take long to plunder it and leave it for dead. Half dead! That was the way Jesus put it.

From the beginning to the end, the Bible teaches us that we are half dead. When God made man, He made him spirit, soul, and body. The body is that part of us which makes us *world conscious*—it enables us to live in a physical universe, able to relate to our surroundings by means of sight and hearing, touch, taste, and smell. It makes us aware that we are part of a space, matter, time universe. The soul is what makes us *self conscious*—aware that we are individuals, separate and distinct from all others; aware of right and wrong and, consequently, morally accountable and possessed of intellect, emotions, will, and conscience. The spirit is what makes us *God conscious*—aware that there is a God and that sooner or later we must give account to Him.

God had warned Adam against eating the forbidden fruit. "The day that thou eatest thereof thou shalt surely die," He said (Gen. 2:17). Adam and Eve ate, and that day they died. Not physically, for Adam lived to be nine hundred and thirty years of age. Nevertheless the day he sinned, that day he died—spiritually.

Something terrible happened to the God conscious part of Adam. He no longer loved God, longed for God, or lived for the moment when, in the cool of the day, God would come down and walk with him and talk with him. He was half dead. The most important part of him was dead. He was dead in trespasses and sins. All his posterity were born in that condition, robbed and ruined by the fall. We are born out of fellowship with God and unable to know God apart from the quickening of His Holy Spirit.

So that is the first thing we learn from this parable. It is a story of ruin.

B. Religion

"And by chance there came down a certain priest that way: and when he saw him, he passed by on the other side. And likewise a Levite, when he was at the place, came and looked on him, and passed by on the other side." Such is religion. It was of no use at all to this robbed and ruined man. The world is full of religions. Some of them robed in glitter and glamour, some of them philosophical, some of them metaphysical, some of them downright diabolical.

The two men who came by that day represent the best in religion. Both men were schooled in the Scriptures. Both men had ready access to the Word of God, had studied the Word of God, had, indeed, given their lives to the work of God as they understood it. Both were ordained clergy in the only religion that was ordained by God. Both were ministers of Old Testament Judaism. The Lord Jesus introduced them into the story to illustrate what organized religion can do for a human being, half dead, robbed, and ruined by the fall. Nothing! Nothing at all. Let us look first at the Priest.

1. The Priest: The Rites of Religion

In Jerusalem there was an altar and a temple in connection with that Old Testament religion. There were offerings and sacrifices. There was an elaborate system of ritual ceremonial cleansing. There were burnt offerings, sin offerings, meal offerings, trespass offerings, and peace offerings. There were the morning and evening sacrifices. There were feast days and fast days. Since God Himself had initiated this religion (Paul called it "the Jews' religion"), it had a rich symbolism, full of superlative teaching. But it was of no use to that poor fellow on the Jericho road.

Notice the priest was going the same way as the man who had fallen among thieves. "By chance there came down a certain priest that way." He was on his way down too. A large colony of priests lived, in fact, in Jericho. This priest had his back toward God, the temple, and Jerusalem. He had done his duties for the year. He made all the required ablutions, offered all the necessary sacrifices, performed all his religious obligations; much good the whole performance had done him.

He was a minister of a religion that had flourished for fifteen hundred years, but he had nothing to offer the half dead man on the Jericho Road. On the contrary, he passed by on the other side. The rites of religion as represented by this priest were useless to meet even the most basic of human needs.

We need to remember that. Baptism does not save. Communion does not save. These things were never intended to save. They were never given to help a man half dead. They were given to those who have already been saved. Next comes the Levite.

2. The Levite: The Rules of Religion

The Levite belonged to the same religious family as the priest, but he was of a different order. The lawyer who stood up to tempt Jesus would recognize himself in this Levite. His ministry was to expound the law. He, too, had duties connected with the temple, but essentially he was a teacher of the law, called to explain to the people the rules of religion. He was supposed to expound the Ten Commandments and the entire body of Mosaic legislation, found in some six hundred and thirty commandments covering every phase of national, moral, and religious life. He was a teacher of the law of God, a law that taught compassion for a neighbor in distress, even if he was a personal enemy: "If thou meet thine enemy's ox or his ass going astray, thou shalt surely bring it back to him again. If thou see the ass of him that hateth thee lying under his burden, . . . thou shalt surely help him" (Exod. 23:4–5).

The *rules* of religion, however, as embodied in this Levite, could no more help the poor fallen victim lying helpless on the road than could the *rites* of religion. What use would it be to tell him to get baptized? What sense would there be in telling him to recite the Ten Commandments? Organized religion and all its paid representatives could do nothing for this wretched, fallen man. The priest and the Levite were both traveling the same downward path as the man lying beaten up and helpless, bleeding, and half dead on the highway.

C. Redemption

Praise God, the story does not end there. The *robbers* have come. *Religion* has come. The stage is now set for the *Redeemer* to come.

1. A Person

"But a certain Samaritan, as he journeyed, came where he was: and when he saw him, he had compassion on him." In this parable the redeemer was a Samaritan. That is to say he was only half a Jew. He was an outsider, one whom the Jews disdained and despised, refused and rejected. That is the first thing about this person. He is the last person a Jew would have chosen to be his savior. The Jewish authorities, in their hatred of Christ, once called Him a Samaritan (John 8:48).

We have no trouble identifying this Samaritan. He represents Christ. The Lord Jesus, after all, was only half a Jew—He was the Son of Mary, but he was not the son of Joseph. He was the Son of Mary, true enough, but He was also the Son of God. In Him there met and merged two natures, the human and the divine. He was related to the human race and to the Hebrew race by virtue of His human birth. He was related to God in heaven because He was the eternal, uncreated, self-existing Son of the living God. That is the first thing about Him. Both human and divine, God manifest in flesh, that is the Person of our Redeemer.

Then, too, we do not read of the Samaritan what we read of the priest and the Levite: "by chance there came down a certain priest . . . likewise a Levite." There was no chance, no coincidence, about the coming of this redeemer. "A certain Samaritan as he journeyed came . . ." Compared with the other two, this Samaritan was a man with a mission. He was on a journey, his steps were deliberate, ordered of the Lord.

It was no accident that Jesus came into this world. It was part of a journey, something planned and arranged before the worlds began. In the dateless, timeless past, before ever God spun the worlds into space or stooped down to fashion Adam's clay, the Lord's path on earth was planned in heaven, down to the very last step (see John 4:4).

The Samaritan "came where he was and when he saw him he had compassion . . ." He came where he was. That is the whole point and purpose of the incarnation. Jesus came where we are. He entered into human life. He deliberately became a man, put on human flesh and arrayed himself in a body like unto ours. He came where we are when He came to Bethlehem.

He came even closer at Calvary. For there He took upon Himself not just a body, as at Bethlehem; He took upon Himself our sin. He came where we are.

So then, redemption is centered in a Person. Someone who came where we are because He had compassion upon us. He came because His heart was filled with love.

2. A Process

The Samaritan "went to him, and bound up his wounds, pouring in oil and wine, and set him on his own beast, and brought him to an inn, and took care of him." He did something the priest and the Levite never thought of doing. He was willing to get involved. The dangers involved did not deter him for a moment, even though the Jericho road was notorious.

Josephus tells us that, shortly before Christ told this parable, Herod had dismissed forty thousand workmen from the temple. Some of them, unemployed and desperate took to these hills south of Jerusalem and became fierce highway robbers. It has been urged, in excuse for the priest and the Levite, that they figured it was too dangerous for them to hang around in the vicinity where a callous assault and robbery had just taken place. The Samaritan had no such fears.

First, he poured into the victim's wounds oil and wine—oil to soothe and wine to cleanse. Throughout Scripture oil is a type of the Holy Spirit. The Lord Jesus never works apart from the Holy Spirit. Nothing can be done in the redemption of a human soul apart from the Spirit of God. We can plan and organize and hire professional talent, but it will all be in vain if the Spirit of God does not first do His work and meet us in our need.

Then the Samaritan poured wine into the wounds. The wine was a cleansing agent. It speaks to us of the precious blood of Christ. It is only the blood of Christ that can cleanse us from the effects of the fall and from the damage that has been done to us by Satan. His blood alone can cleanse the wounds of sin.

The oil and the wine applied by the tender hands of the Good Samaritan brought health and healing to this man he found half dead. That was the process. The Holy Spirit reproves (awakens us to our need), then He regenerates. That is the process (John 3:1–8; 16:8). But that was not all. He "set him on his own beast." He lifted him up and put him in the seat, which he himself occupied.

Again, we have no difficulty understanding that, for that is what Christ has done for us in redemption. He has raised us up and made us to sit with Him in the heavenlies. This poor traveler was no longer lying in the dust of the earth. He had been raised and seated. Later he would be able to appreciate properly what had been done for him. Just so, at conversion, it does not occur to us that we have been seated by Christ "far above all principality and power, . . . and every name that is named" (Eph. 1:21).

But there was more. The Samaritan "brought him to an inn and took care of him." He did not leave him lying by the side of the road. He brought him to a place where he could be cared for, a place where he found others able to minister to him. The inn here is a picture of the church. The church is God's provision, in this age, for all those who have been redeemed. It is in the church we find these who minister to the spiritual needs of the redeemed. That is the process.

3. A Promise

"And on the morrow when he departed, he took out two pence, and gave them to the host, and said unto him, Take care of him; and whatsoever thou spendest more, when I come again, I will repay thee . . ."

Remember, this Samaritan was on a *journey*. He could not stay with the one he had saved, for he was on a journey elsewhere. Thus too, our Lord. He did not come to stay in this world. He came to seek and to save lost people on life's sad Jericho road and then to go on His journey to His Father on high. Nor could that journey be delayed. He stayed here just long enough to make every provision for us during the period of His absence. Then He went on His way.

But the Samaritan promised to come back, in due time, bringing his rewards with him. That gave added incentive to those entrusted with the care of the saved man. Thoughts of his coming again would be a spur to those entrusted with the care of the saved man.

We are constantly reminded in the New Testament of the Lord's promise to return. "I will repay thee," said the Good Samaritan. The people at the inn were to minister on his behalf. He would enter into an accounting with them upon his return. They would not go unrewarded if they ministered just as he had ministered.

The Scriptures constantly affirm that there is a day of reckoning coming (the judgment seat of Christ) for those of us who have been left here to minister Christ to others. He has given us all we need to get on with the task until His return. We shall have to answer then for the way we have invested the means of grace He has put in our hands. If we do well, He will repay. He is no man's debtor.

But what about those two pence? Expositors have expended themselves seeking to account for them. Some have suggested they symbolize the two sacraments—baptism and breaking bread, the ordinances Christ left with the church to administer grace to the hearts of the saved. Some have suggested they symbolize the two Testaments, the Old and the New, which, together, make up God's blessed Book, wherein we can find all we will ever need to sustain us until the Lord's return.

Another suggestion is based on a man's wage in Bible times—he would work all day for a penny. In other words, the two pennies were to cover the entire period of the Good Samaritan's absence; he was anticipating being away just two days. Then he would come back and settle account. Two pence! Two "days"!

Which reminds us that Jesus has been gone now some two thousand years. The Bible tells us that with God a thousand years is *as a day,* so, looking at it that way, He has been gone two days, or there about. It is about time for Him to return. We have His pledge that back He will come, and we have this hint as to the time.

TWENTY-NINE

Three Rich Men

Luke 12:16–21; 16:19–31; 18:18–30

A. The young man: A likeable person
 1. His search
 2. His sorrow
B. The middle-aged man: A lustful person
 1. His problem
 2. His proposal
C. The dead man: A lost person
 1. His pains: They were real
 2. His prayers: They were rejected

It doesn't seem that these three rich men were, in actual fact, one and the same person. It is certain the same principle is at work. Each one illustrates the advance of the ruling passion in a person's life as time goes by. We get a glimpse of this principle putting down its early roots in a young man's life. We see the hold the love of money already has on this young optimist who came running to Jesus.

When we meet the rich young ruler, we see a likable person. Indeed, he is one of the most attractive people in all the Gospels ever to come in contact with Christ.

A. The Young Man: A Likeable Person

We are told of this young man that "Jesus beholding him loved him." Now, of course, the Lord Jesus loved everyone. He loved the loathsome leper, riddled through and through with a frightful disease so that he looked more like a monster than a man. He loved the man who spat in His face. He loved the Roman

260

soldier whose brute strength was flung behind the scourge that tore open His back until it was just a great, blood-soaked ruin. He loved the embarrassed Cyrenian who was impressed by the Romans to carry His cross for Him up Calvary's hill. He loved the man who held the hammer that drove the spikes into His hands. He loved the priests who mocked and jeered at Him as He hung upon the tree. He loved the dying thief, who, in that dark hour, stopped his cursing and prayed for salvation instead. And He loved the other thief who went on reviling and blaspheming right up until the dreadful moment he was launched headlong into a lost eternity. Jesus loved everybody. He still does. It was to give tangible expression to that love that Jesus came from His home on high to Bethlehem's barn and Golgotha's hill. As He traveled through time for those amazing twelve thousand days or so, our blessed Lord let all men know that He loved them.

But here was a special case. Here was a man of whom we read that Jesus, beholding him, loved him. This young man was an especially likeable man. There was something particularly attractive about him. He was wealthy, probably good looking, and impeccably dressed. Doubtless he had excellent manners and a charismatic personality. He was the kind of man who has more than a little touch of charm. So, in a special way, this man made an appeal to the heart of Jesus. We are told two things in particular about him.

1. His Search

This young man was conscious that there was something lacking in his life. He had everything it would seem, born with a silver spoon in his mouth, so to speak. In the first place *he was rich*. Money was no object to him. If he wanted to refurbish his house, he only had to summon his steward. If he wanted to take a trip to Babylon or to Rome or even to Britain or Gaul, he only had to decide when to leave. If he wanted new horses for his stables, new slaves for his kitchen, new clothes for his wardrobe, he only had to snap his fingers. He was rich but he was not happy.

Then, too, *he was respected*. He was a ruler. We are not told exactly what that involved. Elsewhere we are told that Nicodemus was "a ruler of the Jews." In the case of Nicodemus it probably meant that he was a member of the Sanhedrin, the governing body of the Jews.

In the case of this young man it probably meant he was the ruler of the local synagogue or else that he occupied some seat of authority in his local community.

Whatever the case may be, he had what many people covet—a recognized position that carried with it a measure of authority. He was a ruler, but he was not happy.

Moreover, *he was religious.* When the Lord Jesus tossed at him half of the Ten Commandments, the commandments which involved duty to man, the young man could look into the face of Jesus and say, "I have kept them all. I have never killed anyone. I have never committed adultery. I have never stolen anything. I have never lied about someone. I have never defrauded anybody. I have never shown disrespect to my parents." He was religious, but he was not happy. "What lack I yet?" he cried. He was conscious that some basic element was missing in his life. There was some vital key that would unlock some hidden door, but it was hidden from him. His riches, his rulership, and his religion left him empty, unsatisfied, and unhappy. So, deeply conscious that life, even at its best, could not satisfy the deepest hungers of his heart, this attractive young man decided to try Jesus. Perhaps Jesus would have the answer. Perhaps he could find in Him the thing he failed to find elsewhere in life. So, eagerly and excitedly, he came running to Christ.

At once he got off on the wrong foot. "Good Master," he cried, "what shall I do to inherit eternal life?" He used the right words. He used the conventional language. He said all the right things. He called Jesus "Good."

At once the Lord Jesus challenged him. "Why callest thou me good? There is none good but one and that one is God!" There was no escaping the challenge. Jesus said to him, "Either I am not good (in which case I am a fraud), or else I am God." Thus He confronted this young man with the greatest decision of his life—whether or not to believe Christ's claim to be absolutely God in every sense of the word and, as God, able to command this rich young ruler's total unquestioning allegiance.

The young man was not prepared to admit that. When next he spoke he did not say "Good master," he simply said, "Master!" He was prepared to concede many things to Jesus, but he was not prepared to bow heart and mind and soul and will before Him as God.

The Lord Jesus gave this young man the greatest revelation that can ever be made to a human being. He revealed to him exactly who He was—the awesome fact that He, Jesus, was the Son of God. The young man balked at it.

Next the Lord Jesus revealed to this likeable young man exactly what he was; a self-deceived sinner. When the young man professed to have kept the law of Moses, he doubted not that he had. It was then the Lord threw in His bombshell. He said, "Thou shalt love thy neighbor as thyself." It was an all-inclusive summary of half of the Decalogue. He just recited a number of specific responsibilities a man has to his neighbor and concluded, "Thou shalt love thy neighbor as thyself."

"I have kept all those," the young man said, "what lack I yet?"

2. His Sorrow

"One thing thou lackest," Jesus said, "go thy way, sell whatsoever thou hast, and give to the poor, and thou shalt have treasure in heaven: and come take up the cross, and follow me" (Mark 10:21). Jesus offered him a chance to prove that he loved his neighbor as himself. Go! Sell! Give! You say you love your neighbor as yourself? Prove it! The young man was self-deceived in thinking he had kept the Ten Commandments. The one thing that stood between him and Christ at that moment was his wealth. The Lord put His finger right on that and held it there. It is not always wealth. Sometimes it is pride. Sometimes it is intellect. Sometimes it is a besetting sin. Sometimes it is lust. Sometimes it is a godless friendship. What ever it is, Jesus will put His finger on it.

We can write two words across this young man's life—*too much!* Jesus was demanding too much. God's salvation is free, but only because it has been purchased at infinite cost at Calvary. It is offered to men without money and without price. When we come to Christ, however, we have to face whatever it is in our lives that would cause us to do what this young man did. "He went away sorrowful," we read, "for he was one that had great possessions" (Mark 10:22 ASV).

He had come to Christ. He had made his decision. It was going to cost too much to be a Christian. The demands of Christ were too great. He would like to be a Christian, but only on his own terms. He had been called upon to decide whether he would love Christ or love the world. He chose the world. And we see him now with his back turned toward Christ. We can see the droop of his shoulders, the languid, dangling hand. He has made his decision. He will live without Christ.

So then, we have looked at this young man, a likeable man, a man who decided that the claims of Christ were too much. Now we must look at the second rich man. Time has passed and time, as always, has left its mark. This rich man is not the likeable, attractive, almost artless man who made his decision, years ago, to live life without Christ. The ruling passion, love for money, has had plenty of time to mature and dominate the life of this rich man. The principle is at work: "the love of money is the root of all evil" (1 Tim. 6:10).

B. The Middle-Aged Man: A Lustful Person

The man before us now was not a licentious person. There is not the slightest hint of that. His lust was not for women, it was for wealth. His lust was for the world rather than for the flesh, although his appetites seem to have secured a good hold upon him just the same.

We are told two things about this rich man.

1. His Problem

It was the kind of problem many people would envy. He was too rich. He had too much. He did not know what to do with all his wealth. We know exactly how he got his money. So far as the text records, he got it honestly. In the case of the rich young ruler, he "had great possessions"; this rich, middle-aged man's land brought forth plentifully.

There is no hint of unscrupulous business deals. He had not robbed anybody. He had not engaged in crooked real estate deals. He had not defrauded anyone. Nobody had been hurt by his business activities. His wealth was the result of the blessing of God, that general benevolence of God that sends the rain and the sunshine upon the just and the unjust alike. He had prospered by being diligent in his business. And, as a result, he now had a very real problem. He did not know what to do with all his money. His barns were bursting at the seams. He had more grain standing in his fields awaiting his reapers than he could ever cram into his barns. Grain prices were good, but they would be even better in a few months time. There was no sense in selling now. He could make more money by waiting. But wherever could he store all his goods?

We would not need to look far to see where some of his wealth *could* go. He had laborers working for him at a minimal wage. He was paying the going price for labor. He was not cheating anyone, you must understand. He paid what we would call the union rate, that is, what the labor market would bear. That was just good business. Why pay more? What he needed was not bigger barns. He needed a bigger heart. Or he could have gone into Jerusalem and looked all about him. There were plenty of blind beggars in Jerusalem; he could have helped them. There were plenty of lepers crying for alms out on the hills, living in wretched hovels, utterly destitute, unable even to beg where the people passed by. He could have done something for them. There was no end of orphans and widows. He could have done something for them. He never so much as gave them a thought.

If we want two words to write over this man's life, they are the words *too hard!* *Too hard!* A hard heart, a hard soul. Why should he be interested in the poor? Let the government take care of them. He paid plenty of taxes; in fact, he paid far too much in taxes. If a man was poor, it was because he was lazy. It was no concern of his.

But that brought him back to his problem. What was he going to do with his goods. We can see him looking out from the veranda of his palatial home at the wide fields all golden with grain. He rubs his hands. "Wow," he says to himself, "I have had a good year. I have really done well for myself. Now then, what am I going to do with my excess?" So then, the narrative confronts us—as his prosperity confronted him—with his problem. And all the while the calculating thoughts were going on in that keen, business brain of his. The wheels were turning. The ideas were beginning to come. Dollar signs were dancing in his head. He was weighing liquid assets against fixed assets.

2. His Proposal

The man's selfishness is seen in his use of the personal pronouns "I," "me," and "my." He uses the pronoun "I" six times and says nothing of anyone else. He uses the word "my" five times revealing his covetous love of possessions: "my fruits"; "my barns"; "my corn"; "my goods"; even "my soul"! His proposal is two fold: "First," he says, "I will further enrich myself. I will pull down my barns and build greater. I will expand my fixed assets. I will put some more capital into my business. I will broaden my base. I will lay new foundations for even bigger and better surpluses in the future. I will further enrich myself."

"Then," he says, "I will enjoy myself. After all, I have it coming to me. I have worked hard all my life. I have been a zealous business man. Now I am going to have some fun. I will say to my soul, 'Soul, thou hast much goods laid up for many years, take thine ease, eat, drink, and be merry.'" That was fair enough, surely? Why should he leave it all to someone else to spend. He was going to live it up while he was still alive. "After all," he tells himself, "I am not an old man yet. I am not going to wait until I am too old to enjoy it. I am going to have me a good time now."

So that was his proposal. He was going to increase both his prosperity and his pleasures. He made one fatal mistake. He forgot that he had no control over time.

Even as he was boasting to himself of his fortune and making his plans for the future—plans that left God and His Son as completely out as though they did not exist—even as he was making his plans, God was making His.

"Thou fool!" The voice rang like the knell of doom in his soul. "This night thy soul shall be required of thee, then whose shall these things be?" And did he repent, even with the sentence of death to be executed before the earth could spin once more? Not he! And why? He was too hard. His soul was as hard as the rocks he tossed from the land he tilled. There are not many deathbed conversions.

C. THE DEAD MAN: A LOST PERSON

Which brings us to the third scene in the drama, the third scene and the last. And a terrible scene it is. The likeable man, the lustful man has now become the *lost man*—lost and forever lost. We look now not at the likeable man, not at the lustful man, but at the lost man. For now he is dead.

This is not a parable. A parable never names its characters. This is an incident, torn from life, a page out of somebody's history ripped out of eternity and thrust in here, in the Book of God, for all to read.

The man over whose head the sentence of death was pronounced from on high is dead. The ruling passion for money still operates. He is haunted by the memory of his goods. Gone, and gone forever! Another has them now.

We are told about this man that he "fared sumptuously every day." The Greek word is *lampros,* which simply means "brilliantly." The word is not used in a commendable sense. He had been a man fond of ostentatious display—"he fared flamboyantly" would be a better way to put it. His dinner table was covered with vessels of gold. His banqueting table featured the most exotic and expensive of delights.

No less impressive were his raiment—"purple and fine linen." Along the coast of Tyre, there was found a rare shellfish from which the costly purple dye could be obtained, each little creature yielding a single drop of dye. Woolen garments dyed with it were worn by kings and rulers. The rich man had worn purple. His undergarments were made of fine linen produced from Egyptian flax, which grew along the banks of the Nile. This linen was dazzlingly white and was worth its weight in gold. This rich man, then, lived flamboyantly. He lived utterly and completely for himself.

Mention is made, too, of his gate. Again, the word used is of interest. It is a word that means "a gate of beauty." It was ornate, then, covered with scrollwork and intricate carvings, a gate worth a small fortune in itself. And at that beautiful gate of his, no doubt to his supreme and utter disgust, there lay a beggar. For this rich man, after all, would have no need to go to Jerusalem to find beggars. He had one at his gate.

Imagine this rich man as he spurs his fine horse out of his driveway. The wretched beggar scrambles to get out of his way, otherwise, he will be churned beneath the horse's hoofs. The rich man is filled with contempt and rage that so dirty and despicable an object should sully his gate. Yet it is too much trouble to drive him away, so he leaves him there to starve.

Here was the kind of man no earthly court would ever arrest or condemn. On the contrary, he was possibly a member of the civil court. The other judges would have been his friends. They would have thought well of him, spoke highly of him. He was rich, and that said it all. But God can and does arrest men like that, as in the end He arrests all men. He sent one of His messengers to arrest him. That messenger's name was Death.

At this point the final chapter begins in the story of this man's life. A long chapter it is, and it is not finished yet. It has been going on these two thousand years. And it will go on and on forever.

1. His Pains: They Were Real

The text says that he went to *hades* or *sheol*. Both words, one Greek, the other Hebrew, describe the place and condition of those who have died but who have not yet been raised from the dead.

He was in a place where the torment was real. The man was in utter anguish. He could see and hear and feel and reason and remember. In other words, although he was dead, he was still very much alive. All death had done for him was strip him of his body and change his location. But he was still a rational human being.

The Lord Jesus does not linger long over his sufferings in hades. He tells us enough for us to know that they were real, they were intense, they were endless, and they were deserved. Christless he had lived, Christless he had died. Christless he would be forever. So then, attention is drawn to his pains. They were very real.

2. His Prayers: They Were Rejected

This man woke up in hades, a believer in prayer. Across his dreadful misery, however, can be written two words, *too late!* He prayed for two things. First of all, and this was typical of his selfishness, he prayed for himself. He wanted just a moment's relief from his pains. His request was denied. What he wanted was impossible. His condition was fixed and final. He was getting exactly what he had earned. It is too late to pray once a person is dead. The time to pray is now. The Bible says that "the Son of man hath power on *earth* to forgive sins" (Mark 2:10). We must get our sins forgiven now; it will be too late then.

Then he prayed for his brothers. He wanted Lazarus, the beggar man who had once sat at his gate, sent to his brothers. Again his request was denied. He thought that a ghost sent to his brothers would be more effective than the Bible. Such is the basic delusion behind all necromancy and spiritism.

"They have Moses and the prophets," he was told. They have the Bible. Let them read the Bible. If they will not believe the Bible, then God has no more to say to them. And so stubborn is the unregenerate will, so determined in its opposition to God, so obdurate in its unbelief that, even in that place of torment, the man continued to argue and to want his own way.

"No! No! No!" he says, "if somebody rose from the dead they would believe."

"Nonsense!" he is told. "Even though one rose from the dead, they still would not believe." It is significant that the very next person Jesus raised from the dead was a man named Lazarus. And what did the Jews do with him? They tried to put him to death (John 12:10).

But more! God has raised yet Another from the dead, His only begotten and well beloved Son. But do men believe? Some do. Many don't. Those who will not bow to the authority of the Word of God carry their unbelief to a denial of the resurrection of Christ. Yet *that* is one of the best attested facts of history.

So there it is. The story of a ruling passion. The story of a wealthy young man who rejected Christ, rejected Him deliberately and consciously simply because he did not like what Christ had to say to him. The story of a man who mistook his bank book for his Bible, his body for his soul, and time for eternity. The story of a man who woke up in hades, lost. The story is written large into our Bibles, written for those of whom it must be said that they have

> Room for pleasure, room for business
> But for Christ the Crucified
> Not a place where He can enter
> In the heart for which he died.[1]

---

1. Daniel W. Whittle, "Have You Any Room for Jesus?" 1878.

THIRTY

Lazarus

Recalled to Life

Luke 10:38–42; John 11–12

A. LAZARUS AND HIS SISTERS
1. Their humble home
2. Their happy home
3. Their helpful home
B. LAZARUS AND HIS SICKNESS
C. LAZARUS AND HIS SAVIOR
1. The coming of Jesus
2. The comfort of Jesus
a. For Martha: Truth
b. For Mary: Tears
3. The command of Jesus
D. LAZARUS AND HIS SERVICE
1. Martha worked
2. Mary worshiped
3. Lazarus witnessed

Lazarus belongs to a rare species of human beings. Having passed through death and burial, he knew what it was like to stand on resurrection ground. Imagine his experience! He knows what it is like to die and go to heaven and then to lay aside the glory he had with the Father and come back to a world of sin. He knows what it is like to come "out of the ivory palaces into a world of woe."[1]

---

1. Henry Barraclough, "Ivory Palaces," 1915, a hymn based on Psalm 45:8.

Probably no other living man knew as much as Lazarus did about what Jesus gave up to come down here.

Yet Lazarus's lips were sealed, it seems. He has told us nothing about the streets of gold, the pearly gates, the crystal stream, the tree of life, the jasper walls, the angel choirs, or the shining ones that stand around the throne. Like the apostle Paul, who also had a rapture experience, Lazarus must have decided that some things cannot be uttered.

Having seen the other side, his heart and mind lived over there, although his body stayed here. One commentator has said that forever afterward Lazarus eyed the world like a child.

Let us think about this man who was one of the closest friends Jesus had on earth.

A. Lazarus and His Sisters

1. Their Humble Home

Lazarus and his sisters probably had a modest home on the Mount of Olives. Nearly all of Jesus' friends lived in modest circumstances. As Paul puts it, "Not many mighty, not many noble, are called" (1 Cor. 1:26). Jesus found His friends, for the most part, among the ordinary people of Palestine—a fisherman here, a customs officer there. His closest friends were folk from the unsophisticated countryside of Galilee, despised by the rich, the powerful, and the great.

Jesus sought out people like the brokenhearted widow of Nain, the blind beggar Bartimaeus, and the nameless paralytic at the pool of Bethesda. Most of the people in the Gospels are left anonymous. Jesus loved this world's nobodies, and perhaps that is why He felt at home at Bethany in the house of Lazarus.

2. Their Happy Home

Two sisters and a brother lived in that home in Bethany. Martha seems to have been the dominant one, with Mary coming next, and Lazarus always hovering in the background and saying nothing. Not a single word, in fact, that he uttered is recorded in the Gospels. But he evidently was very much loved by his sisters.

Their home was, of course, thoroughly human. As different as Martha was from Mary, there would have been occasional tension between the two sisters. Martha was essentially a doer, and Mary was essentially a dreamer. When two people like that get together, they are bound to have some hasty words once in a while. Mary at times would have exasperated Martha, and Martha with her restless energy would sometimes have frayed Mary's nerves.

But still it was a very happy home. How they looked forward to the occasional visits of Jesus and His twelve friends! We can imagine the laughter and good fellowship they enjoyed on those occasions.

3. Their Helpful Home

Jesus would not have felt free to take that motley crowd of disciples into just anybody's home. But we can be sure He never hesitated to take them to the home on the Mount of Olives where Martha, Mary, and Lazarus lived.

We can picture the scene in Bethany when word comes that Jesus is in Jerusalem. Expecting Him to visit, Martha rushes off to the market to buy olives, figs, dates, raisins, honey, corn, grapes, and everything else needed for a plentiful supper. As soon as she gets home, she prepares what Jesus likes best (we can be sure she knows what His favorite dish is). Mary hurries around with mop and duster to put the house in order before their honored guest and His friends arrived. And Lazarus kills the fatted calf.

Luke describes one scene when Jesus was present in that home. Martha's busyness and Mary's blessedness are evident. Martha, bustling here, there, and everywhere is "cumbered about much serving." There would be bread to bake, meat to cook, salad to fix, and a table to set. And where is Mary?

Mary, as always, is at Jesus' feet. Three times in the Gospels we meet her, and each time she is at Jesus' feet: in life's most *tranquil* hour, before the shadows of Calvary closed in; in life's most *tragic* hour, when Lazarus lay dead and buried in the grave; in life's most *triumphant* hour, after Lazarus came forth from the tomb. She alone, it seems, had entered into the real secret of the Lord. Mary of Bethany was the only one of the Marys not at Calvary.

Presiding over the scene with humble self-abasement, keeping himself in the background but essential to it all, is Lazarus.

B. Lazarus and His Sickness

John 11 tells the story, and we can supply for ourselves some details the apostle left out. Lazarus comes home from work one day complaining of not feeling well. Martha instantly bundles him off to bed and gathers blankets and warming stones for his chills and cool cloths for his fever. Mary sooths his brow with the cloths, a servant goes for the doctor.

But Lazarus gets worse, and his sisters, of course, think of Jesus. Who else can heal the sick as Jesus can? Had He not healed Simon Peter's mother-in-law of a fever? Had He not healed Simon the leper?

"Where is He?" Martha asks.

"He's away across Jordan in Peraea," Mary answers.

But the crisis in the sickness of their beloved brother is approaching. They send a messenger to Jesus. Their last urgent word to him is, "Hurry! Hurry!" Mary and Martha wait, however, for days.

Lazarus sinks lower and lower, and the doctor gives up on the case. Then the messenger come back . . . alone. "Where's Jesus?" Martha asks.

"He's busy," the messenger replies. "He said not to worry. Everything will be all right. He'll come later."

"Later! But Lazarus is dying!"

Did Lazarus come back for a moment into consciousness? Did he whisper, "Is Jesus coming?" before he lapsed into a coma?

The sisters look at each other, unable to think of an explanation for the extraordinary conduct of Jesus. Why doesn't He come? Or simply speak the word of power from afar and heal Lazarus as He had healed the servant of the Capernaum centurion? They hope against hope until it becomes obvious that Jesus is not coming, and Lazarus is going to die.

And die he did. His struggle over; he lay there cold and stiff. And still not a word from Jesus. The bitterness of disappointment was added to the bitterness of grief.

The funeral was about as sad as a funeral could be. Because of the inexplicable silence of Jesus, the death seemed all the more tragic. Why had He not healed Lazarus? It was one of those inscrutable questions we so often ask when we face the loss of a dear one. Why? Why? Why? Jesus, it seemed, had let His friends down. Did such a thought enter their heads? They would not have been human if they had not entertained it for at least a moment.

C. Lazarus and His Savior

Lazarus was buried, and the days dragged on—one, two, three, four long days. And suddenly Mary and Martha heard the news. Jesus is coming!

1. The Coming of Jesus

Storm clouds were gathering in Jerusalem when Jesus said to His disciples, "Let us go into Judaea again." Thomas rallied the disciples: "Let us also go, that we may die with him." Back across the Jordan they went, on up into the hill country of Judea, across the Kidron, and up the Mount of Olives to Bethany. All the way, we can imagine, Jesus reassures the disciples; in effect He says, "Lazarus is quite all right. His sickness, whatever its outcome, is for the glory of God. His body might well be asleep in death, but he himself, the real Lazarus, is very much alive."

D. L. Moody caught on to that truth. In the halls of Moody Bible Institute there is a picture of Moody's grave and with it a quotation from the renowned evangelist: "One of these days you will read that D. L. Moody of Northfield is dead. Don't believe it! I shall be more alive then than I am now."

When Moody's time came to die, he kept reporting to those around his death-bed what he was seeing and experiencing. He said, "Earth recedes; heaven opens before me." His son thought his father had been dreaming. "This is no dream, Will," Moody said. "It is beautiful. . . . God is calling me, and I must go. . . . This is my coronation day!" Referring to his two little grandchildren who had gone on before, he joyfully exclaimed, "Dwight! Irene! I see the children's faces!" And so in a little while D. L. Moody passed on in triumph to the other side.[2]

Lazarus's body was dead, but his soul, we can be certain, was alive on the other shore. He was wrapped in a tumult of bliss and in "joy unspeakable and full of glory" (1 Peter 1:8).

At last Jesus came and Martha rushed out to meet Him. Mary remained in the house.

2. The Comfort of Jesus

How practical and appropriate Jesus was in His comforting. He met Martha with *truth.* "Thy brother shall rise again," He said.

In response Martha expressed her faith in the resurrection: "I know that he shall rise again in the resurrection at the last day." There was nothing wrong with her theology, but theology, however sound, is cold comfort for someone standing by a brand new tomb.

---

2. W. R. Moody and A. P. Fitt, *Life of D. L. Moody* (London: Morgan and Scott, n.d.), 121.

Jesus looked at her and made one of the truly great statements of the New Testament. "I am the resurrection, and the life," He said. "He that believeth in me, though he were dead, yet shall he live: and whosoever liveth and believeth in me shall never die. Believest thou this?" (John 11:25–26). We can divide this statement into three parts:

1. "I am the resurrection, and the life." Jesus said in effect, "I am the source of *resurrection* life. The resurrection of all believers is guaranteed by Me. I *am* the resurrection. Without Me there is no resurrection."
2. "He that believeth in me, though he were dead, yet shall he live." Jesus said in effect, "I am the source of *spiritual* life. I have come to deal with the source of all death and to impart the very life of God to the souls of those who believe."
3. "Whosoever liveth and believeth in me shall never die." Jesus was saying in effect, "I am the source of *eternal* life. When a person receives the life of God, he can never die. He becomes an heir of eternal life. A brief sojourn in the tomb cannot alter that fact."

Martha was a practical, thinking woman. Jesus comforted her with *truth*. He was able to deal with her sorrow by enlarging her spiritual horizons until they were as wide as eternity, and by focusing her spiritual eyesight on Himself. Martha at once affirmed her absolute trust in Him as the Son of God. "Yea, Lord," she said, "I believe that thou art the Christ, the Son of God, which should come into the world." Then she went and called Mary to come at once to meet with Jesus.

Jesus met Mary with *tears*. Mary's needs were quite different from Martha's. Mary needed her emotions soothed. "Lord," she said, "if thou hadst been here, my brother had not died." Gently Jesus asked her to show Him Lazarus's tomb. Then we read that "Jesus wept." It is the shortest verse in the Bible, yet it preaches volumes.

Jesus wept because He, too, was man, "a man of sorrows, and acquainted with grief" (Isa. 53:3). He wept, as man, out of sympathy for Martha and Mary. The Bible says, "When Jesus therefore saw [Mary] weeping, and the Jews also weeping which came with her, he groaned in the spirit, and was troubled" (John 11:33). The word translated "groaned" is *embrimaomai,* which literally means "to snort," just as a horse does when it is angry. The indication is that Jesus expressed strong emotion. More specifically He was indignant. As He, the Lord of life and glory, stood there amidst all that sorrow, He was indignant at the heartache that sin and Satan had caused on this earth. Moreover He intended to do something about it.

3. The Command of Jesus

First Jesus said, "Take ye away the stone." He never does for us what we can do for ourselves. He does not perform miracles in situations where muscle power or brain power could accomplish the same results. Jesus could have stood in front of Lazarus's tomb, waved His hand over the stone, and seen it dissolve into dust, but He never performs idle miracles.

"Take ye away the stone," He said. Practical Martha objected. Horrified, she said, "Lord, by this time he stinketh: for he hath been dead four days." For a moment she forgot her fine theology and her grand assertion of faith in the deity of Christ. All she could think of was the corruption of the grave and what four days of decomposition in a warm climate had done to the body of Lazarus.

Jesus gently overruled all objections. "Said I not unto thee," He asked, "that, if thou wouldest believe, thou shouldest see the glory of God?" So they rolled away the stone.

Then Jesus prayed. He addressed Himself to His Father in heaven because He wanted the world to know that God was His Father. He wanted to show that although He was the Son—coequal, coeternal, coexistent with the Father—He never acted in independence of the Father. Jesus also wanted to indicate that the mighty miracle He was about to perform was proof of His absolute deity just as much as it was proof of His perfect humanity made available to His Father. "Father," he prayed, "I thank thee that thou hast heard me. And I knew that thou hearest me always: but because of the people which stand by I said it, that they may believe that thou hast sent me" (John 11:41–42).

After praying, Jesus gave a command to the corpse and summoned its soul from on high. "Lazarus," He said, "come forth."

Once an infidel was lecturing an audience and spewing forth his unbelief. In the course of his remarks, he referred to this story of Lazarus and asked a rhetorical question: "Why did Jesus say, 'Lazarus, come forth'?" Before the lecturer could proceed, a man in the audience called out, "Mister, I'll tell you why. If Jesus had not said, 'Lazarus, come forth,' all the dead in the world would have come forth."

Thus it was that Lazarus had scarcely tuned his harp, had barely settled comfortably into his new home on high, had hardly said his first half dozen hallelujahs when he heard that mighty shout echoing through the halls of heaven: "Lazarus, come forth." He handed his harp back to the chief musician, and there was silence in heaven as Lazarus left his heavenly abode and set his face as flint toward Jerusalem and Bethany on the Mount of Olives. The heavenly hosts watched as one of their glorified throng wended his way out of the pearly gates, down the skyways to earth, back to that tomb, and into a body now made perfectly whole.

The watchers at the grave saw a strange sight: what they thought was a corpse wrapped up like a mummy glided out of the depths of the tomb. "Loose him," said Jesus, "and let him go." Again He would not do for the observers what they could do for themselves. He could have waved his hand, and those bandages would have unwrapped themselves. He could have commanded Lazarus to step out of those constricting folds of cloth and spice, just as He Himself would step out of His own grave clothes a short while later. But Jesus was not there to provide spectacles for the curious. "Loose him, and let him go," He said.

D. Lazarus and His Service

We know what would have happened today. After Jesus performed the miracle, someone would have invited Lazarus to appear on TV as the star of a talk show, and then the host would have made an appeal for money. But Lazarus lived in the first century, and he simply went on home.

Scripture allows us one more look into that Bethany home. John 12 tells us how the grateful family made a supper for the Lord Jesus and His disciples six days before Passover—a week before Calvary. In that brief glimpse we see Martha, Mary, and Lazarus doing what each could do best. Martha was working, Mary was worshiping, and Lazarus was witnessing.

1. Martha Worked

Martha was busy in the kitchen with the pots and pans, for she was making a great supper. The three of them plus the twelve disciples plus Jesus made sixteen, not to mention any neighbors who might stop by.

Martha was as happy as she could possibly be. Lazarus was alive again, and the presence of a resurrected man in the home put an end to all complaints. Martha "served," the Holy Spirit said in John 12:2, using the same word Jesus used in Luke 22:27: "I am among you as he that serveth." The word translated "serve" means "to minister." Martha's kitchen had become a cloister. She had elevated her work with rolling pins and colanders to the status of a ministry.

2. Mary Worshiped

"Then took Mary a pound of ointment of spikenard, very costly, and anointed the feet of Jesus, and wiped his feet with her hair: and the house was filled with the odour of the ointment" (John 12:3). Judas glumly put a price tag on the ointment and hypocritically complained that the money might have been better spent on the poor. But Jesus cut him off. "Let her alone," He said, "against the day of my burying hath she kept this."

Mary, then, fully understood what lay ahead. She knew that Jesus was going to die. She must have been sorely tempted to bring out that flask of costly ointment when Lazarus died. But she kept it for Jesus, for *His* burial. The resurrection of her brother, however, opened her eyes to an even greater truth: Jesus was going to rise again. The psalmist had said that His body would not even see corruption. Mary would not need the ointment for His burial after all. She did not have to wait until He died to anoint Him. She could do it right now.

As Mary's act of worship was consummated, the whole place was filled with the fragrance. Jesus had the joy of knowing that there was one person on earth who knew what lay ahead for Him—death, burial, and resurrection.

3. Lazarus Witnessed

"Much people of the Jews therefore knew that he was there [that Jesus was in the home of Lazarus]: and they came not for Jesus' sake only, but that they might see Lazarus also, whom he had raised from the dead" (John 12:9). So we catch a glimpse of Lazarus witnessing.

People wanted to see a man living in the power of resurrection life. There was something wonderfully attractive about the new Lazarus. I don't suppose they would have flocked to see the old Lazarus, but the new Lazarus was something else.

The world still wants to see people living in resurrection power—Christians so identified with Christ in His death, burial, and resurrection that they are living a new life beyond the reach of death. That new life is our inheritance in Christ.

The reaction to the witness of Lazarus was twofold. "The chief priests consulted that they might put Lazarus also to death." That was one result. "By reason of him many of the Jews went away, and believed on Jesus." That was the other result.

Jesus and His people always drive a wedge as wide as the world through the ranks of mankind. We are all to be found on one or the other side of a great divide. We either reject Him or enthrone Him. No one can be neutral. We all line up either for Him or against Him, now and for all eternity.

THIRTY-ONE

Caiaphas

The Crooked High Priest

John 18:13–14, 24, 28

A. CAIAPHAS AND THE CHRIST
  1. The corruption of Judas
  2. The crucifixion of Jesus
     a. What happened at the trial
     b. What happened at the tomb
B. CAIAPHAS AND THE CHURCH
  1. The first step
     a. The threat
     b. The thrashing
  2. The further step
  3. The final step

The ghost of Caiaphas haunts the Gospels and the opening chapters of the book of Acts. He himself has been dead and damned these many long centuries. He was the High Priest of Israel in the days of John the Baptist and Jesus. Having been appointed by Valerius Gratus, Caiaphas held the office from the years A.D. 18–36. He held on to the office through the years that Pilate was procurator of Judea, and was deposed by the Roman proconsul Vitellus. The only other fact we know about him, apart from his treatment of Christ and the church, is that he was the son-in-law of Annas, the previous High Priest.

This wicked man, Caiaphas, sinned against the *light* and against the *law* and against the *Lord*. For he was fully acquainted with the coming and career of Christ. We can be sure he made it his business to know all about the movements and messages and miracles of Jesus. "This man doeth many miracles," he grudgingly confessed (see John 11:47). Just the same, he categorically rejected Christ.

He used the power of his office to rig a false and illegal trial, run through an unjust and iniquitous sentence, and then mobilize Jewish public opinion in a national rejection of Christ that has lasted now for some two thousand years.

It is hard to picture anyone being quite as cold-bloodedly wicked as Caiaphas. He comes and goes in the biblical narrative over a dozen times. It was he who organized, and then rationalized, and then mobilized official Jewish opposition to Christ. God's own Son, the second Person of the Godhead, the eternal, un-created, self-existing Jehovah of the Old Testament had been miraculously and supernaturally born on this planet. Caiaphas arranged to have Him crucified. His name lives in infamy.

A. CAIAPHAS AND THE CHRIST

The problem was that Caiaphas felt insecure in his job. For years the office of the High Priest had been more of a political appointment than a privilege bestowed by the living God on a member of the tribe of Levi, of the house of Aaron and of the family of Eliezer. The Romans had made Caiaphas high priest; the Romans could remove him as well.

Although Caiaphas was High Priest in name and wore the robes of his office, he knew only too well that his formidable and influential father-in-law, Annas, was as much (if not more) the High Priest as he was. Indeed, in all but name, it was Annas who called the shots. Worse still, from his point of view, this man, Jesus, from the half-Gentile province of Galilee and the thoroughly despised town of Nazareth, was stirring up trouble. He claimed to be the Messiah and had gathered a vast following, especially in the northern parts of the country. There was no denying the pungent character of His teaching. It was teaching with an authority singularly lacking in that of the Scribes. And there was no denying His miracles. There were hundreds of them.

Nor was there any denying His lineage. That would, surely, be one of the first things that Caiaphas would check. The temple records would reveal that through His stepfather, Joseph, Jesus was of the lineage of David—a direct descendant of Solomon. Moreover, He was also a direct descendant of David through His mother, through a secondary but equally impeccable line.

The Romans would have little tolerance for trouble-making Jewish Messiahs. They would frown on any nation that harbored them. Any Roman-appointed

High Priest who showed any sign of following Him would be dealt with surely and swiftly. So, it boiled down, with Caiaphas and his cronies in the Council, to a simple equation: It was Jesus, or them. Caiaphas was quite determined it wasn't going to be him. The only alternative was to get rid of this nuisance of a Messiah. He was a growing threat to the religious establishment; so He must go.

1. The Corruption of Judas

Matters came to a head when Jesus raised Lazarus from the dead. The entire surrounding countryside was ablaze with the news. From Jerusalem itself, people were flocking out to nearby Bethany to see the wonder for themselves.

A hasty meeting was called of the Sanhedrin, the supreme national court. It consisted of seventy-one members; Caiaphas, the High Priest, was its president. Normally its meetings were held in the "stone chamber" in the temple precincts. Many think, however, that this emergency session was held in the High Priest's house. To this very day, the traditional site where the house of Caiaphas stood is called "the Hill of Evil Counsel."

The members of the court expressed their frustration. "What do we [do]?" they said, "for this man [performeth] many miracles." *That* was their complaint. Instead of rejoicing that such a mighty and monumental miracle as the raising of Lazarus had been wrought, they wrung their hands in impotent rage. Caiaphas stood up. First he poured scorn on his fellow members of the council, calling them a bunch of ignoramuses. Then, callously adopting a policy of political expediency, he proposed a solution. "It is expedient for us," he said, "that one man should die for the people, and that the whole nation perish not" (John 11:50). If said in the context of the cross, Caiaphas would have bitten off his tongue rather than admit such a thing. But God took hold of the wicked man's tongue and made him say (as centuries before he had taken hold of Balaam's tongue) the very truth itself.

Here, then, was the solution to the problem. They must arrest Jesus by stealth and hand Him over to the Romans as a troublemaker to be put to death. If it was to be Christ or them, they were going to make quite certain it was not them. The majority of the counsel went along with this infamous decision, made by the religious leaders of the nation. Those leaders, however, had a problem. Jesus was immensely popular. Moreover, He had undeniable, awesome, supernatural powers. It would be necessary to exercise the greatest care in clandestinely arresting this unwanted Messiah.

Then Judas showed up. He played right into the crafty Caiaphas's hands. Judas was a disgruntled man. He had staked everything on securing a high position for himself in the expected kingdom. He envisioned a lucrative position with all kinds of pomp and power. But all Jesus could talk about was a spiritual kingdom based on a revolution of love.

Caiaphas let Judas run on until he finally came to the point. "How much will you give me if I betray Him into your hands?" Cynically, Caiaphas offered him thirty pieces of silver—the price of a female slave. Judas snapped it up.

They were a pair well met. How Caiaphas must have laughed when Judas went off with the paltry sum in his pocket. How he must have rubbed his hands with wicked glee. Now it was only a matter of time. He had a spy in the inner circle. He had completed the corruption of Judas.

2. The Crucifixion of Jesus

It was Caiaphas who was responsible for the crucifixion.

In due time Judas sent word that he was ready to earn his pay. He would hand Christ over to the authorities that very night in the garden of Gethsemane. Caiaphas arranged for Judas to be provided with an armed escort, for he was still apprehensive. A Man who could walk upon the angry waves, or still a raging storm, or feed thousands with a little lad's lunch, or raise a man dead and buried in his tomb, and who had the ear of the common people was no Man to trifle with. Never, to date, had Jesus used His power to protect Himself; but one never knew. Suppose He performed a miracle such as Moses had performed when the ground gaped open to swallow alive, down into the pit, Korah and his conspirators? Or what if He performed a miracle such as Elijah had performed and called down fire on His foes?

One could not be too careful. It was just as well the arrest was to take place at night, and in a quiet garden. Still, an armed escort, including a contingent of Roman troops, would be in order.

Things were working out nicely from Caiaphas's point of view. For if Jesus *did* defend Himself, and if some Roman soldiers were to get killed, why, then, Pilate would act. The Sanhedrin could explain that it was on Rome's side, that it was trying to arrest a seditious man when the trouble broke out. And, yes, it would willingly hand over this unwanted Messiah to Rome.

a. What Happened at the Trial

Thanks to Judas, Jesus was taken. True, He had demonstrated His supernatural power by throwing the arresting officers and the accompanying mob flat on their backs. True, too, one of the disciples had waved a sword about. But to little effect. One of Caiaphas's own servants, a man named Malchus, had his ear sliced off, only to have it put back on for him by this unwanted Messiah.

What mattered was that, in the end, Jesus had agreed to come quietly. He had been taken first to Annas. Caiaphas considered that to be a courtesy call. Annas bundled Him off as fast as he could to Caiaphas. The stage was now set for a midnight, drumhead courtmartial, wholly illegal (Matt. 26:57).

The first order of the day was to round up a number of false witnesses. That had been done, but to little effect, because their testimony was so palpably false or thoroughly contradictory that even that corrupt court could not use it.

Finally, along came a prize pair whose testimony seemed a little more promising. They had heard this Galilean Messiah say something about destroying the temple and rebuilding it in three days. True to form, they twisted His words to give them a meaning never intended. Jesus, throughout all this inglorious spectacle, remained silent. Finally, even this line of false testimony broke down. Caiaphas, however, was a resourceful man. He had in mind to lay a trap.

The Sanhedrin sat on opposite couches in a circular hall. The president, usually the High Priest, and certainly so in this case, sat in the middle at the farther end. On one side of him sat the *Ab Beth Din* (the Father of the House of Judgment). On his other side sat the *Chakam* (the Wise Man). The accused was placed opposite him. There was probably at least a quorum present. A quorum consisted of about a third of the total number of members, about twenty-three persons. Probably most of those present were priests.

Caiaphas, himself, was a member of a small elite. The high priesthood at this time was confined to about half a dozen closely connected families. Since the days of Herod, the high priests were little more than puppets of the civil power. They were appointed or discharged at the will of the Roman governor. High priests came and went. There were no less than twenty-eight high priests in just over a hundred years. At this impromptu, special meeting of the Sanhedrin, there could have been at least two dozen living and ex-high priests present. Caiaphas was a prize sample. He had gained his elevation by bribery.

He was thoroughly frustrated by the eloquent silence of Jesus. We can see him as, at last, he jumps up from his couch. He paces up and down between the couches on either side. Finally he stops in front of Jesus and puts Him under oath: "I adjure thee by the living God, that thou tell us whether thou be the Christ, the Son of God" (Matt. 26:63). Was He or wasn't He the *Christ* of God? Was He or wasn't He the *Son of God?* "I AM" He said. Then He added: "And ye shall see the Son of man sitting on the right hand of power, and coming [with] the clouds of heaven" (Mark 14:62).

An exultant Caiaphas rent his clothes, shouting, "Blasphemy! We need no further witnesses! We have all heard Him blaspheme" (see Matt. 26:65). Little did Caiaphas know that the rending of his clothes would soon be followed by the rending of the temple veil. The rending of the temple veil, whereby Judaism was rendered null and void, would be followed in less than four decades by the rending of the nation.

The long, cold night went on. The Sanhedrin eyed Him with angry and malicious dislike. Over the years He had exposed them all. He had exposed the *priests* whose greed and selfishness He had challenged. He had exposed the *elders* whose hypocrisy He had denounced. He had exposed the *scribes* whose ignorance He had unveiled. He had exposed the *Sadducees,* to which order both Annas and Caiaphas belonged. He had refuted their liberal theology as mere empty philosophy. One and all, they were bent on His death.

They spent the rest of the night tormenting Him. They spat in His face. They smote Him with rods. They clenched their fists and punched Him. They slapped Him with their open palms. They invented a new game. They blindfolded Him and hit Him again and again saying, "Prophesy to us, O Messiah, who hit you that time?" (see Matt. 26:68).

Then, when the early dawn broke across the eastern sky, they took Him to the Paved Hall at the southeast corner of the temple and gathered the bulk of the Sanhedrin together to ratify the sentence. It did not take long. Then they were at it again, beating Him, punching Him, deriding Him.

The next step was to secure the compliance of Pilate. At first they had a difficult time of it, for Pilate was filled with superstitious dread when the Jews declared that their Prisoner claimed to be the Son of God. He was of half a mind to chastise Him and set Him free.

Caiaphas and His crowd, however, had not sat up all night, scheming and plotting to get a death sentence, only to have their verdict overturned by a higher court. They knew how to force Pilate's hand. This Man Jesus claimed to be a

King, the King of the Jews no less. If Pilate set Jesus free, he would have Caesar to reckon with. The Jews confronted Pilate with a new fear—fear of Caesar.

That did it. Pilate caved in. Caiaphas had successfully forced his hand. Pilate signed the death warrant. Now Caiaphas could crow even louder. His hated Prisoner would die, not by stoning, but by the even more terrible and disgraceful death of *crucifixion.*

He went home that night aglow with his victory. He had become a candidate for the deepest, hottest corner of hell.

b. What Happened at the Tomb

First, however, there was another matter. *Judas came back.* It had finally dawned on him what he had done. Those cursed coins he had earned by treachery burned in his pocket like coals of fire. He took them back to the temple. He appeared again before the chief priests, of whom, surely, Caiaphas was one. He made confession. "I have sinned," he said, "in that I have betrayed the innocent blood." They sneered: "What is that to us? see thou to that" (Matt. 27:4). Such was their cold and heartless reply.

The wretched man pulled the silver pieces from his pocket and flung them down. We can almost hear them roll and rattle across the marble mosaic of the temple court. The priests went scrabbling after them and counted them up. Good! They were all there.

The priestly conspirators gazed at the coins and debated what to do with them. It would be unlawful to put them in the temple treasury. That was their sanctimonious decision. Still, they would put them to good use; they could buy a potter's field with this blood money and use it as a burial place for strangers. The field became known as *Aceldama,* "The field of blood." In making this decision, they unwittingly fulfilled an ancient prophecy of Zechariah (11:12–13). Pleased with themselves, the priests then hurried on out to Calvary to crown all their other infamies by mocking the dying Son of God.

Then came the doubts. Two members of the Sanhedrin advertised their complete break with Caiaphas and his cronies. Joseph of Arimathea and Nicodemus, both wealthy and influential members of the Sanhedrin, took their stand for Christ. Joseph secured possession of the body of Jesus from Pilate and brought costly linen for His burial. Nicodemus came with a fortune in spices. Joseph then donated his brand new tomb, and the body of Jesus was honorably interred.

Meanwhile, Caiaphas and his gang hurried off to Pilate, too. Dredged up from the murky depths of their dark, benighted souls, came a memory. The Lord had foretold His crucifixion—*and His resurrection*. They could remember His words. He had likened Himself to Jonah. As Jonah had been three days and three nights in the whale's belly, so He, Jesus, would be three days and three nights in the tomb. Then He would rise. His words burned upon the walls of their memory like the fiery letters on the wall of Belshazzar's palace. It is a remarkable fact that the Lord's friends forgot His words, whereas His foes remembered them.

Too late to get custody of the body of Jesus, the Sanhedrin decided to make sure His tomb was sealed. Back they went to Pilate with their request. He concurred; for by now his own conscience was tormenting him, too. He loaned them a contingent of soldiers to seal and secure the tomb for the next few days.

It was all in vain. On the third day *He arose!* Angels came down from on high to open the tomb and show the world that He was gone. Just one sight of those angels and the soldiers fled in terror to report to the Jewish authorities what had happened. Again Caiaphas convened the Sanhedrin. The grave was empty! There was no denying the fact. Caiaphas was now faced with terrifying proof of the deity of Christ, but instead of repenting, he invented a lie. He bribed the soldiers and bought the sullen connivance of Pilate. He circulated the word that the disciples had stolen the body. It was another nail in the coffin of his unbelief.

B. Caiaphas and the Church

The Son of God had come and gone, and Caiaphas had rejected Him. God, in His infinite patience, withheld His hand. As they had nailed Him to the cross, Jesus had prayed, "Father, forgive them; for they know not what they do" (Luke 23:34). Instead of pouring out end-time apocalyptic judgments on Jews and Gentiles alike, God acted in grace. He sent His Holy Spirit into the world, and the church was born.

Caiaphas rejected Him all over again. There were three swift, final, downward steps.

1. The First Step

First came *the threat*. It must have seemed to Caiaphas, in the calm between Passover and Pentecost, that he had won. The disciples lay low, cowed and cautious. True, they still met in that upper room; but if all they did was have prayer meetings and cast votes, they were harmless enough. There wasn't a scholar, soldier, or statesman among them.

Then came Pentecost. Suddenly, those dozen men and their friends and followers were transformed; and Jerusalem was invaded by a massive Holy Spirit revival. People turned to the risen Christ and were saved by the thousands. A new entity had been born, injected into history, the *church!*

It took Caiaphas some time to recover from the shock that it wasn't over after all. It was just beginning. He watched and waited and bided his time. Then one day Peter and John healed a lame man sitting by one of the temple gates. A crowd gathered. Peter began to preach to the crowds. Caiaphas took action at once. Peter and John were arrested. Along with the lame man, they were hauled before the Sanhedrin. The court was stacked with the High Priest's relatives and cronies. Peter and John, mere Galilean fishermen though they were, could not be intimidated. They boldly proclaimed that it was in the saving name of Jesus that the miracle had been performed. Caiaphas gave them a warning: "Don't you ever mention that Man's name again," he said. He backed the order with a threat. Peter and John defied him and departed.

Then came *the thrashing.* The disciples were not intimidated. On the contrary, they filled Jerusalem with their preaching and backed it with the same kind of countless, convincing miracles Jesus had performed. Caiaphas got rid of Jesus, or so he thought. Now vast throngs were flocking from all over the country to see and hear a dozen of His Spirit-filled apostles. Caiaphas was infuriated. He had the apostles arrested and flung into the public jail. But now another miracle happened. The Lord sent an angel to open the prison doors!

We can imagine the frustration and fury of Caiaphas when the word came: "Those men you locked up, Caiaphas, they are out of prison announcing that an angel set them free; and they are preaching in the name of Jesus all over this city."

Caiaphas sent off another contingent of the temple guard to arrest them again. The officers, however, were afraid the multitude might turn on them; so they proceeded with caution. Peter and John, along with the rest of the apostles, appeared before the Sanhedrin. "We told you not to preach in this Name," Caiaphas stormed.

"We ought to obey God, not you," Peter replied. Then he boldly began to preach to the High Priest and his cronies. "You slew Him and hanged Him on a tree," he said. "But God raised this very Jesus from the dead and exalted Him to His own right hand in heaven. We are witnesses of these things. So is the

Holy Spirit. Our commission from God is to proclaim repentance to Israel and forgiveness of sins in the name of Jesus!" (see Acts 2).

Caiaphas had heard enough. "Thrash them," he said. A wise old rabbi named Gamaliel recommended caution, but Caiaphas was beyond all caution. Battered and beaten, the apostles marched away, singing at the top of their voices. Back they came to the temple. They came day after day to preach the gospel of Christ. For the moment, Caiaphas was beaten (see Acts 5).

One would have thought that a man, confronted with so much overwhelming evidence, would capitulate before the very facts of the case and before the irrefutable logic of it all. But unbelief is never rational. Caiaphas, like Pharaoh of old, only hardened his heart.

2. The Further Step

The wily politician in Caiaphas whispered to him to bide his time. Sooner or later circumstances would deliver the leaders of this pestilential movement into his hands.

His chance came with Stephen, one of the deacons appointed by the ever-growing Jerusalem church to handle its mundane affairs. Stephen, full of the Holy Spirit, debated the issues of Judaism and Christianity in the various synagogues around town. He ran into a hornet's nest, however, when he took on the Hellenist synagogue to which Saul of Tarsus belonged. Brilliant as Saul was, however, he could not refute Stephen's arguments. So he, and his group of Cilician Jews, resorted to trickery. They hired men to publicly denounce Stephen to the Sanhedrin as a blasphemer.

That was the chance for which Caiaphas had been waiting. Stephen was arrested and brought before the Sanhedrin. False witnesses were hired, and the stage was set as Caiaphas took his seat. Stephen now stood where, a short while before, Jesus had stood. The false witnesses came and went. Again, Caiaphas hardened his heart.

Stephen's defense was a masterpiece. By the time he was finished, Caiaphas and those with him were cut to the very heart by his terrible charges. They gnashed at him with their teeth like a pack of wolves. Then Caiaphas was stung to even greater fury by Stephen's announcement that he could see Jesus standing in an open heaven. He was standing, indeed, at the right hand of God. Stephen was seized and hurried to the place of execution. There, he was flung headlong and then stoned to death. Caiaphas congratulated himself.

"That will show them!" he thought, "now let another of them raise his voice. I'll show them, too!"

But that was not quite the end of it.

3. The Final Step

It seems Caiaphas reviewed the events connected with the stoning of Stephen. He came across the name of Saul of Tarsus, and that name set off a train of thought. Why not put the weight of the Sanhedrin behind this clever and energetic young man? Why not use him to launch a massive campaign of persecution against this new cult?

That was Caiaphas's final step. A Sanhedrin-sponsored, citywide persecution of the infant church was launched in Jerusalem. At first, Caiaphas was delighted with the result. Thousands fled the city, and, as for Saul, "he made havoc of the church" (Acts 8:3). No believer was safe; houses were invaded, and men and women alike were flung into jail.

Caiaphas likely smiled to himself. *Now they know they can't get away with it any longer,* he thinks. His complacency did not last long. Everywhere they went, the disciples made converts and established churches. All Caiaphas and Saul had done was make sure that the gospel was spread far and wide.

That did it! Caiaphas summoned Saul of Tarsus. He gave him letters to the synagogues of Damascus and elsewhere. He gave him his orders and his warrant. He was to track down Christians and bring them bound to Jerusalem where the Sanhedrin could deal with them. That was the final step.

We read no more of Caiaphas. But we cannot help but wonder how bitter must have been the thoughts of his evil heart when the news came that his star performer, Saul of Tarsus, had been converted on the way to Damascus! Indeed, the news was that he was preaching boldly in Damascus. He was telling everyone he had actually seen the risen, ascended Christ. The thing to do, Caiaphas decided, was to persecute Saul of Tarsus, too. And that is where the curtain falls on Caiaphas.

Paul was converted in A.D. 37. The next year, A.D. 38, Caiaphas was deposed. At that point he passes into oblivion, his name covered with opprobrium.

What are we to make of such people as Caiaphas, who spurn all the evidence for Christianity and harden their evil hearts in determined unbelief? We meet many such people, some of them raised in Christian homes and exposed to the truth since childhood. Then they turn their backs upon the whole thing and espouse wicked causes.

The poet says,

> There is a line, by us unseen that crosses every path;
> The hidden boundary line between God's mercy and His wrath.

Once a person crosses that line, the Holy Spirit leaves him to himself. He goes on denying the truth and rejecting Christ until he finally wakes up in hell. For God Himself warns, "My spirit shall not always strive with man" (Gen. 6:30).

THIRTY-TWO

Pilate
Caesar's Friend

John 19:19

A. A PEOPLE HE DESPISED: "JESUS OF NAZARETH THE KING OF THE *JEWS*"
B. A PLACE HE DERIDED: "JESUS OF *NAZARETH* THE KING OF THE JEWS"
C. A PERSON HE DISOWNED: "*JESUS* OF NAZARETH THE KING OF THE JEWS"
D. A PRINCE HE DENIED: "JESUS OF NAZARETH THE *KING* OF THE JEWS"

When Pontius Pilate left Rome for Palestine, the emperor Tiberius gave him a special gold ring. It identified Pilate as an *amicus Caesaris,* "friend of the Caesar." To keep that ring, Pilate allowed Christ, a Man he knew was innocent, to be crucified.

Pilate's ancestors were Roman nobles of the equestrian order. He had served a tour of duty in Syria as an administrative military tribune with the Twelfth Legion and had earned the reputation of being a tough commander. His wife, Claudia Procula, is said to have been the granddaughter of Caesar Augustus; so Pilate had the highest connections in Rome.

As procurator of Judea, Pilate carried a heavy responsibility. Judea was the capital of the seven million Jews who lived in the Roman empire—seven percent of its entire population. Small though it was, Judea commanded the trade routes and lines of communication between Syria and Egypt. Moreover, Judea was the only Roman outpost that prevented Parthia from moving in and blocking Roman access to Egypt. Rome depended on Egypt for her grain supply. Nor could Egypt itself be allowed to fall into hostile hands. The ships that carried their precious cargoes of wheat to Rome must never be endangered. So to be governor of Judea was a trust of some magnitude.

Pilate was certainly not going to allow some local messiah to imperil his position as friend of the Caesar and as guardian of Rome's Egyptian gate. He caved in to political expediency. As he saw it, he had no other choice. If he let Jesus go, he would incur the wrath of the Sanhedrin. If he let Jesus go, he would, in effect, be an endorsement of Christ's claim to be the King of the Jews.

Pilot rejected the claims of Christ—against the advice of his wife, and the instinct of his own soul. He signed a death warrant that consigned Jesus to a particularly cruel and horrible death. Then he ceremoniously washed his hands of the whole business, a gesture that was useless in absolving him of complicity. It was customary in the case of public execution for the governor to write a placard that described the name of the criminal and the nature of the crime. Much to the annoyance of the Jews, Pilate wrote, "JESUS OF NAZARETH THE KING OF THE JEWS." "This title," John recalled, "then read many of the Jews: for the place where Jesus was crucified was nigh to the city: and it was written in Hebrew, and Greek, and Latin" (19:20). The placard was written in Latin, the language of government; in Greek, the language of culture; and in Hebrew, the language of religion. The title was written in all three languages so that all the world could read and consider both the Christ and His claims.

Doubtless Pilate wrote the title tongue-in-cheek. He was annoyed at the Jews for pushing this case off on him. He knew perfectly well that at the bottom of their maneuvering was a deep-seated envy of Jesus of Nazareth. Pilate knew from his spies scattered throughout the country that Jesus was a good man and that He posed no threat to Roman rule. Had He not said, "Render to Caesar the things that are Caesar's, and to God the things that are God's" (Mark 12:17)? At His trial He had conducted Himself with extraordinary self-control and poise. Pilate had been impressed. Pilate knew Jesus was innocent of the charges brought against Him. Jesus confessed to be a King but at once declared that His kingdom was not of this world. He claimed to have come from another world altogether, and Pilate more than half believed Him and was more than a little afraid of Him.

So to get even with the Jews for the annoyance, inconvenience, embarrassment, and anxiety they had caused him, Pilate wrote, "Jesus of Nazareth the King of the Jews." And he would not change the wording. "What I have written I have written," he said (John 19:22).

The placard that Pilate wrote and had nailed to Christ's cross was more significant than he realized. The title revealed Pilate's stand toward a people he despised, a place he derided, a Person he disowned, and a Prince he denied.

A. A People He Despised:
"Jesus of Nazareth the King of the *Jews*"

As a people, the Jews were much older than the Romans. Before Pompey marched into Jerusalem, the Jews were a great people. When the Romans were still bearded barbarians, the Jews were already a great people. Before the story of Romulus and Remus and the she-wolf was circulated, the Jews were a great people.

Before Alexander the Great was crowned king of Macedonia in 336 B.C., the Jews were a great people. Before the Athenians began building the Parthenon in 447 B.C., the Jews were a great people. Before Xerxes invaded Greece, before Cyrus the Persian conquered Babylon, before Nebuchadnezzar rose to power, before the Phoenicians founded Carthage, before the Assyrians forged their cruel empire, before Ramses the Great began construction of the temple of Abu Simbel—the Jews were already a great people. Their roots and their history go far back—back before Hammurabi of Babylon hammered out his legal code, back before the Hyksos kings subdued Egypt. When the Bronze Age was coming to flower in Egypt, the Jews were already a people to be reckoned with in this world.

Perhaps Pilate did not know his history book, but the Jews, a people he despised, were a people not to be despised. They had a legal code greater than Rome's. They had a religion greater—far greater—than Rome's. In Pilate's day, the Jews were the world's bankers. Pilate despised them, for Rome measured a man by his might, and the Jews were not famous as fighters. The Jews retaliated. They measured a man by his money. Kings could be bought. Armies could be bought.

In sizing up the Jews, however, Pilate ignored the wars of the Maccabees. Before the century was over, though, the Jews would teach Rome a lesson it would not forget. To quell the Jewish revolt, the Romans were forced to assemble an army of eighty thousand men. Alexander the Great had carved out his vast empire with thirty-two thousand men. Julius Caesar needed only twenty-five thousand soldiers to conquer Gaul and invade Britain. To fight the Jews, however, Titus was forced to mobilize ten thousand cavalry men and seventy thousand infantrymen, and even against those odds the Jews kept the Romans at bay for four long years. In the end the Romans won, not because of greater skill but because of greater numbers. After the Romans conquered Jerusalem, they still had to subdue Masada. The Jews, led by Bar Kokhba, would try to resist Rome again in A.D. 135.

The Jews would outlast Pilate, the Caesar he served, and the empire he represented. When the Huns and Goths and Vandals at last descended on Rome, the Jews were still a mighty people. They are a mighty people today. Every nation or empire that has ever turned its hand against the Jews has, in the end, found itself fighting against God.

But Pilate despised the Jews. He wrote his contempt into the title he made for the cross: "Jesus of Nazareth the King of the *Jews*." To him the title was ludicrous. Everybody knew the Jews had no king. The king who reigned over them was Herod. And the king who ruled over Herod was Caesar. Pilate thought of the Jews as moneylenders. He thought of them as religious fanatics. He knew some Jews. He knew of a greedy man like Annas and of a guileful man like Caiaphas. The idea that the Jews should have a king struck him as ridiculous.

B. A Place He Derided:
"Jesus of *Nazareth* the King of the Jews"

Nazareth! Even the Jews regarded this Galilean town with contempt. The Jews of Jerusalem despised the Galileans because they were of mixed blood. Many Gentiles lived in Galilee. Its chief city was Tiberius, doubly unclean since it was named after a despised emperor, and it was built on the site of an old graveyard. Galileans were labeled "unlearned and ignorant men" (Acts 4:13). Moreover, they spoke the native Aramaic with a thick, north-country accent.

The Jews despised Nazareth even more. "Can there any good thing come out of Nazareth?" asked Nathanael when Philip told him he had found the Messiah, a Man named Jesus of Nazareth (John 1:45–46). Pilate had been governor of Judea long enough to know how much Nazareth was despised by the Jews. "Jesus of *Nazareth*," he wrote, hoping to annoy the Jews still further. If the accused had been Jesus of Rome, Jesus of Athens, Jesus of Carthage, or even Jesus of Jerusalem, Pilate may have paid more heed to the case. For Jesus of *Nazareth* to claim kingship struck Pilate as absurd.

Nazareth wasn't much of a place even by worldly standards. There would be some cypress trees reaching toward the sky and terraces of fig and olive trees. There would be some poor homes, a fountain supplying the town's only water, a market, and a carpenter's shop. With a clientele of struggling farmers and agricultural workers, the carpenter was paid likely once a year only at harvest time. Probably he was paid in produce and grain.

Jesus, His mother, Joseph, and His half brothers and sisters would have lived in a room above a cave where a donkey was kept. The room would have been virtually bare of furniture. Bedding mats would be rolled up and tucked away in a corner at sunrise. Such cramped quarters were typical of Nazareth.

Although Nazareth was not in his province, Pilate doubtless knew all there was to know about the place. In a way the town was significant as a dividing line. To its south were Jerusalem and Judea and Old Testament religious norms. To the north was upper Galilee. To go from Judea to Galilee was almost to turn one's back on the Old Testament world. Galilee was crossed by the great north-south military roads and by the east-west caravan routes. Galilee was an international corridor, and Nazareth was its gateway.

The sophisticated Judeans spoke the name of Nazareth with a sneer; Pilate preferred Caesarea any time. Sophisticated Caesarea was a transplant of Rome. It had a fine harbor, where Roman warships could drop anchor. It had magnificent theaters, a hippodrome, a marble temple, and the great palace of Herod. Pilate no doubt chuckled as he wrote *Nazareth* on the sign. It was a place to be derided.

C. A Person He Disowned:
"Jesus of Nazareth the King of the Jews"

"Jesus" was a common name among the Jews of Pilate's day. The name had its roots in the Hebrew for Joshua, pronounced *Yeshua*. Whether Pilate knew or appreciated the meaning of the name is questionable. *Jesus* means "Jehovah the Savior." To the Christian, "Jesus" is the sweetest name on earth. To Pilate it was the name of just another Jew. Ultimately Pilate had to choose between two names: Jesus and Tiberius—the King of the Jews or the emperor of Rome.

Caesar Tiberius was the adopted stepson of Caesar Augustus. In the early days of his reign, Tiberius had the reputation of being an able soldier and administrator. But he had a vicious streak in him; and before long, he was thoroughly detested in Rome, not only for his cruelties, but also for his abominable vices. He retired to the island of Capri and abandoned himself to all forms of lust. When he finally died, there was such rejoicing in Rome that people ran about shouting, "To the Tiber with Tiberius!" Others offered prayers to the infernal gods to give him no room below except among the damned. To this disgusting and debauched individual, Pilate owed his promotion.

Everything Pilate had ever heard about Jesus was extraordinary. We can be sure nothing happened in the provinces that wasn't known in Pilate's palace. "He goes about doing good," his spies would tell him. "He performs astounding miracles. Herod Antipas is dying to see one of them. Jesus heals sick people. He casts out evil spirits. He feeds the hungry. He has even cleansed lepers and raised the dead. Many of the common people take His name to be prophetic and consider Him to be their Savior."

When face to face with Jesus, Pilate felt the awesome goodness and power of the man. Pilate had never met a man like Him before. Indeed the procurator seems to have been superstitious about Jesus, but he banished his superstitious fears and decided that Jesus was just another Jew—a remarkable one, but just a Jew.

Thus, there was little doubt in Pilate's mind about whether he would choose the Caesar or the Christ. Pilate would choose the Caesar. So when Pilate sat down to write the title for the cross, he wrote the name of Jesus without any real understanding of the significance of that name.

It is *the saving name.* When Joseph was trying to make up his mind what to do about Mary, he had a visit from an angel who set his mind at rest. The angel told him that the child about to be born was indeed the very Son of God, then added, "Thou shalt call his name JESUS: for he shall save his people from their sins" (Matt. 1:21). The name was no longer an everyday name; it now embodied an eternal truth. Jesus is the Savior of His own.

"Neither is there salvation in any other," Peter bluntly told the Sanhedrin, who were responsible for the murder of the Messiah. They were responsible, too, for efforts to hush up stories about the resurrection. They tried to stop the spread of the gospel. Peter declared, "There is none other name under heaven given among men, whereby we must be saved" (Acts 4:12).

Years later when the apostle Paul was a prisoner in Rome, he sent some sound advice to the church at Colosse: "Whatsoever ye do in word or deed," he wrote, "do all in the name of the Lord Jesus" (Col. 3:17). We cannot go far wrong when His name governs our character, conduct, and conversation. The name of Jesus is *the sanctifying name.* When it is the dominant color on the canvas of one's life, His name sets a very high standard indeed. James Rowe has taught us to sing "I Would Be Like Jesus":

> Be like Jesus—this my song—
> In the home and in the throng;
> Be like Jesus all day long!
> I would be like Jesus.

Pilate asked, "What is truth?" when Truth was staring him in the face (John

18:38). Jesus had said just the day before, "I am the . . . truth" (14:6). Face to face with Truth incarnate, Pilate sold Him for a lie. The procurator persuaded himself that it was in his own best interest to stay in the good graces of Caiaphas. He would do nothing that the suspicious old tyrant back in Rome might interpret as treason. So Pilate signed a death warrant and wrote a title.

D. A Prince He Denied:
"Jesus of Nazareth the *King* of the Jews"

When Pilate sent Jesus to Herod Antipas, Herod arrayed Him in mocking purple. Pilot seems to have thought that Herod had the right idea. Pilate went further. He let his soldiers crown this King of the Jews with a crown of thorns. Would Pilate himself *crown* Him or *crucify* Him? Would he dismiss all charges against this innocent Man or would he sign the most infamous death warrant in history? Pilate crucified Him and the same day made friends with Herod Antipas. The man who mocked Christ and the man who murdered Christ shook hands that day.

Contrary to all appearances, the man on the center cross was indeed the King of the Jews. But He was more than that—much more. In the book of Revelation He is called "King of kings and Lord of lords!" (Rev. 17:14). Psalm 24 calls Him "the King of Glory."

Pilate soon had an inkling that He was a Prince indeed. A crucified man often lingered on for days in his death agony, but the Sanhedrin urged Pilate to hasten the end of the current victims because of the approaching Passover. Pilate cooperated. He ordered that the victims' legs be broken. The centurion came in to report—Jesus was dead—not from crucifixion, not from further action ordered by Pilate, but by a sovereign act of His own will. He had simply dismissed His spirit. Strange phenomena had occurred. A supernatural darkness had descended on the country from the sixth to the ninth hour. The temple veil had been torn asunder in some mysterious way. An earthquake had shaken the ground. Reports began to come in from all over the country that graves and sepulchers had burst open.

Three days later, Pilate was faced with the news that the tomb was empty and the Man he had murdered was alive, back from the dead. At the same time, the open graves had discharged their dead. As Matthew 27:52–53 records, "Many bodies of the saints which slept arose, And came out of the graves after his resurrection, and went into the holy city, and appeared unto many."

Jesus was more than the King of the Jews. The centurion ventured his own opinion: "This," he said at the cross, "was the Son of God" (Matt. 27:54). Perhaps he was bold enough to repeat those words to Pilate. But Pilate had denied Him. To the end of his days he would carry with him the memory of eyes that had looked into his and read his very soul. Pilate's assessment of Jesus had been wrong. If only he could rewrite that title! If only he had never written it at all! He should have crowned Him. Perhaps when, as one tradition tells us, he was a lonely outcast banished from power, he belatedly did crown Him as King of his own life. We can hope so.

THIRTY-THREE

Simon

The Cyrenian Who Carried the Cross

Matthew 27:32; Mark 15:21; Acts 13:1–3; Romans 16:13

A. SIMON THE CONSCRIPT
  1. He was probably embarrassed
  2. He was probably embittered
B. SIMON THE CONVERT
  1. Touched by the sufferings
  2. Troubled by the signs
  3. Transformed by the Savior
C. SIMON THE CHRISTIAN
  1. Simon and Peter
  2. Simon and Paul
    a. His faith
    b. His family

He was a Cyrenian, one born at Cyrene on the north coast of Africa. He is called "Niger," that is, he had a Latin name tagged on to him (Acts 13:1). The word means "black." It may be that Simon of Cyrene was a Hellenist Jew and that he was nicknamed "Niger" because of his swarthy complexion. Or it may be, as some believe, that he was an Ethiopian, a black man, a proselyte to Judaism who had taken the Jewish name of Simon. The city of Cyrene itself was originally founded by the Greeks on the north African coast as part of what we now call Libya. The city was built on a lovely tableland eight hundred feet above the level of the sea. Although it was a Greek city, it was home to a large colony of Jews, wealthy and influential enough to have had a synagogue of their own in Jerusalem (Acts 6:9). Matthew, Mark, and Luke all mention this man.

He has leaped to fame and immortality as the man who carried the cross to Calvary for Christ.

A. SIMON THE CONSCRIPT

It was a historic meeting, the meeting between this black man from Africa and Jesus, the Son of God, lately from Jerusalem, formerly from Bethlehem, and eternally from the Celestial City in the land beyond the sky.

It had been a terrible day for Jesus, Son of the living God, now on His way to Calvary's Hill. He had commissioned His disciples to make ready for the Passover, and when the time came, had gathered with them in the upper room. He had washed their feet, kept the last Passover with them, and sent Judas the traitor about his business. He had talked to the remaining eleven about His impending departure from this world and about the impending coming of the Holy Spirit. He had sung the collection of psalms that make up the Great Hallel—Israel's "Hallelujah Chorus" (Pss. 113–118). And He had prayed earnestly for them all.

Then He had gone to Gethsemane to weep His heart out and to agonize over the dreadful cup He soon must drink. His agony had been so great He had sweat great drops of blood that fell down to the ground. Then Judas had come, accompanied by a Jewish mob and the Roman military.

He had been arrested and carried off to a preliminary hearing before Annas and Caiaphas. He had been sent to Pilate and then to Herod and then back to Pilate. He had been mocked and scourged—Roman scourging was itself something to be feared. Many a man died beneath that fearful lash, and some who survived it went insane. Then He had been led away to be crucified.

His cross was a heavy piece of rough-hewn timber. It had been given to Him to carry to Calvary. Bravely enough, He had summoned what was left of His strength to drag it on its way to Golgotha, "the place of a skull," as it was called.

We can see the sad procession. There go the two thieves with Jesus in between. There are the soldiers under the command of a centurion stolidly tramping along, clearing a path through the crowd. There is the mixed multitude—the priests, the rulers, the rank and the file of the people, nodding and wagging their hands and making Him the butt of their pleasantries and witticisms. There were the daughters of Jerusalem, weeping and distressed by it all. Onward they go. The streets are narrow, the sun is hot. At last the woeful sufferers pass the city gate and head for the hill of shame.

But at length even the magnificent physique of Jesus reached its end. He fell. Nor could all the blows and curses of the soldiers or the scoffing ridicule of the mob alter the fact that He has reached the end of His tether.

The soldiers were in a quandary. It is evident that Jesus could carry that heavy beam no further. Someone must carry it for Him. The crowd looked at Him with about as much compassion as they would have shown a horse that had fallen in the street. And not one of them would touch that cursed tree. The soldiers, certainly, had no intention of carrying it.

The centurion eyed the crowd. Why not compel one of these detested Jews to shoulder the cross? But he thought better of that. The Jews were already riled up. The contemptuous gesture might give a moment's satisfaction, but it was probably more than his commission was worth to do it. He, himself, drew the line at openly antagonizing them. The centurion was at his wit's end. Then he saw a black man coming into the city. He was coming in, they were going out. He was alone, and it was not likely he had friends in high places. Perhaps he was a Jew or a proselyte, but he looked like a black man, an African. Probably he was on his way to Jerusalem to keep the Passover. He should be safe enough to press into the distasteful service of toiling beneath the weight of a cross.

Simon himself was on his way into the Holy City. His heart, like those of the other pilgrims, likely was full of high hopes and pious intentions and thoughts of the Passover feast. He had no idea that the Man who has just fallen down yonder, crushed by the weight of a cross, was none other than the true Paschal Lamb. Suddenly he was seized by the soldiers and compelled at the point of spear and sword to get his shoulder under that cross.

The text says he was "coming out of the country." The margin suggests he was "coming out of a field." The word used is *agros,* denoting a cultivated field. The time was shortly before 9:00 in the morning. We do not know what he was doing in a field or why he was coming out of a field at that time of the morning. Doubtless he wished he had stayed there. Maybe he had heard the shouting of the crowd and had come out of curiosity to see what was going on. Maybe he was just taking a shortcut across that field.

In any case, he was arrested. "Hey, you there," we hear the Centurion bark. A rough hand is placed upon his arm, a sharp command is given: "Pick up that cross." He knows only too well he has little choice in the matter. With their high-handed way of dealing with conquered peoples, the Romans impress men as they please.

There was no room for debate and no time to prevaricate. Simon saw the face of Jesus, beaten to a pulp. A pair of wondrous eyes said "Thank you" in a way Simon would never forget. We can well imagine, though, what would be his first reaction to the distasteful order he was given.

1. He Was Probably Embarrassed

To be seen carrying a cross! Only criminals were crucified. Crucifixion was not only a terribly painful death, it was a very shameful death. There was a terrible stigma attached to a cross, a Roman gallows. Supposing someone he knew saw him. He would be identified immediately with that cross. He put his shoulders beneath that hated instrument of death as a deep flush of shame crept in a crimson tide across his swarthy countenance.

Little did he think, then, that for the rest of his life he would look back upon this incident with a quiet satisfaction. He was being identified with Christ in His death. He was carrying the cross for the very Christ who, in a little while, would die on that cross for him.

Identified with Christ! Little did he know or understand then (or for many a year afterward until he heard Paul preach) how Christ was identified with him. On that cross now being reared against the skyline, on Golgotha's brow, the Lord Jesus was about to die *for* him. More! He was about to die *as* him. At the time, however, he was simply embarrassed.

2. He Was Probably Embittered

As he plodded stolidly along, the jibes and jeers of the mob were directed toward him. He was the one carrying the cross. Doubtless hatred of Rome and all things Roman gnawed like acid in his soul. How he hated Rome! How he hated the arrogance of Rome! How he hated the all-too-ready use of force employed by Rome!

Yet, from time to time, as Simon sweated and staggered on his way to Calvary's hill, he would catch a glimpse of the Christ. By now he would know who He was. He could hear the mob scoffing at this "Jesus of Nazareth." He had doubtless been hearing stories of Jesus of Nazareth ever since he arrived in the country.

People said He was the Messiah. People said He could heal the sick and cast out demons, cleanse lepers, and even raise the dead. People said He could multiply loaves and fishes, still the storm and walk upon the wild, tempestuous sea.

So why was He going to Calvary? Why was His visage so marred, more than any man's, and His form more than the sons of men? Perhaps, at that thought, Isaiah 53 leaped into his mind. Could it be? Could it be?

So, step by step Simon the conscript made his unwilling way to Calvary. And there, either then or later, when he had time to return in thought and memory, Simon the conscript became someone else.

B. Simon the Convert

At last they reached the brow of that skull-shaped hill. With a sigh of relief Simon put down the cross and melted into the crowd. But surely he waited to see what would happen. Surely, as face answers face in a mirror and the heart of one man answers the heart of another, Simon waited to see what would happen next. We know he became a convert of the Christ of God. What would be more reasonable than his standing well back in the crowd, lingering at Calvary to look and listen, wanting to know what happened next. Perhaps his heart was touched.

1. Touched by the Sufferings

They were the very kind of sufferings described by the prophet Isaiah and described, too, by David in Psalm 69. They pierced His hands and His feet. Well, that in itself, proved very little. The Romans were always crucifying people. There were two common criminals crucified that very morning, one hung on each side of the Man they called Jesus. If Simon read Pilate's sign, *"Jesus of Nazareth the King of the Jews,"* then he would have surely been impressed.

The King of the Jews indeed! Was *this* crucified Man the Messiah, the Son of David? Doubtless he listened with all ears. He heard this extraordinary Person say, "Father, forgive them, for they know not what they do" as the soldiers drove the spikes into His hands and His feet.

Simon must have looked at Him in astonishment. He, Simon, had not prayed like that awhile ago when forced to carry that cross. He, Simon, had likely been more like the two thieves, cursing, blaspheming, and screaming. This Man prayed to One He called His *Father,* begging forgiveness for His foes.

Possibly he watched and listened as the minutes lengthened into hours. He heard the two thieves revile Him. Then one thief changed his mind and rebuked his cursing companion. He addressed Jesus as Lord and as God and begged Him to remember him when He came into His kingdom. Yes, and Simon likely heard the gracious reply: "Today shalt thou be with me in paradise" (Luke 23:43).

He could well have heard Him ask for a drink and probably saw them give Him vinegar. Did he suddenly remember the psalm that said, "They gave me vinegar to drink" (69:21)?

Perhaps Simon closed his ears to the sneers and jeers of the rabble and rulers of Israel and turned his back on the Romans and the rabbis, deeply touched by the sufferings of the Savior. Here was, indeed, One who fulfilled Isaiah 53: "He was a man of sorrows and acquainted with grief."

Perhaps, too, his heart was troubled.

2. Troubled by the Signs

Before long it became evident that strange things were happening all about him. It was as though dumb nature had found a voice with which to protest the murder of its Maker. The rocks rent! There was a terrifying earthquake. Then someone brought word that the veil of the temple had been torn in two. Darkness descended and, at high noon, at brightest daylight, it became darker than blackest midnight. These things convinced the centurion and the soldiers. Why not Simon the Cyrenian?

Then came the mighty shout! For Jesus did not die exhausted, as a victim of crucifixion. He died with the shout of the conqueror. He sovereignly dismissed His Spirit and bowed His head and died of His own accord.

Then, too, as the day wore on, news came from all over the country of mysterious happenings in the graveyards and cemeteries of the land. Graves had burst open. Three days later many bodies of the saints that slept in those tombs arose and came out of their graves and went into the holy city and appeared unto many. Doubtless Simon the Cyrenian was troubled by the signs.

Perhaps, before it was all over, his heart was transformed.

3. Transformed by the Savior

People left Golgotha that day beating their breasts. The centurion and the soldiers left there confessing Christ. Both Nicodemus and Joseph of Arimathea took a sudden, bold stand for Christ and became committed disciples from that day forward. Surely Simon, too, went home a different man. Either then, or on the resurrection morning, or a month or so later on the Day of Pentecost,

Simon, the black man from Africa, was saved. He would go home to his wife and children. He would say, "I carried that cross for *Him*. He died on that cross for *me*." Which brings us to the new man.

C. SIMON THE CHRISTIAN

We have no way of knowing, but we can think of how much Simon really understood that day.

1. Simon and Peter

Perhaps Simon the Cyrenian was so intrigued by all these events that he waited in Jerusalem from Passover to Pentecost to see if anything would happen. In the meantime the resurrection of Christ was the talk of the town. Paul could say to King Agrippa in later years, "This thing was not done in a corner" (Acts 26:26). The empty tomb was public knowledge. It would be an odd thing if hundreds of people did not go out to Joseph of Arimathea's burial plot to see the empty cave for themselves. Millions have been to see it since, from all over the world. Curiosity alone would take many a man that way. It is likely that nobody put much stock in the Sanhedrin's lie that the body was stolen.

Stories had gone around about the ascension, too—after all, some 120 people had witnessed it. It would be passing strange if that story hadn't done the rounds. The Sanhedrin had no explanation for that. Possibly Simon the Cyrenian was on the edge of the crowd that saw Jesus ascend.

Then came the Day of Pentecost. It is possible that Simon the Cyrenian was one of the vast throng who heard Peter preach. When the disciples came down from the upper room, everyone knew something strange had happened. There had been a baptism of the Spirit, a filling of the Spirit, and an anointing of the Spirit.

A strange phenomenon drew the crowd. The gift of tongues had fallen on the disciples. People were astonished and amazed. "How hear we every man in our own tongue, wherein we were born?" they demanded (Acts 2:8). It was not only Latin and Greek and Chaldee and Egyptian they heard, but also the local dialects from their own particular neighborhoods. They heard old familiar idioms and clichés common to their own particular part of town back there in Galatia, in Corinth, in Cappadocia, and wherever.

Parthians were there, and Medes and Elamites and dwellers in Mesopotamia, that is to say, people from the distant East. People were there from all over Judea—Jews of the homeland and heartland of the faith. There were people from Cappadocia and Asia, Phrygia and Pamphylia, that is to say, people from the European mainland. There were people from Egypt and from parts of Libya *around Cyrene.* And who would be in *that* group but Simon the Cyrenian standing with others who were from the north side of Africa?

So perhaps Simon the Cyrenian heard the sermon of Simon called Peter. *"This is that!"* Peter declared. He pointed them to their Bibles, to the prophet Joel, and to other parts of the Word. Perhaps he heard him say, "God hath made this man, whom ye crucified, *both Lord and Christ"* (see Acts 2:36).

Suddenly the Holy Spirit fell on the crowd. In a moment three thousand people were saved and added to the church. What would be more likely than Simon the Cyrenian was one of them?

But there is more than that. We think not only of Simon and Peter; we think of Simon and another.

2. Simon and Paul

In later parts of the New Testament, two broad hints are given to us by the Holy Spirit about Simon the Cyrenian. One has to do with Simon and *his faith.* The gospel took root and spread throughout all Judea and greater Palestine. It even took root in Samaria. Saul of Tarsus was saved, the bitterest enemy of the gospel; a man in the pay of the Sanhedrin, dedicated to stamping out what he considered to be the cult of Christianity. In Antioch in Syria, the gospel broke through the confines of Judaistic Christianity and spread like a prairie fire through the Greek colonies. Paul and Barnabas gave themselves wholeheartedly to that work. Souls were saved, and the church was growing. The teaching was inspired.

Then, one day, Paul and Barnabas announced that God had called them to the real mission field. The pair of them had become burdened for the regions beyond, for the untold millions still untold. They shared their burden with the elders of the Antioch church. The elders decided to fast and pray and to make sure that this thing was of God. Then they commissioned their two best men to the work in the foreign field. They laid their hands upon them and sent them forth with the full blessing and benediction of the Antioch church. There were seven elders in that church. Two of them came from Cyrene. One of them was named *Simon.* He was also nicknamed "Niger." He was a black man, and many agree he was the very Simon who had carried the cross for Christ.

Wonder of wonders! The man who carried the cross for Christ played a part in sending Paul and his colleagues on their way to preach that cross all over the world!

But there is one thing more in connection with Paul. We think of Simon and *his family*. When Mark wrote his gospel he mentioned Simon the Cyrenian and did so almost casually, certainly familiarly, as "the father of Alexander and Rufus" (Mark 15:21). Mark mentions Alexander and Rufus because they were well known in the church at Rome, and Mark's gospel was written especially for the Romans. So Simon the Cyrenian won his family to Christ. We can well imagine he would never tire of telling his wife and children of that unforgettable day when he had been drafted to carry the cross for Jesus.

He had been carrying it, in a different sense, ever since. "God forbid that I should glory save in the cross of Christ by which the world is crucified unto me and I unto the world," Paul said (see Gal. 6:14). Simon the Cyrenian would have said a hearty "Amen!" to that. He would tell his two boys about it over and over again until they, too, picked up the cross to carry it.

But we have not quite finished. Among the Roman Christians, to whom the Apostle Paul sent greetings when he wrote to the Roman Church, was a man called Rufus. Paul mentions both him and his mother. This seems to have been the wife and son of Simon the Cyrenian.

"His mother *and* mine," says Paul. Mrs. Simon Cyrenian was one of Paul's ten thousand mothers in Christ. The Lord Jesus promised His disciples that if they took up their cross and followed Him, they would receive one hundred fold in this life and a great reward in the next one. One hundred-fold works out at ten thousand percent. Paul had given up his mother for the cause of Christ. So the Lord provided him with ten thousand mothers all over the world. The mother of Rufus, the wife of Simon Niger, was one of them.

So it was a good day for Simon when he picked up that cross. It is a good day for us, too, when we do the same.

THIRTY-FOUR

The Man Who Crucified Christ

Matthew 27:33–54

A. CRUCIFYING CHRIST
B. CONSIDERING CHRIST
    1.   He had never seen such dignity
    2.   He had never seen such distress
    3.   He had never seen such deeds
C. CONFESSING CHRIST

We know little or nothing about this man. We do not know his name, how old he was, or whether or not he was married. We do not know whether he was a religious man or an agnostic.

We know he was an officer in the mighty army of Rome. We know, too, that he was on active service in the troublesome province of Judea in A.D. 33, and that he was under the jurisdiction of Pontius Pilate.

We do not know whether he was a volunteer or a conscript, whether a native-born Roman or a soldier from the provinces, whether from Macedonia, Britain, or from Gaul. Nor do we know in what far-flung outposts of the empire he had served. Perhaps he had seen duty on the Danube. Perhaps he had served in Spain. Perhaps he had been based in Britain. We do not know. We only know that this was the man who crucified Christ. Millions have crucified Him since. There are some, today, here and now, who are doing just that—crucifying Christ (Heb. 6:4–6). When it comes to Christ, we either crown Him or we crucify Him. There is no middle ground.

We can picture the man, maybe, a tough, seasoned veteran of Rome's many foreign wars. He was evidently a decent enough fellow, more thoughtful than most. The cross of Christ riveted his gaze. He only speaks once in all the story, but when he does it is terse and to the point. Indeed, "out of the abundance of his heart his mouth spoke." This unknown soldier moved for a moment into the spotlight of all the ages, then he moved back just as swiftly, just as silently into the shadows from whence he came. He has been forever enshrined, however, on the deathless page of the Word of God.

Christ claimed two converts at Calvary on the very day He died. He reached out from His cross once and saved a Jew. A Jew first! There was something symbolic even in that. Then He reached out and saved a Gentile. His first convert was a man who cursed Him. His second convert was a man who crucified Him. Such was the Lord Jesus. Those out flung, widespread arms of His reached out to embrace all mankind—the howling mob that surged and swayed around the cross; the soulless priests; the scornful Pharisees; the sneering Sadducees; the senseless multitudes all drawn to Calvary from the ends of the earth; the soldiers of Rome, along with the man who actually crucified Christ. Into the shelter of those saving arms of Jesus that day there came a Jew. Then, three hours later with a mighty earthquake shaking the foundations of the earth, there came a Gentile. A Jewish thief and a Roman legionnaire. Jesus saved them both.

They have been in heaven now, these many long centuries, that Roman and that Jew—the man who died with Christ and the man who crucified Christ. What friends they must have become! We, who like that Roman centurion are "lost sinners of the Gentiles," can come, too, come and stand with that hardy veteran at the foot of the cross. Let us look at Calvary through his eyes. Let us listen to what this man has to say about Jesus, which is called the Christ.

We shall see this man *crucifying* Christ, then we shall see him *considering* Christ, and finally we shall see him *confessing* Christ. In other words, we shall see this man as he goes through the normal stages of conversion.

We ourselves begin with little or no interest at all in Christ. Our background and upbringing might even make us hostile to Him. Then we start to think about Him. And the more we think about Him the greater the hold He gets upon our hearts and lives. Then, if we think hard enough and carefully enough, we shall end up crowning Him as Lord and Savior of our very lives.

A. CRUCIFYING CHRIST

The centurion received his orders some time before nine o'clock in the morning. A frustrated and furious Pilate would have said in curt Latin, *"I miles expedi*

crucem" ("Go, soldier, get ready the cross.") And with these words he handed the
Prisoner over to the man who crucified Christ.

The scarlet war-cloak was stripped away from Jesus, now dyed with yet deeper,
redder stains, the stains of the blood of Christ. He was clad again in His own
garments. The centurion gave orders for the cross to be brought. It was not much
of a thing. No money had been spent on it. It was made of the coarsest, cheap-
est, rough-hewn wood that could be commandeered. The other two malefactors
were rounded up and forced to shoulder their portable gallows. Jesus, too, was
given a cross to carry to Golgotha's brow. Then the procession headed out into
the morning sun. Jesus had not gone far before He began to stagger beneath the
weight of the wood.

Think of what He had been through. There had been days of increasing
opposition, tension, and struggle as His enemies matured their plot. There had
been an evening of deep emotion in the upper room, climaxing in the departure
of Judas and the final farewells.

There had been a night of sleepless agony in the garden of Gethsemane, followed by His secret arrest and the flight of all His friends.

There had been three trials and three sentences of death before the Jews. There
had been a long and exhausting trial in Pilate's judgment hall. There had been
the examination by Herod. There had been brutal mockings and derisions before
both Jews and Gentiles—from the Sanhedrin, from Herod's bodyguard, and
from Pilate's troops. There had been the dreadful scourging and the crowning
with thorns. No wonder He staggered beneath that cross. He simply lacked the
physical strength to carry it any more. The man who actually crucified Christ
probably had scant patience with that. He simply accosted a man named Simon
of Cyrene and forced him to carry the cross for Christ.

There was another incident, too, another interruption. Some of the women in
the crowd wept at the sight of the Savior making His way down the Via Dolorosa
to Calvary. He raised His head. He looked at them. He saw what they could not
see—Rome's armies, crucifying Jews by the thousands, all around Jerusalem in
a day already on its way. He saw these women and their children suffering the
nightmare that accompanied the siege and sack of a city. "Weep not for me," He
said, "but for your children."

At last they came to the place called Calvary, and there they crucified Him.
The method of executing people by means of crucifixion has been abolished now
for fifteen hundred years by the common pity and abhorrence of mankind. It was
abolished by Constantine. But it was common enough in Bible times.

In Judea there was one custom that allowed a passing touch of humanity to briefly relieve the whole brutal business. The wealthy women of Jerusalem had the practice of providing those about to be crucified with a stupefying drink made of wine mixed with gall or myrrh. Jesus, His body already aflame with thirst, accepted the drink offered to Him gratefully. But the moment He tasted it, and knew what it was, He drew back. With sublime heroism, He refused to have His mind drugged. He had come to look death in the face, to taste of death for every man. He would not be half deadened by a narcotic.

Then the long-awaited moment came. He was stripped naked and positioned on the dreadful instrument of death. His arms were stretched along the cross-beams. A large and rusty nail was placed upon His hand—that hand, which had been placed on the heads of little children, which had touched the loathsome leper, which had multiplied a little lad's lunch into a banquet for a multitude—they hammered home a large and rusty nail, bringing instantly a flash of searing pain.

The same was done to His other hand and to His feet. Then that accursed tree, with its living, human burden, was hauled up by strong hands and its foot dropped, with a sickening thud, into a deep hole dug in the ground to receive it. And so He hung there, *crucified,* within reach of every hand that might choose to strike, close to all who wished to insult and to mock. There, in tortures that grew more intolerable with each passing moment, He hung between heaven and earth as one cast out by both.

That is what this world did to God's beloved Son. This world—the world in which we have been born and raised; in which we have been educated, molded, fashioned, shaped; this world, our world, crucified *Him.* And this unknown Roman soldier carried out the sentence. Suppose we had gone up to him and said, "Excuse me Sir, do you not feel any personal responsibility for what you are doing?"

He would have said, "No! Why should I? I am just carrying out orders. I am not responsible for this. Blame those priests over there. Blame the governor. Don't blame me. I cannot stop it. It has nothing to do with me." The executioner, the man with the hammer in his hand, he would have said much the same. The fact remains. This man, the centurion in charge, the man who supervised the whole terrible business, the man who crucified Christ, went along with the crowd. He raised not a word of protest. Write him down as a partaker in the crime.

The Holy Spirit writes all people on this planet down in the very same way. The crime of Calvary was no ordinary crime. It was this world's verdict on the

Son of God, the Creator of the universe. He, who chose to put on human flesh and who stands astride the ages, forces us to take sides. We either crown Him or crucify Him. We either give our silent assent to what happened at Calvary, or we surrender to the Christ of the cross. The Bible warns of the deadly wickedness of "[crucifying to ourselves] the Son of God afresh, and [of putting] him to an open shame" (Heb. 6:6).

So, first of all, we see this man doing what we all have done—carelessly, casually, criminally, crucifying Christ. But that is not the end of the story. Nor does it have to be the end of the story for us.

B. Considering Christ

Matthew puts it this way: "And sitting down they watched him there." The centurion, the soldiers, the man and the men, those who actually crucified Christ, they watched Him there. Human sin had now reached its apex. Nothing a human being had ever done, could ever do, could more terribly express the hatred of the human heart toward God. The depravity, cruelty, wickedness, and dreadfulness of sin is climaxed here, and crowned. They sat down. They sat down in contemplation of a finished work. Their work was finished. His work was still to be done. Then it was that the man who crucified Christ began to consider Christ.

1. He Had Never Seen Such Dignity

The Man upon that Roman tree graced it with such dignity He might have been reigning on a throne. Never before had this centurion seen such majesty in the face of such misery, such calmness in the face of such cruelty, such patience in the face of such persecution.

He began to listen. "Father forgive them, they know not what they do." That was the first thing that arrested him. Those words were for him and for his men, a prayer for those who drove the spikes through His hands and His feet. The centurion had never heard a man say anything like that before. It arrested him. There was something different about this Jew. Most Jews he had met hated Romans. This Man prayed for them, even prayed for him! He heard the curses and cries of the dying thieves. Their blasphemies and obscenities filled the air. He heard the taunts of the priests, and he heard the words of Jesus: "Father forgive!" This man, proclaimed King of the Jews by Pilate, was acting like the very Son of the God of the Jews. Never before had he seen such dignity.

2. He Had Never Seen Such Distress

It was not the pangs and pains of crucifixion that wrung the agonizing cries from the lips of this Man. He was a brave Man, the bravest of all men. The torn flesh, the wrenched bones screaming in their sockets, the throbbing tendons, the knotted muscles, the raging thirst—these were not the things that caused His cries. Weakened as He was, Jesus was Man enough to bear such tortures with more than stoic calm. It was more than that, much more than that.

In spite of these things, He could think of others. He could think of His foes, and forgive them. He could think of the repentant thief on the cross beside Him and promise him instant paradise that very day. He could think of His mother and make provision for her. It was not the physical pain that caused such awesome distress. He was more than conqueror over that.

The cry of distress that astonished the centurion was that cry that came out of the darkness when He who knew no sin was made sin for us. *Eli, Eli lama sabachthani!* It was spoken in Aramaic, the everyday language of the land. The centurion may have known a smattering of that tongue. He listened to that cry. He did not know it, but it was a quotation from one of the Jewish Psalms: "My God, My God, why hast thou forsaken me?" (22:1). It was a forlorn cry, a friendless cry, a fateful cry.

"What! You too, Brutus?" So had cried Julius Caesar when his beloved Brutus joined the conspirators. "You too, Brutus?" Shakespeare has caught the full pathos of *that* scene. He draws us around the dead body of great Caesar. There are the conspirators! There stands Cassius! There, too, is Casca and over yonder, Brutus. There is the Roman mob. There lies the corpse. There stands Mark Anthony, pointing out the wounds.

> Look! in this place ran Cassius' dagger through;
> See what a rent the envious Cassius made;
> Through this the well-beloved Brutus stabbed;
> And, as he pluck'd his cursed steel away
> Mark how the blood of Caesar followed it,
> As rushing out of doors to be resolved
> If Brutus so unkindly knocked or no;
> For Brutus as you know was Caesar's angel;
> Judge, O you gods, how dearly Caesar loved him!
> This was the most unkindest cut of all;

For when the noble Caesar saw him stab,
Ingratitude, more strong than traitor's arms
Quite vanquished him, then burst his mighty heart.[1]

This Roman centurion must have known something similar to that as He, the Son of God, hanging there upon the cross, cried aloud to God. It would have been in his history book at school. "You too, Brutus!" Caesar said, as Brutus's dagger stabbed at his heart.

"My God! My God, why hast thou forsaken me?" Jesus cried. It was a cry to chill the blood, turn the marrow of the bones to ice. It seemed to echo on and on and on in the dark. It was the cry a lost soul might give. Yet this was no lost soul. This was a good Man, a righteous Man, a truly holy Man. Never before had the centurion seen such dignity, and such distress. He was deeply moved.

3. He Had Never Seen Such Deeds

Such unprecedented power. The Roman centurion came from a race that glorified power, naked power. The passion of the Jew was for religion. The passion of the Greek was for knowledge. The passion of the Roman was for power. This Roman centurion was part of an invincible power structure. Roman soldiers had marched into every capital of the western world. But he had never seen power like this.

Caesar in Rome had power. He could order senators to kill themselves. He could send marching men by the hundreds of thousands to the distant frontiers of the empire by a nod of his head. But Caesar had no such power as was displayed by this dying Man.

Here was power that could extinguish the sun as though it were a candle. Here was power to plunge the world into midnight darkness at the very hour of the sun's midday strength, when it was at its meridian, shining in all its might. Caesar might have power on earth. This Man had power in heaven. That was a language an unregenerate Roman could readily understand.

Here was power to rend creation's rocks. For hours the darkness had been deepening, an uncanny, inexplicable darkness, eerie and horrifying. And now the very rocks beneath Golgotha's brow were shaking. As the blood flowed slowly down the tree and soaked into the sod, so the earth shook itself as though in mortal terror of what man had done to its Maker. The rocks began to rend, and

---

1. William Shakespeare, *The Life and Death of Julius Caesar,* act 3, scene 2.

the heart of that centurion was gripped with a great fear. That Man must be *more* than a Man. All creation was testifying so.

Here was power to rend the temple veil. No Gentile could be long in Jerusalem without knowing a few things about the temple of the Jews. He might come to its outer court but there he was stopped. No Gentile was allowed to penetrate into the inner courts. The Roman authorities were so conscious of Jewish scruples on this point that they ratified the death sentence for this trespass even when it was passed on Roman citizens. The centurion had probably often seen what Paul calls, "the middle wall of partition." Notices were placed there in Greek and Latin, at the foot of the steps leading into the inner precincts, declaring, "No foreigner may enter within the barrier which surrounds the temple and enclosure. Anyone who is caught doing so will have himself to blame for his ensuing death." This centurion knew about that and the fanatical exclusivism with which the Jews guarded their temple against desecration by any foreign presence.

No Roman could be in Jerusalem long without going to see the sights of the city and this would be one of them. Probably, too, the centurion had heard that inside of the actual temple itself was another "middle wall of partition." And one designed to keep Jews out too. It was a gorgeous curtain called "the veil." It was wide as the temple, thick as a man's hand and woven in gorgeous colors—blue, scarlet, purple. It had hung there, with one short exception, for a thousand years. To pass that veil was death, sudden, mysterious death, not death by a human hand, but by the mysterious, mighty hand of God. And now that veil was rent! From top to bottom and by the hand of God. As the soldier on Golgotha took his spear to rend the side of the Man on that center cross, already quite evidently dead, so God reached down and rent the temple veil.

So the centurion sat there that day, on Golgotha's brow, watching Jesus. The riven rocks, the opened tombs, the darkened sky, the rending veil. The sights! The sounds! The centurion was convinced.

C. Confessing Christ

"Truly!" he said, "this was the Son of God." Then and there, fully and forever, he capitulated to the inescapable logic of Calvary. "This was the Son of God!" In that moment he passed from death unto life. He confessed Jesus as Lord.

And his testimony had been picked up by the Holy Spirit and enshrined forever on the deathless page of the Word of God. It is as fresh and as forceful today as when it fell from his lips. He became one of the few, the very, very few who come to Calvary, consider the Christ in the light of the cross, and go away believing in their hearts that this was the Son of God.

Crucifying—Considering—Confessing Christ. Many went away that day beating their breasts. This man went away believing in the Son of God. The voice of Jesus rings down the centuries: "Will ye also go away?"

THIRTY-FIVE

Barabbas and His Cross

Matthew 27:15–26

A. His sin
B. His service
C. His Savior
D. His silence
    1. Did he crown Christ?
    2. Did he crucify Christ?
    3. Did he consider Christ?

Matthew, Mark, Luke, and John all tell us about Barabbas. He was a robber, a murderer, and a rebel. Some think the name Barabbas was not his original name. It means "Son of the Father." It might have been a name he took for himself when he became leader of the band of brigands and insurrectionists with whom his name is linked. Others tell us that this man, Barabbas, had yet another name—Jesus Barabbas. Fredrick Farrar of Trinity College in Cambridge, Canon of Westminster and Chaplain to Queen Victoria gives a measure of credence to this claim. Certainly, the name *Jesus* (the Greek form of the Old Testament name *Joshua*) was a common enough name in Palestine in those days. The name *Jesus* means "Savior." If these inferences are correct, this brigand had a most significant name—Jesus Barabbas! Savior! Son of the Father! A strange name and a strange figure is Alfred Edersheim's comment, and Edersheim was a great Hebrew Christian scholar. He suggests Barabbas was some kind of a political antichrist.

Barabbas was drawn dramatically onto the stage of Christ's sufferings. He was made to stand up alongside of Jesus the Christ. Then he was left hovering in the background for an hour or so as the trial of Jesus seesawed backward and forward. Then he was suddenly released and dismissed from the gospel story.

A. His Sin

Two or three words in the Gospels sum up the life of this man. He was guilty of insurrection and sedition. The same Greek word is used but translated differently. He was a robber. He had also committed murder.

Sedition, the word translated *insurrection*, comes from a Greek word that means "to make stand," "one who stirs up sedition," "a rebel." One of the gospel writers tells us that Barabbas was a member of a gang. Probably he was the leader of the gang. Matthew says he was "a notable prisoner" (27:16). Participating in armed rebellion made Barabbas a criminal under Roman law. We are not told when or where Barabbas led this uprising against Rome. The Jewish historian, Josephus, tells of an insurrection against Pilate's government caused by his taking money from the temple treasury to finance the construction of an aqueduct into Jerusalem. Pilate's fear of sparking off another insurrection would account for his touchiness at the trial of Christ. So, then, Barabbas was a "freedom fighter," an insurrectionist, the leader of a popular Jewish front against the detested Romans. Barabbas was the kind of messiah the Jews had always wanted. Someone who would throw off the shackles of Rome and make Jerusalem the capital of a new world empire. They had always wanted a militant messiah. That Barabbas was in prison for leading a violent insurrection would make him popular with the Jews.

The word translated *robber* means "bandit" or "brigand," what we would call a highwayman. Barabbas was not just a thief who stole by fraud and in secret. He was one who robbed openly and by violence. The two thieves crucified with Christ are also described by this word. They, too, were brigands. They are also called *malefactors*. This word simply means "evildoers." It is not at all unlikely that they were members of the gang headed up by Barabbas. Barabbas was a robber. He was a cut-throat brigand; one who robbed by violence and by force.

The word translated "murder" means just that. The word is in the singular, which suggests that Barabbas was guilty, not of indiscriminate slaughter in the heat of a skirmish with Roman legionnaires, but of cold-blooded, calculated murder. As a robber and a murderer, Barabbas was not only a criminal under Roman law but also under Jewish law.

We do not know where Barabbas had his base of operations and carried out his lawless acts. It might well have been on the Jericho Road. The road from

Jerusalem to Jericho was notoriously dangerous. The Jordan Valley, with its crushing heat, with its nightmare scenery, with its serpentine road flanked by overhanging cliffs and projecting boulders was a paradise for highwaymen. At hundreds of points along the road it would be easy to set an ambush, waylay a traveler, beat him to a pulp, and make off with his goods to one of the thousands of caves in the hills. A search party, a regiment of soldiers, indeed, a whole army might fail to root out a band of brigands once it had retreated to its hideout in the hills. A detachment of troops could wander for years in a fruitless hunt for a brigand in those desolate vastnesses of Judea.

Barabbas was an outlaw. Yet he was one with a dash of color. It has been mentioned that he was a "notable prisoner." The word used means "to have a mark upon." In a good sense, the word means "noted," "eminent," "distinguished." In a bad sense, the word means "notorious." Barabbas was notorious. He was what we would call a marked man. No doubt Rome had long put a price upon his head. And, no doubt, Barabbas justified his behavior. He would say that he was not a criminal, that he was a patriot, a freedom fighter. The things he did, he did for the good of his country. The same kind of arguments that terrorists use today when they hijack planes, murder civilians, and hide their bombs in grocery stores and hotels and blow up bus loads of children. They have their admirers, people who support them, finance them, and justify their deeds.

But, at last, Barabbas was caught.

B. His Service

Barabbas was caught and convicted. He was condemned to death and found himself under lock and key in Jerusalem. The condemned cell became his home. It was only a matter of time, and the iron gates would swing open. The armed guard would take him to Golgotha. There, at "the place of the skull," he would be put to death. There was no doubt about that. He was to receive the due reward of his deeds. Death was an absolute certainty.

We can picture him sitting in his cell with his head in his hands, thinking, perhaps, about the past. He might recall his boyhood days. He had been inaugurated into the Jewish faith by circumcision when he was eight days old. Probably he had learned to read and write. Perhaps he had memorized this and that passage of Scripture. A verse or two might well flit across his mind for a fleeting moment.

He would think of his rebellion against authority, of the dreadful deeds his hands had done. He would look within his heart and see that it was deceitful above all things and desperately wicked, just as the Old Testament prophet had said. At times he would stoically accept his fate. So! He was going to die! So what! Everybody had to die sometime or other. He would stare gloomily at the prison wall. At other times he would rage in his bonds. He would curse and swear. His vile oaths would fill the prison. He would tear at the iron shackles that held his wrists; he would hammer at the cold, stone walls; he would seize the bars of his cell and shake them with fury and fear. At times he might sing the obscene songs of the bandit's cave, or perhaps, at times, he would weep silently in the darkness of the night. At times he would resolve to die like a man. At other times he would wake up with the cold sweat of abject fear and naked horror standing on his brow. He was going to die. And oh! What a death! Death by *crucifixion!* The anticipation was as bad as the actual torment itself.

C. His Savior

Jesus died for Barabbas, just as truly as He died for you and me. This fact was brought home to Barabbas in a memorable way. There he is sitting in his cell, as we've imagined, very, very early in the morning. The sun is hardly up when there is the clank of iron mail outside the cell, the grating of a key in the lock, and the grounding of arms. The chain that binds the prisoner to the wall is unloosed. The moment has come, the dreaded moment. They are not even going to let him live over Passover. He had counted at least on that. Instead, he is seized by two soldiers and marched along the dank corridors, out into the open air, and then on into the judgment hall. There is an enormous mob there, all clamoring for something. They are demanding Paschal clemency! Then Barabbas remembers. It is a standing custom for the Roman governor to release a prisoner at Passover, any prisoner, whomsoever the Jews demanded. Hope blazes up in his heart. The crowd is going to insist that Pilate set him free.

But it is not quite so simple as that, as Barabbas is soon to discover. Pilate is going to use him in a giant gamble. For Pilate has another prisoner this day, a notable prisoner indeed. His name is Jesus of Nazareth, Jesus the Messiah, Jesus the Son of God. Pilate had been struggling for what seemed, to him, a whole eternity to persuade the people to dismiss their false, unfounded charges against Jesus. He knows of Christ's triumphal entry into Jerusalem. He hopes that the same crowd who had cheered Him then would choose Him now. He is going to stake everything on a throw of the dice.

Barabbas finds himself marched into the presence of the Roman governor. There he sees, perhaps for the first time in his life, the Person of Jesus Christ. Pilate puts the two men forward and any hope that had surged in the soul of Barabbas dies a sudden death. He does not have a chance. Not if it is to be him or Jesus.

Doubtless Barabbas has heard of this Man Jesus, of the many and marvelous miracles He has performed; how He made the blind to see, the lame to walk, the deaf to hear, the dumb to speak; how He cleansed lepers; how He fed the multitudes with a little lad's lunch. How He had even raised the dead.

Oh, yes, he has heard of this Man Jesus. He has heard of His wonderful way with words. He has heard some of the stories Jesus has told—of the man who fell among thieves; of the rich fool who lived for time and forgot eternity; of the sower, the seed, and the soil; of the wheat and the tares; of the grain of mustard seed. He has heard about the Sermon on the Mount. Oh! What wonderful words they were that proceeded out of His mouth.

He has heard of this Man Jesus, how He claims to be the Son of the living God; how He went about doing good; how He cleansed the temple and drove out those who made a marketplace of the house of God and merchandise of the people of God; how He had turned water into wine; how He had walked upon the waves; how He befriended the poor, the fatherless, the widow; how He blessed the little children.

If it is to be a choice between Barabbas and Jesus, then surely there can be no choice. But he is thrust forward and made to stand alongside the Christ of God. There they stand, the scowling murderer, the very epitome of rebellion and rage, resentment and ruin, and the meek and lowly Jesus of Nazareth, the only sinless Man who ever lived on earth.

The challenge goes forth. "Whither of the twain? Whom will ye that I release unto you? Shall it be Jesus which is called Barabbas or Jesus which is called Christ?" The heart of Barabbas sinks down into his sandals.

But then comes another moment of hope. There is an interruption, a messenger coming in from the outside. He draws Pilate aside. There is a message from his wife. Barabbas has his eyes glued on the face of the Roman governor. He sees the shadow of fear cross his face. Then Barabbas looks at the mob. The chief priests have not wasted this opportunity. There they are, busy among the people, telling them what to say and how to act. This is not the same crowd that had cried Hosanna a week before. That was mostly a Galilean crowd. The mob that now throngs the judgment hall is a Judean mob, a Jerusalem mob.

The priests were busy. The sacred historian tells us that "the chief priests moved the people." That word *moved* is an interesting word. It means "to stir up" (as by an earthquake). In fact, it is the very word from which we derive our modern word *seismograph*.

Now, straining his ears, Barabbas hears his own name being mentioned, again, and again, and again. His heart leaps with hope. There is an upheaval going on out there. The mob is putty in the hands of the priests, who know how to handle it. A few well-placed words. A few inflammatory remarks. A few chosen leaders to raise the rabble cry. Hope comes back to Barabbas. The crowd will choose him after all! And so it does. Pilate comes back, "Whom will you have? Jesus or Barabbas?" And back from a thousand throats comes the roar, "Barabbas! We choose Barabbas! Long live Barabbas!"

But as quickly as hope flames in the soul of the murderer so it dies again. For evidently that is not the answer the governor had counted on. Again and again, once, twice, three times he tries to argue with the mob. Then, turning his back upon them in utter disdain he retires back into the Praetorium, boldly announcing his decision. He will release Jesus the Christ. He will scourge Him and then let Him go.

So Jesus was taken away by the soldiers and thrashed by the Romans with the horrible scourge, a cruel whip which tore great lumps of flesh off the victim's back. At the same time the soldiers arrayed Christ in a mocking purple robe and crowned Him with a crown of thorns.

Now Pilate brings Jesus back out to the Jews. With a mocking gesture he cries, *"Ecce Homo!"* "Behold the man!" (John 19:5). He thus debunks any claims of this Man Jesus to be a King. But the priests are a tough breed. "Crucify!" they cry, "Crucify Him!" And once more hope flares up in the soul of Barabbas, only to die again a moment later.

"He made Himself the Son of God" the priests continued in order to justify their cry. "He is a blasphemer. By our law He deserves to die." But that shout only frightened Pilate all the more—it added to the message he had just received from his wife. Back he went into the Praetorium, taking Jesus with him to cross-examine Him yet again. He came back from that private session so shaken in his soul that he determined to release Him, no matter the cost.

When Barabbas sees this new mood written all over the governor's face, what hope can he have now that he will be released? Roman law is being pitted against mob rule.

But the priests had one more card to play. It was an ace. It was the winning card. "If you let this man go you are not Caesar's friend!" they cried (see John 19:12). Stunned, Pilate walked over and sat down on the Bema, the judgment seat. The sacred historian fixed the spot by its two names: "The Pavement!" In Hebrew, "Gabbatha!" Thus he underlined for all time the exact spot where the dreadful decision was made. Pilate sat down, shaken to the core of his soul. Gone were all his resolves to set Jesus free. The historian tells us the time. It was six o'clock in the morning.

The eyes of Barabbas are glued upon Pilate's face. He can see the despair, the dismay, the disdain written on the Roman's face.

But Pilate makes one more feeble effort. "Behold your King!" he says.

"We have no king but Caesar!" they reply.

"Shall I crucify your King?" Pilate says.

"Away with him, away with him! Let Him be crucified."

Then, as Barabbas holds his breath, the governor calls for water. He washes his hands. "I am innocent of the blood of this righteous man," he says.

"His blood be on us and upon our children!" yells the mob.

So the sentence of death was signed. Jesus was to be crucified; Barabbas was set free. He lived because Jesus died in his place. A Savior had been found, a Substitute.

D. His Silence

What did Barabbas do after he walked out of Pilate's judgment hall, a free man? Was he carried off by the crowd to the nearest tavern to drink and celebrate? Did he quietly slip away down some back alley and rejoin his gang of cutthroats out on the hills? Did he go home and become a law-abiding man? There are three things he could have done. The Bible is silent as to what he actually did.

1. Did He Crown Christ?

We would like to think that Barabbas wended his way to Calvary, and that he flung himself at Jesus' feet as He hung there on the cross. We would like to think Barabbas asked Him—as did the dying thief, the likely companion of Barabbas in the old days—to remember him when He came into His kingdom. There is no record of any such thing.

2. Did He Crucify Christ?

Drunken with the hails and cheers of the crowd, did he join them on the hill? Did he march with them up Golgotha's brow, head held high, arms swinging, voice lifted in ribald song? Did he join them there as they gathered around to mock and deride and jeer? "If thou be the Son of God, come down from the cross!" (Matt. 27:40). Did he thus vent all the venom of his unregenerate, obdurate, hardened sinner's heart upon the very One sent by God to be his Savior, and ours? The Bible does not say.

3. Did He Consider Christ?

Did he just walk away and ignore the Savior? Did he walk away to do his level best to forget what he had seen and heard? Did he do what the majority do? The great majority of people simply ignore Christ altogether. They ignore His claims. They ignore His death. They ignore everything. Is that what Barabbas did? We do not know.

THIRTY-SIX

The Dying Thief and His Faith

Matthew 27:44; Luke 23:32–43

A. HE WAS A DYING MAN
B. HE WAS A DISCERNING MAN
   1. He began to look at Jesus
   2. He began to listen to Jesus
C. HE WAS A DELIVERED MAN

It was nine o'clock in the morning. We can easily imagine what transpired. The Roman soldiers nail him—screaming, wrestling, fighting, cursing, kicking, blaspheming—to his cross. On a sign they write out his name in letters of Greek, Latin, and Hebrew. They add his father's name so that his family can share his shame. They write out his crime: robbery with violence. They hammer the sign to the cross. Then they heave up the cross and drop its foot into a hole in the ground. The more callous of the soldiers laugh as the wretched man screams aloud with fresh pain when the whole weight of his body tears at the raw wounds in his hands and feet.

A more kindly soul gives him a stupefying drink from a sponge stuck on the end of a cane. For a little while the thief is silent except for occasional heart-stopping groans.

That was nine o'clock in the morning. Before the sun reached its zenith at twelve noon on the day of his death, this condemned criminal was marvelously saved. He was the first convert of the crucified Christ. From His cross the Lord Jesus reached out and saved two people. One was a Gentile; one was a Jew. One was a tried and trusted soldier of Rome; the other was a criminal.

Somewhere between five and six o'clock that afternoon, by special order of the governor who was under pressure from the Jews because of the oncoming Sabbath, the soldiers hastened the thief's end. He was fortunate. Normally, people who were crucified did not die that quickly. They lingered on, sometimes for days.

Death by crucifixion was ghastly. It was accompanied by dizziness, cramps, thirst, hunger, sleeplessness, traumatic fever, tetanus, and tormenting heat and flies. Crucifixion was preceded by the torture of anticipation and attended by horrible humiliation. The only man who ever died with dignity on a cross was Jesus.

Death by crucifixion came with agonizing slowness. The victim suffered the agony of cramped limbs, the mortification of wounds, the stretching of every muscle and ligament to the breaking point, and an increasing strain on his heart. He felt the pain of lacerated veins, crushed tendons, and throbbing arteries, especially of the head and stomach. Added to his miseries was a raging, burning thirst. All these torments gradually intensified until the victim lost consciousness. Death, which sometimes did not come for three days, was not the result of loss of blood, but of exhaustion, starvation, dehydration, or suffocation.

But because of the religious scruples of the Jews who did not want to annoy God by desecrating His Sabbath, the soldiers terminated this man's suffering prematurely. In order to compensate for abbreviating his suffering, they ended his life in a particularly brutal way. One of them took a mallet and dealt a fearful blow to the poor fellow's left leg, then his right leg. His left leg snapped and then his right leg snapped, throwing the whole weight of his body on his arms. That in turn ruptured his heart. And so he died in one final flash of pain—and awoke in paradise.

That morning, then, the dying thief was saved. He was not saved by going to church, for the church was not even in existence then. He was not saved by reading his Bible or giving out tracts. He was not saved by living a good life—he was a condemned criminal paying the penalty demanded in those days by the law of the land. He was not saved by being baptized—how could a man on a cross be baptized? He was not saved by doing penance. He was not saved by going on a pilgrimage to some holy place sanctified by tradition and time—how could he go on a pilgrimage when he was fastened, hand and foot, to a cross?

He was not saved by confessing his sins to the watching priests—they could not have forgiven his sins even if they had wanted to. He was not saved by turning over a new leaf—he only had hours to live and most of those would be spent in mind-searing pain. He was not saved by praying to the virgin Mary, who stood there not far from the cross—such a thought never so much as entered his head.

He was not saved by being a good neighbor—he had been caught red-handed sinning against his "neighbor." He was saved the same way everyone is saved.

Let us consider three facts about this criminal and his salvation.

A. He Was a Dying Man

The burning fires of death were already licking about the dying thief's feet. Each drop of blood that ebbed from his wounds made him weaker. Each pain-wracked, agonizing moment brought him closer to the brink. Death, creeping up on him, was laughing at his terror and suffering.

Driven to madness, goaded on by his companion in crime who was hanging on the third cross, the thief began to curse Christ. With the grave already yawning for his sin-stained soul, this man could think of no better way to give vent to his anguish than to ridicule, blaspheme, and curse the Son of God.

Before long, however, he stopped cursing and, turning fiercely on his companion, told him to stop his senseless blasphemies. What had happened? He had begun to think about his sins. "Our deeds!" he exclaimed. "We receive the due reward of our deeds" (Luke 23:41). He was suddenly haunted by the awful load of his sin and by the awesome legality of his sentence. He likely had not thought much about his sins for years—except to joke about them with the boys in the tavern at night—but the nearer he came to death, the more he thought about his sins.

Someone said, "Conscience is a three-cornered thing in my heart. It stands still when I am good, but when I am bad it turns around and the corners hurt. If I keep on doing wrong, the corners wear off and it does not hurt anymore." Conscience, however, has a way of reviving at awkward times. Often it rouses itself like a roaring lion when death draws near. Sometimes it awakens when some unexpected piece of news arrives.

Think of the case of King Herod. Shortly after he had murdered John the Baptist, Herod heard of the miracles of Jesus. "It is John," he said. "It is John, whom I beheaded: he is risen from the dead" (Mark 6:16). Herod's reasoning was strange, for he was a Sadducee, and the Sadducees denied the doctrine of the resurrection. But conscience is stronger than creed. As William Cowper wrote,

> Conscience in some silent awful hour,
> When captivating lusts have lost their power,
> Starts from the down on which she lately slept

> And tells of laws despised, at least not kept . . .
> Shows with a pointing finger, but no more
> A pale procession of past sinful joys;
> All witnessing of blessings long ignored,
> Of life abused, of guilt now underscored.
> Mark these, she says. These summoned from afar
> Begin their March to meet thee at the bar;
> There thou shalt meet a Judge, Omniscient, just,
> And perish there for loved and unrepented lust.[1]

Thus it was that the dying thief fell silent. His conscience had risen at last and, like a lion with its prey, had torn away at the vitals of his soul. "We are condemned justly," he said to the other criminal.

This was the prelude to his salvation. Before anyone can be truly saved, he has to come under the conviction of his sin. The first work of the Holy Spirit in the human heart is His convicting work. In a deep, quiet, mysterious way He comes and enthrones Himself in the conscience and begins preliminary hearings in view of the great white throne judgment yet to come.

So the condemned thief was a dying man, but he was dying with an awakened conscience.

B. HE WAS A DISCERNING MAN

A few minutes earlier the dying thief had been cursing and reviling Jesus. "If thou be Christ," he had said with bitter irony, "save thyself and us" (Luke 23:39). How did the Lord respond? He practiced what He had preached.

In the Sermon on the Mount the Lord Jesus had declared, "Ye have heard that it hath been said, Thou shalt love thy neighbour, and hate thine enemy. But I say unto you, Love your enemies, bless them that curse you, do good to them that hate you, and pray for them which despitefully use you, and persecute you" (Matt. 5:43–44). Thus it was that the more the foul-mouthed malefactor lifted up his voice in execration, the more Christ lifted up His voice in supplication. "Father, forgive them; for they know not what they do," He said (Luke 23:34). We do not know if anyone else ever prayed for the dying thief, but we can be quite sure Jesus did.

---

1. William Cowper, "Hope," in *The Complete Poetical Works of William Cowper* (Boston: Gould and Lincoln, 1855).

1. He Began to Look at Jesus

It is not difficult to suppose that, while the thief cursed, he glared at Jesus. And in doing so, presently his mind clears. The thief looks at a face that is marred more than any man's. All through the preceding night the Lord Jesus has been badgered and bullied by the temple police. He has been marched here and there across the city; He has been hauled before the high priest and abused; He has been sent to Pilate and then on to Herod, who with his men of war had mocked Him; then He had been returned to Pilate and scourged to the bone.

The face of Jesus is bruised and battered beyond recognition and blood runs down it from a crown of thorns. The Lord's beard has been wrenched with brute force from His cheeks and chin. The face that had once inspired the seraph's song hardly looks human any more.

The dying thief began, then, to look at Jesus by looking at His face. In a coming day that face will be for all men either the first glimpse of heaven or the first foretaste of hell.

Now the thief lifts his eyes a little higher and sees the crown of thorns. The thorns remind him of the curse under which the human race lives. "Cursed is the ground," God had said. "Thorns . . . shall it bring forth" (Gen. 3:17–18).

That curse was expanded, for the Jew at least, to embrace every aspect of his life and every detail of his exile from the Promised Land. And that curse was greatly to be feared, for Galatians 3:13 says, "It is written, Cursed is every one that hangeth on a tree" (see Deut. 21:23). Jesus, just like the thief and his companion in crime, was dying under the curse of God. Did the dying thief think about these things? *Why is Jesus dying under a curse? All I have ever heard of Him has been good. Why is He, of all men, not only crucified, but also crowned with thorns—cursed and doubly cursed?*

The thief lifts his eyes still higher, and he sees the inscription Pilate has written: "JESUS OF NAZARETH THE KING OF THE JEWS" (John 19:19). "Jesus"—the syllables ring like joy bells in his soul and penetrate the depths of his heart, for the name means "Savior!" When the thief reads the rest of the title, "the King of the Jews," he wonders if Jesus could be the Messiah. He does not look like a King, but He acts like one. Never before has this dying man seen such poise, peace, and power in the face of distress, derision, and death.

So, then, the thief began to look at Jesus. At first he looked in growing wonder and awe. But as Israel had discovered in the wilderness, and as Jesus had reminded Nicodemus, there is "life in a look" (see Num. 21:8; John 3:14–15).

Years ago there was a well-to-do English country squire who had a daughter he loved very much. He was a rigid Victorian with deeply ingrained notions of what was right and what was wrong and, like so many of his generation, he was a stern, harsh disciplinarian.

One day a visiting evangelist set up a tent on the village green and began to preach the gospel. The young lady went to the meetings out of curiosity and was soundly saved. She went home and told her father, who was a high-churchman. He was infuriated and forbade his daughter ever to go near the tent again; he swore that he would horsewhip her if she did. She informed her father that as much as she loved and respected him, in this matter she would not be ruled.

That night she returned to the tent even though she knew she would face her father's wrath and his horsewhip the next morning. When she came down for breakfast the next morning, her father was standing there in his riding boots and, sure enough, his horsewhip was on the table. "Before you touch me with that horsewhip, Father," she said, "I want you to read this." She handed him a sheet of paper on which she had written some verses of poetry.

She had been up all night praying for her father and reading her Bible. She asked the Lord to help her tell her father why she had gone to that tent in defiance of his will, to tell him, indeed, what it meant to be saved. She had put her thoughts on paper. The words she wrote that night have found their way into our hymnbooks:

> There is life for a look at the Crucified One,
> There is life at this moment for thee;
> Then look, sinner, look unto Him and be saved,
> Unto Him who was nailed to the tree.[2]

My father used to tell the story. He said the young woman's father was touched and broken by the words of this hymn, words she herself had penned.

"There is life in a look" indeed! The dying thief found that to be gloriously true. But he not only looked at Jesus, he listened to Him.

---

2. A. M. Hull, "There Is Life for a Look," 1860.

2. He Began to Listen to Jesus

The Lord Jesus spoke seven times on the cross. The first three times He expressed His tenderness. The next two times He expressed His travail, once in spiritual terms and once in physical terms. The last two times He expressed His triumph, once in summing up the past and once in summing up the future.

The dying thief only heard one of those seven sayings before he cast himself spiritually into the arms of Jesus. After he was saved, he heard a second saying, in which Jesus assured the dying, discerning man that his sins, which were many, were all washed away.

Before he was saved, the only thing this man heard Jesus say was, "Father, forgive them; for they know not what they do" (Luke 23:34). That statement was enough. It opened the gates of heaven for him.

For the most part, the dying thief heard the gospel unwittingly preached by Christ's enemies. They were standing around the cross—the priests and the leaders of the people. This was their hour. They finally had the One they detested where they wanted Him: on a cross, dying beneath the curse of God. They had labored long for this moment—pulling political strings, applying pressure, paying out cold cash to corrupt an already corrupted man, manipulating the mob. Now they had what they wanted, and they savored every minute. "If thou be the Son of God, come down from the cross," they cried. They added a new note of sarcasm—and this is what the dying thief heard them say: "He saved others; himself he cannot save" (Matt. 27:40, 42).

There it was—the essence of the gospel! The Man dying next to the thief was Jesus—the *Savior,* as His name implied. He had saved others; even His foes acknowledged that. Why could He not save Himself? The thief was enough of a Jew to know what the Law, the Prophets, and the Psalms taught about sacrifices. When a sinner brought a sacrifice, the sacrifice could only save the sinner by being slain itself. It could save others; itself it could not save. So this Man with the saving name of Jesus was a Savior in the sense of being a sacrifice for sinners. He could not save Himself because, like those lambs slain on the temple altars, He could only save the sinner by dying for the sinner.

So like a flash of light, the truth dawns on the thief: *Jesus is not dying for His own sins, for He has done nothing amiss. He is dying for mine!*

But Jesus was not only a Savior. He was also a *Sovereign.* Even Pilate had acknowledged Him to be "the King of the Jews." He was the Christ, and He had a kingdom. Obviously it was not a human domain. The thief realized it must be a heavenly realm. Jesus was leaving the world in a particularly horrible way, but when He left He would enter His kingdom. "Lord," the thief said, "remember me when thou comest into thy kingdom" (Luke 23:42).

That tremendous statement of faith was uttered in the face of all the outward evidence to the contrary. The faith of the dying thief embraced the reality of Christ's position in the godhead, even though natural reasoning would conclude that the mighty Creator and Lord could not possibly be the battered Man on the central cross. The thief's faith also embraced the resurrection of Christ from the tomb. What else could result from the death of the Son of God but life restored? Moreover, taking a mighty leap, his faith embraced the return of Christ in all the pomp and splendor of His kingdom.

It is astounding that amidst shame, pain, and mockery, this crucified criminal could see redemption and royalty centered in the bruised and broken form of Jesus. We do not even know his name, but he laid hold of Christ in a way not exceeded by the great apostle Paul.

"Lord, remember me when thou comest into thy kingdom." Those words must have been the most blissful that ever fell on the ears of the Son of God. The great maw of death was steadily creeping up the sides of the thief's cross, yet that suffering soul in his desperate extremity could see what nobody else could see. Peter could not see it. Neither could James or John. Only the thief could see the significance of Pilate's superscription. And the only voice raised that dreadful day in defense of Christ and in confession of His royalty and redemptive work was his.

The dying thief did not have a tenth of our advantages. He had never read a single page of the New Testament. He was not sitting in a comfortable seat surrounded by people who were interested in his soul. He was wracked from head to foot with pain that should have driven him out of his mind. Every outward appearance militated against his seeing in Jesus the Savior for whom his guilty soul so greatly longed. His only friend was a companion in crime. Organized religion, as it was represented by the priests, ignored this penniless thief. No human eye pitied him; no human hand stretched out to save him. Yet he reached out to Christ, not with a cautious feeler but in confident faith. He will rise up in the day of judgment against some of us.

C. He Was a Delivered Man

Jesus looked at the man who had appealed to Him and spoke His second word from the cross: "Verily I say unto thee, Today shalt thou be with me in paradise" (Luke 23:43). Today! The thief would be with Christ that day; not after years spent in some imagined purgatory. He would be with Christ in a very real and very present paradise, not just in a coming earthly kingdom. The dying man was saved and he was sure, for he had the word of Christ. He could well have sung,

> My sin—O, the bliss of this glorious thought,
> My sin—not in part but the whole,
> Is nailed to the cross and I bear it no more,
> Praise the Lord, praise the Lord, O my soul![3]

Shortly after the thief was saved, a series of miracles confirmed that his faith had not been misplaced. The light went out—"There was darkness over all the land" (Matt. 27:45). When the light returned, the Lord dismissed His spirit. Thereafter all the dying thief saw on the cross next to his was a lifeless battered form. The Savior had gone on ahead into paradise, but we can imagine that just over Jordan He tarried for His friend—one of the only real friends He had that day on Calvary's hill.

Between five and six o'clock that same afternoon (as men count time), the Roman soldiers put a cruel end to the life of the dying thief. They launched his soul into eternity, and he was met on eternity's shore by the glorious Lord Himself. Nail-scarred hand clasped nail-scarred hand. The dying thief, dying no more, was conducted on into paradise by heaven's Beloved. Then all heaven rang with a triumphant shout.

> All thro' the mountains, thunder-riv'n
> And up from the rocky steep,
> There arose a glad cry to the gate of heav'n.
> "Rejoice! I have found my sheep!"
> And the angels echoed around the throne,
> "Rejoice, for the Lord brings back His own!
> Rejoice, for the Lord brings back His own."[4]

---

3. Horatio G. Spafford, "It Is Well with My Soul," 1873.
4. Elizabeth C. Clephane, "The Ninety and Nine," 1868.

But there were two thieves crucified with Christ. One has been in heaven for nearly two thousand years. The other is in hell. He had the same chance to be saved that his companion had, but he chose to die in his sins.

THIRTY-SEVEN

Ananias and Sapphira

Liars Both

Acts 5:1–11

A. A LESSON IN DISCIPLESHIP: GREAT POWER
   1. The men
   2. The message
B. A LESSON IN FELLOWSHIP: GREAT GRACE
C. A LESSON IN MEMBERSHIP: GREAT FEAR

The two names sound like music in our ears—Ananias and Sapphira. The name *Ananias* means "Jehovah has graciously given." It reminds us of words from the old hymn, "Savior, Thy Dying Love":

> Savior, Thy dying love Thou gavest me,
> Nor should I aught withhold, Dear Lord, from Thee.
> All that I am and have, Thy gifts so free,
> In joy, in grief, thro' life, Dear Lord, for Thee![1]

Sapphira, an Aramaic word, simply means "beautiful." One name captures the thought of *bounty;* the other captures the thought of *beauty.* If the pair had lived up to their names, they would have been permanent ornaments of the church—enduring examples of the bounty and beauty of the Lord Jesus. Instead they were a pair of Achans in the camp of the church (Josh. 7). Like their Old Testament counterpart, they perished under the judgment hand of God.

---

1. Sylvanus D. Phelps, "Savior, Thy Dying Love," 1862.

A. A LESSON IN DISCIPLESHIP: GREAT POWER

The story of Ananias and Sapphira was told in connection with the story of the early church. Let us consider the men who established the church and the power of their message.

1. The Men

"With great power gave the apostles witness" (Acts 4:33). The apostles themselves were ordinary men; the Sanhedrin contemptuously, in fact, called them "unlearned and ignorant" (4:13). *What under the sun,* the Jewish religious leaders likely thought, *is there to fear from a dozen fishermen, tax collectors, and peasants? Why, there isn't a single educated man among them. They are not rich. They are not sophisticated. They are not from the upper crust of society. They are common Galileans.* But these men were apostles. They had been with Jesus! That was the secret of their power. The apostles were separated from other men by the amount of time they spent with Jesus.

We do not have apostles in the church today. The gift of the apostle was special and specialized. The nursery no longer exists where apostles can be born and raised. John lived longer than any of the other apostles; and when he died, the office and gift of the apostle died.

The word *apostle,* simply means "sent one." There are many "sent ones" today. Indeed, to some extent, all Christians are "sent ones." The work of the apostle remains although the gift of the apostle has ceased.

The early apostles had spent time with the Son of God. They had been baptized, indwelt, sealed, filled, and anointed by the Spirit of God. In the sense that anyone can become acquainted with the Son of God and make himself available to the Spirit of God, anyone can be an apostle. That is the kind of man God uses to build His church. In the early days the Jerusalem church was uniquely blessed by the presence of about a dozen such men in its ranks.

2. The Message

The early church had only one message: Christ—alive from the dead, ascended on high, seated at God's right hand, and coming again. "With great power gave the apostles witness of the resurrection of the Lord Jesus" (Acts 4:33).

The resurrection of Christ is the one great irrefutable argument for Christianity.

At the time of the French revolution, a Frenchman named Lepeaux was disappointed in the poor success he was having in launching a new religion, which to his mind was far superior to Christianity. He appealed to Charles Maurice de Tallyrand, a statesman-bishop who became a leader of the godless French revolution. Lepeaux asked Tallyrand, "What should I do to get my new religion off the ground?"

"My dear M. Lepeaux," the statesman said, "it is a very difficult thing to start a new religion. But there is one thing you might at least try. I suggest you get yourself crucified and then rise again on the third day."

The resurrection was the predominating theme of the apostles' message. It took such ready root there and everywhere because it was gloriously true. "God hath raised him from the dead," wrote Paul to the Romans (Rom. 10:9).

Eusebius, an early church father and historian, tells us that when the news began to circulate in Jerusalem that Jesus Christ was alive from the dead, Pontius Pilate, the Roman governor, considered the story to be of sufficient importance that he officially referred the matter to Tiberius. Under Roman law the Roman senate had the authority to rule on all claims to deity. Eusebius wrote, "An ancient law prevailed that no one should be made a god by the Romans except by a vote and decree of the Senate. The Senate rejected the Nazarene's claim to deity."[2] Apparently the Lord Jesus did not think it worthwhile to get the Romans' approval before claiming to be God and proving it by rising from the dead.

The well-publicized case of Lord Lyttleton and Gilbert West illustrates the power of the apostles' message. The two men, unbelieving and skeptical, decided that the best way to overthrow Christianity was to undermine belief in its two cardinal, historical facts: the resurrection of Christ and the conversion of the apostle Paul. Lyttleton undertook to discredit the account of the conversion of Paul, and West undertook to disprove the resurrection of Christ. When they met to discuss their progress, they made a tremendous discovery. They had both been so convinced by the evidence that they had both written their books to *prove* the very thing they had set out to disprove. Some years ago I checked West's book out of the Moody Bible Institute library and read for myself its clear message of a Christ who died, who was buried, and who rose again.[3]

For a number of years Allan Redpath was the pastor of Moody Memorial

---

2. *Ecclesiastical History,* bk. 2, chap. 2.

3. West, *Observations on the History and Evidences of the Resurrection of Jesus Christ* (London: R. Dodsley, 1749); Lyttleton, *Observations on the Conversion and Apostleship of St. Paul* (London: R. Dodsley, 1749).

Church in Chicago. At one Moody Bible Institute Founders Week Conference I heard him use the following illustration.

Redpath was an Englishman. Although he had lived in the United States for a considerable time, he retained his love for English sports. He was especially interested in the annual cricket test match (the highest level of competition) between England and Australia. Alas! He could find few people in the United States who even knew what cricket was and still fewer who cared anything about a test match to be held in far-off Britain.

The match began each day at 11:00 AM, stopped at 1:00 PM for lunch, resumed at 1:45 PM, stopped at 3:30 PM for tea (cricket is a gentlemanly sport), resumed at 4:00 PM, and stopped at 6:30 PM. Each year the match went on like that for five days.

One year in particular when Redpath was living in Chicago, he wanted to know how the annual match was going. He bought every Chicago newspaper he could lay his hands on, but he couldn't find a word about the match. The American journalists were only interested in the Cubs and the Sox baseball teams. A friend from England kindly airmailed him a copy of a London paper. The headline on the front page was "England Facing Defeat." This news was more depressing than no news at all. Worse still, nobody seemed to care. But two days later Redpath received another British newspaper. This time the headline read, "England in Sight of Victory." In two days the whole situation had changed.

It was a sad day at Calvary when Joseph took Jesus down from the cross, wrapped His body in grave clothes, and put Him in his tomb. The world went on its way. Few people cared. But the disciples were utterly demoralized and defeated. Thomas became an avowed skeptic, Peter ate his heart out with remorse, and John did his best to comfort the Lord's mother, Mary. Then came the resurrection morning. In three days the whole situation had changed.

That was the point of Redpath's illustration, and *that* was the message of the early church: the whole situation had changed. And the news spread. As Paul said to King Agrippa, "This thing was not done in a corner" (Acts 26:26). Peter, James, John, Matthew, Thomas, and all the rest of the disciples were eyewitnesses of the risen Christ. Their powerful message would turn the world upside down.

B. A LESSON IN FELLOWSHIP: GREAT GRACE

Adding to his description of the early church, Luke said, "Great grace was upon them all" (Acts 4:33). That outstanding characteristic and quality of life that marked the Christ now marked the Christians. The overflow of love among Christians was such that a brother who had money in the bank would share his money with a brother in great need. Before long the prevailing custom was share and share alike. This generous lifestyle was an experiment in pure socialism—that is, socialism based on the utmost ideal and motivated by what the Holy Spirit calls "great grace." The experiment did not last and it did not work, but it was an interesting attempt to share and share alike.

Consider, for instance, the example of Barnabas (Acts 4:36–37). He was a Levite who owned property on the island of Cyprus. Carried away with the spirit of the early church, this "son of consolation" sold his property and put the proceeds at the apostles' feet. The Holy Spirit neither approved nor disapproved the deed. He simply cites it as an example of the overflowing love and fellowship of the early church.

This kind of socialism is neither commanded nor commended in the Epistles. The noble experiment was simply recorded as a phase through which the early church passed. Before long, abuses arose, and Jerusalem was known far and wide for the number of its poor saints. There was never enough money to go around.

Brief though it was, the early experiment in sharing is a lesson in fellowship. Although the Holy Spirit does not require a Christian with means to beggar himself in order to help the poor, He certainly does expect the Christian to be concerned about the physical and material needs of the less fortunate. "The poor always ye have with you," Jesus said (John 12:8). We can find plenty of outlets for our generosity if we have the compassion of Christ in our hearts.

Caring for the sick, the poor, the orphaned, the aged, and the illiterate has always been and still is one of the great concerns of the church. The early church was very much alive to the needs of the unfortunate and the poor. Always a leader in social reform, the church built the first hospitals, asylums, orphan homes, and rescue missions. But the modern church has surrendered half its mission to the government. Such surrender leads to socialism without a soul and a welfare state without a conscience.

The gospel of Christ always quickens the conscience of the individual so that he becomes aware of the social ills of mankind. Lord Shaftsbury, a British aristocrat and a devoted Christian, became aware of the plight of little children working like slaves to feed the jaw of the "Moloch" of Britain's industrial machine. He launched a campaign against this injustice. William Wilberforce, a Christian and a member of the British government, aroused a lethargic British parliament to abolish slavery throughout the empire. George Müller, a Christian, reached out to the destitute orphans in England's streets. Amy Wilson Carmichael, a missionary to India, put her influence to work to help wretched widows escape their sad lot in life. She also helped rescue little children destined for prostitution in Hindu temples. The early Christians were aware of each other's needs and "distribution was made unto every man according as he had need" (Acts 4:35).

After describing the generosity that characterized the early church, Luke told the story of Ananias and Sapphira.

C. A Lesson in Membership: Great Fear

About this time two great protagonists came to the floor of the church. Satan came to battle the Spirit of God. God came to demonstrate His power. As a result, great fear came upon the church.

What Ananias and Sapphira did is linked by a conjunction to what Barnabas had done. The linking suggests that they had been impressed by his generous gift. They had likely noted the applause that, all unsought and unwanted, he had received. His gift seems to have been exceptionally generous since the Holy Spirit draws such special attention to it. Ananias and Sapphira seem to have held a family conference; they decide to emulate the generosity of Barnabas. The Holy Spirit says they "sold a possession" (Acts 5:1).

The next verse says they "kept back part of the price." Within a stone's throw of Pentecost, Ananias and Sapphira entered into an agreement to deceive. (Deception is Satan's favorite device.) Their fall into sin was not sudden. Ananias and Sapphira were not overwhelmed by sudden temptation. Their deception was planned and deliberate.

Ananias and Sapphira sold some property. The proceeds are perhaps more than they expected. "We don't have to give it all," they agreed. Later when Peter demanded an explanation from Sapphira, he said, "How is it that ye have *agreed* together to tempt the Spirit of the Lord?" (Acts 5:9) Peter used the word *sumphōneō* from which our word "symphony" is derived. Evidently Ananias and Sapphira shared a harmony of purpose. (The word *sumphōneō* is used in Acts 15:15 to describe the harmony of the Old and New Testament Scriptures: "To this agree the words of the prophets.")

Little did Ananias and Sapphira realize that there was an unseen Listener to their whispered pact. Picture the scene.

"How much did you get, Ananias?" Sapphira whispers.

"Twice what I asked for," replies Ananias. "The man wanted the land badly. He wants to build a bank on the corner. It's right near the temple."

"Do you think we have to give it all?"

"How about if we give all we originally intended and keep back the extra?"

"That's a good idea, Ananias. Do we need to tell anybody what the real market price was? It was a cash deal, wasn't it?"

"Yes, my friend wanted to deal in cash."

"Well, that's all right then. We'll tell everyone that we got such-and-such a price."

The Holy Spirit knew the market price. He was there when the deal was struck. He knew to whom the property was sold and for how much. And He did not keep the information to Himself. He told Peter.

If the Savior detested one sin more than any other when He trod these scenes of time, that sin was hypocrisy. Honest doubts never angered Him, but He scathingly denounced hypocrisy. He who was and is the truth never made peace with a lie. Nor has His Holy Spirit.

Pretending to have a holiness and a generosity they lacked, Ananias and Sapphira lied to the Holy Spirit and "kept back" *(nosphizomai)* part of the price (Acts 5:2–3). Note that Greek expression. When the translators of the Septuagint came to the story of Achan, they used an almost identical word. They recorded that "the children of Israel committed a trespass in the accursed thing: for Achan . . . *took* of the accursed thing" (Josh. 7:1). This Greek expression means "took for himself." Achan hindered the blessing of God and so did Ananias and Sapphira. Their sin was covetousness, the love of money. They held on to what had been promised to God.

The Spirit of God acted at once. He did something Jesus never did—He smote. Once, twice—and two of God's people lay dead on the floor. That morning they had been wrapped in smug complacency; before the day was done they were lying in their coffins.

How swiftly and terribly Ananias and Sapphira were exposed. Their story is a preview of the judgment seat of Christ. Never once did Peter question their salvation. The church has no business judging people who are "without"—only those who are "within" (1 Cor. 5:12).

Ananias laid his offering at the apostles' feet just as Barnabas had done. "Well, bless you, my brother," we can hear Peter say. "This is a generous sum. I take it this is the full price you received for the property?" Ananias could have told the truth. He could have said, "No, as a matter of fact, I did get more for the land, but

I decided to keep some of the proceeds for our own needs." That would have been perfectly acceptable. The Lord is not against private ownership of property.

The Lord said, "Sell all that thou hast, and distribute unto the poor" (Luke 18:22), but this is the counsel of perfection. It is not an obligation. It is not a necessary part of being a believer. It is not an evidence of grace. We must not confuse conversion with consecration. Selling all that we have and giving it to the poor is an evidence of growth, not grace. In the quite different case of the rich young ruler, the Lord saw that his love of money was a stumbling block to his salvation.

Ananias was a free agent as far as his property was concerned. He could keep it, sell it, give it away, or give part of it away. There was no physical necessity, church necessity, or spiritual necessity for him to sell the property and give some or all of the proceeds away. The only compulsion was love—the compulsion to be like Jesus, to express the compassion of Christ for the poor, to lay up treasure in heaven.

Ananias could have told the truth, but he told his lie, and judgment fell. "Thou hast not lied unto men," Peter said, "but unto God." The man dropped dead on the spot, and within an hour he was in his tomb.

Three hours later his wife came in. Where had she been the past three hours? Maybe she'd gone to the bank to deposit the nice little nest egg they had left over. Perhaps she had been in the market deciding how to spend the extra money. Possibly she had been at home waiting for Ananias to return and had decided to go to the church to see if he was there.

At the church's meeting place Sapphira came in, and we can imagine that she was all smiles. By now their generous gift is the talk of the church. She nods to this one and that one. Too eager to receive the praise of men, she does not notice the strained silence. Casually Peter asks her the fateful question: "By the way, Sapphira, how much did you get for that piece of property? Ananias was here a little while ago. He did mention a price. Do I have the figure right? Was it such and such?"

Apparently Sapphira took no alarm at Peter's question. She failed to detect the tenseness of the atmosphere and the pointedness of the question. Or did she suspect something at the last moment, but tried to protect her husband?

Alarmed or not, Sapphira answered Peter's question with a barefaced lie and her doom was swift. Peter's terrible words fell on her ears: "How is it that ye have agreed together to tempt the Spirit of the Lord? behold, the feet of them which have buried thy husband are at the door, and shall carry thee out." She had no time for reflection, no time for repentance. Caught red-handed lying to the Spirit of God, she dropped dead at Peter's feet.

"Great fear came upon all the church." Suddenly people woke up to the fact that the church was a place of terrifying holiness. Fear fell on the unsaved and on those who came to church for the loaves and fishes (the fringe benefits of Christianity). Nobody dared join the church.

Nowadays almost anyone can join a church. The only requirement for membership is a letter of transfer, a glib profession of faith, or an agreement to get baptized. Why does not God's judgment fall today? People get away with lying to the Holy Spirit. They promise to tithe, teach a Sunday school class, study their Bibles, go to the mission field, or visit the sick. Then they break their promises and nothing happens.

In contrast to many churches today, the early church was energized by great power, great grace, and great fear. If the church of today had the *dynamic* of the church of that day, it would have the *discipline* of that day. And if the church of today had the *discipline* of that day, it would have the *dynamic* of that day.

THIRTY-EIGHT

Stephen

The First Martyr

Acts 6:1–7:60

A. The faithful minister
B. The fearless messenger
C. The first martyr

The deacons of the early church were excellent men. Two of them, Stephen
and Philip, leaped almost immediately to high prominence, outshining
even the apostles.

Stephen became the first great *martyr* of the church. He was the vanguard of
that vast army of faithful Christians who, through the centuries, have died boldly
for the cause of Christ. Nero would sew Christians up in blood-soaked sacks and
throw them to wild beasts. He would dip believers in tar and use them as living
torches for his revels. Torquemada would torture Christians to death during the
Inquisition. They would be burned at the stake and massacred by the thousands.
Leading the way into martyrdom was Stephen, one of the deacons.

Stephen's friend Philip (the evangelist) became the first *missionary* of the
church. He took seriously the words of the Lord Jesus: "Ye shall be witnesses unto
me . . . in *Samaria*" (Acts 1:8). None of the apostles wanted to go to Samaria,
although James and John had once been willing enough to call down fire on
Samaria (Luke 9:54). So the deacon Philip went. Soon revival broke out there.
The ranks of the Jewish church were breached, and it was forced to take its first
mighty step toward becoming an international community of called-out ones.
Leading the way "into all the world" was Philip, one of the deacons.

The early church would not appoint anyone, then, to be a deacon unless he
was filled with the Spirit. Stephen was just such a man.

A. The Faithful Minister

The early church expanded rapidly. Thousands were saved and added to its ranks. The apostles were busy. Extraordinary things happened. There was a great outpouring of love in the church, and the Christians were generous in giving money to fund their social welfare program. The Devil saw his opportunity. Some of the Gentile widows complained that they were not getting their fair share from the common fund. A stream of people with petty complaints soon began to distract the apostles. We can imagine the grievances. "Mrs. Smith was given four dollars more than I was, and I have two more children than she has." "Mrs. Jones got beef and I got only chicken." "Mrs. Murphy was given a wool blanket and I received only a cotton one."

Peter, who was a practical businessman, decided enough was enough. It was time to delegate the secular and social side of the ministry to others. But not to just anybody. Anyone can wait on tables in a secular soup kitchen, but only those with the highest qualifications should "wait on tables" in the church. The apostles did not say, "Find someone who has proved himself successful in handling money." They did not say, "Find someone who has a degree in business management." The qualifications for a deacon were much more stringent than that. The apostles said, "Look ye out among you seven men of honest report, full of the Holy Ghost and wisdom, whom we may appoint over this business." *Manward* the deacons had to be "men of honest report," *Godward* they had to be "full of the Holy Ghost," and *selfward* they had to be "full of . . . wisdom."

In other words, deacons had to be men of *sterling character,* their integrity beyond question. They had to be people who could be trusted, people who had impeccable reputations. They not only had to *be* honest; everybody had to *know* they were honest.

Deacons also had to be men of *spiritual capacity.* In the early church nothing less than a complete filling of the Holy Spirit would suffice—even to do the most humble, menial task.

Finally, deacons had to be men of *simple competence,* men full of wisdom, able to make sensible decisions. (It is unfortunate, though, that spirituality and common sense are often strangers to one another.)

Stephen met the qualifications. He was honest, capable, and Spirit-filled—that is to say, the loveliness of the Lord Jesus characterized everything he did. A person who is filled with the Spirit is controlled by the Spirit, is Christlike in his walk and in his talk.

The Holy Spirit says about a deacon, "They that have used the office of a deacon well purchase to themselves a good degree, and great boldness in the faith which is in Christ Jesus" (1 Tim. 3:13). In other words, the office of a deacon is one of God's schools for the development of spirituality, character, and ability.

Stephen certainly developed boldness in the faith. He was "full of faith and power, [and] did great wonders and miracles among the people" (Acts 6:8). What those miracles were is of little or no importance today. What is important is that Stephen manifested the power of God in his life. He made an impact for God on his generation. He waited on tables, as Dr. Luke put it. He ministered in ever-widening circles to the physical and spiritual needs of the flock.

Stephen was not famous just for his mighty works. He became an effective preacher of the gospel. We read, "Then there arose certain of the . . . Libertines, and Cyrenians, and Alexandrians, and of them of Cilicia and of Asia, disputing with Stephen. And they were not able to resist the wisdom and the spirit by which he spake" (Acts 6:9–10). These hot debates probably took place in the Jerusalem synagogue frequented by Hellenist Jews.

The mention of Cilicia draws attention to the Roman province of Asia Minor and to its capital city of Tarsus. The strong inference is that the brilliant young Jew, Saul of Tarsus, was a member of the synagogue where these fiery debates took place. Saul was a trained rabbi, a former disciple of the famous Jewish rabbi Gamaliel, and a formidable opponent in debate. He was a dedicated Jew, a convinced Talmudist, and a bigoted Pharisee. Saul was convinced that Jesus of Nazareth was an apostate and that Christianity was a blasphemous and dangerous cult. He had a mind for the universe—narrowed by rabbinic Judaism. He had a mind capable of writing such world-shaking epistles as Romans, Ephesians, and Thessalonians. But to begin with, his horizons were limited by the traditions and teachings of men like Hillel and Gamaliel.

We can well imagine that Saul and Stephen frequently locked horns over the issue of Jesus of Nazareth. Stephen would calmly point to the Old Testament Scriptures and say, "There were not to be two *Christs*—one to suffer and one to reign. There were to be two *comings*.

"Look at the evidence of the life that Jesus lived, Saul. Jesus was not a blasphemer. He was the Son of God. He walked on the waves and stilled the storm. He turned water into wine and fed hungry multitudes. He healed the sick and cleansed lepers. He cast out evil spirits and raised the dead. It is impossible to deny the supernatural life that He lived. And as for His death—that was redemptive. He died, the just, for us the unjust, to bring us to God.

"He fulfilled the law and the words of the prophets. He fulfilled such Scriptures as Isaiah 53; Psalm 22; and 69. The Scriptures say that His hands and feet were to be pierced. The prophet said He was to be numbered with the transgressors.

"Then, to crown it all, He rose from the dead. Come, come, Saul! The Sanhedrin says that the disciples stole the body, but you are an intelligent man. You know that can't be true. Why didn't the Sanhedrin arrest Peter and John and the rest and put them on trial? Why didn't Caiaphas make them show where the body was hidden? You know as well as I do, Saul, that they did not dare to do any such thing. There was no body to produce. I can introduce you to more than five hundred people who saw Jesus alive after His resurrection. You can cross-examine them if you like. All Jerusalem knows He rose from the dead. This thing was not done in a corner . . ."

Stephen taught the Scriptures with authority. And so the debate went on until Saul and his friends gnashed their teeth in rage.

B. The Fearless Messenger

"If you can't persuade them, persecute them!" That was Saul's philosophy. Before long the Jewish leaders arrested Stephen, put him on trial, and indicted him on two counts. They accused him of attacking the *Scriptures* and the *sanctuary*. His spoken defense is a masterpiece, one of the truly great sermons in the book of Acts. Stephen's defense of the gospel ranks alongside Peter's Pentecostal sermon, Paul's sermon in Pisidian Antioch, and Paul's message on Mars Hill.

Throughout the ages, the church has produced magnificent preachers and powerful sermons. We think of Jonathan Edwards and his "Sinners in the Hands of an Angry God," and of Henry Drummond and his "The Greatest Thing in the World." We think of Spurgeon and D. L. Moody, men who could move the masses with their words. Stephen stands in the forefront of them all.

Stephen's defense revolved around three major points.

God had given the Jewish people *saviors* like Joseph and Moses, but Israel had rejected them. False witnesses accused Stephen of speaking against Moses, whereas Israel's whole national history had been characterized by rebellion against Moses. Stephen's accusers were far more guilty than he was.

God had given Israel the *Scriptures*. The Jews had broken the law. The nation had plunged into the grossest idolatry despite many warnings in Scripture about such folly. More than that, the Jewish leaders were deliberately undermining the

Mosaic Law by imposing all their vain traditions on it. Stephen's accusers were the ones who were guilty of speaking against the Scriptures.

God had given Israel *sanctuaries*—first a tabernacle and then a temple. The temple was David's idea, not God's, although God accepted David's generous thought. Later, Solomon built the temple but had enough sense to see that his sanctuary—ablaze with gems as it was—could not house a God who inhabited all the vast reaches of time and space. Stephen's enemies called their temple a holy place, but all too often they had defiled it.

The tabernacle was different. It spoke of the transient and temporary, for God never stands still. God cannot be locked up in a temple, although it be made of gold, silver, precious stones, costly wood, and rich fabrics, and although it be served with expensive offerings and rare perfumes.

"The very idea! To think that the great, eternal, uncreated, self-existent God of the universe, the Creator of stars and worlds unknown, could be shut up in a tiny temple on an obscure hill by a stiff-necked and rebellious crowd of religious fanatics . . ." Stripped down to its bare essentials, that was what Stephen told his accusers, the religious elite of the nation. It made them mad!

But Stephen was not through speaking. Amid a growing uproar of fury and dissent, he hammered home his conclusion. They had accused him of *reviling the holy place.* He accused them of *resisting the Holy Spirit.* They had accused him of *slighting Moses, the man of God.* He accused them of *slaying Jesus, the Son of God.* They had accused him of *blaspheming the Law.* He accused them of *breaking the law.* Stephen took the charges leveled against him, picked them up, and flung them back in the faces of his accusers. We read, "When they heard these things, they were cut to the heart, and they gnashed on him with their teeth." (Doubtless Luke heard of what happened at this trial from Paul, who was among that mob of angry men). They were turned into a pack of wolves. Everywhere Stephen looked he saw faces distorted with fury and rage.

C. The First Martyr

Having hammered home God's truth, noble Stephen looked away from that ring of furious faces. He looked up. Luke records, "He, being full of the Holy Ghost, looked up steadfastly into heaven, and saw the glory of God [that is, the Shechinah glory cloud, long missing from the earthly temple], and Jesus standing on the right hand of God" (Acts 7:55). Stephen instantly bore witness to what he saw.

Two short years before, Jesus had returned to heaven, having been absent from His homeland for more than thirty-three years. He had come from glory to visit a distant planet (earth) in the remote galaxy that men would one day call the Milky Way. He had returned home in a battle-scarred human body, but He had been given a triumphal entry into heaven. He had assumed once more the glory He had with the Father before the worlds began. We can almost picture His welcome. The gates of glory swing wide. The trumpets blare. The angel choirs, massed along the streets of gold leading to the great white throne, sing the Hallelujah Chorus until it echoes off the everlasting hills. Angels and archangels, thrones and dominions, cherubim and seraphim, join the grand procession. Cheering, chanting, and applauding, the mighty throng parade up to Zion's hill. All heaven rings with the praise of the shining ones: "Holy! Holy! Holy is the Lord!" The twenty-four elders cast their crowns at His feet, and He sits down at the right hand of the Majesty on high.

That is where Jesus was when Stephen saw Him. No less than sixteen times in the Bible Jesus is said to be at God's right hand. No less than thirteen times Jesus is said to be seated at the right hand of God. The word *seated* shows that the work of salvation has been completed to the eternal satisfaction of God. The word *seated* shows that, although He is man, Jesus is also God. He is God the Son—coequal, coeternal, and coexistent with the Father—God over all, blessed for evermore. Jesus is seated, "henceforth expecting till his enemies be made his footstool" (Heb. 10:13).

The day Stephen was tried down here, admiring angels still crowded around Jesus up there. They gazed on the face of incarnate deity. They looked in awe and wonder at the marks of Calvary. Their eyes were riveted on Him, but He was not looking at them. He was looking back to earth where He could see Stephen standing alone, surrounded by a howling mob of scribes and Sadducees, rulers and rabbis, priests and Pharisees. Their faces were distorted with rage, their lips drawn back from gnashing teeth. Hatred was in their eyes and death was in their hearts. And there Stephen stood—one lone man, careless of his life, a latecomer to the ministry—bravely telling the mob the truth about Jesus. This is the scene Jesus saw and it was all too familiar.

The slow fuse Stephen had lighted with his very first word had reached the powder keg. It exploded with fury and violence. The mob seized him and dragged him from the chamber into the blazing sunshine. They marched him through the city streets, dragged him to the foot of a skull-shaped hill, and prepared for the assault.

Saul of Tarsus was there, and he no doubt cheered them on: "Here, you fellows, let me hold your coats," he would say. The stones began to fly. And with every stone the mob threw at Stephen they were guaranteeing for themselves a full measure of God's righteous wrath. Was it stones they were looking for? He would give them stones. Within a few decades or so He would tear down their precious temple stone by stone. He would summon the Romans to bring their catapults and engines of war and throw stones at the Jews. First they had rejected the Savior and nailed Him to a cross of wood. Now they had rejected the Holy Spirit and were murdering a blood-bought, Spirit-baptized, Spirit-indwelt, Spirit-sealed, Spirit-filled, and Spirit-anointed child of God.

Luke wrote, "They stoned Stephen, calling upon God, and saying, Lord Jesus, receive my spirit. And he kneeled down, and cried with a loud voice, Lord, lay not this sin to their charge. And when he had said this, he fell asleep" (Acts 7:59–60).

Saul was also destined to wear a martyr's crown, although nothing could have been further from his thoughts the day he witnessed Stephen's death. That day, iron entered into Saul's soul. Whether it was Stephen's face, or his message, or his calm assurance, or his forgiveness, or his testimony that he had seen the standing Christ, something affected Saul that day. Saul would never forget Stephen. That angel face would haunt him until the face of Stephen was replaced in his soul by the face of Jesus, the Son of God.

When the stoning of Stephen was over, devout men picked up the battered body of the first Christian martyr. They washed it, wrapped it, and gave it a decent burial. Then they met to decide what to do. It was evident that savage persecution would now be let loose on the church. They had seen the face of Stephen, but they had also seen the face of Saul. They had seen the bloodlust, the hatred, the zeal, the fanaticism, and the determination of that young man from Tarsus.

Doubtless they also wept for Stephen. He had shown such promise! *Why,* they must have wondered, *why did God allow this to happen?* Ah, but they could not see the Stephen on high. While they mourned, he was given "the stephanus"—the martyr's crown. If they could have seen Stephen at that moment, they would not have wept. They would have laughed for joy. They would have seen angels crowding around him to welcome him home. The mourners would have seen him conducted amid triumphant anthems to where Christ sat at God's right hand. They would have seen him bow at Jesus' feet. They would have seen him—the spirit of a just man made perfect—enter into the joy of his reward. They would have heard all heaven echo with the Lord's "Well done!" They would have heard Christ say, "Welcome home, Stephen. Now let me tell you about that young man Saul . . ."

THIRTY-NINE

Cornelius

The Noblest Roman

Acts 10:1–11:18

A. THE ROMAN
B. THE REFUSAL
C. THE REVIVAL
D. THE REACTION

The conversion of Cornelius is a landmark in world history. At that point in time, divine decree and apostolic action flung open the doors of the church to the great Gentile world that stood beyond the pale of Jewish ritual religion. Until that momentous day the Jews had a virtual monopoly on the things of God. Gentiles had to become Jews in order to participate in the divinely revealed way to worship God.

What made matters worse was that the Jews detested the Gentiles and said abominable things about them.[1] The Jews said that Gentile idolaters should be cut down with the sword, that just as the best kind of serpent was a crushed serpent, so the best kind of Gentile was a dead Gentile. The Jews asserted that, of all nations, God loved only Israel. According to the rabbis, it was not lawful for a Jew to help a Gentile woman in childbirth because he would be helping to bring another Gentile into the world. If a Jew were to marry a Gentile, from that time forward that Jew was to be considered as dead. Just entering a Gentile house would render a Jew unclean.

A Gentile visiting the Jewish temple in Jerusalem could only go as far as the court of the Gentiles, which was the first and lowest of the various courts. Even

---

1. Alfred Edersheim, *The Life and Times of Jesus the Messiah* (Grand Rapids: Eerdmans, 1959), 1:90–92.

there the rabbis showed contempt. They turned that court into a marketplace for buying cattle and changing money.

Beyond the court of the Gentiles was the court of the women, then the court of Israel, and then the court of the priests. Finally, on the highest plane, was the temple. If a Gentile approached the court of the women, he was stopped by a barrier that stood four or five feet high. This barrier was called "the middle wall of partition." Prominent notices displayed on the wall stated in both Greek and Latin that no Gentile was permitted to pass the wall and that the penalty for trespassing was death. Paul himself was nearly torn apart by the Jews because of a false rumor that he had taken a Gentile beyond the barrier.

Naturally the Gentiles responded in kind. They hated and persecuted the Jews. But as far as God was concerned, when Cornelius was converted, all difference between Jew and Gentile was abolished, and the enmity between Jew and Gentile was removed.

Paul wrote to the Ephesians that in Christ the old enmity is abolished (Eph. 2:15). Jew and Gentile are made one. There is not a Jewish church and a Gentile church; there is just one church in which all differences of race and caste are forgotten. Before Christ, barriers went up. In Christ, barriers came down, just as the walls of Jericho tumbled before the trumpets of Joshua.

Little did Peter understand the significance of what he did that day when he put his pride and prejudice in his pocket, walked from Joppa to Caesarea, and entered the home of a Gentile soldier to lead him to Christ. Already the Samaritans had been invited into the church. Already an Ethiopian Jewish proselyte had been invited in. Now a full-blooded Gentile and his family were invited in. Soon churches would spring up in Galatia, Corinth, Ephesus, and Rome. The Jewish church headquartered in Jerusalem had tens of thousands of members, but soon Antioch would replace Jerusalem as the center of Christianity, Greek would replace Hebrew as the language of divine revelation, and Gentile Christians would enormously outnumber Jewish Christians.

A. THE ROMAN

In Shakespeare's *Julius Caesar,* Antony said of the fallen Brutus, "This was the noblest Roman of them all." Not so! The noblest Roman of them all was a mere centurion named Cornelius. He was stationed on the coast of Palestine at Caesarea, an important seaport built by Herod the Great.

Herod had a long career in creating monuments of magnificent proportions.

His trophies included the temple in Jerusalem, the winter palace in Jericho, and the practically impregnable Dead Sea fortress of Masada. His crowning achievement was Caesarea, named in honor of Caesar Augustus.

Herod hoped Caesarea would become a great metropolis rivaling Alexandria in Egypt. Caesarea stood on a direct trade route running east and west from Babylon to Rome. Byzantium was only a twenty-day sail away and Rome itself just two months by sea. Caesarea's layout was the grid plan favored by the Romans. The city contained a forum, baths, offices, temples, houses, villas, and marble statues. A great lighthouse guided ships from afar, and an aqueduct brought water from Mount Carmel, nine miles away.

Roman engineers had overcome enormous technical difficulties because the site had no natural advantages. It had no coastal bays, headland, or islands to which the harbor could be anchored. The strong current, heavy silting, and rough seas had all posed structural problems. Herod had even used hydraulic concrete, which hardens under water! The magnificent city with its two harbors was a monumental achievement.

Caesarea, with all its paganism and luxury, was the natural capital of Rome in conquered Palestine. Forty-seven miles from Jerusalem, Caesarea was the place where the governor lived. The Jews hated the place. The Romans loved it. It was here that the centurion Cornelius lived.

Cornelius was a noncommissioned officer in the tenth legion of the Roman army. He commanded a special regiment known as the Italian band, a cohort of one thousand men, whose duty was to help keep the peace in the province of Palestine. The Italian band was made up of troops drawn exclusively from Italy, and since no provincial troops or mercenaries were in the ranks, this cohort was considered especially reliable. Cornelius, the leader of this privileged regiment, was one of those centurions who were the backbone of the Roman army. They were chosen for their ability to lead men, for their courage, and for their willingness to stand and fight to the last man.

Cornelius was an extraordinary person. He was a devout God-fearing Gentile, although not a Jewish proselyte. Being a proselyte involved circumcision and becoming more or less a Jew. A proselyte was offered admittance to the rites and ordinances of the Jewish religion, but most Gentiles felt that the benefits were not worth the cost. Cornelius apparently was one of those men who were disillusioned by the pagan religions of their day and were greatly attracted to the ethical, moral, and spiritual beliefs of the Jews. But they drew the line at becoming virtually Jews themselves.

The Jews called such people "proselytes of the gate" and sometimes "God-fearers." As far as the Jews were concerned, "God-fearers" were still Gentiles, still outside the covenant, and still aliens to the commonwealth of Israel.

Yet the Holy Spirit speaks highly of Cornelius: "A devout man, and one that feared God with all his house, which gave much alms to the people, and prayed to God always" (Acts 10:2). Cornelius had achieved as much as a man of his character, background, training, and ability could achieve, and his name was known in heaven.

But the Jewish Christians did not seem to care about Cornelius and his fellow Gentiles. In the eight years since Pentecost, nobody had come from Jerusalem to tell him, or any member of the Roman garrison, that Jesus had died for sinners on that skull-shaped hill in Jerusalem, that He had been buried, that He had risen from the dead, and that He had ascended to the right hand of the Majesty on high. Nobody had told him that the Holy Spirit had come, and the church was being formed. Nobody had told him that the living God of the universe "so loved the world, that he gave his only begotten Son, that whosoever believeth in him should not perish, but have everlasting life" (John 3:16). Peter, James, and John had never bothered with Caesarea. To enter such a place, they reasoned, would be to contaminate themselves. "The uttermost part of the earth" beckoned from their doorstep, yet they had little concern.

So God sent an angel to Cornelius. He did not commission that angel to preach the gospel to him—preaching is our task, not that of the angels. Had that angel been commissioned to preach the gospel, he would have taken Rome by storm. Soon Britain, Gaul, Parthia, Media, and the ends of the earth would have been reached for Christ. The job would have been completed ten times over in eight short years. God allowed that angel to say but one thing: in essence, "Send for one Simon staying with one Simon." And that is exactly what Cornelius did.

B. The Refusal

Simon Peter was staying in the house of Simon the tanner. That fact is significant. The Jews held the trade of the tanner in horror and disgust because it involved handling the skins of dead animals. Under the Levitical ritual code, touching a dead body rendered a man ceremonially unclean. By rabbinic law a tanner's house had to be located at least fifty cubits outside a city to decrease the danger of accidental contamination of a devout Jew. If a Jewish girl married a man and found out later that her husband was a tanner, her marriage could be automatically declared null and void. Simon Peter's prejudices were wearing thin. A man who would stay with Simon the tanner had already jettisoned a great deal of baggage.

One afternoon Peter announced he was hungry. His host suggested he retire to the flat roof of the house with its grand view of the Mediterranean and rest while a meal could be prepared. Peter fell asleep and had the famous vision of the sheet. Down it came from heaven, full of all sorts of creatures pronounced unclean by the Mosaic Law: creatures such as crabs, oysters, shrimp, rabbits, pigs, and all the rest. He heard a voice saying, "Rise, Peter; kill, and eat." Righteously indignant, Peter said, "Not so, Lord; for I have never eaten any thing that is common or unclean." G. Campbell Morgan points out that "Not so, Lord" is not a strong enough translation. "Lord, by no means" would be a more accurate rendering. Back came the divine decree: "What God hath cleansed, that call not thou common" (10:15).

The vision occurred three times. Then, as Peter rubbed his eyes and tried to decide what the vision meant, the Holy Spirit said to him, "Behold, three men seek thee. Arise therefore, and get thee down, and go with them, doubting nothing: for I have sent them" (Acts 10:19–20). And sure enough there was a knock at the door. We can hear Peter's host call up the stairs, "Peter, are you awake? There are three men to see you—Gentiles from Caesarea. A soldier sent them."

"Ask them in, Simon," Peter replies. "I'm coming right down."

The men had a message and an invitation: "Cornelius the centurion, a just man, and one that feareth God, and of good report among all the nation of the Jews, was warned from God by an holy angel to send for thee into his house, and to hear words of thee" (Acts 10:22).

So that was the meaning of the vision, Peter may have thought. *I must not call Gentiles like Cornelius common or unclean for God has cleansed them. I must go.* It didn't take long for Peter to decide. For the first time in his life, he would go to a Gentile city and accept the hospitality of a Gentile home.

It was too late to walk the thirty miles to Caesarea that day so Peter threw caution to the winds. "This," we can hear him say, "is my host, Simon the tanner. I am Simon Peter, an apostle of the Lord Jesus Christ, the Messiah of Israel and the Savior of the world. You fellows had best stay for supper and spend the night here. We'll leave first thing tomorrow morning."

We can imagine, too, the lively discussion Peter and his guests might have had that night. Peter asks, "Have you met a man named Philip? He's a friend and colleague of mine. I understand he's living somewhere in Caesarea."

"No sir, we have never heard of the gentleman. Is he a purveyor to the garrison?"

"No, as a matter of fact he's a preacher."

"I wonder why the centurion sent us all the way to Joppa if there's a preacher here in town."

"My visit to Cornelius involves something much bigger than just talking to a preacher. It involves a revolutionary and radical departure from anything we have ever done before. This involves opening the door of the church to Gentiles. Until now it has been made up of Jews. This step calls for the involvement of a prophet and an apostle. Let me tell you about the dream I had this afternoon just about the time you were approaching Joppa . . ."

Perhaps Peter asked questions about Cornelius. Perhaps the men asked questions about Christ. The night must have been far too short for answering all the questions.

Wasting no time, off they went the next day—Peter, the three men, and some Jewish Christians invited by Peter to come along and be impartial witnesses to the historic event that would soon take place in this Gentile city. Significantly, Caesarea faced the Mediterranean Sea and looked toward an enormous Gentile world.

C. The Revival

The centurion treated Peter as though he were more than a man. That is not surprising when we think about it. How many people have ever been given your name and address by an angel? In all the years I have been preaching, nobody has ever asked me to come to a meeting because an angel gave him my name and address.

When Peter arrived, the house was packed. The word had spread to friends and relatives that Cornelius had seen an angel. *Cornelius?* They may have thought. *The centurion? Surely not. He's not the type. You don't get to be a centurion in the Italian cohort if you're the type who sees angels.*

Peter had an eager and receptive audience. He began by explaining why he, a Jew, was willing to accept an invitation to the home of a Gentile. Then he went straight into the story of Jesus.

Peter's sermon in the house of Cornelius is usually considered to be the draft for Mark's gospel. The book of Mark was the first of the four Gospels to be written. It was written especially for Romans and reflects the preaching of Peter. Mark's gospel divides into two parts brought into focus by the key verse, "For even the Son of man came not to be ministered unto, but to minister, and to give his life a ransom for many" (Mark 10:45). Mark shows us the Lord Jesus giving His life in *service* and then shows Him giving His life in *sacrifice*.

The message of Mark is just what Peter preached to Cornelius. First Peter spoke about Jesus giving His life in service. "God anointed Jesus of Nazareth with the Holy Ghost and with power: who went about doing good, and healing all that were oppressed of the devil; for God was with him." Then Peter spoke of Jesus giving His life in sacrifice. "Whom they [the Jews and the Gentiles alike] slew and hanged on a tree: him God raised up the third day, and showed him openly" (Acts 10:38–40).

And then it happened. Revival broke out in that home. The Holy Spirit came down just as at Pentecost. The same signs appeared. God did not send these signs to convince the Gentiles. They needed no convincing. They were ready to believe whatever Peter told them. God sent the signs to convince Peter and the Jewish brothers who accompanied him.

Probably nothing less than such a dramatic pouring out of the Holy Spirit on the Gentiles would have convinced the Jerusalem church that it was no longer an exclusive Jewish club. The "middle wall of partition" came tumbling down. Judaism, even in its Christian form, was obsolete. Gentiles did not have to become Jews in order to become Christians.

It took the conversion of the apostle Paul, the outbreak of revival in Antioch, the first church conference in Jerusalem, the united testimony of Peter and Barnabas and Paul and James, the writing of the letter to the Galatians, and the writing of the letter to the Ephesians to make the truth begin to sink in. The Jerusalem church was broken up, its people were scattered and deported, the temple was destroyed, and the nation of Israel was dissolved before the truth finally sank in. Judaism was not essential to Christianity; in fact, Judaism was a ball and chain around Christianity's leg.

Even to this day, some people have the idea that messianic Jews should have their own separate church in which the various dead forms of Judaism can be observed as part of Christianity. That kind of thinking shows how difficult it is to slay error.

Peter and his friends stayed on at Caesarea for a few days. Perhaps he did some sightseeing, but that was not the reason why he stayed. He stayed to teach the new Gentile Christians the rudiments of New Testament faith, and then he hurried back home.

D. The Reaction

While Peter was preaching and teaching and building up the infant Gentile congregation in pagan Caesarea, news filtered back to Jerusalem. (It is amazing how things get around.) One would think that the Jerusalem church would have been delighted to hear what had happened in the home of Cornelius. Not so! The elders in Jerusalem were horrified. They could hardly believe their ears. Peter had disgraced himself. He had betrayed the church and practically denied the faith. He had not only gone to the pagan city of Caesarea, he had actually entered a Gentile's house. Worse still, he had taken others with him. Worse yet, he had remained there. Rumor and gossip embellished the story so that by the time Peter came back, the Jewish church was ready to excommunicate him.

It says something about the spiritual state of the Jerusalem church that so soon after Pentecost and giving of the Great Commission, the chief apostle could be put on trial for doing exactly what an apostle was supposed to do—what the whole church was supposed to do. It was supposed to preach the gospel to all men everywhere without regard to color, class, or creed. Peter had failed to dot his i's and cross his t's the way they expected him to, so the Jerusalem believers were outraged. Here was legalism at its worst.

Peter must have been thankful for his independent witnesses as he told the Jerusalem church the story from beginning to end. "The Holy Ghost fell on them, as on us," he said. "What was I, that I could withstand God?"

Jewish Christians would not have believed for a thousand years that God could love Gentiles the way He loved Jews. The gift of the Spirit, the baptism of the Spirit, tongues, the awesome power and presence of the Holy Spirit! It was Pentecost all over again. Tongues were a sign to the Jews, and in the end, they were convinced. Grudgingly, they conceded that Peter's preaching to Cornelius was of God, but they didn't like it, and they did nothing to follow it up. They sent no missionaries to Caesarea. They did not invite Cornelius to come to Jerusalem and meet the church. But God already had His man in Caesarea. Philip was there to do, as before, what they failed to do.

As for us, we can say, "Peter, we are glad you went to Caesarea. We are glad you met Cornelius. We are glad that a second Pentecost put Cornelius and us on the same spiritual footing as you have before God. The Lord knew what He was doing when He enrolled you in the apostolic band."

FORTY

Barnabas

A Christian Gentleman

Acts 4:34–37; 9:26–27; 11:20–26; 13:1–13; 15:1–2, 35–41

- A. A SINCERE MAN
- B. A SYMPATHETIC MAN
- C. A SPIRITUAL MAN
- D. A SENSIBLE MAN
- E. A SURRENDERED MAN
- F. A SOUND MAN
- G. A SEPARATED MAN

The Holy Spirit says that Barnabas was a good man. That is the clue to his character. The Holy Spirit also says in Romans 5:7: "Scarcely for a righteous man will one die: yet peradventure for a good man some would even dare to die." In other words, Barnabas was the kind of man for whom a person would willingly die. We should carefully note that feature in Barnabas. He was *lovable.* A man other men would die for is a man worth following.

Then, too, the Holy Spirit says in Psalm 37:23 that "the steps of a good man are ordered by the LORD." In other words, Barnabas was *leadable.* He was a man well worth following because he was a devoted follower himself.

With these two clues in hand, let us piece together the story of this lovable, leadable man and note seven of his characteristics.

A. A SINCERE MAN

We first meet Barnabas in the very early days of the church, when it was ablaze in its first love for Christ. Barnabas appears at that time in the church's history when men were setting up what G. Campbell Morgan once called "a fanatical communism," governed "not by rules and regulations but by the driving force of love" (see Acts 4:34–37). It was a glorious experiment that failed, not because the impulse to share was wrong, but because the fire died down.

Barnabas, a Levite, had estates on the island of Cyprus. That in itself is of interest because the Levites, in God's Old Testament economy, were not supposed to own land. When God divided up Canaan among the tribes, Levi received no province of his own. Instead, the Levites were scattered throughout the various tribes in the land—some here, some there—to become fulltime workers for the Lord, supported by the freewill offerings of the Lord's people in the other tribes.

Barnabas, good man that he was, exemplifies for us the disastrous failure of the Jewish faith. He was a Levite, and he owned land. Moreover, he owned it in a foreign country, not in the promised land.

In ancient times Cyprus was famous for its vineyards, wheat fields, oil, and figs. It was a secular Canaan, a land flowing with milk and honey. Anyone who possessed land in Cyprus was likely to be both rich and influential.

In the early days of the church, many people sold their possessions and put them at the feet of the apostles. Barnabas outdid them all. He evidently decided that he would become a Levite in deed—a Christian Levite, a landless man dedicated to the social and spiritual welfare of the church.

He was a sincere man. His great wealth, generosity, noble character, and splendid services to the family of God earned him a new name. To his old name, *Joseph,* they added the new name, *Barnabas.* The name means "son of consolation, son of exhortation, and son of prophecy." *Barnabas!* It was a name cut from the same piece of cloth as the name the Lord Jesus used for the Holy Spirit. Jesus called the Holy Spirit the *Paraclete*—"the Comforter, the One called alongside to help." The apostles called Joseph, the Cypriot Levite, *Paraklesis.* His character was such that they identified him with God's Spirit as a comforter and as a man gifted to communicate the Word of God.

This, then, is our introduction to Barnabas. He was a sincere man.

B. A Sympathetic Man

It was Barnabas who introduced Saul of Tarsus to the apostles. Three years had passed since Saul's conversion. Nobody knew where he had gone. The church had heard rumors that he had become a believer. All they knew for sure was that he had vanished. God's saints thoroughly enjoyed a blessed rest from persecution.

But now Saul was back. Worse still, he was back in Jerusalem. More, he was seeking to join the fellowship of the church. Everyone was frightened to death of him. Join the church indeed! Worm out its secrets! Compile lists of its members! Saul of Tarsus was the most dangerous man of the age. Nobody would speak to him. In Jerusalem he was the most hated, most feared, and most friendless man of all. The blood of so many Christians was still red on his hands. No wonder that every door in Jerusalem was bolted and barred against him. Christians considered him to be a sinister Sanhedrin spy.

Against the first rays of that fast-rising sun, Saul of Tarsus, we get our first real glimpse of Barnabas's true stature. Barnabas alone, of all the disciples and apostles in Jerusalem, opened his door to Saul. James the Just—brother of the Lord, chief elder of the Jerusalem church—wanted nothing to do with Saul. Peter, with the keys of the kingdom in his hands, wanted nothing to do with Saul. John the beloved, the apostle of love, wanted nothing to do with Saul. Andrew, who liked introducing people to Christ, and who had a rare gift for seeking out those who needed to know the Savior, wanted nothing to do with Saul. As for doubting Thomas, the scenes in the upper room may have washed all doubts about the deity of Christ out of his skeptical soul, but unless he could have tangible, positive, irrefutable, solid, material proofs of Saul's salvation, Thomas wanted nothing to do with *him*.

In contrast, Barnabas opened his door to Saul. He took him in, sat him at his table, and listened to his story. And he believed him. We can picture Barnabas taking him around to Peter's place and saying, "Peter, I want you to meet brother Saul." Peter was so convinced he entertained Saul in his home for two whole weeks.

What an eventful two weeks that must have been. We can picture the two men up early in the morning to pray together and then off to the house of Martha, Mary, and Lazarus. Or was it to Gethsemane they went first? "Here, brother Saul," Peter says, "here I fell asleep while Jesus prayed. How well I remember the bloodlike sweat on His brow and the tone of His voice as He said, 'What, could ye not watch with me one hour?' [Matt. 26:40]. And here, Saul, right here Judas kissed Him. Here I cut off the ear of Malchus. Here the Lord stooped down and picked the ear up, turned it over in His hands, and put it back on again. And here my nerves broke, as did the nerves of us all. We fled like so many frightened sheep, pursued by nothing but our craven fears."

We can picture the two men going to Gabbatha. "Here, brother Saul, here is where the world's crowd lit their fire. Here is where three times I denied our

Lord. Over there He stood being bullied . . .well, you know the kinds of things they do. I stood here. I warmed my hands. I said I didn't know Him. I spiced my denials with fishermen's oaths. And then the cock crowed. Then He turned and looked at me, and I went out—back to Gethsemane—to weep like He wept. I wept in sorrow, shame, remorse, and regret."

Doubtless they traveled up Golgotha together, that accursed hill of shame, and in silence gazed at the spot where the cross had stood and where the ground had soaked up His blood. Surely they went to the tomb of Joseph of Arimathea, now empty, forsaken, silent, and deserted in its garden of flowers. "And Saul," Peter recalls, "John and I came running, but he outran me. He's quite a bit younger than I am, you know. However, I blundered in first. There lay the grave clothes, just as they had been wrapped around His form. Here, right here, lay the napkin that had been bound about His face."

So Peter would wake up early in the morning and, over breakfast, would give Saul of Tarsus the benefit of his many memories. On into the night, beneath the fig tree in Peter's garden, it was Saul's turn. He would expound to Peter the true meaning of the Jewish Bible as the Holy Spirit had taught it to him during those silent years. Doubtless Peter gasped, amazed at this man's gigantic grasp of truth. Only one man—Jesus—had spoken like Saul, who also spoke with authority, and not as the scribes.

The day would come when it would be the greatest honor in thousands of homes across the wide Roman world to entertain the apostle Paul. But Barnabas was the first—the very first man of influence and responsibility—to open his heart and house to Saul. Barnabas was a sympathetic man.

Nor would Barnabas have been the least bit jealous to see Peter making such a fuss over Saul. Barnabas would have been glad—heartily, humbly glad—that such a pillar of the church would make so much of Saul.

C. A SPIRITUAL MAN

The scene shifts to Antioch. Antioch was wealthy and magnificent, and, after Rome and Alexandria, the third greatest city of the world of that time. A four-mile-long street ran through the heart of Antioch. It was a thoroughly Greek city, yet it was the home of the Roman prefect and his court. It had a large Jewish colony, yet it was the seat of idolatry. Here was the world-famous grove of Daphne, where heathenism flaunted itself in its must alluring and filthy forms.

It was here at Antioch, and quite apart from the officialdom of Jerusalem, that the Holy Spirit began a new work. Here in voluptuous, sinful Antioch the work of taking the gospel to the Gentiles took root and spread. It neither sought nor needed apostolic support. It was an immediate success, and large numbers of Gentiles were saved.

Reports filtered down to Jerusalem. The apostles decided to investigate this new and startling beginning. The heads of the Jerusalem church chose Barnabas to go and see what was going on. It was a wise choice. After all, it was Cypriots and Cyrenians who were spearheading the work in Antioch, and Barnabas was a Cypriot Jew.

Barnabas was indeed a spiritual man. The Holy Spirit tells us that he was "a good man, and full of the Holy Ghost and of faith." Because he was spiritual, he did not lecture the new believers. He did not say, "There are no authorized teachers here. No provision has been made for the proper administration of the sacrament."

He did not say, "We need a manual of theology so that these new believers can be systematically trained in sound Christian doctrine."

He did not say, "There is too much emotionalism in this work. This work needs a stronger emphasis on the moral side of the Christian faith, especially in such a vile city as Antioch."

No! Barnabas was spiritual. We read that "when he came, and had seen the grace of God, [he] was glad, and exhorted them all, that with purpose of heart they would cleave unto the Lord. . . . And much people was added to the Lord" (Acts 11:23–24). He preached Christ, and the revival fires spread.

D. A Sensible Man

It did not take Barnabas long to realize that the work in Antioch was growing so fast that it needed a stronger hand than his to steer it. What should he do? To whom should he turn? Should he go back to Jerusalem and recruit help there? His mind must have scanned the list of apostles. *What about Peter? No. Peter is too impulsive. What about James, the Lord's brother? No. He is too rigid. What about Thomas? No. Thomas is too skeptical. What about John? John is too emotional. What about Philip the evangelist? No. He is no longer in Jerusalem; he is in Caesarea and is too busy.* Indeed, Barnabas could not think of anyone in Jerusalem who could guide what was going on at Antioch. *What a pity Stephen was dead. Stephen would have been the man. . . . What about Saul of Tarsus?* The very man!

"Then departed Barnabas to Tarsus, for to seek Saul: and when he had found him, he brought him unto Antioch" (Acts 11:25–26). It was a bold move. Instead of going to Jerusalem, he went to Tarsus. The word rendered "to seek" suggests that Barnabas did not really know where to find Saul. He went to "hunt him up." He took on himself the risk and immense responsibility of bringing Saul of Tarsus to Antioch without first submitting Saul's name to church authorities in Jerusalem. The Spirit of God led Barnabas to make this decision.

Saul and Barnabas worked together in Antioch for at least a year to enlarge the church, to encourage the believers, and to evangelize the city. It was at Antioch that the pagans coined the term *Christians,* as a nickname of contempt, for believers. A sensible man, Barnabas had been absolutely right in his judgment. Saul was indeed the man for the job at Antioch.

Barnabas must have known that by bringing in Saul of Tarsus, he was bringing in a bigger man than he was—bigger in talent and genius, bigger in his grasp of truth, bigger in breadth of vision and boldness of action. But, as Alexander Whyte said, "To have the heart to discover a more talented man than yourself, and then to have the heart to go to Tarsus for him, and to make way for him in Antioch, is far better than to have all Saul's talents to yourself. . . . Speaking for myself," said that fiery Scottish preacher, "I would far rather have a little of Barnabas' grace than have all of Saul's genius."[1] Or, to again quote Spurgeon's unforgettable lines from "The Unsung Hero of the Early Church,"

> It takes more grace than I can tell,
> To play the second fiddle well.

It is rare, indeed, to find an older man, held high in the opinions of his brethren, who will allow himself to be eclipsed by a younger man. Barnabas was sensible enough to recognize his limitations.

E. A Surrendered Man

Then came a fresh word from God: "Separate me Barnabas and Saul." The elders of the Gentile church at Antioch recognized the voice of the Holy Spirit. He, Himself, had called Barnabas and Saul. He had called, no less, their two best men, their two ablest preachers and personal workers. It was a missionary call,

---

1. Alexander Whyte, *Bible Characters from the Old Testament and the New Testament* (Grand Rapids: Zondervan, 1967), 139.

the call of God to the regions beyond. It was a mighty mandate from on high, a mandate to reach out now to "the uttermost part of the earth," to take the glad tidings of the gospel to untold millions. Barnabas and Saul had been chosen.

Barnabas could have said, "I'm needed here. I want to stay here. I like it here. I feel much more suited to this kind of work than to pioneering work on the foreign field. I think I have done my share. Let another, younger man go. I'll stay here and mobilize the church to give, pray, and support others on the front lines of Galatia and Gaul. What about John Mark? He's willing enough. I'll give him a crash course in evangelism and soul-winning. Paul can take him."

But Barnabas did not say these things. He was a surrendered man. For months now he had been aware—as he and Paul had pioneered together at Antioch, as they had prayed together about the great, lost Gentile world—that the Spirit of God was burdening, calling, separating him to world evangelism.

Then, the Holy Spirit began to exercise the godly elders in the Antioch church regarding the great world of the lost. And, let them face it, they must send Barnabas and Saul. As for Barnabas and Saul, they were ready. They were good men, full of the Holy Spirit, and full of faith—the three great qualifications for a missionary. Education, zeal, or financial support does not make a missionary. A good man, a man full of the Holy Spirit, a man full of faith—these are the marks of a missionary.

Barnabas's goodness gave him the *compassion* that he needed. He was a man touched by the feelings of others' infirmities. He wanted to see other men discover the goodness that is of God.

Barnabas was full of the Holy Spirit. That gave him the *competence* he needed—competence to make a thousand decisions, to deal with spiritual needs, and to know when and where to go.

Barnabas was full of faith. That gave him the *compulsion* he needed—the willingness to do and dare, the ability to trust God for provision, protection, and progress.

F. A Sound Man

When the Jerusalem church wanted to send a man to Antioch to investigate the new work among the Gentiles, what sounder man could they have found than Barnabas? Now a fresh crisis had arisen in the Antioch church. False teaching was being sponsored by teachers from Jerusalem. There was a need now to send a man from Antioch to Jerusalem to settle the matter. What sounder man could be found than Barnabas? And so Barnabas (along with Paul and some others) was sent.

The issues at stake were enormous. The false teachers asserted that Gentile Christians must be circumcised. Indeed, unless they were circumcised, how could they possibly be saved? That made sense to these legalists. The converted Jew looked upon his Christianity as the natural outcome of his Judaism. He had come to Christ by way of circumcision, the law, and a hundred rituals. How could Gentiles be allowed to be saved by starting halfway?

Had it not been for Barnabas, Paul would probably have broken with the Jerusalem church altogether. That would have permanently divided the church in two—a Gentile church and a Jewish (Hebrew Christian) church. There must be a conference to settle the dispute. A sound man would be needed to mediate between the fiery zeal of the apostle Paul and the false zeal of the legalists. Who could be more conciliatory than Barnabas?

G. A Separated Man

The question about the Gentiles and Judaism was settled at the Jerusalem conference. There would not be two churches, just one. Gentiles need not become Jews in order to become Christians. The good news was brought back to Antioch and the work flourished. Peter came up to see it for himself and was thrilled. Then, certain legalistic Jewish brethren from Jerusalem showed up in Antioch. Peter tried sitting on the fence. And, alas, so did Barnabas.

The first crack in an otherwise flawless character surfaced. Barnabas came within sight of being an altogether perfect man. But, after all, he was made of the same clay as we ourselves.

Fiery Paul gave Peter the greatest dressing down of his life for his cowardice. He said nothing, however, to Barnabas. On the contrary, shortly afterward, Paul proposed to Barnabas that they set out on a second missionary journey.

Barnabas agreed. But then the separation came; the hairline crack in Barnabas's character split wide open during a lamentable quarrel with Paul over the missionary candidacy of John Mark. Barnabas wanted to take his young nephew along again, despite Mark's failure on the first missionary journey. Paul adamantly refused even to consider it.

The Holy Spirit draws our attention to "the contention" between them. The Greek word translated *contention* is one of Luke's medical terms. It is the word from which is derived our English word *paroxysm*. It means to have a "fit" or a "sudden attack" or an "outburst of rage." This was not a small disagreement. Its thunder reverberated throughout the whole church. No doubt people took sides—as they have ever since.

G. Campbell Morgan said, "My own sympathy is entirely with Barnabas."

Alexander Whyte said, "Barnabas's ship strikes the rocks till one of the noblest characters in the New Testament is shattered and all but sunk under our very eyes."[2]

Who, then, was right? Consider the arguments that Paul and Barnabas might have offered during their more lucid moments when discussion took the place of dissension.

First listen to Barnabas:

> Mark is my nephew, and I feel personally responsible for his spiritual well-being. What a travesty it would be if I, having risked my life for the heathen in foreign fields, had no concern about my own relatives. I admit that Mark failed, that he turned back after putting his hand to the plow. But I could point out many of my own failures, too. Can we not at least credit Mark with enthusiasm for the cause of Christ? At least he started on the journey when thousands of others stayed comfortably at home. And now, fully alive to the perils and pitfalls of the way, he wants to go again. He is thoroughly ashamed of himself and thoroughly repentant of his past disgraceful actions. Can we afford to break this bruised reed and quench this smoking flax? Shall we act in a way that is contrary to the Spirit of the Lord Jesus Christ, who picked up even Peter when—not once, not twice, but three times—he denied his Lord? Yes, indeed, Jesus picked Peter up and gave him an honored place in the forefront of the apostolic band.

Now listen to Paul:

> Barnabas, I must confess that I am deeply moved by all that you have to say. My heart if fully alive to a similar debt I owe you. Were it not for your influence in the face of opposition, perhaps I would not be where I am today. Because Mark is your nephew, I fervently wish that I could bow to your wish. But there are larger considerations than those of

---

2. Ibid.

family and friendship. The cause and claims of Christ dwarf all lesser relationships.

Mark might render excellent service to the Lord in other fields. For instance, he has a way with words. Let him write an account of the life of Christ for the blessing of all mankind. But for this particular enterprise—for a mission that calls for a cool head, an iron nerve, a steady hand—Mark is totally unequipped. He deserted the cause right when he was needed the most, right when difficulties and dangers loomed largest. We cannot afford to run that risk again. To have a missionary play the coward before pagan converts facing the world's bitter hostility, would be disastrous. It would put Christ to open shame. It would bring mockery on the mission and the message. People would say that we did not practice what we preached. They would say that we expected them to face perils from which we ourselves shrank.

I have long ago forgiven Mark, freely and with all my heart. I pray for him and long to see him greatly used of God. He has a gentle spirit. Everyone loves him for his sincerity, for his sweetness of disposition, and for his willingness to work for God. It would not be fair to Mark to expose him to situations that might be beyond him and that the Spirit of God never intended him to face. One plows and plants, another waters and weeds, and another garners and gleans. Let Mark recognize his limitations. It would be unkind to expose Mark to the kind of situation we faced at Lystra, for instance, where we were first worshiped and then stoned. I foresee rods and shipwreck. I foresee many journeys. I foresee perils of waters, perils of robbers, perils of our own countrymen, perils of heathen, perils in the city, perils in the wilderness, and perils among false brethren. I foresee weariness, pain, hunger, thirst, fastings, cold, and nakedness. I will not expose John Mark to these things—and that's that.

Who was right? Well, as in so many quarrels, both men were right, and both were wrong. Barnabas parted company with Paul, and the Holy Spirit left him to his choice. He Himself marched on with Paul.

FORTY-ONE

Saul of Tarsus

Apostle to the World

Acts 9:1–31

A. THE MIRACLE OF SAUL'S CONVERSION
   1. The vigor of his personality
   2. The violence of his persuasion
   3. The vindictiveness of his passion
B. THE MANNER OF SAUL'S CONVERSION
   1. A tremendous revelation
   2. A total revolution
   3. A typical resolution
C. THE MEANING OF SAUL'S CONVERSION
   1. Complete the church's sacred manuscripts
   2. Commence the church's sacred mission

Young Saul of Tarsus had his first taste of blood at the stoning of Stephen. It turned him into a tiger. "Here, you fellows," we can hear him say to the men who are marching Stephen to the place of execution. "Put your coats down here. I'll keep an eye on them." Off those coats come, and down they go in a heap at the feet of that imperious young man. "Now then, you fellows, let's see what you can do. Fifty shekels to the man who bounces the first stone off that apostate's head. . . . Well hit, sir. . . . Come on! Hit him again. He's still alive. Listen! Now that renegade is praying for us. Come on! A hundred shekels to the man who finishes him off."

Stephen will receive a *martyr's* crown at the judgment seat of Christ, the first in a long and noble line of people who have washed their robes in the blood of the Lamb and who gave their lives for the Lord. Doubtless Stephen will also receive a *soulwinner's* crown for the subsequent conversion of Saul. Saul came away from Stephen's blood-splashed Golgotha with three truths embedded deeply in his soul.

Saul came away from the stoning of Stephen possessed of some *unforgettable facts*. It seems likely that Saul of Tarsus had debated the great truths of the gospel with this keen, Spirit-filled deacon of the Jerusalem church. What a debate that must have been.

Saul brought to the encounter a formidable mind, schooled by the brightest religious teachers of his day. He was a trained rabbi, far ahead of all others in his class. He was the future Gamaliel, the future high priest of Israel perhaps. Saul had the drive, the determination, the discipline, and the dedication required.

He was quite sure, in debate, he would easily defeat Stephen. Stephen defeated him. Saul should not have been surprised. He was debating a man full of the Holy Spirit. He was up against the Mind that designed the universe, the Mind that inspired Moses, David, Daniel, and Isaiah. Saul was up against the One who wrote all thirty-nine books of the Old Testament and who was busy writing all twenty-seven books of the New Testament. Saul was up against the Holy Spirit.

We picture Stephen as he looks into Saul's flushed face, straight into his fiery eyes. We hear him say, "But Saul, it was necessary for Christ to suffer. David said, 'They pierced my hands and my feet.' Of whom did the prophet speak, Saul? Of himself or of some other man? Did not Isaiah say, 'Who hath believed our report?' Was He not to be led as a lamb to the slaughter?"

Saul hated what he heard, but he could not gainsay what the Scriptures said. After such a debate, the stubborn facts of Scripture lay dormant like seeds in his soul. These facts waited like lurking lions in the underbrush of his mind for the moment when they could leap out and overwhelm him. He could stone Stephen, but he could not silence him. Even when Stephen was dead, that probing, persuading voice of his haunted Saul.

Saul came away from the stoning of Stephen with the vision of an *unforgettable faith*. Never could Saul forget Stephen's testimony before the Sanhedrin. Friendless and forsaken, alone in the arena, surrounded by hostile and bitter men, Stephen had been bold under God. His words rang out. Stephen's faith was based on the whole Old Testament. The Scriptures poured out of him like molten lava, heated seven times in the furnace of Calvary. Saul beat his ears with his hands, but that noble testimony still rang in his soul. He considered himself to be a man of faith, but his faith was like a tea cup full, compared to the vast ocean-fullness of Stephen's faith.

Saul came away from the stoning of Stephen with the memory of an *unforgettable face*. Saul had never seen anyone die looking like an angel. Saul had known that men would die for their faith. He had known that men would die out of a fanaticism in spite of the fear that their eyes betrayed. But he had not known anyone could die the way Stephen did. The religious elite of Israel had gnashed at Stephen with their teeth like so many wild animals. Yet the more they had allowed hate and wrath to distort their faces, the more the face of Stephen had shone. It had glowed with the light of another world.

That angel face haunted Saul. It looked at him through the darkness of his bedroom. It hovered over every landscape. In *Oliver Twist*, Charles Dickens told how the face of Nancy haunted Bill Sikes, her murderer, and drove him to distraction. Similarly the face of Stephen haunted Saul, until at last it drove him to Jesus. When at last on the Damascus road he saw the face of Jesus, it reminded him of the face of Stephen. Stephen had become so like his Lord that the likeness even showed in his face.

A. THE MIRACLE OF SAUL'S CONVERSION

The conversion of Saul of Tarsus was a miracle of grace that may still be the talk of every quarter and canton of the celestial city.

Picture yourself in Jerusalem some time before Saul's conversion. Here comes a member of the Sanhedrin. Ask him if he thinks Saul will ever become a Christian.

"Saul? Saul of Tarsus become a Christian?" he exclaims. "Why he'd rather eat pork or worship Jupiter!"

Here comes a new widow with her fatherless children. Ask her. The activities of Saul, grand inquisitor of the Sanhedrin, led to her husband's death.

"Saul? Saul of Tarsus become a Christian?" she responds. "It would take a special dispensation of God's grace to make a Christian out of that man, but I pray for him."

But Saul of Tarsus *did* become a Christian in spite of all the obstacles of birth, breeding, background, belief, and behavior.

1. The Vigor of His Personality

Some people are pliable and easily molded, but not Saul. His personality was hewn out of rock—he was all granite and iron. He would not even bow to the established party line, although it was enunciated by his teacher and mentor Gamaliel. "Leave them alone lest you end up fighting against God" was Gamaliel's advice. *Nonsense!* Saul must have thought. *Coexist with Christianity? With all due respect, Gamaliel is getting old and soft.*

Saul was hard as a diamond, inflexible and adamant. He summoned all the power of his forceful personality for the fight ahead. He summoned all the flaming fervor of his natural eloquence, all the thundering energy of his being, all the drive of his unbridled will. He became a mighty vehicle of destruction. No Alexander, Caesar, or Napoleon ever outshone Saul of Tarsus in determination. All his mind, soul, heart, and strength were set ablaze by his hatred for Jesus and the detested cult of the Nazarene.

2. The Violence of His Persuasion

Saul had his own convictions about the Christ of God and what kind of a Messiah He would be. The meek and lowly Jesus of Nazareth was certainly no Messiah according to Saul's book. Jesus was nothing but a weak impostor.

Saul envisioned a militant messiah—a true son of David, a man of war. The messiah would smite the power of Rome and make Jerusalem the capital of a new world empire founded on the Mosaic Law in accordance with the sayings of the prophets.

Saul was looking for a martial messiah, not a meek messiah. The very expression *meek Messiah* was a contradiction in terms to him. Saul wanted a messiah who would let himself be crowned, not a messiah who would let himself be crucified. Saul wanted a messiah who would reign, not a messiah who would redeem.

The thought of Calvary was revolting. That scene should not be the grand finale of the Messiah's sojourn on this planet. The idea that great David's greater Son should come down here, only to be crucified by the Romans was preposterous!

Saul knew his Bible. He knew by heart the Scripture "Cursed is every one that hangeth on a tree" (Gal. 3:13; see Deut. 21:23). That God's Son should hang on a tree was outrageous. It was blasphemy! Away with anyone who preached such wicked heresy! With Saul of Tarsus it was no matter for mere discussion and debate. It was a matter of life or death.

3. The Vindictiveness of His Passion

Saul nursed in his soul such a fierce hatred of Christianity that he offered himself to the Sanhedrin as their grand inquisitor, their Torquemada, their licensed agent to stamp out this heretical cult. The wealthy aristocratic men who ran the Sanhedrin were only too glad to have their dislike of Jesus of Nazareth confirmed by the fiery eloquence of young Saul and to have someone do their dirty work for them. They gave him a mandate and a free hand.

In later years Saul himself said, wonderingly, that he had been "exceedingly mad" against the Christians (Acts 26:11). Acts 8:3 says that he "made havoc of the church," and Greek scholars tell us that no stronger metaphor could have been used. It was used in classical Greek to describe the ravages of a wild boar uprooting a vineyard. This metaphor occurs nowhere else in the New Testament.

Saul had one controlling passion. It drove sleep from his eyes and mastered all other passions and lusts. He wanted to beat, brand, bully, and bludgeon every man, woman, boy, and girl who named the name of Christ. He was in just such a mood when he was saved.

He was on his way to Damascus, heedless of the blazing sun. His attendants must have cursed him underneath their breath. At high noon, when the merciless Syrian sun beat down from a brazen sky, any sensible man would stop by the side of the road, find shade and shelter beneath some palm trees, and have some lunch and a refreshing siesta. But Saul was driven on by his hate. He was like a man possessed. He was in a fever of rage, afraid someone would get to Damascus before him and spread word he was coming. Perish the thought.

So the salvation of Saul of Tarsus was a miracle. He was saved when, humanly speaking, everything was against his being converted. He was saved in spite of the vigor of his personality, in spite of the violence of his persuasion, and in spite of the vindictiveness of his passion. He was saved even though he could not be reached with reasoning—one cannot reason with a man who knows he's right, who is as stubborn as a mule, and who is driven by a burning hate. Saul's conversion was nothing less than a miracle.

Every conversion is a miracle. That someone "born in sin, shapen in iniquity," blind to the truth of God, deaf to the gospel, dead to the Son of God, and determined to go his own way should come face to face with the risen Christ and enthrone Him as Savior and Lord is a miracle indeed. It is a miracle that happens hundreds of times every day.

B. THE MANNER OF SAUL'S CONVERSION

Some souls seem to be born gradually into the kingdom of God. Others seem to be hurled in headfirst. For some the light dawns so slowly they can never say for sure exactly when they were saved. For others the light dawns like a lightning flash, and the truth penetrates like a thunderclap. When Saul was saved, there was a burning voice and a blinding vision, and all of a sudden, he was prostrate in the dust confessing his newfound faith.

1. A Tremendous Revelation

In all his later writings Saul hardly ever referred to the human life of Jesus of Nazareth. Saul first saw Him, first knew Him, and first enthroned Him as "the Lord from heaven" (1 Cor. 15:47). Ever afterward that was how he thought of Jesus.

"Who art thou, Lord?" Saul cried. "I am Jesus whom thou persecutest," the Lord replied. At once Saul's world collapsed like a house of cards. His religion was useless.

Saul was a circumcised Jew, a Benjamite, a Hebrew of the Hebrews, a Pharisee, a firebrand of the Jewish faith, a moral man, and a law-abiding citizen. He observed the rites of religion and performed the deeds of the law, but his every thought had been sinful. All his religion had done for him was make him an active enemy of Christ. It had simply confirmed him in his sins and persuaded him he did not need a Savior. As a religious man, he felt no need to confess his sin and accept Christ as Savior.

What a tremendous revelation it was to Saul that he was lost and undone and on his way to a Christless eternity. He realized he was the enemy of the gospel and the committed foe of the living, risen, ascended Son of the living God. Without such conviction of sin, no religious man can ever hope to be saved.

2. A Total Revolution

One moment Saul of Tarsus was the chief of sinners; the next moment he was a devout believer with his feet set on the road to becoming the chief of saints. One moment he thought Jesus of Nazareth to be an impostor; the next moment he owned Him as his Lord and his God. One moment he was a terrorist committed to the ruthless extermination of the church; the next moment he was a new creature in Christ Jesus. In Acts 9:1 he was breathing out threats; in Acts 9:11 the Lord said, "Behold, he prayeth."

There was a total revolution within Saul. He was changed in a moment, in the twinkling of an eye. He did not go through a long drawn-out process of psychological reconditioning. He experienced *conversion:* a life-transforming change that affects the mind, heart, will, conscience, body, soul, and spirit.

3. A Typical Resolution

"Lord," Saul said, "What wilt thou have me to do?" Before his conversion Saul had served the Sanhedrin; now he wanted to serve the Savior. He knew that "faith without works is dead" (James 2:26). Saul resolved from that day forward he would allow no rivals in his life, no refusals, and no retreat. Jesus would be Lord of every thought and action.

So Saul of Tarsus, in these early moments of his conversion, was already well on the way to becoming the great apostle Paul. Within a decade the world was going to hear from this man. He was an apostle "born out of due time" (1 Cor. 15:8), but he would be "not a whit behind the very chiefest apostles" (2 Cor. 11:5).

C. The Meaning of Saul's Conversion

What does a newly saved person do? To a large extent, it depends on the person. We probably would have said, "The best thing for you to do, Saul, is to go to Jerusalem and attend the services of the church and learn all you can about the Christian life. There are some good Bible teachers there like Peter and John. You can learn a lot from them."

Well, that is just what Saul did *not* do. He decided to get away from people altogether. He needed time to think, read his Bible, and pray. So off he went toward the silences of Sinai—to Horeb, the mount where God had met with Moses (Gal. 1:16). He dropped so completely out of sight that even his name was thankfully forgotten by the persecuted saints of God.

Saul, however, was not forgotten by God. He was in God's school. His teacher was the Holy Spirit and his textbook was the Bible. God was preparing him for the greatest of all ministries, second only to that of his beloved Lord from heaven.

Saul "is a chosen vessel unto me," God said. God had built into him a combination of qualifications He had not built into any of the other believers in the ever-growing Christian community. Saul was a Jew, a Roman, and a Greek. He was a Jew by birth, training, religion, and education. He was a Greek by scholarship, learning, and language. He was a Roman by citizenship—freeborn. Saul of Tarsus was a cosmopolitan, a man made for the world. With the conversion of such a uniquely qualified man, the time had come for God to complete the inspiring of the Word and commence the evangelizing of the world.

1. Complete the Church's Sacred Manuscripts

There were new truths to be conveyed to men. Saul was the man for that. He was an intellectual giant with a mind commensurate to the task. A major part of the New Testament had not yet been written. Saul was chosen to write it. God needed a man with his genius, boldness, and authority. Saul knew that from the time of his birth he had been meant to do that.

When Saul of Tarsus departed for Arabia, the Christian vocabulary did not yet exist. Words like *Adam, Moses, law, sin, death, grace, works, atonement, redemption, adoption, justification, faith,* and *righteousness* existed in the general vocabulary of the Hebrew people. But such words had not yet attained their full stature in Christ. Words inspired by the Holy Spirit came to the mind of Saul when he was in Arabia. He later wrote, "I conferred not with flesh and blood" (Gal. 1:16). Saul took Genesis, Leviticus, Psalms, and Isaiah in his backpack when he went into the wilderness. He returned with Romans, Ephesians, and Thessalonians in his heart.

2. Commence the Church's Sacred Mission

There were new nations to be converted to God. Saul of Tarsus was the man for that task, too.

When Saul was saved, the church was exclusively Jewish. When he died, churches dedicated to the worship of Jesus existed in every major city of the Roman empire. Saul took the pagan world by storm, and Gentiles poured into the church in a living tide.

When Saul was saved, Jerusalem was the geographic center of the Christian world. Peter, James, and John were the pillars of the church. When Saul died, Rome was the center of the Christian world, and Jerusalem had become a mere suburb, relegated to the backwaters of history. It would soon be wiped off the map for centuries.

What was the meaning of Saul's conversion? His experience on the Damascus road was a major turning point in the history of mankind. Every conversion is intended to be just such a turning point. The conversion of men like Martin Luther, William Carey, David Livingstone, D. L. Moody, and the like have all been high-water marks in the history of this planet. God intends that your conversion and mine would be the same. May each of us make sure it is.

FORTY-TWO

Paul

The Ablest Apostle

Acts 28:30–31

    A. How Paul reviewed the past
        1. His unregenerate past
        2. His unrecorded past
        3. His unrivaled past
    B. How Paul redeemed the present
    C. How Paul regarded the future

The book of Acts ends with Paul in prison in Rome. His terms of imprisonment appear to be light, as would befit the detention of a Roman citizen. He was probably chained to a soldier and could not come and go as he pleased, but he was free to receive any visitors he wished.

We can visualize the great apostle running his house like the courtroom of a king. Correspondence flows in from all over the empire, and a constant stream of visitors come and go. His attendants, including his beloved physician, execute his decisions. There is no pomp or ceremony; Paul has no use for that kind of thing. But even the most disinterested jailer is impressed by the power, influence, and diligence of this extraordinary Jew who possesses Roman citizenship, speaks flawless Greek, and writes words that command greater respect than those of the emperor.

Paul was permitted to live in his own rented house. Let us spend some time with him there and see how he reviewed the past, redeemed the present, and regarded the future. We will see a man who has few regrets (and all those under the blood), who is wholly committed to a single cause, and who is quite unafraid of the dangers ahead.

A. How Paul Reviewed the Past

Everyone has a past. It must be a good feeling to be comfortable with one's past. We can do nothing about the past except applaud it, apologize for it, and overcome it. What has been done has been done and can never be undone. Only God can do anything about a sinful past. He promises to blot it out. He promises even more. He says He can restore the years that the locusts have eaten (Joel 2:25).

1. His Unregenerate Past

Paul was raised by devout Jewish parents in the port city of Tarsus on the coast of Asia Minor. His father was a Roman citizen. How he acquired this priceless honor we are not told. Most likely a Roman general or administrator in southeastern Asia Minor granted citizenship to him for rendering some valuable service. The service may have been rendered to Pompey or Mark Antony. As Roman citizens, Paul's family must have associated with the cream of Gentile society in Tarsus and Cilicia, even though their strict observance of Jewish law made it impossible for them to exploit their advantages fully.

Paul described himself as a Hebrew of the Hebrews—a Hebrew sprung from Hebrews (Phil. 3:5). He was proud of his heritage as a Jew and of his status as a Roman. He grew up in a bustling seaport thronged with sailors and merchants from all over the known world. He was a cosmopolitan Hellenist and a Greek-speaking Jew. He was also a trained rabbi, one who had sat at the feet of Gamaliel. That in itself set Paul apart from the rank and file, even among the Jews.

Gamaliel was the grandson of the illustrious rabbi Hillel. He was a Pharisee, and his learning was so great that he was one of just seven doctors of Jewish law given the title *rabban*. Upon his death, this proverb was circulated among the Jews: "Since Rabban Gamaliel died, the glory of the law has ceased." They were wrong, of course. They would have been more correct to say, "Since the Lord Jesus died, the glory of the law has ceased."

At the feet of this distinguished teacher, young Saul of Tarsus imbibed his views of Judaism. Already the first branches of the Talmud were flourishing. A Jewish student, taught by a learned rabbi such as Gamaliel, would learn more about the Midrash and the Mishna than about the Bible.

Paul, no doubt, memorized all 613 commandments of the Mosaic Law. But he was probably more conversant with the work of Hillel (who brought to full flower that system of exegesis that applied Greek reasoning to the Hebrew Scriptures) than he was with the Scriptures. He would have known by heart all the intricate rules, regulations, teachings, and traditions that the Jews had hedged around the law. Paul doubtless had at his fingertips all the dos and don'ts the Jews used to hedge around and protect the Sabbath. (Christ swept all these rules away as so much high-sounding nonsense.)

Yet this star pupil—brilliant, sincere, protected, privileged, and promoted— later wrote the word *ignorant* over that early period of his life. Ignorance was his only excuse for his rabid persecution of the church. "I did it ignorantly," he said (1 Tim. 1:13).

Paul was sadly ignorant of the law of God all the time he was studying it in those days. He played with it as a child plays with an ornament. But no one—father, mother, schoolmaster, or fellow student—ever took that swift and terrible Sword out of its sheath to show him its glittering edge, its divine workmanship, and its ability to pierce the conscience, stab the soul, and bring fearful conviction of sin. Gamaliel taught those eager young men who thronged his academy what Rabbi So-and-So said and what Rabbi Such-and-Such said. He distorted, dissected, and dissipated the Word of God. And young Saul drank it all in. He was Gamaliel's star pupil, the one he thought most likely to succeed. The church marked him down as the young man most likely to persecute Christians.

A persecutor is what Paul became. He made havoc of the church. It is easy to imagine that he cheered those who stoned Stephen and held their coats. He obtained warrants from Caiaphas and Annas to persecute the church at home and abroad with a single-mindedness and savagery that struck terror into the hearts of Christians everywhere.

Paul's later words reveal a deep pang of remorse: "I persecuted this way unto the death, binding and delivering into prisons both men and women. . . . I imprisoned and beat in every synagogue them that believed" (Acts 22:4, 19). "When they were put to death, I gave my voice against them. . . . [I] compelled them to blaspheme" (Acts 26:10–11). "Beyond measure I persecuted the church of God, and wasted it" (Gal. 1:13).

How Paul thanked God after his conversion for the precious blood of Christ! All his sins against the Christians were under that blood that washes white as snow. God forgave his sins and forgot them, but Paul could not forgive himself, nor could he forget. The faces of men, women, boys, and girls rose up to haunt him. At night he would see faces, hear voices, and wake up bathed in a cold sweat—even after he had been saved for years and those sins had been cast behind God's back, buried in the depth of the sea, and blotted out as by a cloud.

No wonder Paul had such a burden for the poor saints of Jerusalem. No wonder he took collections for them everywhere he went. No wonder he begged and pleaded with his Gentile converts in city after city to contribute funds for the needy Christians in Jerusalem. Many of them he had widowed, orphaned, and beggared himself. Their faces were ever before him even though God had eternally banished his sins from His mind.

2. His Unrecorded Past

With constant delight the great apostle remembered that never-to-be-forgotten experience on the Damascus road, the startling heavenly vision of the risen ascended Christ. How that experience colored all his thinking ever afterward! Paul had never known Jesus during the days of His flesh; he knew Him only as "the Lord from heaven" (1 Cor. 15:47). That blinding vision was the beginning of his understanding of the Great Commission. "Once I was blind, but now I can see," he must often have said.

The Holy Spirit draws the veil of silence over the next few years in Paul's life. But the new convert was not wasting his time. In Arabia, under the guidance of the Holy Spirit, Paul hammered out the theology of the New Testament. Those years in Arabia were essential for him to sort out fact from rabbinical fable. He had so much to unlearn. Much of the teaching he had received from Gamaliel was worthless to him in his new life in Christ.

During this silent period Paul seems to have been disinherited by his family (Phil. 3:8 says that he "suffered the loss of all things"). He had already received the "mighty ordination of the nail-pierced hands" for his work among the Gentiles (see Acts 9:15), so there was nothing to prevent him from getting busy for God. He was not the kind of man to sit around waiting for a call from the Jerusalem church—they were glad he was somewhere else. Paul, saved or unsaved, was trouble as far as the Christians in Jerusalem were concerned.

As Paul reviewed his past, he remembered his first visit to Jerusalem after his conversion. He remembered the incredible loneliness he felt. The whole church eyed him with the greatest suspicion. They thought he was simply pretending to be saved in order to worm his way into the congregations in Jerusalem as a Sanhedrin spy and informer. Then Barnabas, a true son of consolation, befriended him and introduced him to the apostles.

Paul looked back with pleasure on the time he spent in Jerusalem with Peter. "Here's the upper room, brother Paul," we can hear Peter saying. "Here's where Jesus entered into Jerusalem to the hallelujahs and hosannas of the crowd. Here's where He overturned the tables of the money-changers. Here's where we all went to sleep while He wept and prayed over yonder. Here's where I denied Him, to my shame."

God warned Paul emphatically that Jerusalem was a dangerous place for him. He felt drawn to it just the same. Ultimately, events there led to his imprisonment. He spent years of his life in prison at Caesarea and Rome, thanks to the disinterestedness of the Jerusalem church.

3. His Unrivaled Past

Paul never forgot the day when the real call came. First the Antioch church needed a teacher, and his friend Barnabas came to recruit him for that ministry. Then the Antioch church needed a missionary, and Paul and Barnabas, with young Mark in tow, set out to evangelize the regions beyond.

Paul thought of his years as a missionary. His first missionary journey was to Cyprus, where he experienced the thrilling confrontation with Elymus the sorcerer and the conversion of Sergius Paulus, the island's Roman governor.

Then the great Taurus mountain range beckoned to him to come back to Cilicia where he had already labored for years on his own. Taking a firm hold on the leadership of the missionary team, he announced his decision: "We'll head north, pass through the Cilician gates," we hear him say, "and then travel on into Galatia. Danger? What's the matter with you, John Mark? If we're in the will of God, so what if there's danger? There's danger everywhere. You're quitting? Well, my young friend, all I can say is that you have a great deal to learn about discipleship."

Paul conducted evangelistic campaigns in Pisidian Antioch, Iconium, Lystra, and Derbe. A pattern soon developed. Paul's policy was to go to the Jews of the local synagogue first. Inevitably the synagogue divided right down the middle. The unbelieving Jews were invariably bitterly hostile. Rage, jealousy, blasphemy, and persecution always followed.

Paul remembered being hailed as a god at Lystra one moment and being stoned as a troublemaker the next. *It was just as well that John Mark went home,* Paul must have thought. How he valued dear, patient Barnabas, always willing to play second fiddle. He never complained and was willing to suffer with Paul for the cause of Christ.

Paul remembered the joy of planting churches everywhere. Hundreds of people became Christians, were baptized, and learned the rudiments of the gospel and sound exegesis of the Old Testament. Going back to ordain elders was a wonderful memory also.

Then came the Jerusalem conference and his confrontation with the Jewish church over the freedom of Gentile Christians from the law of Moses, from circumcision, from Sabbath keeping, and from Israel's dietary laws. Even in prison, as Paul sat reminiscing, he could not hold back a grateful *Amen!* for God's sovereign overruling of that conference. It was still hard to believe that Peter and the ascetic, legalistic, narrow-minded James took his side. He would have liked to free Jews as well as Gentiles from the bondage of the law, but God would take care of that in His own time. Paul was sure the destruction of the temple, foretold by Jesus, would help.

Paul thought, also, of his next two missionary journeys. The disagreement with Barnabas over John Mark was sad, but God stepped in and provided Silas, Timothy, Titus, and a host of other young men to take Barnabas's place. Paul went back to Galatia and on to Troas.

Then God overruled again. Paul met the man from Macedonia, first in vision, and then in the flesh, as dear Dr. Luke walked into his life to confirm Paul's call to evangelize Europe.

Memories arose: Philippi and the jail; Thessalonica and revival; Berea and a people zealous to test all teaching by the Book; Athens and the once-in-a-lifetime opportunity to speak for God on Mars Hill. *How strange,* Paul must have mused, *that the Greeks could be so brilliant in philosophy, politics, art, and science and be so blind in religion.*

When Paul traveled on to Corinth and Ephesus, hundreds of thousands of people found Christ. Paul planted church after church in city after city in country after country. Almost single-handedly, in cooperation with the Spirit of God, he evangelized all the Eastern European Mediterranean. What a life he had lived since Jesus came into his heart. Perhaps the soldier chained to his wrist awoke with a start as Paul shouted, "Hallelujah!"

B. How Paul Redeemed the Present

We picture Paul looking at his prayer book. It listed so many places and so many people. Barnabas, Mark, Timothy, Titus, Priscilla, Aquila, Aristarchus, Apollos, Rufus, Alexander, Demas, Crispus—name after name was listed. Paul thought of the hundreds of men he had discipled. Now in the ministry, they were blazing gospel trails to vast regions beyond. Paul's prayer list was enough to keep him busy from morning to night.

He was praying for others too: Lydia; the Philippian jailer and his wife and children; the poor little slave girl; Alexander the coppersmith; Festus; Felix; King Agrippa; that poor lost man known to the world as Nero Claudius Caesar Augustus Germanicus; the soldiers; the members of the praetorian guard, many of whom he had already won to Christ.

Reminded of the soldier chained to him, perhaps Paul said, "Tell me, my friend, you're new to the guard, aren't you? Where are you from? Are you married? Two little boys, eh! What are their names? Tell me, Marcus, has anyone ever told you about Jesus? Let me tell you how I met Him."

We picture Paul witnessing, praying, and redeeming many long hours by writing letters. From his rented prison-house in Rome, Paul carried on a voluminous correspondence. Some of his letters have been preserved. No greater letters have ever been written than Paul's prison letters to the Ephesians, the Philippians, the Colossians, and Philemon. Paul wrote these letters under the direct control of the Holy Spirit. They are God-breathed, inerrant, divinely inspired, and part of the living fabric of the Word of God. They will outlast all the suns and stars in space. These jewels of inspiration will dwell in our minds for the endless ages of eternity.

Much happened to Paul between the time he wrote his epistle to the Romans from Corinth and the time he wrote his epistle to the Ephesians from Rome. He had called at Philippi and Ephesus on his way to Jerusalem. He had warned the Ephesian elders that heresy was on the prowl and that they were responsible for the flock. He brought to Jerusalem a magnificent financial gift from the Gentile churches of the West. He was asked by James to go into the temple court and to offer a sacrifice—to prove his Jewishness. He was beaten up by the mob and rescued by the Roman garrison. He addressed both the multitude and the Sanhedrin. A conspiracy to murder him was set afoot, and he was hurried off to the Roman city of Caesarea. There he lingered in jail for two long years. He appeared before Felix, Festus, and King Agrippa. An exasperated Paul appealed to Caesar, as was his right as a Roman citizen. He was packed off to Rome in chains, installed in his own hired house, and allowed considerable freedom to carry on his church affairs.

The wheels of justice creaked on slowly in Rome, as they did everywhere else. Paul, though, faced an added element of danger. It was well within the bounds

of possibility that he would be executed. When he had appealed to Caesar in
A.D. 59, there were no indications that Nero would degenerate into the monster
he became. But, by A.D. 62, the official attitude toward Christians had changed.
Nero's wise tutor Seneca retired. The Jewess Poppaea wound the imperial tyrant
around her little finger. The corrupt Tigellinus had Nero's ear. In just two years
Nero would set fire to Rome and blame the Christians for the holocaust.

Between the writing of the epistle to the Romans and the writing of the epistle
to the Ephesians, Paul grew to the full measure of his stature in Christ. His letters
from prison had a new emphasis on the lordship of Christ and on the mystery
of the church and its relationship to Christ.

So we picture Paul redeeming the present by writing, by witnessing, and by
worshiping. The past was gone. The future was still unknown. He still had today.
He saw to it that each passing moment was freighted with precious cargo to be
weighed in for reward at the judgment seat of Christ.

C. How Paul Regarded the Future

Paul never worried about the future. Whenever he tried to lift the veil and
peer into the future, all he could see was Christ. The Lord Jesus dominated
every horizon.

If Caesar should set him free, then for him to live was Christ. He would evangelize Spain. Beyond Spain lay Northern Europe, the Germanic tribes across the
Danube, and the Angles on the island of Britannia. If Nero set him free, Paul
would fling himself into global evangelism with a passion and a purpose that
would make the past seem like wasted time.

If Nero were to command his execution, then hallelujah! To die would be
gain. He would be absent from the body and present with the Lord.

Paul had already had one glimpse of glory. He had been caught up to the third
heaven and had seen things untranslatable. He could never decide afterward if
he had been in the body or out of the body during that experience. He knew
for sure, though, that the experience was real, tangible, and audible. What lay
beyond the grave was as solid as what lay on this side. What he saw and sensed
over there filled him with "a desire to depart, and to be with Christ; which is
far better" (Phil. 1:23).

The word Paul used for *desire,* in writing to the Philippians, is the usual word
for *lust* in the New Testament. Indeed the original word is translated "lust" some
thirty times. Paul was lusting to go to heaven. He had tasted the powers of the

world to come and had become, as it were, an addict of heaven. Let Nero execute him. All Nero could do was promote him to glory. Paul's future would be Jesus! Paul's future would be forever. His future would be one of "joy unspeakable and full of glory" (1 Peter 1:8). Neither Caesar nor the Sanhedrin nor Satan could rob Paul of his future. His future would be glorious.

In the end Paul witnessed before Nero, and Nero had him executed. But when Paul arrived in glory, Jesus had him crowned.

FORTY-THREE

Onesimus

A Runaway Slave

Philemon 1:1–25

A. THE GRIEVING MASTER
B. THE GUILTY MAN
    1. His dangerous condition
       a. Defiance
       b. Distance
       c. Debt
       d. Dread
       e. Death
    2. His dramatic conversion
       a. Salvation overtook him
       b. Salvation overcame him
       c. Salvation overwhelmed him
    3. His determined consecration
C. THE GRACIOUS MEDIATOR
    1. The pledge
    2. The plea

A. THE GRIEVING MASTER

Onesimus was a slave. Worse still, he was on the run. He belonged, body and soul, life and limb, talent and ability, to another—to Philemon. Philemon is one of those exceedingly rare individuals who has a whole book of the Bible to himself. There was no room, in the world in which Onesimus lived, for him to act in defiance, self-will, and rebellion. Nothing but disaster and death awaited him along that line. Moreover, he had no need to rebel, for his master was a good master. All we are told, or can deduce about Philemon, emphasizes that. He was good, generous, thoughtful, loving, and kind.

All that was expected of Onesimus was simple obedience. That was to be the one basic all-embracing law of life for him. He was expected to be loyal and diligent to his master. If he fulfilled that law, he could be consciously happy, right, and fulfilled. All his needs in life were provided by his master. Obedience was the sole principle upon which his life was to be built. He must not act in defiance of his master. In all things he must say, "Not my will but thine be done." Within the compass of that one prohibition, he could live a full life, loved and cared for by a good and gracious lord.

God made us subject to the rule of life—obedience. He made us to be happy in the circle of *His* will. We were made to be inhabited by God, the human spirit controlled by the Holy Spirit and monitored by the indwelling Holy Spirit. The Holy Spirit was to control the intellect, the emotions, and the will. Our thoughts would be wise thoughts and right thoughts. Our emotions would be pure emotions. Our decisions would be proper decisions. Our inward life would be pure and spiritual because it would be controlled by the Holy Spirit of God. Our inward life would be expressed outwardly through our physical body, the seat of our various senses. That was to be the law of our being. God's plan was to make us consciously happy, good, and right.

We have vast scope for developing our own personality, for the exercise of our talents, and for accomplishing our Master's will. God, however, drew a line. We must do always those thing that please God. There was no room for self-will, re-bellion, sinful independence. Adam was well warned: "In the day that thou eatest thereof thou shalt surely die" (Gen. 2:17). If he crossed that one forbidden line, he would violate the law of his being. He must live within the compass of God's will. Nothing else would do. If he defied that will, he could expect wrath.

Onesimus lived for some time within the benevolent circle of his master's will, but then, as Adam had done in the garden, he rebelled. Philemon was greatly wronged, for Onesimus not only ran away, but he robbed his master as well. And worse, by rebelling and robbing and running, Onesimus advertised to the world a false concept of his master. He proclaimed his master to be a hard man, a man impossible to please, a man whose service was unkind. It was not the least of the wrongs he did to Philemon. Philemon must have been greatly grieved. His good name, his loving nature had been dragged in the mud by this unthankful rebel.

More. By his rebellion, Onesimus had exposed himself to the full weight of the law. The wrath of a slave master in the Roman Empire was a thing to be feared. Philemon would be well within his rights to invoke the full penalty of the law against Onesimus. Then woe betide him if he were caught. There were no limits to what a master could do to a slave. The law was all on the side of the master.

"Thou shalt surely die," God warned Adam, and all his fallen race. By our rebellion and self-will, we have greatly wronged Him. We have denied His claims, defied His commands, distorted His character before the whole universe. We have grieved Him to His very heart. We have spurned His love, scorned His grace, trampled on His rights, refused His rule, and earned His wrath.

Man in sin is a rebel, exposed to the wrath of a thrice-holy God. The only reason God's wrath is not unleashed at once is because it is held back by His grace. We will not be permitted to outrage God's mercy and live in high-handed rebellion indefinitely. Right now, however, like Philemon, God is patiently waiting, grieved to His very heart. He has the right and power to pursue us, but He holds back.

B. The Guilty Man

1. His Dangerous Condition

Five things marked out Onesimus at this stage of the story. The same five things mark the rebel sinner in the world today.

First, he was marked by *defiance*. Onesimus hated being told what to do. He wanted to please himself, do his own thing, run his own life. Why should he obey Philemon? Why should he not assert his independence and be his own man?

God did not make man so that he could be independent. When Jesus came, the world's only perfect Man, He said, "I do always those things that please the Father" (see John 8:29). "Lo, I come, in the volume of the book it is written of me, I delight to do thy will, O my God" (Ps. 40:7–8). In Gethsemane He said, "Not my will but thine be done" (see Matt. 26:39).

Man in sin is not like that. Man in sin is a rebel. He wants his own way, wants to be master of his own fate, captain of his own destiny. The last thing he wants is to acknowledge a Master, one it is his duty to obey. It was "by one man's disobedience" (Rom. 5:19) that "sin entered . . . and death by sin" (Rom. 5:12). We are all "children of disobedience." Defiance against God is the bottom line of unregenerate human behavior.

The second thing that marked Onesimus was *distance*. He wasted no time fleeing as far as he thought advisable from his master's house. He ended up in Rome. Surely he would be safe from discovery there in that vast metropolis. There was safety in numbers, he thought. He could become an anonymous member of the crowd. If he ever felt a longing for the grand home he had lost, he stifled it. There could be no going back. Distance was his safest choice.

Man in sin is far from God. It had once been Adam's delight to meet with God in the cool of the day, but sin changed all that. Fallen Adam's first instinct was to hide. The first question ever asked on earth underlined that fact of distance: "Adam, where art thou?" (see Gen. 3:9). It was not that God did not know perfectly well where Adam was; Adam needed to know. His lostness was pointed out to him in terms of distance.

Man in sin wants to keep as much distance as possible between himself and God. The thought of God makes him uncomfortable. He wants to hide from God. That is why the theory of evolution is so popular. It gives people a working hypothesis for atheism, or so they think. Evolution is a false theory and full of flaws; but it is taught with zeal as gospel truth because, without it, people have to face the fact that there is an omnipotent, omniscient, omnipresent Creator. That brings God too near for comfort.

Men are far from God in their behavior. Cain described himself as "a fugitive and a vagabond in the earth" (Gen. 4:14). Man's sin makes him an outlaw. Man cannot stand to think he lives under the eye of God. His behavior is such he has to hide. He loves darkness rather than light, because his deeds are evil.

The third thing that marked Onesimus was *debt*. The story suggests he had robbed Philemon. Since he had no means of paying his debt, his life had become one great liability.

Sin has robbed God. Sin began in Eden with an act of stealing when Adam and Eve ate of the forbidden fruit. God's generosity was as wide as the world: "Of *every* tree of the garden thou mayest *freely* eat . . ." (Gen. 2:16, emphasis added). There was only one prohibition. "The tree that is in the midst of the garden" (Gen. 3:3) was reserved for God. It was His alone. *That* was the one they wanted. Moreover, they took it and became such confirmed thieves that God had to bar the way to the tree of life. He placed a cherub with a flaming sword at the garden gate to guard the way to that tree.

When Pilate gave the Jews the choice between Christ and Barabbas, they chose Barabbas. The Holy Spirit adds, "Now Barabbas was a robber" (John 18:40).

"Will a man rob God?" was almost the last word of the last prophet of the Jews before a four century silence fell (Mal. 3:8). Man is a born thief. He has robbed God of His creatorial right of being honored and worshiped by His creature. He has turned Eden into a desert and filled the world with woe. He has used his powers to promote interests detrimental to those desired by God. We have accumulated an enormous debt of sin. We are ten-thousand-talents debtors. We are bankrupt, and we have nothing with which to pay.

The fourth thing that marked Onesimus was *dread*. He was terrified at the thought of being sent back to Philemon. He desperately needed Paul's covering letter when, finally, he agreed to go. In his unregenerate days, every day was haunted for him by the fear of discovery. The sight of a Roman soldier or an officer of the law filled him with dread.

"I was afraid!" (Gen. 3:10) confessed Adam when God found him hiding among the trees of the garden. Men posture and parade and pretend they are not afraid of God, but it is all bluster and bravado. They have every cause to fear Him, and fear Him they do.

God is indeed a God of love; He is also a consuming fire. "Knowing," says Paul, "the terror of the Lord, we persuade men" (2 Cor. 5:11). The Holy Spirit declares, "It is a fearful thing to fall into the hands of the living God" (Heb. 10:31).

God knows how to imbue men with His terror. He wakes them up at night and fills their souls with horror. Voltaire, the atheist, died with such terror in his soul that his atheist friends guarded the way to his death chamber lest others might see how terrible were his torments. The woman who nursed him swore that not for all the wealth in the world would she ever attend the deathbed of another atheist. Lenin, too. It is reported that, in the end, Lenin, who taught millions to become atheists, died howling like a dog, his great mind having snapped under the torment of having finally to face the God in whose face for so long he had shaken his fist.

The fifth thing that marked Onesimus was *death*. He was under the sentence of death, and he knew it. Runaway slaves in the Roman Empire were crucified. From the moment he became a rebel, Onesimus lived with the fear of death. It was a ghost, and it haunted him. It gibbered at him in the form of every soldier he saw, and in the form of every law enforcement officer he spied coming his way.

We, too, are all under sentence of death. We cannot escape it. It is hard on our trail. It pursues us as relentlessly as a weasel pursues a rabbit. It has our scent and will never lose it.

Moreover, death is not the end. It is the first and lightest of the torments that rebels against God's mercy, love, and grace must face. "It is appointed unto men once to die," says the Spirit of God, "and after this the judgment" (Heb. 9:27). There is a second death described by God Himself as "a lake of fire." These are not horror stories invented by the ministers of religion to keep people subservient to priests and their like. They are dread truths revealed in God's infallible Word.

Such was Onesimus's dangerous condition. Such is the condition of all outside of Christ. The church has very largely given up preaching on hell. The fact, however, remains. There is a heaven to be gained and a hell to be shunned for each child of Adam's ruined race.

2. His Dramatic Conversion

So then, Onesimus was a fugitive from justice. He was a stranger to grace, lost and alone in a far country, when *salvation overtook him.* He was not looking for it. It was the last thing Onesimus had on his mind. His only hope was that somehow he could make it on his own, elude the long arm of the law and the terrible wrath he had earned.

Then one day he was arrested. Not by the government, but by the gospel. The exact details of his encounter with Paul, of his consequent conversion to the Lord Jesus, are left unrecorded. God's plan of salvation is universally the same, although the exact details are different in every case.

Onesimus was arrested. Salvation overtook him. As fast and as far as he fled, God chased him down with a fleetness of foot moved by love. For God loved lost Onesimus, an anonymous slave in the surging crowds of lower class Rome, as much as He loved wealthy Philemon and Philemon's privileged son, and as much as He loved the great apostle, the ambassador of His grace to the court of the Gentile heart.

Then, too, Onesimus was overcome. *Salvation overcame him.* He capitulated before the powerful logic of the gospel and the revelation to his soul of the perfect love of God.

One wonders how Paul laid his approaches to Onesimus's soul. Did he take him by storm along the line of fear? Onesimus feared the wrath of his master; there was One he should fear much more. He had sinned with a high hand against

Philemon—and Paul knew Philemon, knew him to be a kindly, generous, sincere Christian gentleman. But worse than his sin against a loving human master was his sin against a loving God. He had awakened God's wrath. He had best come at once to the cross.

Did he take him along the line of his servitude? No. Onesimus was a slave. Nobody wanted to be a slave. Bondage was a hateful thing. Paul might have rattled his own chain; he was a prisoner himself. God Himself had a Son. That Son had taken upon Him the form of a slave. He had become obedient unto death, even the death of the *cross*. Looking meaningfully at Onesimus, Paul could have reminded him, "The *cross* Onesimus. He died the death of a slave on a cross so that you might forever go free."

Paul was a master at laying his approaches to the sinner's soul in order to storm the bastion for Jesus. We witness as Onesimus is overcome. Down go the arms of his rebellion. Away goes the resentment and rage, the frustration, the fear, those passions that burn in a human heart and that are set on fire by hell. He gives in to Jesus and passes from death to life, from slavery to freedom, from darkness to light; and his name is written by God in the Lamb's book of life.

But more! *Salvation overwhelmed him.* Watch Paul put his arms around him and call him, "My *son!* My son, Onesimus! My profitable son! My son begotten in my bonds!" He told Philemon that Onesimus was "a *brother,* a brother beloved." He told the Colossian church that Onesimus was "a faithful and beloved brother which is one of you" (Col. 4:9).

Salvation brought Onesimus into a new world, a world where love reigns, where people are no longer slaves and masters, Jews and Gentiles, Greeks and Barbarians, but brothers and sisters, loved ones in Christ. Onesimus was simply overwhelmed. For salvation purchases for us not only eternal life, but a new dimension of life here and now.

3. His Determined Consecration

"And now Onesimus," says Paul, "we are going to send you back to Philemon."

Salvation cancels our debt with God; it does not cancel our debt to society. It awakens, in fact, a new moral awareness, a new social obligation, a quickened conscience about what is right and what is wrong.

Onesimus was a slave. He belonged to Philemon according to Roman law. That law was unfair and often inhumane. It was terribly oppressive, a blot on Rome's passion for justice, a gross outrage against human rights. But it was the law. Paul did not argue the civil rights issue. He simply accepted the law as the law.

Onesimus belonged to Philemon, so back to Philemon he must go. That was the *right* thing to do. Moreover, he had stolen money from Philemon. He must go back and confess that and throw himself on the mercy of the one he had wronged. There was no way to escape that. Salvation saves a sinner from hell, but it does not necessarily save him from prison.

Moreover, he must go back to Philemon a new man in Christ, determined henceforth, if his life was spared, to be the best slave in the Roman Empire, the most obedient, conscientious, loving, eager slave that ever was. If *that* was God's calling for him in life, so be it. God's will was good and acceptable and perfect. God made no mistakes. And great would be his reward in heaven.

And what if Philemon demanded his pound of flesh? Paul did not think that he would, but what if he did? Then Onesimus must pay the price. God would give him grace and would be glorified in him whether by life or by death. Paul's gospel has little enough in common with the cheap gospel preached in some quarters today, a gospel that demands no repentance, requires no change of heart, makes no moral demands, and promises a new life free from poverty and pain.

Jesus must be Lord! That is the only gospel, and it is costly, indeed. There are to be no rivals, no refusals, no retreat. Such was the gospel Onesimus embraced.

C. The Gracious Mediator

The uncompromising terms of Paul's gospel were softened by there being a mediator between Philemon and Onesimus, one who came between to smooth the way. Paul himself.

Note *the pledge.* As to the debt Onesimus had accrued, Paul said, "Put that on mine account." The Greek word is *ellogeō,* and it occurs in only one other place in the New Testament. In explaining the gospel to the Romans, Paul said, "For until the law sin was in the world: but sin is not *imputed* when there is no law" (Rom. 5:13, emphasis added). But Onesimus had invoked the wrath of the law by his behavior. His debt had to be imputed to him or to someone. Paul says, "impute it to me, charge it to me. I'll take full accountability for his debt." He adds, "I will repay."

Thus our glorious Redeemer took our debt, our guilt and shame, and paid it all. The law's debt was not ignored. It was honorably discharged, paid in full by the shed blood of the Son of God on the cross on Calvary's hill. There is no more debt.

Payment God cannot twice demand,
First at my bleeding Surety's hand
And then again at mine.[1]

Then we note *the plea*. As to the defiance Onesimus had exhibited, Paul said, "Receive him back for ever." Eternal life was now in the scales. "Whosoever believeth in Him," God says of His Son, "shall not perish but have everlasting life" (John 3:16). He is "My son . . . begotten in my bonds," said Paul. "Now look here, Philemon," Paul, in effect, writes, "the same relationship exists between Onesimus and me that exists between you and me, and the same relationship exists between me and the Father in heaven that exists between you and the Father in heaven. We are all one. That is how I want you to regard him and treat him now and forever."

The whole epistle is a plea. Paul stood between the wronged Philemon and the newly converted Onesimus and brought them together in a new family relationship of love and life. That is exactly what our Mediator has done. Jesus could speak to Mary Magdalene of "My God and your God, of My Father and your Father." He says to the Father, "This erring one belongs to Me as I belong to You. He is as much Mine as I am Yours. I want You, Father, to look on him as You look on Me. I want You to see him as You see Me. You see Me as Your Son; see him as Your son. Bring him into a new family relationship of eternal love and everlasting life."

"If thou count me [as] a partner," wrote Paul, "receive him as myself." The word for "partner" is *koinōnos* and is translated elsewhere as "companion" and as "partaker." Peter uses the word when he says we are *"partakers* of the divine nature" (2 Peter 1:4) and when he says that he was "a witness of the sufferings of Christ, and also a *partaker* of the glory that shall be revealed" (1 Peter 5:1).

So, through the work of our gracious Mediator, we, with Him, become partakers of the divine nature and the coming glory. God has received us as He has received His own beloved Son. He sees us, He sees us in Him, and He sees no difference at all. We are "accepted in the Beloved." We are sons of God, joint heirs with Jesus Christ, seated with Him in heavenly places, crowned with glory and honor.

---

1. Augustus Toplady, "From Whence This Fear and Unbelief?" 1772.

FORTY-FOUR

Simon the Sorcerer

A Deceiver

Acts 8:5–24

A. THE MAGIC SIMON PERFORMED
B. THE MARVELS SIMON PONDERED
  1. The preaching he faced
    a. Preaching about God's sovereignty
    b. Preaching about God's salvation
  2. The power he faced
C. THE MIRACLE SIMON PERCEIVED
D. THE MONEY SIMON PLEDGED

The Samaritans had been slighted and scorned by the Jews for centuries. One of the worst insults one Jew could offer to another was to call him a Samaritan (an insult that was hurled in the face of Jesus by His foes). Jews would go miles out of their way to avoid going through Samaria in their journeys north and south between Galilee and Judea. Nor was the hatred one-sided. There was indeed a great gulf fixed between Samaritan and Jew.

But the whole city of Samaria was stirred one day by the sound of a voice. It was the voice of a Hellenist Jew by the name of Philip. He was a deacon of the newborn Jerusalem church. Heaven's man was in town! He was not pointing out the glaring inconsistencies in the Samaritan religion, which was a mixture of paganism and Judaism. He was telling the Samaritans about Jesus: Jesus once went to Jerusalem, he doubtless reminded them. But now He had gone home to heaven. By way of a cross. But this same Jesus was alive from the dead, alive for evermore, and He was seated at the right hand of the Majesty on high. And here was the good news: Jesus was mighty to save.

Revival broke out. Souls were saved, people were baptized. There was rejoicing. Indeed the Holy Spirit says, "There was great joy in that city." Something far better than a half-baked Judaism tacked onto a half-tamed paganism had come to Samaria. Christ had come! The church had come!

Heaven's man was in town! But hell's magician was in town too. He called himself Simon Magus. He watched Philip closely and with greedy eyes. He took note of the miracles Philip was able to do. Simon had a professional interest in these miracles, for he was a sorcerer.

Acts 8:9 says that Simon "used sorcery, and bewitched the people of Samaria." The word translated "sorcery" here is *mageuō*, which means "to practice magic." The word translated "bewitched" here is *existemi*, which literally means "to drive someone out of his senses." Simon had everyone in town thinking that he was "some great one [possessing] . . . the great power of God" (vv. 9–10). The word translated "power" here is *dunamis*, which refers to inherent power. The same word is used in 1 Corinthians 1:24: "Christ the power of God." Indeed the people thought Simon was the divine *logos*.

The man was overwhelmed, however, by the miracles that Philip performed. Acts 8:13 says, "Simon himself believed also: and . . . wondered, beholding the miracles." The word translated "wondered" here is another form of *existemi*, which means "to be amazed and dumbfounded." So the Devil's man made a profession of faith.

Before this narrative in Acts is completely told, however, it becomes evident that Simon was an impostor who saw a profession of faith as a means to an end. He was the father of all those who see a path to power in joining a church, a useful way to promote social, economic, or political advantage.

A. THE MAGIC SIMON PERFORMED

There seems to be little doubt from the text that Simon Magus possessed extraordinary supernatural powers. He was a practitioner of the black arts and a minister of the mysteries and magic of Satan. Secular sources such as G. H. Pember's *Earth's Earliest Ages* provide some interesting information about the man.[1]

Simon is said to have boasted, "Once when my mother Rachel ordered me to

1. G. H. Pember, *Earth's Earliest Ages* (Glasgow: Pickering and Inglis), 295–99. Pember's chief source is the second of the Clementine *Homilies*.

go to the field to reap, and I saw a scythe lying, I ordered it to go and reap, and it reaped ten times more than the others."

He claimed that he made statues walk about, and that he could roll over fire without being burned. He said he was able to fly; to turn stones into bread; to change his appearance, sometimes assuming the form of a serpent or a goat; to open locked doors without a key; to melt iron; to produce various kinds of phantoms at banquets; to cause dishes to move about, as if they were spontaneously waiting on him at the table; to use witchcraft to murder people; to use abominable incantations to separate a soul from its body.

We do not know whether these claims are true. We do know that those who embrace the mysteries of occult religions can do strange things, wholly beyond the capabilities of people in a normal state. Satan has great power, and he confers power on those who dedicate themselves to him. Judging by the language the Holy Spirit used to describe Simon Magus, we can conclude it not unlikely that he was an initiate into the deep things of Satan. In any case Simon held the Samaritans in thrall.

Then Philip the evangelist came. He had been chosen to be a deacon of the Jerusalem church because he was a man of impeccable testimony and integrity, a man full of wisdom, and a man filled with the Holy Spirit. Faced with Philip, Simon and his magic paled into insignificance. The Devil, for all his wiles and devices, is no match for the Holy Spirit.

B. The Marvels Simon Pondered

Philip, full of the Holy Spirit, was clothed with an authority and power beyond any that Simon had heard of or experienced. The sorcerer pondered the evangelist's preaching and power.

1. The Preaching He Faced

Simon heard the truth, absolute truth, truth preached with concern and conviction. Most of his life had been wrapped up in lies. He was both the deceiver and the deceived. Probably most of his so-called magic was done by means of hypnotism and optical illusion. A Satanist of sorts, he worked hand in glove with the Father of Lies.

But Philip's preaching was direct and to the point. He preached on two simple subjects: God's sovereignty and God's salvation.

a. Preaching About God's Sovereignty

Acts 8:12 says that Philip preached "the things concerning the kingdom of God."

It has always been God's intention to establish a kingdom on our planet. The "mystery of iniquity" was already abroad in the universe when God stooped down to fashion Adam's clay. It was imported to our planet by fallen Lucifer and brought wreck and ruin to our world (Gen. 1:2).

When God made Adam and Eve, He said, "Let them have dominion" (Gen. 1:26). The Holy Spirit added that He "crownedst him [Adam] with glory and honour, and didst set him over the works of [His] hands" (Heb. 2:7). When Adam fell, he surrendered his sovereignty to Satan, and Satan set up his empire over this world. Legions of fallen angels rule this world as Satan's agents. They are described as principalities and powers, as the rulers of this world's darkness, and as wicked spirits in high places. God's sovereignty has been challenged by all this, and to all outward appearances, He has been defeated. Not so! God is still on the throne.

Satan's triumph in Eden did not outlast the day. God came down into the garden Himself and set up His judgment seat. Satan was summoned and sentenced. God would bring on the scene a Second Man, a Last Adam. This glorious One would be virgin born, truly man and truly God, seed of the woman, and Son of God most high. The serpent and his nefarious host would succeed in bruising His (Christ's) heel (an early intimation of a death involving the wounding of the feet). But He in turn would crush the serpent's head. The guilty human pair would know sorrow and suffering, toil and travail, and the bitterness of death. Their ruined race would be born in sin. How sadly true those fateful words. But the judgment was a message of both horror and hope. Salvation full and free would be offered to all.

Satan wasted no time. Moved by an implacable hatred of the human race and by a tormenting fear of the coming One, he launched upon the systematic enslavement of Adam's race. And he kept a sharp watch for the first sign of the coming promised "seed of the woman." He so corrupted the race that within several generations God had to send the flood. But the line to the coming Christ was preserved aboard the ark.

God left the world at large to its own devices. Just the same He pursued His plan of sending His Son when the time was due. The promised "Seed of the woman" was to be the seed of Abraham, then of Isaac, then Judah, then David.

And just so, it occurred. Isaac was chosen over Ishmael, and Satan attacked Isaac. Jacob was chosen over Esau, and Satan attacked Jacob. Judah was chosen over Reuben, and Satan attacked Judah. David was chosen over all of Jesse's sons, and Satan attacked David. Solomon was chosen to be David's heir and his successor on the Hebrew throne, and Satan attacked Solomon.

Satan watched as the Hebrew kingdom was divided because of the chosen people's sins. He concentrated on the southern kingdom and corrupted all its kings. Then he turned on the kings in David's line and corrupted most of these. In the days of Athaliah, Satan nearly succeeded in wiping out the royal seed altogether. On and on the events took place. Satan so debased the royal line that by the time of Jehoiakim, shortly before the Babylonian captivity, he had brought down God's curse upon it.

Satan's efforts were all in vain. Too late, Satan discovered that God's secret plan was to fulfill His promise not through Solomon, but through Nathan, a younger son of David and Bathsheba. So in time the promised seed arrived, born of the virgin Mary, and conceived of the Holy Spirit.

Then Satan attacked Christ—with every weapon he had. He tried to have Him murdered as a babe. He tried to have Him murdered as a man. Ultimately Satan turned the nation against Him and succeeded in getting Him crucified. It seemed as though he had won. But Christ rose from the dead. He ascended into heaven, sat down on His Father's throne, and set a new date for the establishment of the kingdom. In the meantime, He puts all those who trust Him into the kingdom of God.

Simon had never heard anything like the message that Philip preached. Even the sorcerer's devious heart was stirred.

b. Preaching About God's Salvation

The evangelist proclaimed God's salvation as well as His sovereignty. Acts 8:12 says he preached "the name of Jesus Christ." Philip told the Samaritans that God had provided a Savior for the lost and guilty children of Adam's ruined race. Jesus was His name, and He was mighty to save.

Doubtless Philip told the Samaritans about the virgin birth of Christ, of His immaculate life, His marvelous miracles, His wonderful teaching, His atoning death, His bodily resurrection, His bodily ascension, and His promised return. No doubt he told them how He healed the sick, gave sight to the blind, cast out evil spirits, raised the dead, walked on the waves, stilled storms, and fed multitudes. Simon Magus listened with wide open ears. But there was something else, something that made a far deeper impression on his mind than Philip's preaching.

2. The Power He Faced

Simon might have been prepared to write off some of the preaching. Jesus had passed through Samaria not too long before, and the testimony of the woman at the well had made no little stir thereabouts (see John 4:1–43).

Moreover, the mighty miracles of Jesus were the talk of the surrounding countryside. Galilee and Samaria and Decapolis and Peraea and Judea, all put together, comprised a very small country. The miracles of Jesus were too well known to be denied. The Jewish authorities had a blasphemous explanation for them—they accused Him of being in league with the Devil. But the common people knew better.

Now Simon saw miracles for himself. Acts 8:7 says, "Unclean spirits, crying with loud voice, came out of many that were possessed with them: and many taken with palsies, and that were lame, were healed." Here was living proof that Philip had power over demons, power over disease, and power over disability. The sorcerer was impressed.

The Holy Spirit says, "Then Simon himself believed also: and when he was baptized, he continued with Philip, and wondered, beholding the miracles and signs which were done" (Acts 8:13). Simon "wondered"! In other words he was amazed—he was dumbfounded.

Aware that his own miracles were just silly Satanic tricks and not very beneficial to anyone except himself, Simon decided he needed to get in on Philip's power. Apparently the way to get the power was to profess faith and be baptized. So Simon professed faith and was baptized. He kept hanging around, hoping to see how Philip performed all these amazing miracles.

C. The Miracle Simon Perceived

Then Peter and John arrived in town, the most notable apostles and leaders of the infant church. The two newcomers were a cut above Philip. They had been close acquaintances of Jesus. And, Simon noticed, Philip gave way before them.

Simon watched eagerly to see what Peter and John would do—and he did not have long to wait. They "prayed for them, that they might receive the Holy Ghost" (Acts 8:15). They prayed that the born again Samaritans might receive the baptism, the gift, the filling, and the anointing of the Spirit of God. "Then laid they their hands on them, and they received the Holy Ghost" (v. 17). Luke does not record that any special phenomena accompanied the giving of the Holy Spirit to the Samaritans. There was no speaking in tongues or anything like that. But something must have happened, because it made a profound impression on Simon Magus. Here was power indeed.

The power behind Philip was the Holy Spirit; and Peter and John, it seemed, had the power to give the Holy Spirit. Simon wanted that power. We can almost hear his thoughts: *Added to powers I already have, this new power will put me ahead of the two apostles themselves. I can start my own church. I can make Samaria the capital of this new religion instead of Jerusalem. Then I will go to Rome.* Simon coveted Peter and John's apostolic gift more than anything else he had ever coveted in all his covetous life.

D. The Money Simon Pledged

Perhaps Philip was pleased with himself for having made such a notable convert as Simon the sorcerer. Perhaps the evangelist told Peter and John what a Satan-driven man Simon had been before he professed faith, and how he had submitted to baptism and now seemed like a model believer: he attended all the meetings, exclaimed over all the miracles, and did not seem jealous or resentful because Philip was the most talked about man in town.

Such a report would have filled Peter and John with suspicion. They realized that the man might be playing a game, for Satan does not easily yield possession of such an excellent tool as Simon.

Then Simon Magus and Simon Peter met face to face. Simon Magus went straight to the point: "Give me also this power, that on whomsoever I lay hands, he may receive the Holy Ghost" (Acts 8:19). There was nothing to find fault with in that request, but the man betrayed himself. He had a big bag of money with him and offered it to Peter and John in return for the gift of power. Peter saw right through him and rebuked him with words that rang out like the knell of doom:

> Thy money perish with thee, because thou hast thought that the gift of God may be purchased with money. Thou hast neither part nor lot

in this matter: for thy heart is not right in the sight of God. Repent therefore of this thy wickedness, and pray God, if perhaps the thought of thine heart may be forgiven thee. For I perceive that thou art in the gall of bitterness, and in the bond of iniquity. (Acts 8:20–23)

Simon had deceived Philip, but he did not deceive Peter—or God. It is easy to deceive the saints. Still today people join the church in hope of commercial gain. It is easy for a man to act the part of a believer while hiding some entrenched wickedness that holds secret sway over his soul. Judas did it for years.

Thoroughly frightened by Peter's words, Simon Magus exclaimed, "Pray ye to the LORD for me, that none of these things which ye have spoken come upon me" (Acts 8:24). Why couldn't he pray for himself?

The Bible doesn't tell us what happened next. According to one ancient tradition, Simon Magus went to Rome where he greatly harassed the church by subverting many people and winning them over to his own cult. He astonished the Gentiles by a display of a magical power, including levitation (the demonic ability to fly through the air). About all this, however, the Scripture is silent.

The Holy Spirit leaves us with a Simon Magus afraid for his life but not frightened enough to show genuine repentance and fling himself unreservedly upon God. The story of Simon is a beacon light warning all mariners on life's stormy sea that it is possible to profess the faith, to be baptized, and still not be saved at all. It is possible to deceive evangelists and the church, but God sees the heart. Simon's heart was as rotten after his profession of faith as it was before.

FORTY-FIVE

Doctor Luke

Paul's Physician

Colossians 4:14; 2 Timothy 4:11; Philemon 1:24

A. DISTINGUISHED DOCTOR LUKE: THE HISTORIAN—A VERY BRILLIANT MAN
1. The historian of the Christ
2. The historian of the church
B. DEVOTED DOCTOR LUKE: THE HELPER—A VERY BELOVED MAN
C. DARING DOCTOR LUKE: THE HERO—A VERY BRAVE MAN

There are no lack of ideas and suggestions to fill in the blanks of our actual knowledge of the great, good, and gifted man we know simply as Luke. We are indebted to him for two of the greatest books in the New Testament, but he keeps himself in the shadows as much as he can.

It has been suggested, for instance, that Luke may have been one of the two Greeks who desired to see Jesus about the time of the raising of Lazarus (John 12).

Professor Ramsay thinks that Luke was the "Man from Macedonia" who met Paul at Troas and turned the apostle's feet toward Europe.

It has been suggested that he was once a slave in the household of Theophilus. This wealthy government official, it is thought, arranged for Luke to be trained as a physician and that when Luke became a Christian he told his master about Christ. As a result, Theophilus, too, became a Christian and gave Luke his freedom. At least, this would account for the fact that Luke dedicates both his books to a beloved benefactor.

It is thought, also, that Luke was "the brother" whose praise was in all the churches (2 Cor. 8:18) and that Titus, also a Greek, was his brother (see 2 Cor. 12:18—where "a brother" has the force of "his brother").

It has also been suggested that Luke and Paul first met when they were fellow students at the University of Tarsus. The three great centers of medical studies in the Roman world were Alexandria, Athens, and Tarsus.

When driven to the wall for hard facts, we discover that Luke is actually mentioned only three times by name in the entire New Testament. From Colossians 4:14; Philemon 24; and 2 Timothy 4:11, we learn that Luke was a physician, that he was one of Paul's fellow laborers, and that he was with Paul at Rome during Paul's last imprisonment.

Thus, we now look at Luke the *historian,* and at Luke the *helper,* and at Luke the *hero.*

A. Distinguished Doctor Luke: The Historian—A Very Brilliant Man

There can be no doubt about Luke's scholarship. By birth he was both a Greek and a pagan. See Colossians 4:10–14 where Paul speaks of "they of the circumcision"—that is, Jewish believers—and other Christians, the Gentile Christians, the group in which he places Luke. This sets Luke apart. He was the only author, among all those the Holy Spirit used to write the Bible, who was a Gentile.

That Luke was a physician is important, too. At the time of Imperial Rome, there was an accrediting college at Rome that supervised the licensing of medical doctors. It was called the Collegium Archiatorum. It was responsible for examining all those who wanted to practice medicine in every city of the empire. Those newly admitted to the medical fraternity were interned under older physicians. Their methods of treatment were closely supervised, and their mistakes were severely punished. A doctor could even lose his diploma.[1] Thus we can be sure that Luke was well-educated. He thus stands apart from the other evangelists. Paul found in Luke a man with a kindred mind, a man of scholarship and education and attainment, a man to whom he could talk as an equal.

Joseph Ernest Renan, the French philosopher, skeptic, and historian, declared that the gospel of Luke was "the most beautiful book in the world." There is a very old tradition that Luke, as well as being a physician, was also a painter. He was certainly an artist with words. He paints very vivid vignettes.

We know him best, though, as a historian. First and foremost, he recorded the history of the great Man.

---

1. Frédéric Louis Godet, *A Commentary on the Gospel of St. Luke* (n.p., n.d.), 1:17.

1. The Historian of the Christ

It is likely that Luke wrote his gospel either at Caesarea or at Rome—or perhaps it was begun at Caesarea and finished at Rome.

Paul, at the end of his third missionary journey, made his way to Jerusalem. He brought with him considerable monetary gifts from his various Gentile churches to help alleviate the poverty in the Jerusalem church. Far from being thanked, he was railroaded. James persuaded him to take part in some ceremonial activities in the temple. There, he was mobbed by the crowd and barely escaped with his life. All of a sudden Jerusalem was rife with plots to get rid of him. Consequently, he was taken into protective custody by the Romans, who imprisoned him for two years at Caesarea, the Roman capital of Palestine.

Luke appears to have been Paul's attendant all this time. It was an excellent opportunity for the distinguished doctor to travel the length and breadth of the Holy Land in order to talk to anyone and everyone who had firsthand knowledge of Jesus, collecting material for his first book. He met and interviewed Mary, the Lord's mother, for example, and she unburdened her heart to this attractive scholar and told him how it had all happened. Luke translated into Greek, as exactly as he could, the story she had to tell. She expressed her thoughts in Hebrew, Luke rendered them into elegant Greek.

And so his historical record became more and more complete.

We can picture him hurrying off to talk to officials at the Court of Herod—his close friendship with Theophilus would doubtless open those kinds of doors for him. He would spend time with Philip the Evangelist, who now lived with his daughters at Caesarea. He would talk to the disciples of John the Baptist. He would, of course, spend as much time as possible with the apostles in Jerusalem. He would talk to people whom Jesus had healed. He would seek out those who had heard Jesus teach in order to get their impressions and their stories. He would seek out, perhaps, the Gaderene demoniac and the widow of Nain, and the woman who once had an issue of blood, and the Samaritan leper who, alone of all ten, came back to give Jesus thanks. He would seek out Jairus and his daughter. He would find the little lad who had loaned his loaves to the Lord—and seen an extraordinary miracle. He would find blind Bartimaeus and Zacchaeus and the soldier who had crucified Christ. His source material grew and grew.

Perhaps he had Mark's gospel in his possession, well-thumbed and underlined and covered with his own marginal notes. And, of course, there were many other written attempts to record the story, and to all those he, no doubt, referred. None of them have survived because Luke's gospel, once it was published, eclipsed them all.

He would hurry back to Paul with his latest findings. The two would discuss the stories, sifting fact from fable. And Luke would write.

For the Preface, he wrote in what has been called "remarkable elegant and idiomatic Greek." Coming to the story of the Incarnation, derived in Hebrew from the Virgin Mary, he changed his style and wrote a couple of chapters in Hebraistic Greek. Thereafter, he returned to his every day Greek style.

Luke had a rich vocabulary. The Grimm-Thayer Lexicon shows that no less than 312 words are found in this gospel that are found nowhere else in the New Testament.

He tells us of six miracles of Jesus nobody else mentions. He records thirty-five parables altogether—of these no less than nineteen are recorded by him alone. If Luke had not written, we would not have known, for instance, about the good Samaritan, and the rich fool, and the prodigal son, and the rich steward, and the rich man and Lazarus, and the Pharisee, and the publican.

And through it all we detect the quiet influence of Paul, for Luke emphasizes faith and repentance and mercy and forgiveness, just as Paul does. Luke has a Pauline view of Calvary. He is fond of the words *grace*, *salvation*, and *Savior*. His gospel illustrates Paul's concepts of justification by faith.

Throughout, when quoting from the Old Testament, Luke uses the Greek Septuagint version of the Bible. That would be what you would expect from a Greek writing to Greeks.

Distinguished Doctor Luke!

But Luke was not only the *historian of the Christ,* he was also historian of that great Man's body.

2. The Historian of the Church

We do not know for sure when Luke first met Paul. The first indication we have from the book of Acts is in Acts 16:10. Paul had been moving steadily westward across the Roman Province of Asia Minor. Doors were closed to him everywhere by the Holy Spirit until he came to Troas. There, Paul had a dream of a man from Macedonia urging him to come over into Europe. The next morning who should walk into Paul's camp but a man from Macedonia—Dr. Luke, who was possibly an old acquaintance of Paul's from college days in Tarsus.

In any case, the famous "we passages" begin at this point, indicating that Luke was now a member of the missionary team. He sailed with Paul over to Macedonia. He went with him to Philippi but escaped the persecution aimed at Paul and Silas in that Roman colony. When Paul left Philippi, Luke stayed behind.

The next time we see Luke is when Paul arrived back at Philippi at the end of his third missionary journey, some seven or eight years later. Luke joined Paul on his journey to Jerusalem and so had a firsthand knowledge of what happened there. He seems to have remained with Paul during his imprisonment at Caesarea, and he accompanied him on his journey to Rome. Thus, he shared in the shipwreck he describes so graphically before continuing on with Paul to Rome.

We learn from Paul's epistles that Luke remained with Paul as his "fellow-labourer" until the end of his first imprisonment. The last glimpse we have of this distinguished doctor is when he and Paul were back at Rome at the time of Paul's last imprisonment.

So, from his acquaintance with many of the leading figures in the Jerusalem church and his close friendship with the great apostle to the Gentile church, it is evident that Luke was well-qualified to write this first history of the church.

That narrative begins at Jerusalem and ends at Rome. It begins with a Pentecost and ends in a prison. It begins with a small, despised Jewish sect in a remote and insignificant Roman province and ends with members of the prestigious Praetorian Guard being won to Christ by the greatest missionary of them all. It begins in a narrow Jewish fold and ends in the capital city of a world empire.

The Acts narrative begins with the church having some severe handicaps. Its Founder had been accused of sedition and had been crucified by a Roman Governor. It ends with churches dedicated to the worship of this very Man, established in every major city of that part of the Roman Empire. Thus, the faith that began in Asia, in the end is identified with Europe.

Much of the success of the church's mission can be attributed to Luke's hero, the apostle Paul. In a little more than ten years he established the church in four provinces of the empire (Galatia, Macedonia, Achaia, and Asia). Before A.D. 47, no churches existed in these provinces. By A.D. 57 Paul could speak of his work having been completed in these parts as he fixed his eyes on the far west. Paul based his activities on four centers. From Damascus he penetrated the Nabatean kingdom in Arabia, making Tarsus his center for ten unchronicled years. Thereafter his centers were Antioch, Corinth, and Ephesus. Most of the knowledge we have about these things comes from Luke.

The book of Acts forms the essential link between the Gospels and the Epistles. Without it we would be greatly mystified by many things. We have letters, for instance, written to churches in such places as Rome, Corinth, Galatia, Ephesus, Thessalonica, and Philippi. But, without the book of Acts, we would have no idea how these churches came into being. We read of a monumental man named Paul, but there is no hint of him at all in the Gospels. He claims, however, to be an apostle and acknowledges himself once to have been a bitter persecutor of the church. How could we explain these things apart from the book of Acts.

Luke carries the story forward in three movements. He begins with *the founding emphasis* of the church. He tells us of those early days in Jerusalem and Judea, and centers that part of the story around Simon Peter. Beginning with Pentecost and until the time Peter opened the door of the church to the Gentiles, he was the driving force of the church, the Holy Spirit's man of the hour.

Luke continues with *the forward emphasis* of the church. There were new victories and new voices. Two of the church's very first deacons sprang to prominence—Stephen became the church's first martyr, and Philip became the church's first missionary. Then Saul of Tarsus was saved—soon to leap to fame as the apostle Paul.

Luke concludes with *the foreign emphasis* of the church. He tells us about *Paul the Pioneer,* chronicling for us his three great missionary journeys, and he tells us about *Paul the Prisoner* and of his fruitful captivities, both at Caesarea and at Rome.

And we can be sure that he was just as meticulous, just as careful to verify his facts, just as thorough and exact in writing the history of the church as he was in writing the history of Christ. We thank the distinguished doctor. He was even more than historian, however, and to another of his roles we now turn.

B. Devoted Doctor Luke:
The Helper—A Very Beloved Man

Paul was not a well man. He carried with him everywhere something he calls his "thorn in the flesh." We do not know for sure just what it was. Some have concluded Paul was an epileptic. Some have surmised he had a disfiguring eye disease. Then, too, when we think of all the beatings and scourgings Paul suffered, and all the hardships, and shipwrecks, and imprisonments, it is little wonder that he needed the constant attendance of a physician. And there was dear Dr. Luke always at hand, eager to help, able to minister to the great apostle's physical needs.

We cannot help but wonder what Luke thought the first time he saw Paul's back! Did Dr. Luke, before Paul left Philippi for points south, take him home first and exercise all his healing skill on Paul's lacerated back. Perhaps he made up some ointment for him. "Rub this in before you go to bed each night, Paul, and see that Silas does the same. It'll take some of the soreness away."

And when Paul finally got back to Philippi after some of the horrendous experiences he describes in 2 Corinthians, Luke would insist on a complete physical overhaul. "That does it, Paul! From now on I'm traveling with you . . ."

And so he did. Devoted Dr. Luke! So when Paul was mobbed in Jerusalem, Luke was there. When the chains on his hands and feet galled him in the prison at Caesarea, Dr. Luke was there. Dr. Luke seems to have made it his great ministry in this life to keep Paul alive as long as possible.

Doubtless Paul had his bouts with rheumatism, or arthritis, or migraine headaches. No doubt like everyone else he had his attacks of such things as the flu, or its old-world counterpart. And ever at hand was this devoted doctor. Perhaps Paul would not have lived long enough to write his prison and pastoral epistles without the constant ministry of his personal physician. So the whole church, in all ages, owes the devoted doctor a vote of thanks.

Not that Paul was the kind of man to mollycoddle himself. He was no hypochondriac. "How are you, Paul?" Luke might say after some particularly sleepless night. "Just fine, Luke, just fine," says Paul. And Luke would say, "Just lie down, Paul, and I'll massage your back and relieve those cramped muscles of yours."

When we read that long list of beatings and shipwrecks and perils and anxieties (forced out of Paul in sheer self-defense in his second surviving Corinthian letter), we think Paul must have been made of iron. Oh no! He was made of the same kind of flesh as we are. How often he must have thanked God for Luke. To that role of companion in toil and troubles we now turn.

C. DARING DOCTOR LUKE: THE HERO—A VERY BRAVE MAN

Times changed. When Paul appealed to Caesar he was confident that, as a Roman, he would receive a fair trial, even though Nero was the Roman Emperor when Paul pronounced the fateful words: *"Ad Caesarem prouoco!"*

Nero came to the throne of the Empire in A.D. 54, and it seemed to one and all that, at last, Rome had found itself a decent emperor. The first five years of his reign Nero was under the beneficial influence of his tutor, Seneca, the Stoic philosopher. He was also greatly helped by Afranius Burrus, the honest prefect of the Praetorian Guard. The first five years of Nero's reign were among the best years that the empire ever had. Certainly, when Paul appealed to Caesar in A.D. 59, there was no warning of the diabolical and drastic change that was soon to come.

Paul was kept under house arrest in Rome for two years. During that time the Sanhedrin's case against him was, presumably, allowed to run out by default. Doubtless the Jewish authorities had not bargained on an appearance before the Imperial Court in Rome. The Roman authorities dealt severely with those who brought frivolous and vexatious charges.

It seems likely that Paul was released in A.D. 61, and that he continued his missionary activities. Then, in A.D. 62, there was a marked turning point in Nero's administration. Burrus died and was replaced by the corrupt Tigellinus. Seneca retired from public office. Nero divorced Octavia and married the Jewess, Poppaea, a warm friend of the Jews and no friend of Christianity. In A.D. 64 Nero set fire to Rome and, to escape the wrath of the general public, blamed it on the Christians and inaugurated a holocaust against Christianity. Paul was rearrested and taken back to Rome.

He was marked down, now, as a ringleader of a hated sect. This time his imprisonment was not the light kind of house arrest he had enjoyed before. Now he was incarcerated in the dreaded maximum security ward. He was led up the Steps of Groaning to the terrible Mammertine prison, and there handed over to four of the assistants to the public executioner. Stripped of his outer garments and left naked except for his tunic, he was hauled to a trapdoor. Ropes were put under his armpits, and he was lowered into the terrible lower dungeon, the infamous Tullianum. The ropes were withdrawn and the trapdoor closed.

The floor consisted of patches of mud and filth. Some straw was provided for a bed, and a spring provided water. Now all he had to do was sit in the dark and wait. Some of his colleagues he sent away. Some abandoned him. Daring doctor Luke remained true to the end.

Perhaps he was allowed a candle. Perhaps Luke was allowed to visit him. One way or another Paul managed to write 2 Timothy. Perhaps enough influence was brought to bear to relieve him to the extent that he could gain access to the upper chamber where, at least, he would have some light.

One thing we know. He was now friendless and forsaken. Just one man stood by him—although others were willing to come; Timothy for one, and presumably Mark, for another. Paul was cold, so he asked Timothy to bring his coat. Time hung heavy on his hands so he asked Timothy to bring his books and parchments. He had one steadfast friend, however, who stuck to him through it all—doctor Luke, daring doctor Luke.

Luke remained with the aged apostle until the morning he was led away for execution. He did what he could to relieve his sufferings. Heavy chains weighted down the apostle's hands and feet and galled them with open sores. Luke dressed them as best he could. Paul was dependent on Luke for food, and Luke dared the hostility of the guard and the dangers of the marketplace to feed his friend. He was to Paul that "friend that sticketh closer than a brother."

At last Paul was led away to execution. His head was struck from his body, and his soul soared upwards to the gates of light. And Luke vanishes into oblivion—next to be heard of at the judgment seat of Christ to hear the Lord's *"Well done, Luke!"*

FORTY-SIX

Demas

Paul's Judas

Colossians 4:14; 2 Timothy 4:10; Philemon 1:24

A. THE DILIGENT MAN
   He is linked with:
   1. Aristarchus: A resolute believer
      a. A daring man
      b. A dependable man
      c. A devoted man
   2. Luke: A reliable brother
   3. Mark: A recovered backslider
B. THE DOUBTFUL MAN
C. THE DISILLUSIONED MAN

The name *Demas* means "of the people," or, as we would say, "one of the crowd." Some lexicons give the meaning as "popular." We are left in the dark as to whether Demas was popular or whether he simply wanted to be popular. Popularity can be a great asset in the cause of Christ, but it is a poor foundation on which to build a ministry. The same crowd that applauds us today might just as easily vilify us tomorrow. We can quickly fall from the world's good favor into its bad ones. The same crowd that cheered Christ's triumphal entry into Jerusalem howled for His death before Pilate a few days later.

Demas is mentioned just three times in the New Testament. These three references are brief, but they give us enough clues to form an estimate of his character.

Paul, in his brief memo to his friend Philemon, called Demas a "fellowlabourer."

The apostle was in Rome at the time he wrote to Philemon, under house arrest, accused of treasonable acts by his Jewish enemies. He was, however, accorded all the rights that accrued to him as a Roman citizen. Although constantly chained to a soldier, Paul had a great deal of liberty. He was able to entertain a stream of visitors, retain the services of a personal physician, and carry on a marvelous correspondence. During this time he wrote Ephesians, Philippians, and Colossians—three of his greatest works—in addition to his remarkable epistle to Philemon. Paul was quite prepared to cope with the worst if things should turn sour at his impending trial, but he was optimistic about the possibility of being released from prison and returning to his evangelistic ministry.

Demas was one of the men who ministered to Paul and was with him during this imprisonment. Paul referred to these men in Philemon 24: "Marcus, Aristarchus, Demas, Lucas, my fellowlabourers." The word translated "fellowlabourers" is *sunergos,* which means "companions in labor." Today we would say they were Paul's coworkers.

It seems that during this period, Demas used his popularity and his gift for making friends to further the cause of Christ. Evidently he was a man Paul trusted and used. Later Demas would become a doubtful man and then a disillusioned man, but at this time he was a diligent man.

A. THE DILIGENT MAN

First we see Demas as a man who was not afraid of work and was active in the Lord's service. Paul was able to send him on errands here and there throughout the great Roman metropolis. Paul had friends in influential places, for some of the Caesar's household had been converted through his ministry. It seems the apostle had won members of the powerful praetorian guard to Christ. Possibly Paul sent popular Demas to minister to them.

Paul also had contacts in the large Jewish community in Rome. Perhaps Demas was able to use his popularity to make friends for Christ among the Jews.

The majority of the people in the Roman capital were slaves, and we can be sure that Paul had a great work going among them. As a prisoner he could not go much beyond the front door of his house, so men like Demas had to be Paul's hands, feet, eyes, ears, and mouth.

Years before, Paul had sent his now-famous epistle to the church in Rome. No doubt Paul took an active interest in the church at Rome, its local ministry, its missionary outreach, its ministers, and its teaching. Possibly Demas was involved in helping the apostle keep in contact with the various congregations of Christians in the city.

Perhaps Demas also helped Paul with his voluminous correspondence. The apostle told the Corinthians he had "the care of all the churches" on his shoulders (2 Cor. 11:28), so his New Testament epistles must have been just a small portion of his actual written ministry. With no trouble at all, a man like Paul could keep half a dozen scribes busy.

At the time Paul led runaway Onesimus to Christ and sent him back to Philemon in Colossae, Demas was acknowledged as one of Paul's most valued helpers. There was not a cloud in the sky.

It seems Paul and Demas had a mutual friend in Philemon, so in the epistle to Philemon, Paul mentioned Demas—and put him in some very good company indeed. The Holy Spirit matched Demas up with Mark, Aristarchus, and Luke to fortify him for the hour of temptation that lay ahead. He could have learned much from each of these men. He failed, though, to take advantage of the opportunity. When the time of testing came, Demas the diligent became Demas the deserter.

1. Aristarchus: A Resolute Believer

From Aristarchus, Demas could have learned to be daring, dependable, and devoted. Aristarchus was a native of Thessalonica, a man from Macedonia. He seems to have been one of Paul's wealthier converts, able to leave his ordinary occupation to accompany Paul on his travels. He did this for about three years (from Acts 19:29–Acts 27:2).

a. A Daring Man

When Demetrius, the silversmith of Ephesus, stirred up a riot against Paul because sales of silver images of the goddess Diana had fallen off due to Paul's activities, the mob seized Aristarchus. It must have been a terrifying experience, for no mob is more savage than one whose passions have been aroused by the belief that their god has been insulted. For a while his life hovered in the balance, but in the end he was saved by the boldness and common sense of the town clerk.

That experience made no difference to Aristarchus, for he was a resolute believer. A hairbreadth escape or so was not going to deter that daring man from standing shoulder to shoulder with Paul. Demas could have learned something from him, resolute believer that he was. He could have learned not to quit when the way gets rough, even if taking a stand for Christ put him in a life-threatening situation.

b. A Dependable Man

When Paul collected money from the Gentile churches for the poor saints in Jerusalem, he decided that a representative delegation from various contributing churches should be the bearers of the gift. Paul was eager to send relief. He himself had made many of the saints poor when he so bitterly persecuted the Jerusalem church. One of the men he chose was Aristarchus the Thessalonian. Aristarchus was a dependable man who could be trusted to carry an assignment through to its completion.

Many volunteers start well. They are full of enthusiasm and eager to help. Before long, however, the novelty wears off. They are not prepared for the long haul and they drop out. But Aristarchus was made of sterner stuff. Paul knew that once he gave his word, Aristarchus would stand by it—all the way to Jerusalem and back. Demas could have learned from his example.

c. A Devoted Man

When Paul was arrested in Jerusalem and accused by the Jews of causing a riot in the temple, Aristarchus stood by him. Paul was moved on to Caesarea and was arraigned before Felix, a venal governor who looked expectantly to Paul for a bribe to secure his release. The apostle was not the kind of man who would bribe anyone; he had too much respect for his own conscience and too much regard for the other man's soul. So Felix left Paul in prison for two years. Then matters came to a head. Goaded by the new governor, Festus, Paul appealed to Caesar and shortly afterward, arrangements were made to send the apostle in bonds to Rome. Aristarchus, loyal to the core, accompanied him (Acts 27:1–2). Others might flinch at the sight of Paul's chain, but not Aristarchus.

In the epistle to Philemon, Paul called Aristarchus a fellow laborer, but in the epistle to the Colossians, Paul called him "my fellowprisoner" (4:10). The word translated "fellowprisoner" literally means "fellow prisoner-of-war." Some commentators think Aristarchus voluntarily made himself a prisoner in order to be near enough to Paul to minister to him. Others think Aristarchus's activities in Rome and his close association with Paul led to his arrest. In any case Aristarchus was a true soldier of Jesus Christ. Tradition says that he was martyred by Nero. Demas could have learned a lesson from such a loyal, devoted companion.

2. Luke: A Reliable Brother

Paul also linked Demas with Luke. The great apostle never had a better or more faithful friend than Luke, whom he described as his "beloved physician." Probably Luke was a Gentile since he was not counted among those who were "of the circumcision" (Col. 4:11). He had accompanied Paul from Troas to Philippi, and when Paul and Silas left that town, Luke remained behind in Philippi. Assuredly he was a devoted helper in the infant Philippian church. Seven or eight years later Paul came back to Philippi (on his third missionary journey), and there was Luke waiting for him. From then on, Luke was Paul's constant companion, accompanying him to Jerusalem, ministering to him in Caesarea, accompanying him to Rome, sharing in his shipwreck, and continuing with him to the end.

Our last glimpse of this faithful friend is in Paul's last letter to Timothy where the apostle wrote, "Only Luke is with me" (2 Tim. 4:11). By that time, Paul was under much severer arrest, for by then Nero had shown his true colors. It was becoming increasingly evident to him that Christianity was not just a form of Judaism, but a new faith altogether, with daggers drawn against paganism. Nero ordered the imperial police to intensify their scrutiny of Christians, and he sought for an opportunity to persecute them openly. The opportunity came with the burning of Rome in A.D. 64. Nero blamed the Christians for that disaster and launched a widespread, fearful persecution against them.

One by one Paul's adherents left. Some he deliberately sent away from the storm center. Luke alone remained. Demas might have learned something from such a willing companion and reliable brother.

Already Luke was collecting the material that eventually found its way into his peerless gospel and the book of Acts. He had talked to everyone who mattered both in Palestine and throughout the Roman world. What a mine of information Demas might have found in a man like Luke. What a pity Demas didn't stay closer to him, for God surely brought Luke into his life for a purpose.

3. Mark: A Recovered Backslider

Finally, Paul linked Demas with John Mark. This Mark, a cousin or nephew of Barnabas, was the companion of Paul and Barnabas on Paul's first missionary journey. Mark seems to have been a native of Jerusalem where his mother Mary owned a house. It was in her home that a prayer meeting was held to plead for Peter's release from prison right after the martyrdom of the apostle James. Peter called Mark "my son," so it is likely that Peter had won him to Christ.

When Paul, Barnabas, and Mark arrived at Perga on the coast of Asia Minor, Mark decided to quit and go back home to his mother. Probably he was horrified to learn that Paul intended to head up into the Taurus mountains, through the Cilician gates, and on into Galatia. Stories of the untamed nature of the region may have influenced Mark's decision. Wild bands of brigands haunted the passes and preyed unmercifully on lone travelers. In any case, Paul was much vexed with Mark's decision, and his defection led to a serious break between the apostle and Barnabas at the time of Paul's second missionary journey. Mark and Barnabas went back to the island of Cyprus; Paul, with Silas as his companion, headed back to Galatia.

But Paul never held a grudge. Later we find Mark in Paul's company during his first imprisonment at Rome (Col. 4:10). And during his second imprisonment, Paul pleaded with Timothy to "come before winter" and bring his cloak, his books, and Mark, whom he described as "profitable to me for the ministry" (2 Tim. 4:11, 21). Evidently Mark had made a complete recovery from his stumbling start. He had even traveled to far-off Babylon with Peter (1 Peter 5:13).

There is something poignant in Paul's earnest plea to Timothy to bring Mark. What changed Paul's mind? Perhaps at some time during Paul's first imprisonment someone showed him a manuscript so new that the ink was scarcely dry. Even a cursory glance attested its worth. Its burden seemed to be the Roman people. It bore the image and likeness of Peter, but the penmanship and signature were indisputable. It was the first-written gospel—the gospel according to Mark! "I never knew the young fellow had it in him," Paul would have declared as he perused the pages with increasing delight. "Here, Luke!" we can almost hear the apostle exclaim. "Come and have a look at this. Mark has beaten you to it!"

Mark was a recovered quitter. From him Demas surely ought to have learned about the ease with which one can quit and about how long and painful the road to recovery is. Mark did not come casually into Demas's life; Mark was sent Demas's way by God.

So then we first see in Demas a diligent man. In those bright days he was a helper to the great apostle and as such he deserves honorable mention. Demas was Paul's fellow servant, a true yokefellow in the work of the Lord. But that was before Nero persecuted the church.

B. The Doubtful Man

In Colossians 4:14 Demas is simply named; that's all. "Luke, the beloved physician, and Demas, greet you," Paul wrote. Perhaps between the writing of Philemon and the writing of Colossians, Paul detected the dry rot in Demas's soul. Perhaps Paul saw the first hint of worldliness. Or maybe he noticed the first almost imperceptible trace of cooling in Demas's spirit. Possibly only a man as spiritually sensitive as Paul would have been able to detect the change.

Pausing pen in hand, Paul apparently realized he could not say anything to the Colossians about Demas—good or bad. The apostle certainly was not going to say anything bad. The man had to be given the benefit of the doubt. But he needed to be watched carefully, to be prayed for more diligently.

Backsliding never occurs overnight. A backslider's affection for the Lord Jesus cools gradually. He loses his first love; he begins to neglect his daily quiet time with God; and he starts to absent himself from the place where the people of God gather together for fellowship, ministry of the Word, worship, and prayer. His service becomes more and more perfunctory; he still goes through all the motions, but the heart has gone out of his efforts.

A famous concert violinist was once asked what would happen if he stopped practicing the usual number of hours every day. He said, "After the first day I would notice the difference in my performance. After the second day the conductor would notice. After the third day the rest of the orchestra would notice. And after the fourth day everyone would notice." Demas had not backslidden to the point where it was public knowledge, but Paul already knew or had a very good idea that Demas's fervor was beginning to cool.

C. The Disillusioned Man

By the time Paul started to write his last letter, he no longer had any doubts about Demas. "Demas hath forsaken me," the apostle wrote, "having loved this present world, and is departed unto Thessalonica" (2 Tim. 4:10). Demas wanted to put some distance between himself and Rome, where the fire of persecution was the hottest. He wanted to go away from Paul since Nero's spies watched the apostle's every move and reported on his friends.

Demas "loved this present world," said Paul. The word translated "loved" here is *agapaō*. The apostle's use of *agapaō* shows that Demas was not just fond of the world or merely infatuated with the world. He was in love with the world; it commanded his heart, mind, soul, and strength.

The word translated "world" in this verse is *aiōn*. It does not refer to the physical planet on which we live. *Aiōn,* which can also be translated "age," refers to this present span of time. So the affections of Demas were now taken up with this life—this present, brief, passing age. He had lost sight of the world to come.

"Demas hath forsaken me," said Paul. The word translated "forsaken" is *enkataleipō,* which literally means "to leave or to abandon." The same word was used by Peter on the day of Pentecost when he quoted from Psalm 16:10 in his reference to the resurrection of Christ: "Thou wilt not leave [abandon] my soul in hell" (Acts 2:27). Demas had abandoned Paul. It was too dangerous to be near Paul anymore.

What appeal of the world finally overcame Demas's heart? Was it the lust of the flesh? Was it the lust of the eyes? Was it the pride of life? Was it an unsaved woman? Was it a safer pulpit? Was it the fear of man? Was it the thought that Paul was too fanatical in both belief and behavior? All we know is that Demas went to Thessalonica. Maybe his wife was a social climber and had already departed for Thessalonica where the stigma of being a Christian was not so pronounced as it was in Rome. Maybe being a Christian would be less of a hindrance to her ambitions there. Maybe Demas was simply tired of being poor.

We do know he joined the very doubtful company of people like Lot, Absalom, Orpah, Solomon, and Jonah. Lot's backslidings in Sodom cost him family, fame, and fortune. Absalom's pride led him to plan his father's murder and led Absalom himself to an early grave. Orpah went back to the demon gods of her people. Solomon ended up turning Jerusalem into a second Babylon. Jonah ran away from the path of duty and became a menace to all those about him. Demas became like the followers of the Lord Jesus who, after His hard teaching on the bread of heaven, decided they'd had enough and left Him. "Will ye also go away?" Jesus asked the handful who remained (John 6:67).

As the Neronic persecution began to mount and Christians were dipped in wax, tied to stakes, and then kindled to provide light for the wild parties on the emperor's lawn, many began to leave town. One by one the little circle around the apostle dwindled. We wonder if Demas came to say goodbye or if he quietly packed his bags and slipped out of town one moonless night. We can almost hear Paul saying to his beloved physician, "Will you also go away?" And we can hear Luke say to his beloved Paul what the Twelve had said to Jesus: "To whom shall we go? thou hast the words of eternal life" (John 6:68).

So Demas left. This world got the best of him at last. He passed into the night, and we will see and hear no more of him until his name is called at the judgment seat of Christ.

FORTY-SEVEN

Antichrist
Otherwise Called "the Beast"

Revelation 13; 17

A. His parentage
B. His prophet
C. His policy
D. His persecution
E. His paralysis
F. His punishment

He is known by many names. He is called "the Assyrian," "the lawless one," "the Man of Sin," "the son of perdition," "the little horn," and "the prince." We often call him the Antichrist. In the Apocalypse he is usually called the Beast.

The Antichrist has been foreshadowed in history time and time again. *Cain* was the first in a long series of men who by their wicked works and willful ways prefigured him. Cain went out from the presence of the Lord a marked man. Having refused to become a pilgrim and a stranger on the earth, he became instead a fugitive and a vagabond. He laid the foundations of a thriving and energetic civilization that became so utterly godless and vile that it had to be divinely overthrown by the waters of the flood.

Nimrod was another type of the Antichrist. His name means "the rebel." He determined to build a society to suit himself. It was to be both humanistic and rebellious against God. Three times the words "Let us" occur in the story of the tower Nimrod's civilization built. All the emphasis was on man. "Let us make us a name," they said (Gen. 11:4). Nimrod's society was to be a new age civilization, a united nations organization, a world federation of nations—with

God left out. There was to be a one-world *sovereignty* symbolized by the city, a one-world *society* symbolized by the common language, and a one-world *sanctuary* symbolized by the tower. And Nimrod, the great rebel himself, the mighty hunter, would preside over it all. Babylon was to be center of his empire, and idolatry was to be its religion.

One of the strongest types of the Antichrist, both in history and in biblical revelation was *Antiochus Epiphanes.* This Syrian tyrant conquered Jerusalem in 168 B.C. and massacred the worshipers in the temple. He issued a decree that everyone had to join a universal religion and obey universal laws—or face death. He seized the Jewish temple and consecrated it to Jupiter (Zeus). Antiochus identified himself with this pagan god and ordered everyone to worship him. He also ordered an immediate cessation of all Jewish sacrifices and suspended all Jewish religious observances. He destroyed all the copies of Scriptures he could find. He replaced the annual Feast of Tabernacles with a feast dedicated to Bacchus. Antiochus built an idol altar over the brazen altar in the temple court. In the temple itself he installed an image of Zeus, the thunderer of Olympus. Then Antiochus sacrificed a sow on the altar, made broth of its flesh, and sprinkled the broth all over the temple. He perverted the youth of the city and taught them vile practices. Although he massacred thousands of Jews, there were numerous apostate Jews who admired and followed him. Antiochus was one of Satan's forerunners of the coming Antichrist.

There have been other men in the long course of history who have staged dress rehearsals for the coming of the Antichrist. The devilish *Nero,* for example, launched a fearful persecution of the Christian church. *Napoleon,* who aimed to resurrect the old Roman empire and conquer Palestine, used the Roman Catholic Church as a pawn. The Antichrist will do the same. *Hitler* sought to bring Europe under his control, and his holocaust against the Jews was a fearful foretaste of an even worse persecution to come.

A. His Parentage

In Revelation 12 the great red dragon shows up in heaven. He has seven heads and ten horns and is easily identified as the Devil. His malice is directed against the nation of Israel. He was thwarted, however, in his effort to destroy the man-child (the Lord Jesus) at His birth.

In Revelation 13 we see "a beast rise up out of the sea" (v. 1). It, too, has seven heads and ten horns which indicate his kinship with Satan. Revelation 17 emphasizes the Beast's seven heads and ten horns and provides the additional information about him (v. 3).

The great red dragon is Satan. The scarlet-colored beast is the Antichrist. The Beast betrays his parentage, for he looks and acts like the great red dragon. In other words, the father of the Beast is the Devil himself. He is the incarnation of all wickedness.

Revelation 17 tells us that the Antichrist is to be killed and then brought back to life again. So, like Christ, the Antichrist has two comings. When he comes the first time, he rises out of the sea. In other words, the Beast is an ordinary human being who rises out of "the sea," that is, out of the Gentile nations. Reference to "the sea" points to the Mediterranean world. He will probably be a Roman because he is identified with the little horn of Daniel 7:8.

Some people think that the Beast will actually be fathered by Satan. Jesus said concerning Judas, "Have not I chosen you twelve, and one of you is a devil?" (John 6:70). Some assume that both Judas and the Antichrist are of Satanic origin. Since Jesus called Judas *the* son of perdition" (John 17:12), and this title is only used elsewhere for the Antichrist (2 Thess. 2:3), some suggest that Judas and the Antichrist are the same individual. Acts 1:25 says that Judas, after he had hanged himself, went "to his own place." The implication is that Judas is presently being groomed in the underworld to come back as the Antichrist.

More likely "the beast out of the sea" will be a Gentile, probably Roman. He will revive the old empire and rule as the last of the Caesars. He will also be the final heir to Nebuchadnezzar's lordship of the world. The Antichrist, at his first coming, will be a very attractive, dynamic, and brilliant individual who will charm and fascinate the nations of the world. Probably he will sell himself to the Devil, as Hitler did. The Antichrist will be taught and led by principalities and powers, by the rulers of this world's darkness (see Eph. 6:12), and by "wicked spirits in high places."

Revelation 17 tells us he will be killed, but it does not tell us how. Perhaps the Antichrist will be slain when God's two witnesses (Revelation 11) and Satan's two representatives (the Beast and the False Prophet) wage war against each other. That war will be a battle of miracles similar to that which took place in Egypt when Moses and Aaron confronted the pharaoh's two false prophets.

God will permit Satan to bring the Antichrist back to life. Thereafter, he will be known not as "the beast . . . out of the sea" (Rev. 13:1–4) but as "the beast out of the bottomless pit" (11:7; 17:8–11). From this point on, he will be a supernatural being and will be universally worshiped. The Antichrist will be Satan incarnate, the visible expression of the invisible Devil, and the vehicle through whom Satan will try to accomplish his purposes for this planet.

B. His Prophet

Revelation 13 chronicles the coming of two beasts. The first, as stated, rises out of the sea and is therefore a Gentile. The second (not to be confused with the second coming of the first beast) becomes up out of the earth and is probably a Jew. The sea, in Old Testament typology and symbolism, refers to the Gentile nations, and the earth to the Jewish people. The second beast will be subordinated to the first one (like Hitler and Himmler), but they will be soul twins. The second beast looks like a lamb, but appearances will be deceptive. When he speaks it will be as though a dragon speaks. He soon betrays his Satanic origin. He is called "the false prophet" (Rev. 16:13), and he will exercise all the power of the first beast. The False Prophet will be the first beast's high priest and spokesman. The False Prophet will persuade the world that the first beast is the long-awaited Messiah and that the world's interests lie in submitting to him.

The Lord Jesus warned that, as the last days begin to dawn, numerous false prophets will arise and deceive many (Matt. 24:11). All the world's false religions have been founded by false prophets. The church has had its false prophets, too. Today false cults in Christendom deceive millions. But these false prophets are simply part of Satan's general attack on the Christian faith. He is the father of lies, and deception is the idiom of his speech. He uses false religions to keep lost people lost. Satan is not against religion; he is all for it; he invented most of it.

The second beast, the false prophet, will be known as *the* False Prophet. He will come with deceit and with lying wonders, wielding all the power and authority of his master, the Antichrist. The False Prophet will be a golden-tongued orator and will appear to be harmless. Satan will enable him to speak as one inspired, and only those enlightened by the Holy Spirit will be able to withstand his persuasive tongue. The False Prophet will make wickedness seem right. His miracles will dazzle and deceive. Except for those whose names are written in the Lamb's book of life, the human race will fall for him and follow him. He will lead them to the Antichrist, the Antichrist will lead them to Satan, and Satan will lead them to hell.

The only safeguard for the human race will be the Word of God. But since men will long since have abandoned that for the countless false religions and philosophies abroad in the world, the False Prophet will persuade men that the Antichrist is their long-sought savior.

C. His Policy

When the Antichrist first appears, he will be just a "little horn" (Dan. 7:7–8, 16–26)—that is, he will not have much power, but he will be the consummate master of craft and cunning. He will arise somewhere in southern Europe, probably in the sphere of the vast Roman church. He will be given a seat in the councils of the ten kings, the European leaders who control a shadow Roman empire. He will make short work of three of them and then control all ten.

The details in Scripture are sketchy, but we do know from Revelation 17 that the Antichrist will make common cause with the Roman Catholic Church. The Vatican will think it can control him, but it will soon discover that it has allied itself to a tiger. The Antichrist will use this religious system to gain the upper hand in Europe and in all countries where Catholicism is entrenched. The Vatican will think it can use this "little horn" to get back its lost power and authority in the world, but as soon as the Antichrist has made the ten kings subservient to his will, he will turn on the ecclesiastical system itself and tear it to pieces. The ten kings themselves will gleefully fall upon the enormous wealth and riches of the Roman Catholic Church and divide the spoils among themselves.

As soon as the Antichrist is securely enthroned as the ruler of the European Union, he will act swiftly to expand his power. We are not told specifically what part the United States and the western hemisphere will play in all this. The "old lion" (the European powers—Isa. 60:9; Ezek. 38:13) will be loose. The lands of the Americas are the young lions spawned centuries ago by the old lion. Probably the Antichrist will pull the economic rug out from beneath the United States and bankrupt the United States, Canada, and Latin America. Then he may forge a new Atlantic alliance in which the countries of the western hemisphere participate but take their orders from Rome. Once he has the western world at his command, the Antichrist will prepare to satisfy larger ambitions, for his goal is to rule the world.

A global empire was granted in principle to Nebuchadnezzar by God. With him the "times of the Gentiles" began (Luke 21:24). He only ruled a tithe of the whole. His successors in the prophetic world were the leaders of Medo-Persia, Greece, and Rome; but none of these men ruled the whole world. With the revival of the Roman empire and the formation of the new Atlantic alliance, the way will be clear for the Antichrist to pursue his plans for a truly global empire. All the economic, industrial, and military might of the West will be at his disposal, and he will be ready to further his schemes.

The Antichrist will sign a treaty with Israel, what the Bible calls—an agreement with hell (Isa. 28:15). This seven-year treaty will activate the seventieth and final "week" (of seven years) still hanging in abeyance (see Dan. 9 for the vision of the seventy weeks). Under the terms of this treaty the Antichrist apparently will guarantee Israel's security and authorize them to rebuild their temple. He has secret plans, though, for that temple.

We can imagine the howl of rage that will come from the Muslim world when the Jews start to rebuild their temple on its ancient site. But the Islamic Nations will be powerless. At the slightest hint of opposition, the Antichrist will occupy all Arab territory down to the Euphrates. He will not want a roll call of quarrelsome Middle East Arab states to spoil his global plans. He will want to get rid of Islam. It will be an obstacle to the accomplishment of his ultimate goals.

The Islamic peoples will appeal to Russia at a time when Russia will be looking for a way to reassert itself as a world superpower. Russia, according to Ezekiel 38, will seize this opportunity to move into the Middle East, and Germany will join forces. The Islamic states will join this massive anti-Semitic alliance. Russia and its allies will move swiftly, and the combined armies will cross into Israel. Then God will act. The terrible disasters spoken of in Ezekiel 38–39 will overtake the invading powers, and their armies will be virtually annihilated. Their homelands will also be visited by divine judgment. Suddenly Russia, Germany, and the Islamic powers will no longer exist.

The way will thus be open for the Antichrist to achieve his goal of global sovereignty. Before the rest of the world can recover from the astounding news that Russia and her allies have been destroyed, the armies of the Antichrist will occupy their territories. He will issue an ultimatum to the eastern nations: "Join—or else." They will say, "Who is like unto the beast? who is able to make war with him?" (Rev. 13:4)

The eastern nations will quickly submit to the all-conquering Antichrist, who will now have three capitals: *Rome,* his political capital; *Jerusalem,* his religious capital; rebuilt *Babylon,* his economic capital. He will have achieved the goal sought by hundreds of would-be world conquerors; he will rule the whole world.

D. His Persecution

Now the Antichrist has no more use for the Jews. The Antichrist will tear off his mask of friendship and show his real face. He will seize the rebuilt temple in

Jerusalem and install an image of himself in the Holy Place. The False Prophet will give life to the image and endow it with power to destroy those who refuse to worship it.

The Antichrist will then order a global test of allegiance: Everyone will be required to prove their loyalty to the new world order by receiving the Antichrist's mark on their right hands or on their foreheads. Without that mark no one will be able to buy or sell. A total economic boycott of those who do not display this badge will be universally enforced. A little boy will not be able to buy even an ice cream cone without the mark.

"The mark of the beast" (Rev. 16:2; 19:20) will be related to the name of the beast. Revelation 13:17–18 tells us "the number of his name." In Hebrew and Greek, every letter is also a number. Every word is not only a collection of letters but also a collection of numbers. In other words, every word has a numerical value. The Greek letters that make up the name of Jesus add up to the number 888. The numerical value of the Antichrist's name, when it is finally revealed, will be 666.

Those with a Judeo-Christian background, those who have been converted by the preaching of the 144,000, and those who fear God more than they fear man will be hounded to death. Satan will launch his most determined effort to rid the world of all lingering traces of the true and living God. The resulting holocaust will make the horror camps of the Nazis look like a Sunday school picnic.

But God will not abdicate the throne. Not for one moment will He surrender His sovereignty. The Antichrist's day of reckoning will come.

E. His Paralysis

Even as the Antichrist rides the crest of his power, things will begin to go wrong. The vials of God's wrath will be outpoured. The first four vials (bowls) will be aimed at the Antichrist's power structure on the planet. Under the hammer blows of heaven he will lose his grip, and his might will begin to ebb away.

The eastern half of the Antichrist's empire, the nations east of the Euphrates, will break away. (The Euphrates has always been the Bible's dividing line between East and West.) A new eastern coalition will be thrown together, and the "kings of the east" will mobilize and march westward (Rev. 16:12). Japanese technology will be married to Chinese manpower. The great eastern hordes will rally to the rebel cause, and the united armies of the East will march to confront the rapidly mobilizing west. They will cross the Euphrates and deploy on the plains of Megiddo. The Antichrist will move his Western allies to deal with the approaching "Kings of the East." The vast armies of East and West will now face each other, determined to decide once and for all who is going to rule the world, East or West? The stage will be set for the battle of Armageddon.

F. His Punishment

Before the battle can begin, however, there will be an invasion from outer space. It is Jesus; He is coming again! This time He will be backed by the armies of heaven. The church will be there in all its glory. All the Lord's might and majesty will be revealed. The sword will go forth from His mouth. The conflict will be over. The armies of earth will be swept away. The Antichrist and his False Prophet will stand alone, gazing at an enormous field strewn with the bodies of the slain.

The judgment of the Antichrist and the False Prophet will be swift and sure. They will be seized and flung headlong into the lake of fire, and the smoke of their torment will rise up on high. The Antichrist's rickety empire will be quickly dismembered. The survivors—Jew and Gentile alike—of the years of famine, pestilence, earthquake, persecution, and war will be summoned to the valley of Jehoshaphat. There, near the site of Gethsemane, the Lord Himself will separate the "sheep" from the "goats." The world will be fully cleansed of all those who wear the Beast's mark. Those who survive the judgment will be regenerated and sent to help pioneer the millennial kingdom in the name of Christ.

Explore the

BIBLE

in greater depth with the
John Phillips
Commentary Series!